Kind of Blue

Born in Nottingham in 1940, Ken Clarke was educated at Nottingham High School and Gonville and Caius College, Cambridge, where he studied law and was called to the bar in 1963. In 1970, at the age of twenty-nine, he became MP for Rushcliffe in Nottinghamshire, a seat he has held ever since. He held many ministerial posts in Margaret Thatcher's Cabinet, including Secretary of State for Health and Secretary of State for Education. He subsequently served as Home Secretary and Chancellor of the Exchequer under John Major and Secretary of State for Justice and Minister without Portfolio under David Cameron. He lives in London and Nottinghamshire.

KIND
OF BLUE

A POLITICAL MEMOIR

Ken Clarke

PAN BOOKS

First published 2016 by Macmillan

First published in paperback 2016 by Macmillan

This edition first published with a new appendix 2017 by Pan Books
an imprint of Pan Macmillan
20 New Wharf Road, London N1 9RR
Associated companies throughout the world
www.panmacmillan.com

ISBN 978-1-5098-3720-5

Typeset by Palimpsest Book Production Limited, Falkirk, Stirlingshire
Printed and bound by CPI Group (UK) Ltd, Croydon, CR0 4YY

For Gillian

Contents

FOREWORD

This memoir was largely dictated into a tape recorder, usually over a late-night brandy and cigar, as a conversational recollection of a life spent actively engaged in politics and government with some asides about my personal life. My family and I prize our privacy so, by and large, it concentrates on the political narrative. I had no intention of producing an academic and erudite historical text with footnotes based on extensive research. Instead, I hope I have produced a readable and very personal recollection of my involvement in events which will also underline my driving commitment to my political principles and to my view of the national interest of the United Kingdom.

I have always believed that the sanest route to prosperity and social equality is to combine free-market economics with a strong sense of fairness. Capitalism in the West is currently – and not altogether unreasonably – being undermined by people who feel it is unfairly rewarding the wealthy few and doing nothing for the vast majority of our citizens. But those of us who espouse modern capitalism and those who, like me, are members of the Conservative Party, should be even more concerned than the most ardent left-winger with ensuring that society is fair. That belief has underpinned my entire political career.

These veteran meanderings could only be turned into a book with the assistance of very efficient and well-organized friends and colleagues. They helped the Dictaphone interpret my narrative. They edited and sorted out the text and checked my assertions of distant facts. I had made personal written notes on some of the more dramatic events in my career two or three nights after those events had occurred. But since I have never kept a diary, my off-the-cuff remarks needed considerable sorting out and checking.

I am particularly grateful to Kathryn Laing, my last so-called special adviser, or political aide, who first insisted that I should try to do this and gave me the crucial Dictaphone. With great persistence, she encouraged me to record my reminiscences and, whilst on maternity leave, made steady progress in setting out the text in a presentable and readable order. When she eventually returned to full-time work she bullied me into approaching a literary agent, Natasha Fairweather of United Agents, and through Natasha I obtained a publisher, Pan Macmillan, and the editing services of Deborah Crewe. Deborah in particular drove me on to complete the composition and to improve the language and clarify the meaning I intended as I did so. I am extremely grateful to both of them as well as to Georgina Morley, my editorial director at Macmillan. I am also grateful to all the other people at Macmillan who have helped see the book into print, including my copy-editor David Milner, Laura Carr, Tania Wilde, Ena Matagic, Stuart Wilson, Wilf Dickie, Iram Allam and Philippa McEwan who has the unenviable task of organizing the publicity schedule.

I would also like to record my thanks to the staff in my office, Debbie Sugg and Jamie Hall, who worked at arranging the logistics of all this and made some comments. I am particularly grateful to many other friends who, like Debbie Sugg, have read relevant parts of the text and given their comments and reminders. People like Norman Fowler, Nick Macpherson, Anthony Teasdale and several others have kindly given their time to check and prompt my recollection of the incidents that they experienced with me. I am extremely grateful for the time and effort they put into it.

I would like to take this opportunity to pay tribute to the huge number of good friends and colleagues that I have had throughout my political lifetime. The effect of being reshuffled from department to department and serving on and on from parliament to parliament is that I have spent my time surrounded by a collection of friends and collaborators to whom I have been very close for the periods of time during which we worked together. I have then quite frequently failed or been unable to maintain contact with them as I have moved on to another sphere and become equally dependent on private secretaries, parliamentary private secretaries, special advisers, junior ministers, senior civil servants and all the other people that have to form part of a closely knit team in my next department. I can only apologize to Colin Moynihan, Michael Jack, David Trippier, Angela Knight and many others, with whom I worked very closely and who, alas, do not get commensurate mentions in the text. It is impossible to list all the politicians, civil servants and personal friends with whom I have collaborated but I cannot overstate my appreciation of the trusting personal and working relationships I have enjoyed throughout my career with so many marvellous people. If they read this book I hope that most of them will enjoy being reminded of the particular episodes when they were closely involved and that they will not disagree with either my narrative or my interpretation of events.

Finally, I should thank my late wife, Gillian, to whom this book is dedicated and who had to put up with a largely absent husband throughout our fifty-year marriage. But without her – and without our long telephone calls every evening we were apart – I would never have lasted the course.

1

'Go!'

(Dexter Gordon, 1962)

EARLY LIFE

I have never thought very much of politicians who make a great deal of their poor-boy origins. Nevertheless, I was born on 2 July 1940, impeccably working class.

My parents, both from Nottingham, were living in Aldercar, at the rural end of a Derbyshire pit village called Langley Mill in the heart of D. H. Lawrence country. The landscape was dominated by a huge number of collieries dotted in and around the surrounding villages. Coal tips emerged from the fields, some of them permanently smoking from internal fires. Expanses of farmland filled the remaining landscape, making the setting strangely bucolic. The village itself was home to a closed, very working-class community: the adult men all worked in one of the two or three collieries in the immediate surroundings. My father – an electrician at Moorgreen Colliery – was no exception.

My father's name was Kenneth, and I repeated this confusion when many years later I named my own son Kenneth. My mother was called Doris, a name which was becoming out of date even in the 1940s. Both of them were intelligent and perfectly literate and numerate but neither had had any kind of secondary education, and both had left school at about thirteen. My father had simply never been offered any sort of secondary education. In my mother's case her parents had refused her secondary-school place because they didn't believe that such an education was necessary for a girl. Both my parents had succeeded through their own unaided efforts in making considerable progress through life, despite the disadvantage they had undoubtedly suffered.

We were never remotely poor, though, because my father had a second job as the manager of the cinema in the nearby town of Eastwood. He used to tell me how in his younger days he had in fact operated the projector for the first talking film shown in Nottingham, at the Elite cinema. He also recollected how as a very young employee he had occasionally played the piano for the silent films when the pianist was too drunk to go on. He was actually quite a talented pianist, and I always enjoyed it when he played popular tunes on our piano in the front room.

Unlike the majority of men in our village my father was therefore not a lifelong miner. In fact, throughout the war he combined his two jobs in order to save money to go into business on his own account. The result was that we were rather better off than most other people in the village. We had a pleasant newish semi-detached house and my father always owned a Ford car. We acquired a television set as soon as television came to the Midlands and I can remember sitting in front of the tiny black-and-white screen showing the first pictures from the new Sutton Coldfield transmitter as the wonders of television began.

My childhood was always happy and loving. I was brought up with the children of the other colliery families, joining in the football and the other games on the fields near to my house. From the earliest age I would regularly go to watch the Aldercar football team and the rather good Langley Mill cricket team, which had a large ground and played in the Notts and Derby league. As a very young child I would be allowed to wander round the village entirely on my own, or go with friends to the football, the cricket and other games.

The war barely touched me. My father and most of the men in the village were of course in a reserved occupation and so were never called up. It did, though, provide one dramatic note in an otherwise uneventful childhood. We used to see the German aeroplanes flying over us on their way to bomb Nottingham, and I learnt the difference in the engine tone between our planes and their bombers. One night a German plane unloaded a bomb when returning from a raid. A cowshed was demolished, and some cows killed, and our house was faintly shaken. It was very exciting.

My sister Patricia, known as Pat, and brother Michael came along after the war. They were five and seven years younger than me and though I got on well with them both, we were never close because of the gap in age. Regretfully, in adult life we have been in only occasional on–off contact, always friendly with my sister and usually friendly with my brother. Pat was briefly a librarian before she married a farmer, and Michael became an antiques dealer. Neither was ever remotely interested in national politics, or in my career.

My extended family all lived ten miles away in Nottingham and we regularly went to visit my grandparents and my uncles and aunts. Grandfather Clarke lived with my father's stepmother in a typical terrace house in Sneinton, a poor district of Nottingham. My father was the second of three children by an earlier partner, all of whom had married and moved away. Grandfather Clarke lived with his current wife and another six unmarried sons, my uncles, who never moved away.

My grandfather was a cheery man who would settle down with me around the black-leaded fire in his sitting room and recount stories of his wayward life, with an occasional uncle interjecting to correct his wilder flights of fancy. He had been raised in a large farming family in the village of Tostock in Suffolk, but had run away from home at thirteen or fourteen, and ended up at sea. My uncles used to say that this was because he could not bear working in the fields topping turnips in the rain. My grandfather used to show me pictures of warships and tell me very romantic stories implying that he had served in the First World War. However, one of my uncles later told me that he had actually left the navy before the war started. He had since then lived as an occasionally employed house painter. He was clearly a happy layabout who just about managed to provide for his family.

Grandfather Clarke's matrimonial history and therefore my origins are remarkably obscure. He had apparently been deserted by his first wife who had fled on her wedding night. He then took a mysterious mistress who was my grandmother and whom I never met. Family legend had it that she was a gypsy, and in the one and only surviving photograph of her it does look as though she might have been Romany. She lived with my grandfather for many years, along with another woman described as her sister. It was my family's opinion that the sister was probably in fact her daughter. In a further twist, the 'sister' married my grandfather after the death of my natural grandmother. This was the step-grandmother who I got on well with on my child-hood visits to Sneinton. To this day, I have never discovered whether the second marriage was actually bigamous because nothing had been done about divorce from the first wife.

My father ran away from home himself when he was about fifteen years old after an argument in which he struck his stepmother. He found digs not far away with a landlady in West Bridgford, the suburb of Nottingham I would represent as an MP many years later. It was there that he began working as an electrician and also received training as a watch repairer.

Grandfather Smith, my mother's father, was a fairly remarkable man. A toolmaker at the Raleigh bicycle factory, he was a classic skilled blue-collar worker and was extremely proud of his craft skills. His great hobby was to enter competitions in magazines and he turned out to be quite expert in one in particular, the *John Bull*'s 'Bullets'. This was a literary competition which invited respondents to come up with a witty phrase to shed light on a particular given topic. Grandfather Smith obviously acquired quite a lot of money from the cash prizes that he won entering this and other competitions over the years. He and my grandmother lived in a very nice large detached house in Lenton in Nottingham, and he continued to win foreign cruises and other prizes quite regularly throughout his life.

Grandfather Smith was the only person in the family with the faintest interest in politics. He was a Communist. He did not address me with his views very often but as I grew older he always tried to persuade me to read the *Daily Worker*, which he said was the only newspaper that told the truth. He and my grandmother were also ferocious pacifists and they had persuaded their son, my uncle Harold, to keep out of the war by pretending to be a committed pacifist himself. I do not know whether a similar conversation between my parents had resulted in my father taking the electrician job in the mines.

Talking with my grandfather, I eventually discovered that he had actually been a committed follower of the Labour Party's George Lansbury before the war. When Lansbury was expelled from the leadership for his pacifist opposition to the rearmament programme, my grandfather resigned from the Labour Party in disgust. He was not remotely a Marxist. He was one of those Communists who regarded Uncle Joe Stalin as a kindly old man who presided over a working-class paradise in the Soviet Union. He looked on all suggestions that the Soviet Union was the home of any kind of totalitarianism or repression as simply CIA propaganda designed to protect our capitalist masters. Fortunately he never persuaded me, perhaps because my avid reading of my father's *Daily Mail* began at around the same time.

I have no clear recollections of Grandmother Smith (née Harper) although she seemed a quiet, sweet person. Family legend had it that the Harpers had been a rather prosperous Yorkshire family who had come down in the world because of the behaviour of my great-grandfather who had allegedly drunk and gambled away the family fortune at Doncaster races. This, I strongly suspect, was a quite cruel defamation of the old man who had difficulty when in his later years he came to live in Lenton with my very strict teetotaller grandparents. I became aware of occasional rows when he attempted to smuggle the odd bottle of beer into the house, but he was quite obviously not remotely a man with a drink problem.

It was my Communist Grandfather Smith who introduced me to one of my lifelong habits. From the age of seven I would walk every Saturday into Langley Mill and get onto the trolley bus which ran from Ripley to Nottingham, the longest trolley-bus route in the country. My grandfather would meet me off the bus and we would go to watch the football. One week we would go to Notts County and the next to Nottingham Forest. All of my school friends supported the then much bigger Derby County football club, but thanks to my grandfather these two Nottingham clubs had my avid backing. Occasionally Great-Grandfather Harper would join us, but neither of my parents showed the slightest interest or ever accompanied me.

Both clubs attracted enormous crowds in the post-war era and I would walk surrounded by shuffling feet into packed grounds. The small boys like me would be hoisted overhead and passed from hand to hand down the stands to the front where we were plonked on the side by the touchline.

Notts County were the better-followed and more fashionable side because they had some great fading stars playing for them in the Third Division South. I still have vivid recollections of watching the wonderful centre forward Tommy Lawton heading the ball, and Jackie Sewell playing alongside him. I decided, though, that I was going to be a Nottingham Forest supporter, I think because their peculiar name reminded me of other romantic team titles like Plymouth Argyle and Crewe Alexandra. I retain to this day an addiction to going on alternate Saturdays to each football ground.

I began school at Aldercar Infants School just after my fifth birthday. It was within walking distance of our home and on my first day my mother dutifully accompanied me, pushing the pram with my sister inside. I was so keen to attend that I ran far ahead of her and was already inside the school by the time she arrived. I enjoyed school instantly and my mother decided that it was quite unnecessary for her to accompany me backwards and forwards ever again.

My mother had already taught me to read. I can remember making very good progress, and at first sat with the two or three other children who could read on their own whilst those of the others who could manage it were taught to read. I am fairly certain that I was regarded as one of the brightest in the class by the old schoolmistresses who taught us. We were given extremely bad meals with root vegetables boiled to death and a paucity of meat, but the whole atmosphere was pleasant and I think I was a cheerful and diligent young schoolboy.

When I was seven years old, I moved from Aldercar Infants School to the all-age Langley Mill Boys School. This was a very boisterous gathering of boys and lads in the middle of the village with large fields including playing fields at the back. The vast majority of the pupils were the sons of miners and the games in the playground were very rough.

Occasionally one of the brighter boys had a chance of going to Heanor Grammar School at the age of eleven. I don't think that it crossed anybody's mind that one might aspire to any kind of higher education or professional life, and I genuinely suspect the school sent more boys to borstal in my time than it ever did to university.

The standard of academic teaching for the brighter boys was, however, remarkably high. We all sat in class in strict order of our performance in the previous term, with number one at the back of the class and number forty or thereabouts at the front under the eyes of the teacher trying to maintain discipline. I sat at the back and competed for the top two or three places with the son of the pub landlord from nearby Stoneyford, and another boy whose father was a garage manager. Discipline was enforced with considerable strictness and the help of a cane. I had a bad habit of rocking back on my chair from our old-fashioned Victorian bench desks. One day I crashed over backwards having already been warned not to do this. I remember my shock and surprise when my teacher Mr Burnett gave me six of the best on each hand for having caused such disruption. I did not do it again.

Mr Burnett must actually have been a remarkable teacher because, despite the class size, he inspired me to work hard and to enjoy my schoolwork. Now, looking back, I am eternally grateful to him. His teaching was old-fashioned, and included a lot of rote learning. But in his stern and unbending way he ensured we made extremely good progress.

I don't think, though, that I was an out-of-place swot. I was just another lively child running in and out of the school during the breaks, with all the same enthusiasms as my schoolmates. The one possible exception was that I continued to be an enthusiastic reader of my father's *Daily Mail*, which was almost the only reading matter available at home. I would usually begin with *Flook* which was a cartoon drawn by Wally Fawkes with words by Humphrey Lyttelton. (I later knew this duo as jazz players – Wally Fawkes on the clarinet, and Humphrey on the trumpet. Wally Fawkes as Trog also became one of my favourite political cartoonists when I was older.) I would then read the football or cricket before turning to all the political pages and avidly following the activities of the Attlee government.

It was at this astonishingly early age that I became utterly absorbed in politics. Aged nine I kept a full scrapbook of the 1950 general election. Before that I had followed closely the stern economic policies of Mr Cripps who was then Chancellor. I was familiar with the various other leading politicians involved and rejoiced at the fall of the minister of fuel and power, Mr Shinwell, who the *Daily Mail* and I held responsible for the coal shortage of 1947 and the power cuts that we had regularly suffered during that freezing winter. I loved the dramatic narratives that politics provided. I read the news each day like the latest chapter of an adventure story and, as with all my childhood enthusiasms, became obsessively interested and knowledgeable. One day, at school, I was one of two or three pupils called to the front of the class to say what we wanted to be when we grew up. The other two wanted to be a coal miner and a locomotive driver. I announced to an astonished teacher and classmates that I intended to be a Member of Parliament.

After the war, my father had used his savings from working two jobs to buy a small shop in the nearby town of Eastwood, which overlooked the Erewash Valley and Langley Mill. Thereafter he earned his living as a watchmaker and jeweller and achieved some modest success. His customers were at first his fellow miners: in post-war England they were a comparatively prosperous part of the working class.

Eastwood was the birthplace and childhood home of D. H. Lawrence, but in those days the town refused to acknowledge its most famous son. My father knew many men who had known the Lawrence family and they all took the same view of the people that I so enjoyed reading about in *Sons and Lovers*. To them, old man Lawrence had been a marvellous individual and hugely popular. They all deplored his stuck-up and snobbish wife and son. The son was particularly repudiated because he had gone away to write 'all those mucky books'. So far as I am aware, D. H. Lawrence reciprocated these feelings, never having anything to do with Eastwood from the moment that he first left to go to Nottingham High School, a path I would also take.

My father was a wonderful man of whom I have nothing but the proudest and fondest memories. He was very short, as was my mother, and he was embarrassed when I discovered that his nickname at school had been 'Titch'. He was a relaxed workaholic who enjoyed the hard work of running his shop. Indeed he was never happier than when he was sitting at his workbench behind the shop with his eyeglass in his eye repairing his beloved watches. He was pleasant and talkative and generally content with his life, and he cannot have had an enemy in the world. After he died, about three years after I had become an MP, I was constantly approached by people in Eastwood and Nottingham who just wanted to tell me what a wonderful man my father had been.

My mother was very fond and loving, although she frequently quarrelled with my father, which he found difficult. She was a tense and somewhat neurotic person, not happy and untroubled like my father and me. Looking back now, I think she probably suffered quite badly from clinical depression. But it didn't have the slightest adverse effect on my upbringing, nor on her relationship with me. She always looked after me. My brother once told a biographer of mine that she had a drink problem when we were children but I do not believe that she did. She certainly did not follow the temperate habits of her parents, but she never appeared to me to be affected by drink and I do not think that was down to my naivety. Decades later she would spend Christmas with my wife and me so we had plenty of opportunity to see her take part in the festivities without the slightest apparent intoxication, beyond the normal festive standard. But in her last one or two years she became depressed and isolated and we then undoubtedly had trouble trying to keep drink out of her flat, without much success as she died of cirrhosis of the liver in October 1978.

I don't like to discuss these things at length because it is unfair on my mother and gives them more emphasis than they deserve. The important thing, to me, is that my parents between them enabled me to have a happy and balanced home life, first at Langley Mill and then when we moved on. Did my laid-back temperament come from my happy upbringing? Or did I experience my upbringing as happy because of my even temperament? I don't know and don't care to dwell on it. But I do know with absolute certainty that I have no unhappy memories of my early childhood.

2

'Giant Steps'

(John Coltrane, 1959)

NOTTINGHAM

On 1 June 1950, when I was nine, we moved from Langley Mill to Bulwell, a working-class district in the north of Nottingham. This must have made a considerable impact upon me because I still recall the date without difficulty when I forget practically every other family date that I am supposed to remember. Nottingham was bigger, noisier, livelier and more open to the world than Langley Mill. It must have been dawning on me even then how narrow and restricting life in a small old-fashioned pit village was in a changing world.

Nothing captures the Nottingham I knew in the 1950s as well as Alan Sillitoe's *Saturday Night and Sunday Morning*. My father had bought a second shop in a row of local shops on Highbury Road, Bulwell, and the family moved into the rooms behind it. I had a bedroom upstairs which I shared with my young brother, which I was to do until I left home after university. The living accommodation was quite small but we had a drive and a garage and a huge garden that extended into a large field which for some reason belonged to our shop. Above that was a high embankment along which steam trains ran between Nottingham Victoria and Derby Friar Gate. For a short time my father tried to keep chickens in a henhouse on this piece of land but he hated feeding them in the morning, and so tried to press me into doing it for him. My duties came to an end when I released a flock of hens from the henhouse before their wings had been clipped and my father and I had to spend hours recovering them from the thick bushes and undergrowth on the railway embankment to which they had flown. The garden and then the field eventually became an overgrown wilderness in which I enjoyed playing and climbing into the fruit trees with my brother and sister and occasionally our friends.

I began to attend Highbury Primary School which was a walk of only a few hundred yards. Its bland name belied the fact that it had originally been the rather more down-to-earth Albert Street School. I quickly settled in as a newcomer although I had to have a fight in the playground with the class bully before I could be accepted. This had probably been partly provoked by my striking Derbyshire accent, full of 'thee', 'thou' and 'tha wouldna', which did differ from my fellow pupils' very strong Nottingham accent. The accent was soon modified, as it continued to be over the next decades, steadily becoming classless BBC English at secondary school, enjoying a short period of being rather plummy, and then eventually settling into whatever my mature accent can be described as.

I found myself far ahead in my schoolwork and moved very quickly into the top class. I was taught by the splendid Mr Fletcher, who obviously believed that I was a highly intelligent and able pupil. He was the second teacher, after Mr Burnett at Langley Mill Boys School, who really took me in hand and drove me through the necessary teaching process to prepare for the 11-plus examination. He was so impressed by my abilities that when I had passed the exam, which would normally have meant that I went on to the High Pavement Grammar School, he entered me for a city scholarship to Nottingham High School. Nottingham High School was the city's great independent day school, and at the time the city and county council bought about a third of its places, meaning that there were a fairly large number of scholarships available. Unfortunately, increasing left-wing 'anti-elitist' orthodoxy meant that this practice was discontinued a few years later.

I duly visited Nottingham High School where I was interviewed by a panel of the staff, whom I seemed to impress. The only answer that I can recall giving was when I was asked about reading comics. I rather loftily announced that I preferred comics like *Hotspur* which were full of written stories to the others which were only strip cartoons. That probably confirmed my place at the school. With hindsight, going to Nottingham High School transformed my whole life.

I think that six boys and six girls from Highbury Primary School had got through the 11-plus and they should all have gone to High Pavement Grammar School or Manning Grammar School for Girls. But not all of them were allowed to take up their places because their parents either did not wish them to belong to such grand establishments, or possibly – and perhaps more likely – they could not afford the compulsory uniform. And two of the girls were not allowed to go to Manning because their parents could not see the point of girls having a secondary education at all.

I quite enjoyed my twelve months at Highbury Primary School, where my knockabout life followed a normal course. I played for the school football team and we actually reached the final in that year's citywide competition, which was remarkable for a small school. I played in the semi-final but sadly was dropped for the final which at least meant that I was not totally disappointed when we were defeated by a larger school. This modest primary school also ran a cricket team during the summer which I occasionally played for, although I was usually reduced to being twelfth man and scorer. The few friends I made were largely amongst the neighbouring children but I carried none of those friendships forward when I went to secondary school.

Nottingham High School, founded in 1513, was a ride on a city trolley bus away at a large site surrounded by green parks just north of the city centre. In those days it was a grand academic sweatshop where the top class in each year group was almost fully made up of the scholarship boys, together with a few of the brightest fee-paying pupils, who were the children of the local professional and business classes. There was no great social distinction between we 11-plus boys from the council estates and the poorer districts on the one hand and the middle-class boys from the outer suburbs for which I would one day be the MP. I look back and regard this period, which we enjoyed as a result of Rab Butler's 1944 Education Act, as one of the United Kingdom's brief phases of meritocracy and social mobility.

I enjoyed lessons and began to take on board Latin, French and serious mathematics. I had always hitherto been accustomed to being top of the class and it came as rather a shock when in my first term I was rated at about twenty-sixth out of the class of thirty. This was no doubt a result of my idle assumption that I could do well without having to make any particular effort. From then on I steadily began to improve my performance and rise up towards the ranks of the academic high-flyers.

This was possible largely because I always found it easy to pass the end-of-term examinations. I look back and see myself as having been almost a professional examinee for a period of more than ten years until I eventually ceased academic education when I was called to the Bar. My performance was quite sufficient for the school to be satisfied with my presence and enabled me to avoid any problems over my lack of interest in a lot of the school activities. I behaved myself reasonably well and I showed all the promise they were looking for, as the whole institution was driven by a desire to produce good results and the maximum number of scholarships and places at Oxford and Cambridge.

I enjoyed my almost eight years at Nottingham High School. Most boys who can remember me at all from school associate me with trainspotting, an enthusiasm that I had acquired at school in Bulwell. The majority of Nottingham boys of my generation seemed to collect books in which we would write down the numbers of the steam trains that we saw, aided by a collection of spotters' guides listing all the steam engines in the four regions of British Rail. I steadily moved on from collecting numbers to becoming an ardent enthusiast of railway and locomotive history and spent a quite disproportionate amount of my spare time travelling great distances to collect the numbers of as many varieties as possible of the hugely variegated steam engines that pulled trains across the country. I became really quite captivated by the magic of the steam engine. Many dated back as far as the nineteenth century and the trains that went along the embankment at the bottom of our family garden in Bulwell were still the steam trains of the Great Northern Railway which had built that line in the 1880s.

Eventually I became the driving force of the school Locomotive Society and when I was in the sixth form I organized coach trips to locomotive depots all over the country. Despite taking such an avid interest throughout my secondary-school career, and probably to the great surprise of my trainspotting friends, I abandoned it almost entirely as soon as I went away to university. Academic study and adolescence had widened my interests.

I was also active in school cricket, but once again achieved no success. I had one game for the first team at about the under-fourteen stage when I was dismissed first ball. I did better watching the game, starting the visits to Nottinghamshire County Cricket Club at Trent Bridge that would continue throughout my life. The school played rugby which I dutifully did for as long as I was obliged to. I used to get roped in for house matches where I played in the forwards with instructions to make strenuous efforts to restrain smaller but better players on the other side. Unfortunately the school did not play soccer as it was regarded as a game for the lower orders and not suitable for a pretentious academic institution like our own, which was trying to create gentlemen. However, like all my friends, I played vigorous football in the playground and at every other opportunity. Eventually, in the sixth form, I did two seasons with a local amateur team called Sherwood Amateurs where I did reasonably well.

Although supposedly voluntary, the school required all but the most resistant to join the Combined Cadet Force which obliged us to have military uniforms and parade with rifles in the playground. The school was proud of its military tradition but I certainly was not suited for a military career, although I expected, naturally, to have to serve two years National Service in due course. (In fact I missed National Service by just a few months, to my pleasure and relief.) Because I had a very low level of interest in drill and was rather negligent in such matters as polishing brass and looking after my gaiters, I was eventually moved from the infantry to the artillery section. This was quite engaging as it involved some training on a 25-pounder field piece instead of cleaning and dismantling rifles and Bren guns. When the time came for the summer camp we abandoned the strict lines of infantry tents in Catterick and instead spent an entertaining few days at Otterburn, the UK's largest firing range, in Northumberland. During the day we practised firing live shots from our 25-pounders. In the evenings we cowered in our tents, terrified of the hard-drinking Black Watch regulars who went on the rampage every night, their bagpipes keeping us awake.

Another camp I attended was at Buckenham Tofts in Norfolk where it rained continuously and we slept in leaking bell tents. Each of the many schools represented there had its own line of tents, but the schools quickly allied themselves into one of two gangs, one led by Epsom and one by Lancing. There were a large number of fights as we were all so bored and idle because of the rain. Military policemen broke up a fight one night in the NAAFI tent using batons with quite some vigour. It was all rather *Lord of the Flies* for four or five days.

Eventually I became the senior NCO in the artillery but I was kept at sergeant because it was quite obvious that my own lack of taste for discipline and conformity did not justify the elevation to company sergeant major that my role would otherwise have warranted.

These diversions were all very secondary to strict adherence to academic study as I moved up the school in the top academically selected A class – although I slipped into the B stream for French as I lacked any flair for languages.

It was in my third year at Nottingham High that I went into the class of the third and last remarkable schoolmaster to transform both my education and my attitude to life. David Peters was a strict form master but he was also a historian and he began to drive on my increasing interest in history. It duly became my favourite and best subject throughout my school career. I was particularly keen on medieval history and eventually, in the sixth form, I chose European and British medieval history as my main subject, again taught by Mr Peters. He not only helped to instil my initial enthusiasm, he also appeared to like the long wordy essays which I would turn out for him on such subjects as the investiture contest.

Mr Peters was instrumental in my first encounter with 'abroad', too. He was something of a pioneer for school trips, and my first visit outside the country was to the medieval town of Bruges in Belgium. I was overwhelmed by the extraordinary experience of being in a

French- and Flemish-speaking country, by the medieval architecture and by Flemish painting which I love to this day.

Thereafter I was able to go on the school trip every year including one to Paris. My parents, who had never left England, were so intrigued that they were tempted to make a day trip from our family holiday in Jersey to Saint-Malo, where they of course discovered that my five years of school French was of no great use. Fortunately they became as interested in the outside world as I had become and I am glad to say they had quite a few opportunities for foreign holidays in their later years.

At O level, which was the first public examination level, several of us refused to sit any science subject. I found the laboratories boring and the subjects of physics and chemistry tedious, and insisted on taking art and architecture instead. The school was not happy but yielded. My own graphic abilities were minimal but I was able to make up for that by passing the examination in medieval church architecture. I acquired a lifelong interest in art and architecture from that limited beginning. In later years, together with my wife Gillian, a committed medievalist, I made many trips to Romanesque churches all over Europe.

I passed all my O levels, about eight in total, including an additional maths paper which I only passed by rote learning, as my comprehension of calculus was exceedingly limited. All my learning in mathematics was forgotten immediately. I also passed a French oral examination although, as my parents had learnt, no native French-speaker was able to understand any word that I said.

In the sixth form we were divided into subject-based groups on a very traditional basis. The academically brilliant were encouraged to enter Sixth Classics to study Greek and Latin. The next most able were encouraged to go into Sixth History, which is where I found myself. The reasonably competent found themselves in Sixth Science doing physics, chemistry and maths. The comparative duffers were put into Sixth Economics because it was assumed that they would only be suitable for jobs in business and banking.

As a member of Sixth History I was expected to do three A levels:

history, English literature and either French or Latin. Again four of us were very awkward and refused to do a language. We insisted on taking economics instead and were academically head and shoulders above the other pupils in the class. I am afraid that our little group was somewhat disruptive in the lessons. We turned them into an almost permanent political debate with the unfortunate economics teacher, Mr Thompson, which had a rather bad effect on the success level of some of the other pupils in the necessary examination. This was the only academic qualification that I ever acquired for my job, many years later, as Chancellor of the Exchequer. When I met the then retired Stan Thompson, he expressed pleasure and amazement that he had ever taught a Chancellor!

I continued with all my outside interests and in addition became rather good at the game called fives, which is a bit like squash and played in an enclosed court according to the rules of Rugby School. I became the captain of fives, which I enjoyed greatly – and at least it kept me fit. I combined this with my football, cricket and train-spotting, and I also began to go into the bars and jazz clubs of Nottingham as soon as I looked old enough to appear a legal drinker in the eyes of the more tolerant barmen. I became a regular customer for at least part of every Saturday night at a trad-jazz club in West Bridgford. It was called the Dancing Slipper and in later years was in my parliamentary constituency, although by then it had become a more respectable tea room. I first met several of the Tory ladies who became the backbone of my constituency association as young girls at that club. I began to collect jazz records and discovered that Charlie Parker and Miles Davis were rather different from the bands of Chris Barber, Humphrey Lyttelton, Acker Bilk and other regulars at the Dancing Slipper.

Despite my continued interest in politics, my political activities within the school were very limited. From my O level year onwards I joined the school debating society and was an active participant in as many debates as possible. I think I developed a dreadful public-speaking style as I could not be restrained from talking at the speed of an express train. I espoused all manner of political opinions as my views veered about in these formative years and gave speeches expressing views ranging from the extreme left to the extreme right and back again.

I must have become a little more polished at some point because I was a strong contender for the only elected office in the debating society, which was that of secretary. Unfortunately, I was defeated by my friend Bill Woodward who was already a good speaker and would later go on to be a successful barrister and QC. It was my first but not last experience of electoral defeat.

Our most stirring and controversial debate was about the Suez Crisis. I was going through a phase of being an enthusiastic supporter of Anthony Eden's ill-judged venture and spoke accordingly, no doubt with suitable patriotic fervour. My favourite teacher David Peters attended with several other members of the teaching staff as the whole country was dramatically gripped by the issue. I remember being very impressed by Mr Peters' passionate and well-argued speech against the invasion which, because of my admiration for him, surprised me and also stirred some doubts in my own opinion which I had already given. My reflections on the Suez debate over the next year or two played quite a large part in forming my lifelong opinions on Britain's role in the modern world and the end of our national delusions of being a Victorian imperial power in the new global order.

It was at about this time that I had my introduction to the House of Commons, again through school trips organized by the energetic Mr Peters. I took to it immediately and I remember being utterly absorbed in the proceedings. Two quite particular occasions stick in my mind. On my first visit, I remember sitting in the gallery and seeing a very aged Winston Churchill on the government front bench below the gangway. He sat there in a crowded House listening to some minister at the Despatch Box before suddenly heaving himself to his feet plainly intending to leave the Chamber. A senior Tory backbencher instantly leapt to his side to give him an arm to lean on as he moved towards the Bar of the House. The unfortunate minister continued to drone on whilst the whole House and all the visitors in the gallery gazed in wonder at this slow-moving awesome figure making his way in short slow steps towards the exit. Alas, that was the only time in my life that I ever set eyes on Winston Churchill.

On another occasion, I remember sitting in the gallery about two rows directly behind Nikolai Bulganin (premier of the USSR) and Nikita Khrushchev (First Secretary of the Soviet Communist Party), who were making a governmental visit to London and were obviously being invited to observe bourgeois democracy in action.

These were merely memorable celebrity occasions on visits where I otherwise absorbed the extraordinary Victorian atmosphere of an institution still at its height. It merely confirmed my determination to become a participant there if I possibly could.

I successfully passed all my A levels and, as was usual at that time, all those believed to be Oxbridge contenders were invited to spend a third year in the sixth form. I put my name down to do the rounds of the Oxbridge colleges, which then held their own entrance examinations in groups. David Peters sent a lot of his pupils to Jesus College, Cambridge, but he asked me to have a go at Gonville and Caius College in my first Cambridge group, as he hoped to establish a contact there. If I was unsuccessful, I was lined up to travel to about four other groups at both universities to see if I could find a slot. I had never been to either city in my life. I had never even heard of Caius College.

I went to Caius, sat the examination in history, and was interviewed. They offered me an exhibition and I accepted. I remember that, as a matter of courtesy, I rang someone at Balliol College, Oxford, to say that I no longer needed to attend their examination next week. A very snooty fellow of Balliol made it clear that his college was quite happy to miss me if I was really someone who was content to go to Cambridge.

As with the move from Langley Mill to Nottingham High School, going on to higher education would be another life-changing journey to a different and wider world for a provincial professional examinee.

3

'Blues for a Reason'

(Chet Baker, 1984)

CAMBRIDGE

College life in Cambridge is a completely closed unreal world but it can be a wonderful experience for a young person leaving home for the first time. I arrived determined to become a politician and in Cambridge I did just that. The world of student politics and debate occupied a huge proportion of my time and brought me into close contact with all the other political activists from every college.

Caius was one of the larger colleges, with a reasonable academic reputation, although almost half the students were medics. The medical students lived in a slightly different world from me and they seemed to have been selected largely for their ability to fill the college eights on the river, which was not an activity with which I was ever even tempted to experiment.

The admissions tutor and history don Neil McKendrick had admitted me with a view to my becoming one of his high-flying history students. The historians were a very distinguished group, but I annoyed Neil, who was only about five years older than I was and would become a lifelong friend, by being very utilitarian and switching to law. I thought that a law degree would give me a good professional living and, more importantly, I believed that it would be easy to combine with politics. (This view did prove to be somewhat out of date by the 1960s.)

My director of studies was a Mr Michael Prichard, who patiently sought to educate the little group of lawyers that included me. He was a splendid, slightly eccentric academic whose most striking physical feature was the totally artificial and obvious wig that slipped about on his bald head during our tutorials. He patiently persevered with inculcating some legal knowledge into us despite being perfectly well aware that I was spending more of my time on politics. My days and nights in Cambridge were spent in the Cambridge Union society, the political clubs and the bars of the city. I spent my Christmas and summer holidays doing paid work to keep my overdraft down, catching up with law in the Easter vacations.

The law tripos was very old-fashioned and my studies were interesting but quite useless for any subsequent practice. In my first year we did a lot of Roman law and I duly learnt how to free a Roman slave.

I got a first in my first-year examinations and was made a scholar of the college. Thereafter, however, my swotting in the vacations only earned me a 2:1 degree. To misquote Supreme Court Justice Oliver Wendell Holmes, politics is the right career for anyone with a good second-class mind. My excuse is that political life in Cambridge made legal study impossible, but Mr Prichard was very annoyed and I was rather disappointed myself.

I had tested my interest in the law in the summer between finishing school and starting at Cambridge by taking on the role of office boy in a legal practice in Nottingham called Huntsman, Donaldson and Tyzack. There I mostly drafted conveyances. More interestingly, I was sent to sit behind the barristers whom we had instructed in criminal trials at the Nottingham assizes or quarter sessions (the predecessors of today's Crown Courts). This confirmed to me that I would much rather be a barrister than a solicitor. At the beginning of my second year at Cambridge, I duly entered Gray's Inn, because it was Mr Prichard's inn. In the summer after my fourth and final year at Cambridge, during which I studied international law and added an LLB to my BA, I borrowed a Bar Council postal course from my fellow law student and political enthusiast Michael Howard, which I swotted over. I passed my Bar finals and was called to the Bar in November 1963, the autumn after I went down.

*

The most significant event of my life, however, occurred in a totally different sphere in my first term. I went with some friends one evening to a Trinity College barbecue on Jesus Green. There I approached an attractive girl with shoulder-length hair and invited her to have a dance, which must have been my incompetent jiving to the inevitable trad-jazz band. She proved to be Gillian Edwards, a first-year history under-graduate at Newnham College and like me a product of the 11-plus system. I was struck with her very quickly although she politely declined to let me have a kiss when I walked her back to her college at the end of the evening. Gillian became my girlfriend for the whole of my university career. The Sixties hadn't really got going at this stage: those were simple, innocent times. We had tea in each other's college rooms, and, conforming to the undergraduate fashion, sat through bleak and boring nouvelle vague films at the Arts Cinema. I was interested in Gillian's passion, medieval history. She was less interested in my passion for politics, but coming from a politically active family she understood and accepted it. Gillian was one of the cleverest undergraduates of her generation and she would have taken a brilliant first if she had not met me and spent too much time with me. She would have become a history don if she had not married me. As it was, she cut short her academic career and became my rock, for over fifty years. She provided me with security, a family life, love and affection – a sane and stable background through all the crazy ups and downs of the political life I had chosen to pursue.

My immersion in politics at Cambridge was wholly typical of most undergraduates at the time. We were a small and privileged minority amongst our generation, as less than 10 per cent of the population went to university at all. Those of us at Cambridge all assumed that we were on the way to securing lifelong careers with whomever we afforded the eventual privilege of employing us. There were full-time rugby players, some of whom played internationally, full-time actors and entertainers and full-time cricketers. David Frost was one of the distinguished undergraduates at Caius but I usually only saw him as a cabaret performer at the bigger parties or the May Balls. The staggering under-graduate success was Mike Brearley, who combined captaining the first-class cricket team in the summer with getting a starred first in his degree.

I had no idea what my political convictions really were at the time I first went up, and had not decided which political party was going to have the good fortune to have me as a member. There were a large number of enthusiastic Conservative students at Cambridge, rivalled in number only by the Campaign for Nuclear Disarmament which provided the majority of the Labour Society's ranks. I joined the clubs of all the political parties and attended most of them at first.

The big issue at the time was Secretary of State for the Colonies Iain Macleod's drive to move the remains of the British Empire, particularly in Africa, to independent status. This was a hugely controversial subject and one that caused immense dissension inside the Conservative Party throughout the country. Most undergraduates were of course in favour of this move. The Macmillan government was combining this with cautious steps towards market economics and social reform. The Labour Party in contrast was really dominated by traditional post-war socialism and by institutions such as the trade unions and the co-operative movement, which I associated with everything that was old-fashioned, reactionary, and too dominant in my own county of Nottinghamshire. Labour seemed backward-looking and quite unable to engage with the emerging issues of the late twentieth century. I was tempted by the social democracy of Roy Jenkins, Tony Crosland and Shirley Williams, but more attracted in the end by the forward-looking younger Tory ministers in the government.

As a result, by the end of my first year I was standing for office in the Cambridge University Conservative Association, or CUCA. I still kept some connections with the Labour Party, and for a brief time I was an active member of both the Bow Group in the Tory Party (the thriving national political club and pressure group for young reforming Tories), and the Campaign for Democratic Socialism in the Labour Party. This enabled me to meet people like Roy Jenkins at the same time as coming into regular contact with most of the senior members of the Conservative Cabinet, who at that time saw Cambridge as an important recruiting ground.

As I became more politically active I met a quite remarkable number of people who became lifelong personal and political friends.

One of the first was Norman Fowler, whom I met at a freshers' 'squash' or party in my college for CUCA. Norman, hitherto unknown to me, made a rousing recruiting speech. I not only joined the association but we were soon firm friends. Years later, he would be my ministerial boss.

The first policy discussion evening I attended was at Pembroke College in the rooms of Peter Lloyd, later my Minister of State at the Home Office. The discussions were rudely interrupted and then brilliantly taken over by a flamboyant and voluble John Gummer, who arrived late dressed in a long priest's cloak which in the evenings he was accustomed to wear as his outdoor coat. Leon Brittan, who seemed to be the most outstanding member of CUCA and was already ex-president of the Union, Michael Howard, Norman Lamont, Peter Lilley and many more were all active members. My first office in CUCA was as assistant librarian to the librarian, John Gummer. My only duty was to keep the 'library' – a battered suitcase full of old pamphlets. Somehow we lost it. Nevertheless I was elected upwards through the ranks and became chairman in my third year.

I held my twenty-first birthday party jointly with my close friend Martin Suthers, later prominent in local government in Nottinghamshire, in Leon Brittan's rooms overlooking Trinity Great Court. The riotous assembly, in a long, rowdy drinking session involving a great deal of dry sherry and a small fire started by I know not whom, included many people in the governing leadership of the country thirty years later. I enjoyed it but was slightly distracted by Norman Fowler, who spent the entire party in pursuit of Gillian.

We were so politically enthused and competitive that more than a dozen of the undergraduates that I overlapped with eventually became Conservative Members of Parliament and six of us became Cabinet ministers. We became publicly notorious in the Thatcher years when we were described as the Cambridge Mafia. At the time, we were all attracted by the modernizing and reforming 'One Nation' views of some of the key members of Harold Macmillan's government, including Rab Butler, Ted Heath and Reginald Maudling. My particular hero was Iain

Macleod – a brilliant platform orator, an original thinker, and a man of real political courage as he withstood the hatred – which it was – of the diehard imperialist right of the party.

By the time I left Cambridge I was firmly taken by the principles of free-market economics combined with a social conscience, and a supporter of a foreign policy that accepted the realities of the new post-war world. I remained a One Nation Conservative for the rest of my life.

One of the more memorable student political controversies in which I became involved occurred when, as that term's chairman of the Conservative Association, I invited Sir Oswald Mosley to speak. Perhaps unsurprisingly, there were no fascist sympathizers in Cambridge at all. Mosley had, however, not lost all of his commanding presence; he could be a brilliant orator and had spoken at the Cambridge Union at least once in the previous year or two. I had seen him give a gripping performance in a Union debate where he had started talking for a few moments before a student approached him and slapped a custard pie in his face. This silenced the barracking and produced shocked silence whilst Mosley wiped the custard from his face and the student was removed. He used the incident to capture everyone's attention and thereafter gripped the audience with his commanding delivery of a case which did not persuade but was compellingly delivered. I invited him in order to add colour to the card for the term. It was an early illustration of my belief that the principle of free speech should extend to listening to arguments you violently disapprove of, and facing them with debate, not prohibition.

Brian Pollitt, the Communist son of Harry Pollitt, the former Communist MP, was a very active political student and one of my circle of political friends. He began a forceful campaign against providing a platform for Oswald Mosley ('no-platforming' might be a new term but it is not a new concept) in which he was joined by Michael Howard, who was a CUCA officer. This became a typical student wrangle which led all the way up to that term's Cambridge Union elections.

The Cambridge Union was a debating society, with a membership

– separate from but overlapping with that of the political clubs – of politically ambitious students of all stripes. I was by then a committee member and was overwhelmingly likely to be elected at the end of the term to the post of secretary, which would in turn pave the way to president of the Union – probably the most prestigious position that any aspiring politician at Cambridge could hold. Michael Howard resigned from CUCA in protest against the Mosley meeting and briefly joined the Labour Party. He stood against me as secretary of the Union as part of his anti-Mosley campaign and defeated me.

None of the fuss changed my mind. The Mosley event went ahead in the form of a debate, before a packed audience in the Corn Exchange, between Sir Oswald on the one hand, and John Gummer and myself on the other. It was largely a debate about Mosley's political record. Mosley was not at his best and I may be a little biased but I think that Gummer and myself got the better of the arguments.

I was convinced that if the debate had been held before the Union election I would not have suffered this setback to my political progress. (In the end, it merely delayed my progress by a year, but it did mean that Michael overtook me in the queue to be president, a position he attained about a year before I eventually did.) But I had enjoyed the row and the controversy and so was fairly relaxed about it all. Thankfully, the incident had no effect at all on my friendship with Michael Howard, which has lasted throughout our lives.

I also rose through the ranks of the national body, the Federation of University Conservative and Unionist Associations (or FUCUA), to become its chairman in 1963. Of my Cambridge contemporaries, only John Gummer really got as involved as I did: I succeeded him as chairman. We both attended two big FUCUA conferences a year, one of which was held at Swinton Hall, the Yorkshire home of Lord Swinton, a veteran minister under Chamberlain and Churchill. Hordes of ministers came to address these conferences but our main efforts were put into writing and performing a cabaret at the end. These were high-quality examples, I think, of the newly fashionable art of political satire, mainly at the expense of Macmillan and his government. I took part adequately enough but John Gummer was a brilliant cabaret performer.

FUCUA was an institution of the Conservative Party and as such the chairman had a seat on the party National Executive. I therefore began to attend distinguished meetings of leading party figures at Conservative Central Office, the Carlton Club and other great Conservative centres in London, where I found myself surrounded by tall patrician men with cultured establishment accents and expensive suits. The most interesting issue being raised at the time in the executive was the crisis over the MP John Profumo and the model Christine Keeler, which had created a sensation and shaken the Macmillan government to its foundations. My most memorable moment from these meetings was rising to my feet to address a rather combative question to the then chairman of the party, Lord Poole, to enquire why the prime minister, the chief whip and others had been so gullible as to believe Profumo's denials of any improper relationship between him and Miss Keeler, and to oblige him to make a statement to the House of Commons to that effect. The resignation issue was, as always, supposed in theory to be based on the lie denying the offence, rather than the offence itself. I shocked some of those present but of course I also discovered that I had had the temerity to express the views of a considerable number of the older members of the executive. Ironically, forty years later, when he had completed his decades of penance, I got to know John Profumo quite well. He and I were both members of a dining club called the Other Club, where I discovered him to be a charming and delightful man.

The first party conference that I attended was at Llandudno in 1962. I attended practically every party conference thereafter every autumn for the next fifty years. At this first gathering, I enthusiastically supported from the floor and elsewhere a speech by Harold Macmillan arguing the case for the application he had made to join the European Community. His aspirations fitted my developing political beliefs perfectly. Britain had recently suffered the ignominy of the Suez debacle, after which the former American Secretary of State, Dean Acheson, had notoriously explained that 'Great Britain has lost an empire and has not yet found a role.' Our economic development was lagging behind that of the nations who had been occupied, or whom we had helped to defeat, in the Second World War. We were still having this ridiculous internal debate about the justification for Macleod 'giving away' the empire, which we had to do if we were to avoid the post-colonial wars in which the French had been immersed. Macmillan held out for my generation the prospect of a better role for a modern Britain in the future world. This idea that our destiny lay in Europe became one of my core convictions from then on.

The following year, 1963, I was at the conference in Blackpool when it received the announcement of Harold Macmillan's resignation as party leader. This astonishing move plunged the conference into an agitated and extraordinary debate, which I think I enjoyed more than any party conference I have attended before or since. The conference's media profile leapt to sensational heights and every delegate was plunged into the plotting and campaigning which we assumed was more the atmosphere of an American party convention than the usual measured debate of our Tory gathering. As the chairman of FUCUA, I was charged with collecting the opinions of students and submitting them as part of the so-called consultation process which eventually turned out to be the totally bogus precursor to the fix by the 'magic circle' of the party. I hoped myself that Macleod or Heath would stand but plainly neither of them was going to do so. It seemed to me obvious that the great bulk of the members of FUCUA would support Rab Butler despite the dull and dismal speech that he gave at the conference. I duly submitted this opinion to the executive.

Butler was of course quite unacceptable to the Conservative establishment who had never forgiven him – and never would – for his prominent role in appeasement before the Second World War, and probably also for his renowned cunning and guile. A move was organized for a certain Lord Home, who seemed a most unlikely candidate even from his position as Foreign Secretary. However, as the conference went on it became obvious that his candidature was emerging. The ruling oligarchy invited another student, Jonathan Aitken, who held no office in FUCUA at all but had impeccable family connections, to carry out a parallel consultation amongst students.

Jonathan duly reported that student opinion favoured Alec Douglas-Home.

The darling of the conference delegates was Quintin Hogg, Viscount Hailsham. I was in the audience at a packed fringe meeting, the annual Conservative Political Centre lecture, when he suddenly announced that he was renouncing his peerage in order to be a candidate. Pandemonium broke out as a weeping Quintin stood before us to acknowledge the cheers. I had been standing at the side whilst he spoke and I now made futile attempts to find somewhere to sit down as a symbolic gesture to dissociate myself from the extraordinary rally atmosphere which had broken out.

Randolph Churchill, Winston's erratic son, rushed to the conference to support Quintin, although that support was probably damaging to his candidate. I found myself alone in a lift with Randolph and was quite unable to prevent him pinning a lapel badge with 'Q' on it onto my jacket. I removed the offending object within seconds of leaving the lift.

I regarded Quintin as brilliant and entertaining but an unguided missile politically. Later when I was a junior minister he was Lord Chancellor. I then liked and admired him but I occasionally had the effrontery to clash with him at Cabinet Committee meetings when I attended as Norman Fowler's deputy. As the years went on, he would always arrive late for such meetings, burst through the door into the discussions and walk noisily with the aid of two sticks to his place, sometimes carrying a small dog which he would place on his lap. He would then give his firm views. He once dismissed me angrily as a 'Midlands road hog' in a discussion on speed limits. He was in his less eccentric prime at the time of his leadership bid but he would have been too erratic as prime minister even then.

Alec Douglas-Home duly emerged from the establishment manoeuvrings as prime minister. He was one of the most delightful and likeable men I ever knew in politics; but he was a disastrous political campaigner against Harold Wilson and the 'white heat of the technological revolution'.

During my time at Cambridge, I lived at a level which was financially far beyond anything that my student grant or my father could afford.

An indulgent bank manager, George Noon, at the local branch of Barclays in Eastwood, allowed me to run an overdraft without apparent limit. Appropriately enough for my lifestyle, I tried to keep it under control in the vacations by working night shifts at a bakery, manning a machine in John Player's cigarette factory and taking a job at a brewery. Work at the Home Brewery was usually at a bottle-washing machine but I also spent two alcoholic weeks as a driver's mate on a brewer's wagon with a pint at every pub we stopped in – I always say that this was the best job I ever had. I also worked for the Post Office at Christmas where the number of extra staff hired seemed to exceed the number of people really required for Christmas mail by a comfortable margin. I played a lot of poker in the canteen.

When I came to leave Cambridge in the summer of 1963 I had an overdraft of about £3,000 (nearly £60,000 in today's money). I nervously went to see Mr Noon who asked how I was going to repay it. I explained that I was broke but hoped to enter a barrister's chambers. He sighed, looked me over, and agreed that the bank would lend me whatever it would take to buy a black jacket and waistcoat, striped trousers, a good overcoat, a bowler hat, and a rolled umbrella. Duly acquired, these made me look like a very juvenile Chaplinesque figure. I also purchased – courtesy of the growing overdraft – a set of barrister's robes.

I was now a Cambridge graduate and postgraduate, an ex-president of the Cambridge Union, and a barrister-at-law. I also took steps to prepare to be a Conservative parliamentary candidate. I went to Conservative Central Office in Smith Square, London, to meet Sir Paul Bryan MP, the party vice chairman then in charge of candidates. The system was not as formal and elaborate as it is now. He did not interview me but merely asked me where I would like to stand. I told him that I couldn't afford to win a seat just yet since I had to earn some money, and said I would like to gain experience in a Labour seat in the Midlands. He explained that at this point in the electoral cycle most constituencies had already adopted candidates, but wished me luck in the search and entered me onto the approved candidates list.

I now fondly imagined that I was ready to enter the real world.

4

'Workin''

(Miles Davis, 1956)

BIRMINGHAM

I had been given an introduction to a chambers in Birmingham by a don at Cambridge. I had specified Birmingham because I had calculated that I could not possibly afford to start in practice in London. My understanding was that the competition for work in London was so great, and the cost of living so high, that it would be almost impossible to keep myself solvent for the first few years. I hardly knew Birmingham, except that I had trainspotted at its two railway stations from time to time, travelling between the stations on the tram. My legal expectations had been raised by my observation during my holiday job as a solicitors' clerk that all the serious court work in Nottingham had been done by Birmingham barristers. I had also formed the view (I cannot now remember how, but it turned out to be true) that there was more work for beginners on the Midland Circuit.

I travelled to Birmingham for an interview with Michael Davies, who was the head of a chambers in the old Victorian terrace at 41 Temple Row. Unbeknown to me, this was the strongest set of chambers in Birmingham at the time. There was then no organized way of applying and being considered for a pupillage. I had about ten minutes in casual conversation with Michael during which we got on together reasonably well. He then promptly offered me a place and took me outside to introduce me to the people who would be my colleagues for the next sixteen years. They seemed a very pleasant crowd and they appeared to accept Michael's impulsive decision to admit me without query. He may have been struck by my outstanding personality but it is also possible that he had noted the reference to the presidency of the Cambridge Union on my CV.

I moved into digs at Olton, a 'nice' suburb in Solihull, and began the short commute by steam train from the local station into Birmingham's Snow Hill very shortly thereafter. I had fallen on my feet. The Bar had been almost impossible for beginners for several years before, but as a result, I think, of some extensions to criminal legal aid there was now a glut of work available and the chambers was desperately short of barristers. I sat with and behind my pupil master Michael Davies from time to time but I was also almost immediately propelled into cases of my own, not only in the magistrates' courts and the county courts but in jury trials at quarter sessions and at the assizes.

My academic career had given me no training of any kind in the day-to-day intricacies of the criminal law or the law of negligence. I acquired the necessary practitioners' books, mainly Archbold on crime, and learnt my trade as I went along, beginning with the imitation of my better opponents. I actually made my first appearance before the Court of Criminal Appeal when I was still in pupillage: fortunately the judges, who could be very aggressive, seemed to treat me indulgently.

Within a few months, Michael Davies became Recorder of Derby and then took silk. Following the custom of the time this required him to transfer to London chambers, and for my last six months in training I became the pupil, where my workload allowed, of Philip Cox.

Both became my great friends, as did most of my colleagues in chambers. We were a very lively and gregarious collection of men. A great deal of hard drinking accompanied a very great deal of serious practice of all kinds, enlivened by the odd practical joke. In one instance my great friend David Jones snapped handcuffs on one of my wrists during a court adjournment, only for the judge to come back in for a quick word with me. I had to keep a straight face while

I answered his enquiries with the handcuffed arm firmly behind my back. On another occasion at Warwick Crown Court, David, acting for the prosecution, picked up a slip of the tongue I had made while acting for the defence. I had referred to my client stealing a Ford Meriden in Granada, rather than the other way around. David passed me a note informing me that the Spanish police had a warrant for arrest, which unfortunately I read out to the whole rather unimpressed courtroom before realizing I had been had. Most days, after usually rather more serious business than this, the younger men would congregate in one of the pubs before heading for home. This created considerable difficulties for me with my landlady who was trying to cook supper for me at a set time. Gillian at this stage was continuing her PhD in medieval history at Cambridge. I used to drive over to see her at weekends as a relief from the hard work and play during the week.

The result of all this was that I rapidly became – at least to a certain extent – financially independent, although as endless patient letters from my long-suffering bank manager attest, I only ceased to live on some kind of a bank overdraft when I finally became a Cabinet minister more than twenty years later. To the relief of my landlady I left my digs at Olton after less than a year and acquired a lease on a newly built flat in Harborne.

Meanwhile I had been pursuing my hopes of a Conservative candidature, having become an active member of the Birmingham Bow Group. Early in 1964, just a few months into my pupillage, Central Office contacted me to enquire whether I was interested in being the candidate for Mansfield in Nottinghamshire as the adopted candidate had recently 'gone mad', which was the insensitive way of describing a nervous breakdown in those days. I immediately agreed. I was appearing at an inquest in Shifnal, Shropshire, on the day of the selection meeting and spent the evening driving across the country in my recently acquired second-hand Hillman car in order to be interviewed by the Association Executive at the Swan Hotel in Mansfield.

Mansfield was a very traditional mining constituency with a large number of coal mines in and around the town and the few surrounding villages which were the basis of the whole local economy. It was an unwinnable seat for the Conservatives. Nevertheless I was up against some quite strong opposition for the candidacy, including the magazine proprietor and man about town Jocelyn Stevens, who later became a prominent business figure. I took my turn with about four others being interviewed for half an hour by a panel of twenty or thirty people. To my amazement they selected me.

It was Gillian who, in conversation with one of my new constituency officers, discovered that they had chosen me because of the honesty of one of my answers. Every candidate apparently had been asked why they wanted to be the Conservative candidate in Mansfield. Every other candidate had replied with a passionate assertion that they were confident that with a considerable effort the seat could be won for the party. This was obviously untrue. I had replied that I could not possibly afford to be an MP until I had established myself at the Bar and that I was looking for experience in a safe Labour seat to help me in future years. The Tory ladies of Mansfield had looked upon this young man who at twenty-three seemed still a schoolboy, and decided to reward him for his common-sense reply. I was the first Tory candidate for Mansfield in living memory who had not been educated at Eton.

As this was the spring of 1964 with an election only a few months away at most, I was immediately plunged into a short frenzy of campaigning. I was soon regularly driving my old car the four-hour round trip on the pre-motorway roads between Birmingham and Mansfield.

This made life very difficult for those making the arrangements for my forthcoming wedding. Gillian and I had never really formally become engaged, but had just rather assumed that we were after I left Cambridge. My mother-in-law Betsy Edwards had therefore resigned herself to her daughter's determination to marry this brash young man and had begun to make preparations for the wedding. She found it quite impossible to maintain sufficiently regular contact with me to make any clear arrangements, as the three weeks of the full-time election campaign in October were held immediately before my wedding. In the end I fear my solitary contributions to the day were asking John Gummer to be my best man, and buying a ring from a friend of my father in the old jewellery quarter in Birmingham.

The 1964 campaign nationally was a vain attempt led by Sir Alec Douglas-Home to preserve a Conservative majority. For me, though, both the campaign and the election went entirely according to plan. My agent was an untrained local enthusiast named Joyce Maddison who was the wife and mother of coal miners. She and I enjoyed ourselves enormously improvising an active campaign with no resources at all except a small office in the Mansfield Conservative Club. The association had no money so one of my first tasks was to visit the head of the local family brewery which produced Mansfield Ales. As all brewers were in those days, he was a Conservative and agreed to give us enough money to at least enable us to pay the telephone bill and order some printing. I had to go out with a helper and a ladder to put up my own posters, and I canvassed vigorously amongst the somewhat bemused electors of Mansfield who were a very challenging but pleasant lot of people. I looked so young that many electors thought that I was campaigning on behalf of my father.

The sitting Member of Parliament was a man called Bernard Taylor who had first been elected during the war, unopposed as was the custom during hostilities, as a pacifist and a left-wing union activist.

I addressed many public meetings during the campaign which were well attended and sometimes quite noisy. These included one or two head-to-heads with Bernard Taylor. He had a classic stump speech which began with an emotional reference to his memories of his mother's careworn hands. He had been blackballed in the 1920s as a union activist and condemned to unemployment for long periods of his youth as a result. He would turn to me and wave his finger at me saying, 'You said that grass would grow on the headstocks before you would let us back in the lockouts.' I would sit there protesting, 'Bernard, I wasn't even born then,' but he was not deterred.

Joyce and I had set ourselves the reasonable objective of keeping Bernard Taylor's majority below 20,000. When the votes were counted we were very pleased to discover that we had achieved that modest ambition with 1,000 votes to spare. As a result of this triumph I was rapidly readopted as Mansfield's candidate for the next general election, whenever it might come. I still could not afford to go into politics.

Our wedding was held on 7 November 1964, three weeks after the end of the campaign. It took place at Lamorbey Church in Sidcup and was a hugely enjoyable occasion. A large number of our old Cambridge friends attended as guests and I had lunch with a number of them at the Station Hotel in Sidcup before going to the ceremony. Several of those attending would eventually become Conservative Members of Parliament, and my future colleagues in Conservative Cabinets.

John Gummer as best man pleased my mother-in-law by bringing to the proceedings an atmosphere of religious devotion which she had sadly discovered I quite obviously lacked, despite the devout High Anglican beliefs of my new wife. Gillian was solely responsible for our spiritual well-being from that moment and would remain so for the rest of our lives together.

After the ceremony, I drove Gillian in my old Hillman up the long road to Birmingham and to our new home in our flat in Harborne for the first night of what was to be a long and happy marriage. I was too busy in court for an immediate honeymoon so we took a very enjoyable long-weekend honeymoon in Paris the following Easter.

I was twenty-four years old, and am sure that I was delighted to be marrying Gillian with both my legal and my political careers under way. But I remember no particular sense of glowing achievement. I knew what I wanted to do – I wanted to get married, practise at the Bar and become a politician – and I just got on and did it. I was very lucky that it all panned out. Looking back, my whole life has been coloured by good fortune, which I fear at the time I rather took for granted.

Thereafter we spent several happy years with me fully occupied at the Bar and in pursuit of my political career. Our first child, Kenneth, was born in October 1965, a little under a year after we were married, and our daughter Susan arrived three years after that in November 1968. A stray cat with kittens adopted us and became the first of

many until in our later years, much to our mutual regret, we became
too busy to be able to care for one.

It quickly became obvious that Gillian's intention of pursuing her
academic career was fairly hopeless. She cut short her work on the
supply of food to Edward I's army in Wales, took an MLitt, and
immersed herself in bringing up the children. Gillian also happily
threw herself into being a political wife: she had, I would plead in
mitigation, always known I was going to be a professional politician,
and indeed she had strong political views of her own. These were
fortunately similar to mine – she was as liberal a Conservative as I
was and in fact was always even more pro-European than me. Gillian
willingly adapted to the constant car journeys across to Mansfield, a
couple of hours' drive away, to help me nurse my seat. We used to
drop off the children for the evening with my parents in Bulwell and
they became very attached to each other. Susan developed a particularly treasured relationship with my mother, bringing her great joy I
think. Happily, my practice developed to the extent that I was able
to acquire a large second-hand Ford Cortina estate car – the Hillman
having become no match for the pushchair and our array of children's
accessories. This was followed by a large second-hand Ford Zephyr
with the most enormous bonnet.

Around this time I made a political trip to Berlin with the Konrad
Adenauer Foundation, an educational and political organization allied
to Germany's centre-right Christian Democratic Union party with
which I remained in fairly regular contact for the rest of my career.
It was my first trip to Germany and the proceedings involved a lot
of debate with young people from all over Europe during which I
argued strongly for the European project. Our political discussions
continued in the evening in cafes and bars along the Kurfürstendamm.

This trip gave me a striking insight into the realities of the Cold
War and had a profound effect on my political views. The Berlin Wall
had gone up as a crude wire fence and concrete-block wall in 1961
and it was still very raw. In some roads the terraced houses on one
side of the street had had their residents evicted and their doors and
windows to the West bricked up. I was able to exercise my right as

a citizen of one of the occupying powers to make visits into East Berlin through Checkpoint Charlie. This was a shattering move from one world to another.

West Berlin and East Berlin were extreme parodies of their respective societies. The West was lively and neurotic and full of drinking dens and clubs alongside its commercial life. At the checkpoint, I found that I had to deal with the 'Volpos', the appalling East German border guards. They resentfully allowed a young British man through, but only after herding me through little rooms and quizzing me aggressively and insisting that I took some Ostmarks with me to prove that I would spend the legitimate currency in the East at the ludicrous official exchange rate that they charged. I very recklessly soon discovered that American cigarettes were a much more reliable means of exchange in any shop or bar in East Berlin.

Where West Berlin was noisy, lively and busy, East Berlin was quiet, calm and almost dead after six o'clock in the evening. The capital's heart, a boulevard called Unter den Linden, was eerily silent and deserted. Only a few cars ever travelled the streets and they were the large Zil limousines built in the East and conveying party officials. The whole place had an air of depression about it. The great public buildings had been rebuilt after the devastation of the Second World War but they were a mere facade along the major streets and in the main square, with near decay and neglect in every street behind them.

On another occasion a fellow delegate and I travelled into East Germany on the S-Bahn, the clapped-out elevated suburban railway that crossed the line between West and East but was operated by the East Germans. We were unaware that the Communists had imposed a rule that Westerners had to return to West Berlin through the entry point by which they had left. We tried to go back through Checkpoint Charlie and were waved away by one of the Volpos. My companion recklessly tried to argue and insisted on trying to walk on to get back to the West where he and I were quite entitled to go. A policeman confronted us both at short range with his automatic rifle pointed at us, and pushed us backwards to comply with his firm instructions.

Over the next few years I made a number of visits to Berlin. On one of my early trips I deliberately travelled out to East Berlin's border with the rest of East Germany. I observed the strict control through a border manned by armed guards who were regulating the movement of every East German citizen trying to travel onwards.

The whole experience clarified my views of the Cold War. There were then many fellow travellers in British politics and their attempts to persuade me of the marvellous qualities of a socialist society would never trouble me again. I was also amused to remember how Brian Pollitt, my Communist sparring partner from Cambridge, had tried to persuade me that the 1956 Hungarian Rising had all been organized by fascists trying to revive the cause of the pre-war Ustaše with the help of the CIA.

I had an excellent clerk in chambers, Norman Allcock, who put up with my political jaunts and rapidly developed and managed my practice. He was later succeeded by his junior Norman Jones, who was equally proficient. The clerks were the men who really managed all the barristers and arranged the court activities. They were paid a significant percentage of each barrister's fees which probably made them the best-paid members of the whole set. The camaraderie of the chambers remained as strong as ever and we were all thriving. My own practice consisted of criminal trials, largely in Birmingham, Warwick and Coventry, combined with a common-law civil practice comprising mainly plaintiffs' cases in industrial accident claims. Indeed, I became one of the favourite barristers for a firm of solicitors instructed by the Union of General and Municipal Workers.

As I had discovered in my student vacation jobs, standards of health and safety at work were quite appallingly bad. The Black Country teemed with old foundries which couldn't have changed much since Victorian times, with frequent explosions if water got into molten metal. Presses would often have had their guards removed. I developed a small speciality in accidents involving the giant steel drop hammers from which huge hot 'billets' (white-hot slabs of glowing metal) would occasionally be flipped out, escaping from the massive tongs being used by the men holding them so that they would fly across the workshop and strike some unfortunate victim. This must have had quite a formative effect on my views on good employment regulation in later years. It also prevented me from ever romanticizing this hard, dirty, dangerous blue-collar work.

I also did some matrimonial cases in my first few years, although I found the emotion and bitterness of family disputes unattractive. Many aggrieved wives would not contemplate divorce but instead sought maintenance from estranged husbands in the magistrates' courts. Some of the lay magistrates in the Black Country particularly had very reactionary views which would be regarded as shocking today. I will not name the towns in which old men in shabby court-rooms above police stations would dismiss any claims from women complaining that they were on the receiving end of a few thumps when their husband returned home each Saturday night. There were many of them, however.

The most remarkable case that I was ever involved in was what must have been the last case in England brought by an indignant husband seeking damages against another man for the enticement of his wife. This attractive but dim-witted young woman had been hired as a secretary but rapidly became a director of her boss's company with a very large car in suspicious circumstances. Led by my former pupil master, Michael Davies QC, I was acting for the husband, a flower seller who traded outside Dudley Zoo, quite obviously one of the many prosperous illegal bookmakers who thrived at that time. The extraordinary proceedings went on for three days until suddenly none of the parties arrived but sent us a message saying that the case had been settled personally, presumably on the basis of the busi-nessman paying a suitable sum by way of damages to our client for his insulted honour. This archaic form of action was soon after abol-ished.

Amongst my occasional opponents in criminal cases was a young man from a London chambers called Igor Judge. We remained friendly over the subsequent years, and many decades later during the Cameron government we were amazed to discover ourselves together again in an extremely amicable professional partnership as Lord Chancellor and Lord Chief Justice.

In later years, Igor would often relate a particular case in which we had been acting against each other – I had been representing a co-respondent who was facing a claim for damages for adultery from the husband. Igor on behalf of the husband, and I on behalf of the wrongdoer settled the claim on the payment of a few hundred pounds. I remember these offbeat cases vividly because with hindsight they represented an extraordinarily archaic and sexist concept which would be regarded as quite horrific by today's society.

Gillian and I left our little one-bedroom flat in Harborne quite quickly and bought a large Edwardian house in Woodstock Road in Moseley, Birmingham. It had many bedrooms, making it suitable for our young family, and was quite near the city centre, although the area was a little faded and was something of a red-light district.

Our son Kenneth had been born in a hospital maternity ward but Susan was born at home in Woodstock Road, as was then the custom for a second child. Gillian later told me that the midwife had enquired which lavatory and bathroom we had the use of. She was astonished to be told that we occupied the whole house.

I was in court on both occasions but I got back home whilst Gillian was still in labour with Susan. The midwife and my mother-in-law sent me out to the garden to mow the lawn until after delivery and until mother and child were ready to receive me. I was, of course, back in court the following day.

I was eventually able to earn the money to buy a much smarter house in a much better part of Moseley, in Amesbury Road, to which we moved in 1979 and began to enjoy an extremely comfortable lifestyle. Like every house we ever owned thereafter this was within walking distance of a Test cricket ground. I became a keen follower of Warwickshire in the summer and of Aston Villa and West Bromwich Albion in the winter. It was at this time that we developed the habit of vanishing abroad for the whole of August with our children to houses that I rented in beautiful parts of every country in southern Europe. For years to come, it would be the closest and happiest escape of the year for the whole family.

When the 1966 election came, I of course contested the Mansfield seat. The experience was a little duller than the first time round in 1964, but we fought a good campaign. Bernard Taylor suddenly announced his retirement when the election was called and was succeeded by Don Concannon, a younger miner who did his last shift at Clipstone Colliery about two weeks before he was successfully elected. He and I startled the outside world by asking for a recount. We all liked the Liberal candidate, a local shopkeeper called Reg Strauther, and we urged the returning officer to try to find a few more votes to help him to save the £150 deposit, which we knew he would have to pay out of his own pocket. Given that the 1966 election was, nationally, a walkover for the Labour Party, it must have surprised radio listeners to hear of a recount in Mansfield.

Another part of my political apprenticeship was a trip to the United States set up by a strange organization called the American Council of Young Political Leaders which was probably financed by the CIA. The purpose of the trip, on which I was joined by my old friend Michael Howard, was to observe the midterm elections of 1966. We toured several states in the East including New York and Washington and we also observed Ted Kennedy's first campaign for the Senate seat in Massachusetts.

This was a very striking introduction to American democracy and most of it was of course hugely enjoyable and impressive. Even then, I was amazed by the vast amounts of money being spent on the individual campaigns by the candidates for seats in both houses of Congress. The trip also had some rather more offbeat and extraordinary features.

We travelled into the South and the state of Mississippi where the civil rights movement was under way and our hosts were young men engaged in that campaign. I was struck by the reminders of the Old South, with an impoverished black population still living in the countryside on estates in little shacks which seemed to date back to before the Civil War. And the extraordinary racist attitudes amongst some of the white campaigners, their extremism and the crude racist language in which they expressed their views was totally startling to me.

I also attended a fundraising dinner with a huge number of people supporting the candidature of the incumbent governor or perhaps mayor of Philadelphia, I don't remember which. I was struck by the modest occupations and ordinariness of hundreds of people paying large amounts per plate to support the unimpressive candidate. A companion at our table explained to us wearily that we obviously did not understand the patronage system. Everyone there was an employee of the city administration. The governor or mayor was trying to get a second term. Not only did the jobs of all the office workers and porters present depend on his re-election, but a second term would give them all sufficient tenure to qualify for the spectacularly generous city pension scheme.

Fortunately on my many subsequent visits to the United States I was able to see more and more of the better, albeit spectacular, features of American political life. These tended to be an improvement on the more basic pork-barrel elements that were still in play, and which I observed, in the mid-1960s.

I began to search seriously for a safer Conservative seat as soon as the 1966 election was over, at the beginning of Harold Wilson's longest period of government. With all my young friends from my student days, I prepared to do the rounds of those seats in the Midlands which had seen Labour gains in the recent election and where Conservative Associations wanted a candidate as soon as possible to begin the fightback.

My first selection attempt, alongside an enormous number of my contemporaries, was at South Bedfordshire. John Gummer and I were both indignant to find that we had been rejected after our interviews and we had the temerity to enquire of Central Office why. They politely said that we were considered too young. More illuminating was the comment that the selection committee had been shocked that some of the young men seeking selection had turned up for interview wearing ties and socks that were not of matching colours. Matching socks and ties had certainly never been my practice and was never to become so. The argument that we were too young was somewhat dented when South Bedfordshire adopted David Madel who was another of my friends and no older than I was. His sartorial elegance must have been exceptional on the occasion, together of course with his undoubted abilities as a charming speaker.

I next traipsed to Wellingborough where I gathered that I was regarded as the favourite. I got through to the last three and was invited to address a large final meeting in which the entire membership of the association was involved. My speech and questions were ruined by the persistence of one member of the audience who was a keen supporter of Ian Smith and his breakaway independence movement for Southern Rhodesia. I typically engaged in a robust debate about the merits of Smith's unilateral declaration of independence. The stormy controversy that this provoked in the audience was obviously fatal to my chances and the seat was won by Peter Fry. Despite this, we later became colleagues on very good terms.

I was then helped by a particular incident which had occurred during the 1966 election campaign. The former chief whip Sir Martin Redmayne had been defending the seat of Rushcliffe in Nottinghamshire. He was not a particularly vigorous campaigner and he assumed that his seat was as safe as it had been since he had first won it in 1950. After a week or two he had become bored with campaigning and suddenly announced that he had urgent business in London. This left the association with problems, particularly with a public meeting at the Agricultural College in Sutton Bonnington at which all the candidates were supposed to be speaking. They appealed to Central Office for help and I was asked to take an evening away from Mansfield to speak on Martin's behalf. The hall was packed with huge numbers of students as well as villagers, and an extremely noisy and combative debate took place. For me, it was as if I were back in the familiar arena of student debating.

Perhaps not wholly surprisingly, Sir Martin's laid-back approach to campaigning resulted in his majority being narrowly overturned by the Labour candidate, a young academic social worker called Tony Gardner. By that time Sir Martin had had a very distinguished parliamentary career and was happy to accept a peerage and move to the House of Lords. As a result Rushcliffe was the next stop on my tour of constituencies and I was interviewed by the executive. The chairman of the association was a farmer called Norman Beeby, who later became a close friend into his very considerable old age. He had been sitting in the hall in Sutton Bonnington when I had stood in for Sir Martin and had obviously already decided that he wanted to have the young man he had seen there as his candidate. I was duly put on the shortlist.

The officers of the association fixed the shortlist so that only two people went before the whole membership at a mass meeting. They deliberately left out the seemingly best-qualified candidate on the basis that he was too likely to beat me.

The night before the final selection meeting, open to all paid-up association members, Norman Beeby rang me to give me some tips. He assured me that he was almost certain that he had arranged for me to win. However, he solemnly advised me that I must change my opinion on two important subjects: Europe and capital punishment. I think that Norman first began to understand that he would have difficulties with his candidate when I politely but firmly assured him that I had no intention of changing my pro-European and abolitionist opinions.

Despite this early encounter with the sensitivities of the Conservative right wing, I was adopted in a meeting of several hundred people as Rushcliffe's new, very young Conservative candidate.

Thereafter Gillian and I settled down to the slightly shorter journeys between Birmingham and the southern part of Nottinghamshire to maintain a long four years of nursing a constituency which I had every hope of winning. Tony Gardner was defending a majority of only a few hundred against me, amidst the disasters of the Wilson government and the threat of a Tory resurgence.

I fought my new constituency with the assistance of a very agreeable and active collection of members from branches in every village in the whole patch. It was a marginal seat: there were still coal mines in the constituency, and Stapleford and Kimberley were very much working-class districts, but the farmers now outnumbered the miners and there were, particularly in Beeston, some business and professional people. The farming villages to the south of the river, including Kingston on Soar where Norman Beeby lived, were amongst the more attractive areas and would be the only parts of my original constituency to survive the boundary changes which were to become a constant feature over the succeeding decades.

Just before the association had adopted me, they had hired a young agent of about my age called Roger Stewart. He became a good friend and we remained close until his sadly early death. He was the best Conservative agent that I ever encountered, with a fierce professionalism and a very persuasive way of inducing the volunteers and the candidate to work harder than they thought they could. Rushcliffe was regarded as a key marginal seat and we threw ourselves into very vigorous campaigning, helped by the many luminaries of the party who descended on us at regular intervals. These visits were tremendously exciting for a young aspiring politician, but we did struggle to work out what we were going to do with the likes of Margaret Thatcher, Reggie Maudling, Keith Joseph, and the then rising star, Michael Heseltine.

During the final three-week campaign I had a supporting visit from Ted Heath. We went on a walkabout in a crowded shopping centre surrounded by press. He was stiff and awkward and quite unable to communicate with any member of the public. He merely shook hands and gruffly said hello to everyone who approached him. The party chairman, Tony Barber, was better. I have a great photograph of both of us on the back of a lorry with him holding a microphone haranguing the crowd.

My days were filled with the by then routine business of leafleting, canvassing and making speeches. Roger had a slick team in the office who used to measure by column inches the coverage we were getting in the local press compared to the sitting Labour MP. His aim was to equalize the coverage, which is quite a task against an incumbent. It required the constant creation of events the local papers would consider newsworthy. The most unlikely I can recall was a Miss Rushcliffe Young Conservative beauty competition, with pictures of the aspiring candidate and the finalists appearing in the local papers the next day.

Far more importantly, the disasters began to pile up for the Wilson government and so my hopes remained very high. Ted Heath was not the most popular Leader of the Opposition, but the party surged in the opinion polls as was then typical in the midterm of any government. Towards the end, however, Wilson began to recover as a result of the success of the economic policy of Roy Jenkins as Chancellor. The outcome nationally began to seem less certain.

After an exhausting schedule of daily canvassing, morning and afternoon, an opinion poll in the final week seemed to suggest that Labour had recovered the lead and that the result was going to be strikingly similar to 1966. Roger and I discussed this with a certain alarm. We were both completely confident that we were winning our constituency and we eventually told ourselves that Rushcliffe must be in a well-disposed part of the country. Nevertheless I continued to be concerned that my four years of remorseless and punishing effort might prove to have been in vain. In those days Rushcliffe was one of the large minority of constituencies which did not count overnight and only began to count the following morning. Indeed, throughout my political career, Rushcliffe was always one of the last constituencies to declare its result. This was because the chief executive of the council was always so sensibly careful with public funds that he would never hire a large number of tellers. My fears were greatly abated, though, in the course of the overnight count. The neighbouring seat of Nottingham South was being fought by Norman Fowler against another Labour incumbent with a small majority of a few hundred votes. I was hugely relieved when Norman's result eventually was declared and he had a comfortable majority.

The long tedious process of bringing, sorting out and counting the votes in Rushcliffe was eventually resolved only quite late in the afternoon. When the result was finally declared, I was elected with a majority of over 6,000.

5

'Hot House'

(Dizzy Gillespie, 1945)

PARLIAMENT

My election to Parliament was followed by a curious lull. No one seemed to have noticed that I had won, except that, to Gillian's amusement, the District Council invited me to the opening of a new sewage works near Awsworth.

Eventually I spoke on the telephone to John Gummer, also newly elected as the MP for Lewisham South. We admitted to each other that no one had contacted us and we did not know what to do. We decided that on the first day of the new parliamentary term we would meet for lunch in London with another newly elected MP, Iain Sproat, and then go to the House of Commons to see if they would let us in.

When we nervously arrived at the St Stephen's Entrance, in the middle of the building's grand western front, the friendly elderly policemen who were then the only security recognized us from photographs they had been given and we were allowed in and beyond the normal public limits of the Central Lobby. We were criticized by a whip for turning up late and speedily marshalled to be sworn in before the Speaker. I was standing in the short queue in front of the Table of the House, waiting to be sworn in, when I was tapped on the shoulder by a new Labour MP, a young man called Gerald Kaufman, who asked politely whether I would mind if he went in front of me as he had an urgent engagement to get to. I agreed of course, which meant that forty-five years later Gerald Kaufman became, by a few minutes, the Member of Parliament with the longest continuous service, and therefore 'Father of the House'. This was a great relief to me as I had no particular desire to attain that curious rank.

I now found that I had the run of the rabbit warren that is the Palace of Westminster, but nobody made any attempt to give me any sort of induction or explain where things were. The only help that I can recall receiving from the Whips' Office was the usual weekly whip telling me what votes were expected. The Badge Messengers dotted at intervals around the House, whose formal jobs were to enforce security and deliver messages within the estate, helped me to find where the lavatories and the cloakroom were, and I eventually discovered important places like the Table Office, which was where one went to table Parliamentary Questions, and the library. In my first months, the MP who was most helpful to me was my old opponent from Mansfield, Don Concannon, who was a quite delightful man and went out of his way to give me advice of every kind on the logistics and customs of this strange institution.

As I had always intended, I continued with my legal practice which meant making almost daily train journeys between Birmingham and London during the week, before my road journeys from Birmingham to Rushcliffe at the weekends. Gillian and I had always known that this was going to happen but it was still a shock to face up to the reality that from that moment on I would be a largely absentee husband and father. With Kenneth aged four and Susan still not two, a huge burden was now thrown upon Gillian to bring up our children at home in Birmingham, which she steadily undertook. I rapidly stopped making jokes about her being a 'one-parent family' as it was dangerously near to the truth. For more than a decade, my daily practice on four days a week was to leave court when it rose in the afternoon and go to London, staying at the House of Commons until at least ten o'clock at night before returning to Euston for the train back to Birmingham, using the train journey to prepare the next day's legal work. I would then spend weekends in Birmingham, usually with one or two drives over to Rushcliffe and back for constituency engagements.

There was a large new intake into the 1970 parliament to give Ted Heath his majority, many of whom became very good personal friends in addition to the many that I had already met through my political activities as a student and a candidate.

The atmosphere of the House of Commons was quite different then from that of today's House. It was essentially a large political club where most MPs would gather in the afternoon and then stay into the evening and often the night in very close proximity with each other. By the evening, most MPs would be eating and mingling in the House, with ministers and Shadow ministers alongside all their backbenchers. It was an exciting political village, with constant discussion, plenty of gossip and many lively events. Debates in the Chamber were well attended because backbenchers were expected to be there at least for the ministerial opening and winding-up speeches. In the summer, attendance levels were no doubt also helped by the fact that the only air-conditioned rooms in the whole Palace of Westminster were the Chamber of the House and the Strangers' Bar. Most evenings were spent in one or the other with a combination of the two usually dominating the late-night sittings.

Dining clubs were another prominent feature. Following the election, motivated by extreme anxiety that we were going to be supporting a right-wing and reactionary government, my One Nation friends and I had formed our own dining club of moderate new Conservative members, imaginatively called Nick's Diner after our leader Nick Scott. In fact our fears proved unfounded. Nick, who had been my hero Iain Macleod's parliamentary private secretary – an 'eyes and ears' role in which a close working relationship often develops between the junior and senior partners – rapidly became an influential figure in the Heath government, and by the end of the parliament many founding members of Nick's Diner had become junior ministers. Nick's Diner is still going today, and I am still a member and it still continues, in an unbroken tradition of total confidentiality, to engage in lively conspiratorial liberal Conservative chatter.

The composition of the House was also very different to that of today. There was a marked class divide between the two parties with many establishment and country-gentlemen-type characters on the

Conservative side, and many working-class and trade union Members on the Labour side. Almost all Conservatives wore the traditional formal black jacket, waistcoat and striped trousers, whereas most of the Labour Members wore inexpensive suits – although the Hampstead set and those around Roy Jenkins were somewhat smarter. There were a grand total of twenty-six female MPs, of a possible 630, and they were almost all of a very particular type. To survive in the macho, aggressively male, clubland world of the House, female MPs had to be absolutely formidable. To use an old-fashioned term, meant entirely respectfully, they were battleaxes, and they had an ability to strike terror into an unsuspecting young minister or indeed anyone else they encountered. The vast majority of MPs were not remotely interested in seeking ministerial office which was only pursued avidly by the minority of men of affairs who dominated the proceedings on both sides.

The 1970 intake represented a break with this pattern. We were the first products of the meritocracy of Rab Butler's 1944 Education Act, a large cohort of 11-plus boys and university graduates, and we brought a new, earnest, professional, careerist political enthusiasm into the place, on both sides of the House. But it was many years before this became the dominant approach.

The most striking new Members came from Northern Ireland. I had been twenty-nine when I was elected but I was not the youngest Member of Parliament because a radical Republican young woman called Bernadette Devlin had been elected in Ulster at the tender age of twenty-two. She became a very prominent, active and unorthodox participant. She sometimes wore blue denim overalls in the Chamber and she once rushed forward to try to punch the then Home Secretary, Reginald Maudling, after he had given a statement about Bloody Sunday. Another new Member was Ian Paisley, who represented the other extreme of Irish politics. He was even then a formidable figure who insisted on addressing the Chamber in a huge stentorian roar. We used to joke that he obviously intended his speeches to be heard by people on the other side of the Irish Sea.

The traditional advice to new Members of Parliament had always been that one should wait a year or two before making a maiden speech. As if to give notice of our enthusiasm and ambition, our intake broke with that immediately.

I duly made my own maiden speech just over a week after being sworn in. Looking back, it was a very poor effort because I decided to intervene on the then very controversial subject of education, although my own views were still rather unformed. Under the previous Labour government, the Education Secretary Tony Crosland and his Minister of State Shirley Williams had begun the move away from the 11-plus and grammar schools towards the new comprehensive system. I largely addressed the confused situation in my own constituency whereby some towns and villages sat the 11-plus but others had already moved to comprehensives. I have always been a believer in meritocracy and academic selection although I steadily formed the view that the old 11-plus system was too primitive and uncertain for those who were not definitely on one side of the ability line or the other. Instead, I soon came to believe that academic streaming within a school where high educational standards were being set for all within the limits of their abilities was the best ambition. I doubt whether my maiden speech in Parliament came to any clear conclusion at all. I had at least got over the slightly nerve-racking experience of making myself heard.

As a quite active new Member of Parliament, I was glad when after a few months my presence appeared to have been noted. I was invited to become the parliamentary private secretary to Sir Geoffrey Howe, who was then Solicitor General. I already knew Geoffrey faintly because he had been one of the leading lights in the Bow Group, and in the wing of the party to which I myself belonged. He had led the way in developing the philosophy of free-market economics with a social conscience that I espoused and was an obvious high-flyer in the new government. He was leading for the Heath government on two of its most important and contentious issues – the reform of the trade unions, and Britain's entry into the European Community.

I soon found myself, as a very junior political adviser, trying to be Geoffrey's eyes and ears on the most controversial piece of business before the House of Commons: the Industrial Relations Bill.

The Wilson Opposition was in some difficulty in opposing the bill, which was intended to put a stop to the constant, often unofficial, strikes that were then plaguing the country. As prime minister, Harold Wilson had himself been persuaded of the necessity of trade union reform, and he had formed a partnership with his Employment Secretary Barbara Castle to introduce a bill on the subject just before the 1970 election. This was all based on Barbara's famous White Paper, *In Place of Strife*. She had heroically tried to take the bill through a parliament with a Labour majority and had failed. Prominent critics like Jim Callaghan had withheld their support, the Cabinet had split, tempers had frayed and the whole thing had had to be abandoned. It was therefore, in my opinion, now a mistake for Barbara Castle to take the lead in opposing our bill. It has to be said, however, that she did it very formidably: she was obviously trying to re-establish her reputation as a staunch socialist and advocate of the left.

Listening to the meetings preparing the bill and then to all the debates in the House of Commons was the first step in my serious political education. I began to understand what the processes of government and Opposition really involved. I also became ever more familiar with the personalities and the politics of MPs on both sides of the House as I listened to and engaged with them. And, of course, it meant that I had to return legal briefs and stay in a friend's spare bedroom in Lambeth when work on the bill required my daily attendance in the House.

When I first arrived in Parliament no office of any kind had been provided for me as no one could see what a junior MP could require an office for. I did share a constituency secretary with two other MPs and I used to see her once or twice a week. Parliament had recently introduced the concept of free postage and free stationery for parliamentary correspondence and I would dictate my letters sitting upstairs in the Committee corridor on a bench with my secretary alongside me taking shorthand on a pad on her knee. Senior MPs were baffled by this, and could not understand why enthusiastic new Members like me bothered to do it. One passing senior Labour MP once enquired what I was doing and, when told, informed me that he simply threw what little constituency correspondence he ever received into the wastepaper basket.

New MPs began to press for office accommodation and when I was made parliamentary private secretary to Geoffrey Howe I was allotted a space in a huge room in a derelict Members' club on the corner of Bridge Street opposite Big Ben, which the House had taken for the purpose. Large numbers of desks were allocated to newly elected MPs of all parties, who were supposed to work from this room, although Norman Fowler and I were amongst the few who actually did. John Prescott, then a new Labour MP, and one of the most outspoken and noisy critics of the Industrial Relations Bill, also worked from there. I was condemned to listen in silence to the debate on the bill in the Chamber, which was the convention for the PPS on their minister's subject. John and I therefore began to carry on vigorous debates in our shabby office. We became so heated on occasions that secretaries would come rushing from nearby rooms thinking that we were going to have to be separated. In fact, John enjoyed a good combative political debate as much as I did, and I think it proved the basis for a reasonably friendly relationship between us for the subsequent several decades we spent together in Parliament, although there was a distinct limit in his earlier years to the extent to which he would consent to become friendly with any Tory.

The bill eventually proceeded to successful enactment as the Industrial Relations Act 1971. Over the next year or two it was then destroyed by a combination of industrial militancy and legal challenge. With hindsight, Geoffrey and I both put a lot of the blame on the parliamentary draftsmen. Geoffrey had prepared a draft bill when he was in opposition and a practising lawyer. The parliamentary draftsmen defended their monopoly right to draft government legislation and must have persuaded the then Employment Secretary Robert Carr and others that their more complicated text should be used. It made the law more difficult to predict and apply in the real world. Geoffrey and I continued to have disagreements with parliamentary draftsmen throughout our political careers.

Curiously, it was this much-maligned Conservative Industrial Relations Act that laid the basis for modern employment law, introducing new remedies for employees for unfair dismissal and discrimination, to be delivered by a new system of industrial tribunals.

The government received no credit for that and the Act was seen as an unpopular failure.

The second great piece of legislation that Ted Heath gave over to the care of Geoffrey Howe was the European Communities Bill. This was intended to achieve Ted's great purpose of taking Britain into membership of the European Union. This was another one of my own enthusiasms and I was delighted to be engaged in it, but circumstances suddenly changed the nature of my involvement.

I had continued to be an unusually active backbencher and had spoken on quite a variety of subjects. Hansard shows that between July 1970 and March 1972, for example, the topics on which I contributed my views included controlled drugs, fowl pest, US forces in Europe, pensions, private zoos, immigration, the M1 (diversion signposting), the Chronically Sick and Disabled Persons Act 1970, the Social Security Bill, the Wild Creatures and Forest Laws Bill, unsolicited publications, drugs, repeals, provisions for determining supplementary benefits, derelict land clearance, language laboratories, employers' liability, legal aid, the Nottingham–Birmingham motorway, education, public expenditure, attendance allowance for the severely disabled, the coal industry, Broxtowe Colliery, out-of-town shopping, housing estates, abortion clinics and – on many occasions – the European Economic Community.

It is just possible that the thought had already crossed the chief whip's mind that a period of silence on my part would be welcome. In any event, matters were brought to a head when in March 1972 I decided to speak on the subject of Northern Ireland, following a visit I had made to improve my knowledge of that part of the United Kingdom, which was rapidly plunging into violent crisis. I had made the trip along with two new colleagues and old friends, Barney Hayhoe, the new MP for Heston and Isleworth, and Chris Tugendhat, the new MP for the Cities of London and Westminster. It proved to be an eye-opening and significant experience. We were all shocked at the startling, bigoted and extreme opinions which were expressed to us by the politicians and leading figures on both sides, who all nevertheless seemed quite eager to meet us. I do not think that any one of us had expected the deep-rooted sectarian prejudices which, as far as we could see, permeated every citizen's opinion. The problem was illustrated most starkly to me when the first thing that many of our interlocutors wished to know was what denomination we three young Conservative MPs were. I was actually the only Protestant in the little group, if I was remotely religious at all. Ulstermen were amazed and baffled to discover that the other two were both Roman Catholics and Conservatives. In particular, they flatly refused to believe my own truthful assertion that I had not known that Barney Hayhoe was a Roman Catholic before I made the trip.

We had made arrangements with the SDLP Member for Derry, John Hume, to facilitate contacts and to enable us to visit him in his own constituency. This was a most remarkable thing for us to do, as large parts of Derry were effectively under the control of the IRA and were officially designated no-go areas for both the police and the army. John Hume assured us that we would have safe conduct and we promptly drove into no-go Derry to have a fascinating discussion with him at his house. Needless to say, this proved very unpopular with the security services who were horrified to find that three British MPs had gone beyond their reach into enemy territory and seemed quite amazed that we had done so unimpeded.

Upon our return to London, the three of us went to see the Home Secretary, Reginald Maudling, who was in charge of the crisis in Northern Ireland. We tried to persuade him that the policy of internment (the arrest and imprisonment without trial of hundreds of suspected IRA activists) had been a dreadful political mistake. It had handed the Republicans massive ammunition for propaganda – particularly as there were plausible claims that some people had been arrested in error and were being interned with no just excuse for their imprisonment at all – and had consequently boosted recruitment and rejuvenated their ranks. Reggie was unfortunately not persuaded although, as a very liberal Conservative himself, he did seem extremely engaged with our views to which he gave a good hearing.

Armed with what I fondly imagined to be my new expertise, I felt emboldened to take part in a debate in the Chamber on Northern Ireland. However, I succeeded in causing considerable annoyance to the Unionists on the back benches sitting around me. Ulster Unionists were then formal members of the Conservative and Unionist Party and were therefore my colleagues, attending party meetings and filling ministerial positions in the government.

The day after my Irish intervention I was summoned to the office of Francis Pym, the chief whip. I expected to be told off for speaking in the Ulster debates and provoking backbenchers on my own side. To my amazement, he invited me to join the government as a member of the Government Whips' Office. I was delighted by this recognition of my political talents. With hindsight, I suspect that it was a very wise move of Francis to shut me up in debate as whips were traditionally totally silent in the Chamber in order to avoid them compromising the government's official spokesmen. He probably also believed it was time that I learnt something more about politics and Parliament and the relationship between a government and its political supporters. Whether this was his intention or not, that was certainly the effect of the next step in my political career. At thirty-one I became the youngest member of the government and the most junior member of the Whips' Office.

6

'Steps Ahead'

(Steps Ahead, 1983)

WHIPS' OFFICE

Francis Pym ran a particularly powerful Whips' Office because of his very close relationship with the prime minister. Ted himself had been a chief whip in the past and I gained the impression from Ted's reminiscences that he enjoyed his reputation as a strict disciplinarian. He spoke with pride and pleasure of his role during the Suez Crisis. He had followed an ancient tradition which dictated that at key occasions the chief whip would personally act as teller, marking off each Conservative rebel as they came out of the wrong voting lobby.

Ted and Francis's personal friendship and the close affinity the prime minister obviously felt for the office of whip combined to make my life fascinating; it was pure politics. We were a wide-ranging group of MPs – although all male – from every generation and every wing of the party. All our parliamentary desks were in the two Whips' Office rooms close to the Members' Lobby and we found ourselves together there for much of the day. Francis also had a large room in 12 Downing Street where we held a weekly morning meeting to put the world to rights. As the junior whip it was my duty to serve the considerable quantities of wine which the office consumed as our pre-lunch discussions deepened.

Inevitably, the culture of the Whips' Office took most of us into the hard-drinking social life of the House of Commons in the after-noon, evening and into the night of almost every day the House was sitting. I was so immersed in the life and work of the House that I had some personal acquaintance with almost every Member of Parliament in every party.

In the early evening I would usually drop into Annie's Bar for an hour or so. This extraordinary institution was only open to MPs and lobby journalists. It was on the ground floor in a corridor next to the House barber's shop. I was always told that in the nineteenth century it had been the office of the great Irish statesman Charles Parnell, who frequently entertained his lover Kitty O'Shea there. On one occasion she had had to exit hurriedly through the window before unexpected visitors could find her *in flagrante*. A small closed group of MPs and journalists were steady regulars there with the result that in Annie's one could acquire a huge proportion of the daily gossip of the political village in which we worked.

Visitors to the Commons could be entertained in the Strangers' Bar and I frequently spent the later evening and part of the night of all-night sittings there. This bar served draught beer, and before our intake arrived it had been used almost entirely by Labour MPs, giving it its nickname, 'the Kremlin'.

Amongst the visitors that I occasionally took into the Strangers' Bar was my Tory councillor mother-in-law Betsy Edwards. She fitted into the atmosphere in a remarkable way given her very typecast Conservative lady background. I well remember her engaging in long, flirtatious conversations with a group of elderly miner MPs, most of whom had by then transferred to the House of Lords and were led by Joe Gormley.

Each Conservative MP was allocated to a whip's 'flock' and we shepherds were expected to keep in close contact with our charges' political opinions. The most striking rumours and reports of the political and private activities of Conservative MPs had to be recorded by each whip in a small book which was kept locked in the chief whip's office and which was only consulted by him. I think that Francis, as all his predecessors did, kept this book as his personal possession and he probably followed what was said to be the practice of all his predecessors by destroying it when he lost office, in order to protect some of our colleagues from the risk of posthumous scandal at the hands of later historians.

A very strange form of discipline was applied to the backbench MPs of the day. Loyalty was then the secret weapon of the Conservative Party so that in response to the written whip for the week – that is, the written voting instructions issued by the chief whip to each Member – one could rely on the attendance of practically all our parliamentary party. There were just a few notorious absentees who could be very occasional attenders.

The best approach to any MP was not to behave like a school prefect and certainly not to try to give military-style orders. While all Conservative MPs would feel bound by duty to obey the two- or three-line whip indications on their weekly whip, they all had shades of personal opinion and expected these to be heeded. Those MPs who had strong opinions on particular subjects, and especially those who were concerned about specific government policies, had to be engaged in conversation. If, following these conversations, we antici-pated difficulties, we would report back and arrangements would be made for meetings between the troubled Member and the relevant minister. Considerable give and take was expected. The government was profoundly influenced by the opinion of its backbenchers and expected to make concessions on the content of bills and on policy positions if any significant disquiet was detected. A rebellious vote was very rare indeed and always accompanied by elaborate expres-sions of respect and regret. Concession and compromise out of the public gaze in response to influential Members' opinions was quite normal.

The result of this gentlemen's club-like atmosphere was that Parliament was profoundly more influential on the government than it is today. I spent my career observing the steady decline of Parliament's influence on public life whilst the campaigning power of the media steadily grew. Eventually Fleet Street acquired more power than Westminster.

Most backbench MPs in the early 1970s were, as I had done before my 'promotion', earning their living outside politics and devoting themselves to national political issues in the afternoon, evening and

night. On the Conservative side, the only MPs with no outside occupation were those with private fortunes and sometimes landed estates.
On the Labour side, many were supported by the trade unions. Labour
MPs who were solely dependent on their MPs' salaries would live in
comparative poverty in a bedsit somewhere near King's Cross with
the wives and families living in a council house in the North.

Most of the established Members concerned themselves only with
national politics and paid little or no attention to local issues, which
they regarded as the work of local councillors. Most did not live in
their constituencies and the very grand and long-established would
only visit the constituency once a year, usually on a very formal
occasion when they would be greeted by the local stationmaster in
ceremonial dress, complete with top hat.

I was one of the keener Members by the standards of the time.
Every weekend I attended constituency events, usually organized by
the local party. I introduced 'surgeries' where my constituents could
come to see me with their problems, something my predecessor had
not bothered with. I replied to the growing volume of letters that I
received from constituents, usually raising personal matters rather
than political issues. However, I am quite sure that my local activity
level was very low compared with that of the typical MP elected forty
years later, when second-guessing local authority decision-making
and involvement in the particularly local issues of planning, road
safety and so on has supplanted some MPs' involvement in national
politics.

The so-called Knights of the Shire – a medieval term that had now
come to refer to a group of rather grand Conservative MPs representing rural seats and eschewing government posts – were a
formidable body of men and it would have been a profound mistake
to regard all these strange people as fools. They were prosperous and
intelligent in the main and had very strong personal views which
they combined with a sense of duty and service to both their party
and their county. Subtlety and respect were the only ways of maintaining sensible relationships with these men, many of whom had
unlikely names like Sir Tatton Brinton, Sir Jasper More and Sir Tufton
Beamish. I often wondered whether a previous generation of parents

had given their sons distinctive names to mark them out as future Tory MPs.

Almost all backbenchers attended the Wednesday afternoon meeting of the 1922 Committee together with all the whips. One of us would be the whip on duty, sitting on the top bench and giving the business of the House for the following week. This would be followed by questions from the floor which could sometimes be a challenging occasion for the novice MPs like myself at the junior end of the office.

On the rare occasions when the government faced serious problems, the mood of the 1922 Committee meeting was easily detected and needed to be taken seriously. Pounding of desks with clenched fists would show approval of any statement made by a whip or a backbencher. Growing dissent would become worryingly discernible in the form of rumbling and growling and would have to be followed by urgent reporting back by the chief whip to Downing Street, in the form of Ted Heath's parliamentary private secretary.

There were of course a number of utter eccentrics amongst the backbenchers. It was not thought very civilized to intervene and give an opinion too early at the 1922 meeting. The result was that a very entertaining and intelligent MP called David Walder invented a reliable rule which became known as Walder's Law. This laid down that the first Member to speak from the floor of any 1922 Committee meeting was by definition mad.

At one memorable 1922 meeting a very noisy argument amongst backbenchers ensued and a crisis seemed to be looming. We were saved by a normally silent country gentleman, Admiral Morgan Morgan-Giles, the MP for Winchester. He stood to attention and gave a six-word speech: 'Pro bono publico, no bloody panico.' He sat down to thunderous thumping of desks and the crisis was over.

The historically significant business of that 1970 to 1974 parliament was the European Communities Bill. Ted Heath achieved his lifelong dominant ambition of leading the United Kingdom into membership of the European Community fairly quickly, thanks to the skills of the minister he made responsible for negotiating Britain's entry in

Brussels, Geoffrey Rippon. Geoffrey Rippon became something of a friend and patron of mine, no doubt partly because he perceived my European enthusiasm. The accounts I heard of his late-night party negotiating style in Brussels seemed rather incredible but were consistent with my personal experience of him. He was a hard-living, hard-drinking, gregarious man. He was quite right wing on a number of subjects but he was fervent in his internationalism and European beliefs. His negotiations in Brussels were combined with a constant social life, which was exhausting for the Foreign Office officials and others who worked with him but which was also, in Geoffrey's opinion, quite essential to the successful diplomatic negotiation of the difficult issues.

Geoffrey was responsible for introducing me to an extraordinary European political club called the Institute of Political Studies. John Gummer had already attended one meeting of this mysterious body. He warned me that I would be receiving a strange invitation to travel to a weekend meeting in Liechtenstein and urged me to accept it. I did so and I never regretted the decision.

The club's members were a very wide range of politicians and businessmen from across the Continent, going beyond the boundaries of the EU to such countries as Austria, Spain and Portugal. It was I suppose a sort of secret Davos. We were all sworn to secrecy about its very existence let alone its discussions, and the rule about the confidentiality of its meetings has always been adhered to rigidly.

The British contingent's travel to the meetings, by flights to Zurich and then a train through Alpine landscape to Liechtenstein, felt bizarrely old-fashioned. The senior MPs who made up the remainder of the British delegation heightened the bygone-age atmosphere – they were a remarkable collection of personalities – and the journeys always reminded me of the train journey across Europe in Hitchcock's famous thriller *The Lady Vanishes*.

This impression was particularly enhanced by two regular attendees, Sir John Rogers and Sir Peter Agnew, both of whom were delightful characters. Sir John was an old-world gentleman who was actually an extremely intelligent politician who had been one of the founders of the influential One Nation dining group in Parliament. He really did behave like an eccentric 1930s Englishman abroad, however. On our travels his younger colleagues had to keep an eye on him to limit his flirting with waitresses and his practical jokes on our Continental trains. Sir Peter was a retired naval captain who had had a distinguished wartime career. He too was straight out of central casting as a stiff-upper-lip colonial Englishman with a detached interest in political affairs. The two of them could have taken the roles of Charters and Caldicott in *The Lady Vanishes* with no difficulty whatsoever.

The institute members spent the whole weekend in a long and earnest discussion of all the great political issues of the day, particularly in Europe. My very first meetings were held in little skiing hotels high in the mountains. Then wealthy French and German members raised the funds to build a clubhouse in the valley. Thereafter we used to meet in a large clubroom sitting around a long table in a manner rather reminiscent of a British Cabinet. The meetings were not always high-powered. Geoffrey Rippon was often inclined to invite the British members to play truant and go for a 'meeting' in the mountains during the afternoon. Nevertheless we held some fascinating discussions on important topics, which hugely improved my knowledge and understanding of Continental attitudes towards the Cold War, the Soviet Union, Britain's relationship with Europe, and the other major problems that concerned us all.

Not every member of the institute was in favour of the European project and the question of possible British membership of the European Community was a constant topic of debate in the first year or two of my meetings. One member was a French ex-minister then regarded as a minor star in Gaullist politics called Michel Habib-Deloncle. He was an animated opponent of British entry and highly sceptical about our value to the European cause. He was quite an agitated debater and simply listening to the exchanges between him and John Gummer was always wildly entertaining, with John able to pursue the British cause with an enthusiasm and lucidity I envied.

In the early 1970s the institute's wider membership ranged so broadly across the political spectrum that its publication would certainly have caused Gummer and myself a little difficulty in London. I ought to add that some members, despite representing very right-wing governments, turned out to be extremely enlightened, such as one or two liberal members of the then Franco and Salazar governments. On some evenings my bridge partner was Salazar's foreign minister. A Spanish minister of tourism was a member who went on to be a successful democratic politician after Franco's fall, and was eventually the leader of the right-wing People's Party in democratic Spain. French ministers, German MPs and Swedish academics mixed with businessmen from across Europe. Some of the members who were not professional politicians were diplomats and, I suspect, intelligence agents. One became president of Germany.

The leading light, however, was a remarkable Swedish journalist. Arvid Fredborg had been a journalist before and during the Second World War, sometimes in Germany, and had obviously played a leading part in maintaining a flow of liberal and democratic information about events in fascist Europe. He had subsequently become a successful political consultant and a resident of Liechtenstein. He was amazingly well informed about global politics and had personally visited almost every country in the world. He was a vast source of wisdom, analysis and information for all the members of the institute.

On only a few occasions was I persuaded to attend conferences of a sister organization called CEDI. CEDI, rather unenlighteningly, stood for 'Centre européen de documentation et d'information'. Slightly but not much more helpfully, it proclaimed itself to be 'An international society with a Christian base, which, once a year, seeks to put the world to rights'. At one CEDI conference, I had the bizarre experience of addressing the floor from the platform in the Spanish royal palace at the Escorial, giving a paper with the rather grandiloquent title, 'Crise des états ou malaise de l'Europe'. Also on the platform was the heir to the Spanish throne, Juan Carlos. I remember the slighting reference a Spanish neighbour made to me when we were listening to the opening address by the future king. My neighbour declared in a whisper that I should realize that this man would be a 'five-minute king' once the Franco regime fell. As it turned out Franco would fall within a very short time and Juan Carlos would play a vital role in moving the country back to democracy, including seeing off another Franco-ist coup in the early 1980s.

After this experience, I gave up CEDI. With my very liberal One Nation conservative opinions, it was a dangerous step too far for me.

However, I have continued to attend the meetings of the institute at least once a year. I still derive great value from them, and also great pleasure from the lively and gregarious social scene, the eating of good meals and the drinking at the bar which inevitably accompany our gatherings. They are a welcome and useful break from the routine of my normal political life.

My forays to Liechtenstein and beyond added rather exotic background political experience to the knowledge that I acquired through my involvement in the European Communities Bill. I had worked briefly on the edge of the bill in my role as Geoffrey Howe's PPS before my transfer into the Whips' Office. Because I knew the newly elected Members better than any other whip, and because of my pro-European views, Francis Pym allotted me as one of the two whips assisting the bill's passage through the House, alongside the excellent and silky Hugh Rossi, the Member for Hornsey. Together, Hugh and I became closely engaged with every MP taking a strong interest in the bill, which was debated at enormous length for very many days late into the night with every stage taking place on the floor of an unusually crowded House of Commons.

As first a PPS and then a whip, I was condemned by long-standing convention to be absolutely silent both in public and on the floor of the House throughout. However, this did not frustrate me unduly as I was deeply involved in my minor role and I think that I attended every minute of the proceedings as they went on.

There was strong opposition to the bill from the majority of the Labour Party and from a substantial number of our own backbenchers. The most numerous opponents were from the anti-capitalist left who regarded the whole European project as some kind of capitalist plot which they rightly felt would prevent any further movement towards the central command economy to which the Labour Party aspired.

The right-wing opponents were the old imperial right who firmly believed that Britain's future role in the world depended on our leadership of the British Commonwealth rather than in treaty alliance with our old enemies on the Continent. It was their view that the economic health and whole future of our old friends in New Zealand was threatened by our pending membership, which would exclude from our market some of the frozen lamb upon which, it was believed, their economy would always depend. There was also a deep conviction amongst many of our anti-Europeans that British agriculture would be ruined by our entry, a feeling that was fomented by the steady briefing organized by the anti-European permanent secretary of the Department of Agriculture, Fisheries and Food.

The dominant issue was the concern about the surrender of our sovereignty. The government and pro-Europeans responded by describing the process as the 'pooling of sovereignty' to enable us to play a more significant role in the modern world. The pro-Europeans argued that this pooling of sovereignty was inevitable in the twentieth century and was already being done through our membership of bodies such as the United Nations and the NATO alliance, both of which involved member-state governments giving up total freedom of action.

The most impressive performers in the parliament of 1970 to 1974 were undoubtedly Michael Foot and Enoch Powell, who were constant participants in the European debates, both of them opposing our bill. The other outstanding opponent on the Conservative side was John Biffen, then a young former Bow Group member who had been elected in a by-election shortly before my intake arrived. I did once make the mistake of trying to address John Biffen severely about one of his threatened rebellions. He quite rightly reacted forcefully to my presumption with such strong language that it gave me a lasting respect for the sincerity of his convictions. He went on to become a very substantial figure in future parliaments and was a rising minister in the Thatcher government until he fell out with her.

The passage of the bill entirely depended on sufficient pro-European Labour MPs either voting with the government or abstaining, to offset the significant number of Conservatives who were rebelling against it. The wing of the Labour Party led by Roy Jenkins voted with us for the initial vote in principle and gave us a very substantial majority. This only happened because Francis Pym, with strong support from his office but with some difficulty, persuaded Ted Heath to allow the party a free vote. It was a crucial decision and I believed that Francis's judgement was wholly correct. The free vote on the Conservative side undermined the Labour Party's attempt to impose political discipline and gave the pro-European Labour Members the political room for manoeuvre they needed to act courageously and vote with us.

The pro-European Labour MPs were, however, extremely nervous about voting with the government during the later committee and report stages of the bill, because the Labour Party was putting them under intense pressure. Many feared deselection in their constituencies if they repeatedly voted with us. The result was that they all voted with the anti-European Labour leadership on most votes at committee and report stage, apart from a heroic little band of six senior MPs who had already determined that they were going to retire at the next election.

It was, though, crucial that we win every vote at committee and report stage. Because the bill gave the government the powers to ratify and then comply with a treaty, no amendment of any kind was acceptable to the bill as drafted.

Because of my friendly contacts with many Labour Party MPs, I was heavily involved, on an almost daily basis, in trying to ensure that enough of them stayed away and abstained on all those days when we knew we would face a significant rebellion from our side. On three or four occasions I had quite detailed negotiations about this with John Roper, a newly elected Jenkinsite. I would always request a number we thought essential and John would try to help his colleagues by negotiating me down to the absolute minimum that would avoid real risk. This highly unusual arrangement proved really quite successful on the key occasions on which we invoked it.

On one occasion, though, John and I made a serious miscalculation – or he had pressed me too strongly. The majority fell to just four which was the narrowest squeak that the bill, the government and the Whips' Office had throughout the whole process.

I hugely enjoyed my unseen and minor role in these momentous proceedings. At the historic moment in October 1972 when the bill finally received royal assent, I firmly believed that at the age of thirty-two I would be extremely satisfied with my political career if it went no further.

As part of its membership of the European Community, the United Kingdom was now to be represented in the new European Parliament by nominated MPs from all parties. (It was a few years before I and others began to advocate a move to elected MEPs.) Francis Pym and the party leadership were very unsure about how to cope with this new species of Conservative MP with this extra role. They decided that the MEPs could not possibly be allowed to go to Brussels and Strasbourg unsupervised by the Whips' Office and beyond all reach of party discipline, and so to my delight I found myself appointed, as a whip, as a member of the Parliamentary Assembly of the Council of Europe. The Council meetings themselves were wholly honorific but enjoyable excursions for a group of backbenchers. I was also charged with travelling with the new Conservative MEPs to every meeting of the European Parliament. I had no serious political problems to deal with and there was no real purpose in my being there, but I entered a fascinating world of political gossip and debate and added to my understanding of the new politics.

The members of our parliamentary delegation were thrilled with excitement at their responsibilities in the European Parliament. Eventually they would discover that their actual role in affairs was extremely limited for any practical purpose. As I travelled with and got to know the group, though, it was brought home to me how much most of the Conservative Party was gripped by excited support for the European project, and how much it entertained the most idealistic expectations of our new membership opening the way to an enhanced role for Britain in international affairs and an advance for the British economy into the ranks of the most competitive and prosperous. I look back and contrast that atmosphere of a new dawn with the growing cynicism and pessimism of later years and the nostalgic yearnings for an older nationalism which were later to divide and consume my party.

*

As the European debate continued, I was also asked to ease the passage of health and education legislation and policy through our back benches.

Keith Joseph was then Secretary of State for Health and Social Security and he embarked on an early attempt to reform the National Health Service, becoming the first Conservative minister to be accused by Labour of 'privatizing the health service': an allegation that they have levelled against every Conservative health minister thereafter throughout my career.

Keith was actually trying to introduce some modicum of business-like management into this chaotic, high-profile and constantly crisis-ridden system. Unfortunately he brought in the management consultants McKinsey to advise him. At that time in the early 1970s, McKinsey were great advocates of a system called 'consensus management' in which a team of executives would run an organization on a consensus basis between themselves without any one person being chief executive. I was the whip on the bill seeking to put this system into legislative effect.

The health-care system is always the most emotional subject in the political life of any Western democracy and there was considerable argument about these proposals. Listening throughout all the debates on second reading and in standing committee and report was an intense educative experience in the way in which the NHS was managed, insofar as it was 'managed' at all. I had to listen to prolonged filibustered debates in which the Labour Opposition dutifully outlined the utter disasters that the measures would cause. There were, however, some Conservative backbenchers who also had serious doubts about the proposals.

Dr Gerard Vaughan, the MP for Reading, and the very distinguished new Member for Aylesbury, Tim Raison, were extremely critical of the strange consensus arrangements that were proposed. It required all my persuasive skills based on my friendship with both of them to stop them voting against the government as members of the bill's standing committee. I was eventually successful in getting the measure smoothly through the Commons, but I must confess with hindsight that Tim and Gerry were entirely correct in their fears and I had ensured a favourable vote for a ridiculous proposal.

The substantial reforms of the National Health Service which I would eventually enact in the late 1980s had as their starting point the complete abolition of Keith's ill-fated management system.

Meanwhile in the late 1970s I would have my first direct experience of its failings when I found myself the barrister instructed to be the lead counsel for a public inquiry into the complete collapse of the management of the Solihull District Health Authority. Unfortunately, I did not earn a fortune and spend months of my life on this particular endeavour, as I would be likely to do today. In those days, judges would conduct inquiries in a brisk and businesslike way, obstructing the kind of fee-spinning that occurred in later years. This particular hearing finished in less than three weeks.

That time was quite sufficient to demonstrate that this tiny district health authority, which had only been created in response to political pressure to keep Solihull separate from Birmingham, had been managed in a disastrous fashion involving all the executives and almost all the members of the authority in permanent personal feuding. I had to agree with the judge's main recommendations which were that all four of the executives should be removed and that every lay member of the authority, save for the rather engaging socialist councillor who had first exposed the scandal, should be dismissed. This first-hand experience of the practical effects of the Joseph and McKinsey reforms was to have a substantial subconscious influence on me by the time I came face to face with the headless bureaucracies of the health-care system as a minister a few years later.

It was my role as the education whip that brought me into my first direct contact with Margaret Thatcher, the then Secretary of State, as she fought a long and losing battle with the educational establishment and her own department. I particularly remember attending the weekly meetings of her ministerial team, which were a fascinating insight into the constant crises that the subject produced.

Margaret's junior ministers were first Bill van Straubenzee and then Norman St John-Stevas. They were both brilliant, able and rather camp in their personal style. I became friendly with them both over subsequent years. It was fascinating to see the very considerable diplomatic skills with which the two junior ministers in their turn managed their aggressive and impetuous Secretary of State. Indeed, the combination of Margaret and her juniors was quite extraordinarily formidable. They were both exceedingly loyal and supportive without being excessively obsequious. They were both quite prepared to work hard to try to deliver Margaret's broad agenda, with which they completely agreed, and they fought in the trenches against the civil servants – or 'officials', as ministers tended to call them – to try to deliver what she wanted.

Margaret in those days was a classic Tory lady straight out of central casting – strident and combative with traditionally conservative values. Her wars with the teachers and the officials made her extremely unpopular with the education establishment and with the public. She became particularly unpopular for her decision to stop giving free school milk to all primary-age pupils. Everyone who had been to school after the war realized that, once the immediate post-war shortages were over, this had become absurd. Schoolboys like me who quite liked a drink of milk at the mid-morning break would down extra bottles to use up the considerable excess supply created by the many pupils who would never touch it. It was a complete waste of public money. The political defence of the policy was really because of the huge subsidy that it provided to the country's dairy farmers. Left-wing opponents of course declared that the change would lead to a return of rickets and malnutrition amongst the nation's young. The proposal got through, but the politics of it were regarded by the public as right yet repulsive.

Francis Pym's informal late-night Whips' Office gatherings over whisky did at one point cover Margaret's position. Francis took the opinion of the office on a proposal from Ted Heath to sack her. The press had given her the persistent nickname 'Milk Snatcher' and Ted, who had never liked Margaret personally, had apparently decided that she was damaging his government's popularity. The whole Whips' Office was fiercely against her dismissal and this coincided exactly with Francis's own personal opinion. We later discovered that the only argument which had enabled Francis to win the day had been that Ted could not as a bachelor prime minister sack the only woman in his Cabinet. I have no doubt that Ted looked back in later years and bitterly regretted acceding to the strong advice of Francis Pym, reinforced by the urgings of the Whips' Office, on this subject.

Margaret came to hate the Department of Education with a deep and bitter loathing which was still with her many years later when as prime minister she appointed me as its Secretary of State. Her conversation in the brief time that I served her in that capacity was always dominated by dire warnings of how I must 'fight them' because they would do everything they could to thwart the reforming policies which she had initiated with Kenneth Baker and wished to continue.

The key point in the life of the Heath government came when Ted decided to make a remarkable economic U-turn. The first warning of this for junior members of the Whips' Office like myself came when Francis Pym asked all the whips for their personal opinion on whether we could survive as a party if the total number of unemployed people reached 1 million. We undoubtedly were not recovering very quickly from the dire economic conditions that we had inherited in 1970, and unemployment had continued to creep up. However, we had up until that point been working on the premise that a steady return to more market-based economics, albeit with all the political caution that the post-war consensus demanded, would eventually turn us round.

I, along no doubt with many others, expressed the view that a figure of 1 million unemployed would be politically rather disastrous. It would create quite a headline and echo the difficulties of the depression for the Conservatives before the war. More significantly, the leading lights in the government obviously shared this view.

After the tragic and politically devastating death of the Chancellor of the Exchequer Iain Macleod just after the 1970 election, Ted had appointed the personally delightful but very weak Tony Barber. Ted now commanded Tony to follow a totally different set of economic policies from the market-based reforms on which we had been embarked, aimed at averting the threat posed by the rising unemployment figures. Ted dismissed two of the junior ministers with particularly strong market economy views, Sir John Eden and Nicholas Ridley, and launched an interventionist and expansionist economic policy based on the premise of social partnership with employers and the trade unions. I have always believed that Iain Macleod would have been the only man tough and powerful enough to have stopped Ted Heath making this disastrous error. His death from a heart attack in his bed in 11 Downing Street, just one month after he had been appointed Chancellor, was a political tragedy as well as a personal one.

Needless to say, the short-term stimulus to the economy from this dash for growth was very short-lived. The policies of statutory control of wages and prices, the constant attempts at consultation with trade unions and employers, and the steady increases in public spending and debt had a predictably catastrophic effect in hastening our eventual removal from office. This was almost entirely Ted's personal initiative so far as I could understand. The only colleague with whom he worked on these policies on extremely close terms was Sir William Armstrong, the then Cabinet Secretary, who became known colloquially in conversation between ministers and whips as the deputy prime minister.

But the ultimate disaster came from disputes in the nationalized coal industry.

We had had a national miners' strike quite early in the government, in January 1972, with the miners demanding a 43 per cent pay rise. (Inflation was running at just under 10 per cent at the time.) The dispute had taken a lurch for the worse a couple of weeks in with the emergence of Arthur Scargill, an activist from Yorkshire. Despite Joe Gormley's moderate leadership of the National Union of Mineworkers, Scargill began to organize intimidating and occasionally violent mass picketing across the country.

He made his reputation at the siege of the Saltley Gas Works in Birmingham. The works had a large store of coke for use as fuel and had remained open throughout the strike, which was undermining its impact. Scargill brought in huge crowds of NUM 'flying pickets' to try to prevent employees and lorries getting in and out of the works.

I had an insight into these activities because Gillian and I by then employed a live-in nanny, who we described as our au pair, called

Pauline. Her mother was the landlady of the public house nearest to the works entrance, and she now asked Gillian if we could release Pauline for a temporary period so that she could come and help behind the bar. Apparently the pub was selling huge and unprecedented amounts of beer to the hard-working pickets and she was rushed off her feet.

Finally, on 10 February 1972, about 10,000 members of the Amalgamated Union of Engineering Workers marched from local factories and joined the picket. The chief constable of Birmingham advised the government that he was no longer able to accept responsibility for the maintenance of public order at Saltley, which would have to close. This resulted in a humiliating retreat and the settlement of the miners' pay claim within weeks, on extravagantly generous terms. Miners in my constituency told me that they had received a far bigger pay rise than they would have settled for. Scargill's power base was established and for the next ten years he never looked back.

The ultimate end for the Heath government came when another miners' strike was called in February 1974. The claim this time was a deliberate attempt to break the terms of Heath's statutory prices and incomes policy. Heath was by now determined not to surrender to claims which would shatter his economic policy, particularly because he believed that he had a private agreement with Joe Gormley, which would ensure a reasonable settlement in the near future.

The whips heard about the growing crisis in informal gatherings held at least once a day over the course of several weeks. Francis Pym would describe to us in utmost candour everything that was going on inside the government, including the proceedings at Cabinet and the prime minister's policy intentions. Our Whips' Office had a very tight-knit corporate loyalty and, so far as I am aware, there was never the slightest leak of any of this information to feed the sort of press speculation that would nowadays be regarded as the greatest possible danger from such a set-up. I have no idea whether subsequent Whips' Offices have managed to preserve this sense of collective loyalty and this depth of information about the affairs of the government in which they serve. I hope that they have.

Unfortunately, on this occasion the information passed on to us was that Gormley, who probably was looking for a settlement, had lost control of his union in which the influence of people like Scargill was now dominant. The country was in a hopeless deadlock, which gravely threatened the ability of the utility companies to provide power to industry and households. This dragged on for weeks. In an attempt both to dramatize the issues, and as a prudent precaution, the government put power supplies on a 'three-day week' basis.

Rumours began to circulate, suggesting that Ted was being put under great pressure to call a general election to resolve the issue. We in the Whips' Office were of course consulted and we were aware of what was being argued. All the good sensible people in the government were on the wrong side of the argument and were advocating this snap general election. People close to Ted like Willie Whitelaw and Jim Prior were indeed pressuring him to move to a quick poll.

Typically, Ted was not instantly persuaded, either by Willie and Jim, or by Francis Pym and his deputy chief whip, Humphrey Atkins, who all told him that parliamentary opinion wanted him to call an election. The prime minister wanted to consult the Whips' Office as a whole.

A dinner was arranged for the whole office at which Ted could hear our individual views and our appraisal of party opinion. It was a very memorable occasion. Barely fitting into a small dining room somewhere on Downing Street or perhaps in the House, every whip took part and expressed his view. We were equally divided and a vote was taken which produced a tie. The arguments in favour of a general election tended to come from those from the Home Counties and the South. I was one of the Members from the Midlands and the North who were all strongly against it. I could not see how on earth an election campaign could be confined to one subject for three weeks. Nor could I see how any result in the general election could resolve the industrial disputes and deadlock between the Coal Board and the NUM.

I hope that I put my own views clearly but I was nothing like as eloquent as a splendid veteran MP called Walter Clegg, who represented North Fylde in Lancashire. Walter was a wonderful bluff provincial solicitor who was not normally the most fluent of orators.

He had probably had a little more to drink over dinner than even the generality of those present, but the wine put greater force into his passionate arguments in a way at which we all marvelled. For a time he and his allies obviously reinforced Ted Heath's own doubts and he delayed yet further before calling the election. Unfortunately he eventually succumbed to the persuasion of his most senior and closest political friends.

The resulting election, fought under the slogan of 'Who Governs Britain?', was a predictable disaster. The campaign did not confine itself to the subject of the strike, and the government's position was completely undermined by a senior official at the Coal Board who appeared to state that a reasonable settlement could quite easily be achieved if the government would give a different interpretation to the terms of its pay policy. These difficulties and the growing signs of economic problems were quite sufficient to defeat the government and return the Labour Party as the biggest party in Parliament.

The Labour leader Harold Wilson was quite amazed to discover that he had won the election and had a prospect of forming a government. However, Ted, who had won fewer seats but more votes than Harold Wilson, clung on for a few days and attempted to form a coalition with the Liberals by negotiating an agreement with their leader, Jeremy Thorpe, who the Whips' Office discovered was to be offered the post of Home Secretary.

The whips were all instructed to ring up our list of MPs and to sound out their opinions of coalition. I set about this task with little enthusiasm and rapidly gained the impression that my particular flock were on balance heavily against the whole idea. Not for the last time, a wise old Knight of the Shire, Kenneth Lewis of Rutland, put his opinions to me briefly and eloquently, including a few mild expletives. 'The whips,' said Kenneth, 'should tell that silly man that he has been defeated and that the only sensible and decent thing to do is to accept defeat and resign as soon as possible.' I passed on that and similar views to my chief with my own personal approval; I had found Kenneth wholly persuasive.

My own election campaign had been rather comfortable. This was because early on in the parliament the Boundary Commissioners had, as they often did, engaged in a substantial redrawing of the constituency boundaries in Nottinghamshire. They had created a new Rushcliffe constituency out of prosperous and solidly Conservative parts of three old constituencies, including mine and my friend Norman Fowler's. Needless to say all three of the MPs involved wanted to become the parliamentary candidate for this very safe Conservative seat.

The biggest share of the population in the new Rushcliffe was actually being contributed by Philip Holland, but he was quickly eliminated. He was a very pleasant but extremely idle MP who had never played any great role in the life of either his constituency or Parliament. Norman and I then had to take part in a whole new reselection process in which we were joined by dozens of rival contenders, including many of my contemporaries and friends who had not been successful in 1970, one of whom was Nigel Lawson.

My former constituents, led by Norman Beeby, were fiercely loyal to me, and Norman Fowler's were fiercely loyal to him. We emerged as two applicants on a shortlist of three. The third hopeful was Tony Newton, who later became a Cabinet colleague of both of us but had no hope in this Nottinghamshire struggle. Norman and I insisted that we were going to have a straightforward and friendly competition, enjoining all our supporters to desist from any personal attacks. We also asked them to get on with it quickly as one of us would have to 'go on his travels' to try to secure another seat.

At the final mass meeting I was the successful candidate. Norman was able to go on a search for a new base and, happily, in a fairly short time he was adopted as the parliamentary candidate for Sutton Coldfield, which in those days was even safer than Rushcliffe. We therefore both acquired secure berths for our political activities for the rest of our parliamentary careers.

The Heath government's triumphant and historic success was Britain's membership of the European Community. I fear, however, that the government was in every other way rather disappointing and quite dominated by the economic and industrial relations problems which eventually overwhelmed it. The 1971 Industrial Relations Act was fatally flawed by its drafting and became impossible to uphold because the only way of enforcing it proved to be by imposing penalties on martyred trade union officials. Economic policy involved a lurch towards a syndicalist system dominated by increasingly powerful trade unions and interest groups. This remained a growing problem for the rest of the decade and was only resolved with the crash of the Callaghan government and Margaret Thatcher's reforms.

The most courageous decision taken by the government was the admission of the East African Asians when various regimes in that part of the world began to persecute their Asian minorities. Ted and his government accepted unflinchingly that they had a moral obligation to provide refuge for these hard-working people who were being victimized because British colonial rule had failed to leave behind a strong enough liberal democratic structure that would defend the rule of law. This decision was not instantly popular in a country where large sections of the population had not adjusted to the growing number of ethnic-minority populations and the steady move to a more diverse culture. The new immigrants moved in particularly large numbers to the city of Leicester near to my home base, and for a time the politics of that city were troubled by underlying racial tensions. But the new arrivals were well educated and enterprising. They have made a very positive contribution to British society ever since they arrived, and eventually emerged in Leicester as one of the strongest and most successful parts of that city's society. Enoch Powell-type views were repugnant to Ted Heath and his closest colleagues and were totally ignored. I fear that as I write some decades later it is almost impossible to believe that any British government in the early twenty-first century would contemplate taking such a firm, ethical decision.

The real problems in the 1970–4 government turned on Ted Heath's own personality and the style of government that he adopted after he made his economic U-turn. He had been a brilliant speaker before he became prime minister, holding student audiences gripped when he came to our gatherings and described the European negotiations that he had then been conducting on behalf of Harold Macmillan. After he ceased to be prime minister and leader of the party he became a very impressive and sometimes amusing speaker as an elder statesman in the House of Commons. Unfortunately, during his time as premier he became an inarticulate hesitant speaker with a somewhat bullying manner. He proved quite incapable of giving very much inspiration as a leader, either from the platform or in the media.

Even worse, he had serious problems with his inability to have normal friendly social relationships with anybody he encountered. I can only presume that he was extremely shy. He found it desperately difficult to conduct conversations with people he did not know and had no small talk of any kind. He would lapse into extraordinary long periods of silence in the course of conversations and discussions. His manner of speaking when he did address people could be extremely brusque and occasionally very rude.

He had a particular difficulty in any conversation with women. Stories abound of women finding themselves sitting alongside him at dinners and Ted failing to address a single word to them throughout hours of the proceedings. My advice to any woman who asked me how to get through this wall of ice was to try to turn the conversation to either classical music or sailing. I had heard Ted suddenly melt and become human and forthright on those two subjects, which were his abiding personal interests. I was quite incapable of conversing about yachts or classical music myself but I was assured that some women found my tip helpful.

Within the government Ted was far too aloof from most of his ministerial colleagues, except for the handful who were very close to him. Even they resented, I felt, the undue dominance which he allowed the Cabinet Secretary Sir William Armstrong in all the crucial decisions. Ted spent his last two years running a very personal form of government which quite obviously was heading towards the economic disaster that Harold Wilson had the misfortune to inherit when he finally defeated Ted in 1974.

The government's final fall was particularly humiliating as we crashed out of office in the middle of a miners' strike. The hesitation and delay before the fatal decision to call the February 1974 election was very damaging to Ted's reputation. The problem was made worse by the fact that both sides of the argument remained convinced that their advice had been correct. Those who had been urging 'forward' blamed the defeat on Ted delaying and missing the best moment. Those who, like me, had been urging 'back' were of course convinced that the decision had been fatally flawed.

The outcome was therefore a sad one and brought Ted Heath's political career to a premature end. I hope, however, that he was always able to console himself with his one overriding achievement, that he had secured the United Kingdom's place in Europe.

Ted was always friendly enough towards me because he appreciated that I was as enthusiastic a European as he was, although there was one occasion when he found even me lagging behind. After he had lost office I remember a conversation in the corridors of the House of Commons when I had for some reason been stressing the need to explain that the European Community was not a federal organization but was destined to be a Union of Nation States bound together by a treaty. Ted angrily dismissed this. He brusquely said that in his opinion the age of the nation state was now over. He never gave himself the opportunity of undertaking the Herculean task of selling that proposition to the British political class and the public, and he would never have succeeded in persuading even me.

7

'Don't Get Around Much Any More'

(Duke Ellington, 1942)

OPPOSITION

After the election, there were changes in the Whips' Office. Humphrey Atkins, who had been our genial deputy chief whip in government, became chief whip when we went into opposition. He tried to persuade me to stay in the Whips' Office, appealing to my loyalty to the party at this difficult time, when he wanted everyone to rally round and steady the ship. I explained sadly that, though my years as a junior whip had been the happiest of my life (a confession that I think startled Humphrey a little), I had to refuse. I had not been able to live on my salary as a government whip, needing homes in both London and Birmingham and supporting a young family, and I needed to get back to the law in order to get my overdraft down and return to solvency.

I therefore went back to my practice as a barrister in Birmingham and to the very arduous lifestyle that implied. Once again I became a regular passenger on the afternoon train down to Euston and the midnight train back up again. Fortunately there were only two occasions over the next six years when I slept through the stop at Birmingham to wake up in Wolverhampton around 4 a.m. Sleeping on a bench on Wolverhampton Station waiting for the first train of the morning to take me back to Birmingham was a rather tiresome way of spending the night, even when I had my red bag of robes to use as a pillow.

During my time in the Whips' Office, I had been obliged to take a sabbatical from the Bar, so I was a little surprised to find that quite a few of the barristers I appeared against had not noticed my absence. They had merely assumed that I had not been in a case against them for a year or two. For most of my legal colleagues, it seemed that I was merely resuming my ordinary daily existence.

All this was only possible because Norman Jones, now the chief clerk in my chambers, was most exceptionally helpful in accommodating me. My friend Nick Budgen was also a Conservative MP in practice in Birmingham. His practice effectively died out because his clerk found his parliamentary obligations an irritating nuisance. Norman was a genuine friend and he obviously found it an amusing diversion to try to accommodate the demands of my double life.

However, this could be difficult when I was put under pressure in the House to stay for all-night sittings. On one occasion we were trying to filibuster a government bill covering various aspects of the criminal law, and appeared to be setting out to take the bill through the night and into the following day. I had to return to a trial in the morning so I did a deal with the whips: I made the longest speech that I ever made in Parliament at about two o'clock in the morning, relating entirely to one particular clause of the bill which dealt with obscure and technical points concerning the law on trespass and squatting, in order to keep the debate going whilst other people slept. In return the whips agreed that I could leave by the early morning train. With the help of one or two friends intervening in my speech from time to time from the back benches, I spoke for about an hour and a half arguing that the House should not give leave to an unfortunate government backbencher to withdraw an amendment which he had foolishly moved on some trivial point. I could have gone on for considerably longer but a whip eventually came into the Chamber, sat down beside me and pulled my jacket. He told me the party had settled the main dispute at issue and the bill would now complete its passage through the House in the normal way. I was free to go home.

I had cause to reflect on this lunatic lifestyle many years later during the MPs' expenses crisis of 2009–10. Received wisdom at that point viewed it as wholly unacceptable for a Member of Parliament to hold down any other paid employment. The scale of abuse that was uncovered made it impossible to hold any reasoned conversation on the subject. However, I felt – and I still do feel – that my constituents genuinely benefited from the experience and knowledge I gained while practising at the Bar. It is all too easy to become out of touch from normal day-to-day living at Westminster. My work at the Bar certainly helped avoid this. It was also entirely necessary if I was to be a Member of Parliament at all.

Another person, equally as helpful and wonderful as Norman Jones, now entered my life. My original secretary, whom I had shared with Julian Critchley and Brian Walden, and to whom I had dictated correspondence in the Committee corridor, was rather grandly swiped from me by newly elected MP Tim Sainsbury, who invited her to come and work for him in the family firm. She quickly found that she disliked working for 'Mr Timothy' at Sainsbury's stuffy and old-fashioned head office and asked for her old job back but unfortunately it was too late. I had appointed a new secretary, Hazel Slater, who proved a huge success and continued to work for me as secretary and PA for another twenty-five years, handling all the logistics of my life that I was incapable of handling myself.

Harold Wilson's Labour Party had won by a surprisingly small margin in the February 1974 election. It was quite obvious that, apart from paying the coal miners everything that Arthur Scargill had asked for, he was merely waiting for the first convenient opportunity to call another election to obtain a proper majority. The Conservatives were keenly aware that it was not in their interests to fight this campaign too soon. I remember more than one occasion when the new deputy chief whip, Jack Weatherill, approached me in the House to ask me to go home before a crucial vote because we were extremely worried that the government might be hoping that we would defeat them on the issue of the day. But such tactics only delayed the inevitable and a further election was called in October 1974, a mere seven months later.

It was one of the least satisfactory elections that I can recall. Harold Wilson fought a disingenuous campaign saying that he could see 'the light at the end of the tunnel' and that economic prosperity was over the horizon. This was misleading and proved to be excessively optimistic. Ted Heath meanwhile was persuaded by Ian Gilmour, one of his few close confidants, and others, to fight an extraordinary campaign calling for the formation of a National Government including ministers from all major parties, in the manner of what the Germans later came to call a Grand Coalition. Despite the failure of this bizarre approach it would later be resurrected by Tony Blair in the 1990s in the form of the 'Big Tent' into which he hoped to woo left-wing Conservatives and Liberal Democrats when he started the New Labour 'project'. I suspect it had as little impact upon the general public then as it did back in the 1970s.

I fought an orthodox Conservative campaign in Rushcliffe, as I personally believed both Harold Wilson's and Ted Heath's propositions to be ridiculous. The Conservatives were in a worse state than they had been in February of that year and in fact went backwards in the polls. Nonetheless the victorious Labour Party still had to make do with a tiny overall majority of only three seats. The country was obviously still essentially right-of-centre in its politics and this eventually proved fatal to the ability of first Wilson and then James Callaghan to govern strongly.

In February, after our narrow defeat at the ballot box, I had been invited by Geoffrey Howe, now Shadow Secretary of State for Health and Social Security, to join him on the front bench as a junior Opposition spokesman. At first I demurred, citing as I had to Humphrey Atkins my need to get back to the law. 'Oh,' said Geoffrey, waving his hands, 'don't worry about that, you'll manage.' It was true that the demands would be less onerous than they would have been in the Whips' Office. So, despite the further complications it would cause my long-suffering legal clerk Norman Jones, I willingly accepted.

I took to the frontbench-spokesman activity like a duck to water and enjoyed it enormously. Geoffrey was nervous about my first speech challenging the minister on the floor of the House and he assumed that I would be nervous as well. He gently advised me to try to begin by making a speech which concentrated on asking the minister to respond to questions. I had the usual boundless self-confidence of most young MPs, which was almost certainly not justi-fied, and I simply made a straightforward Opposition speech. Geoffrey was obviously reasonably satisfied, as he never tried to give me advice again.

Over the next few years I became a very considerable expert, in my own opinion, on the subjects of pensions and social security. I will not burden the reader with the details of the complex bills on these subjects where I led for the Opposition in committee and usually wound up for the Opposition in debates on the floor of the House. Pensions and social security are vitally important subjects which are extremely complicated and extremely boring to all but the fixated enthusiasts and specialists. Very few members of the House of Commons know all that much about the variety of important subjects on which I became a committed campaigner. I still have volumes of committee proceedings on various bills which fellow political anoraks are welcome to study if they really wish to relive the issues of so many years ago.

One similarly enthusiastic young campaigner was Frank Field, then the founder and spokesman of an excellent pressure group which he called the Child Poverty Action Group. I came to know Frank well and he and I often consulted and debated issues on which we might covertly campaign on the same side. After a few years he joined me in the House of Commons and became one of the most impressive and influential figures in the Parliamentary Labour Party.

The most remarkable event in the early years of the new Labour govern-ment was Harold Wilson's extraordinary decision to hold a referendum on Britain's membership of the European Community. He did so purely for the purposes of managing his divided party, for which it proved a total failure. He thought he could unite the warring factions by saying that he was going to renegotiate what he considered to be the inadequate terms agreed by Ted Heath and Geoffrey Rippon. He solemnly nego-tiated some minor changes then put them to the country.

The whole political class in the 1970s was totally opposed to the idea of referenda playing any part in the government of a complicated modern nation state. Margaret Thatcher spoke for many people when she dismissed such notions as the tools of dictators like Napoleon and Mussolini. The only purpose of holding a referendum is of course to get around and override a majority in Parliament. Personally, I have always preferred parliamentary democracy with its continuing accountability of representatives for the consequences of their decisions. The only prominent advocate of referenda in 1970s political life was the very radical Tony Benn.

Harold Wilson had fondly imagined that he would take a fairly neutral role in the campaign and leave it to the general public to tell him what his opinion on continued membership should be. He was infuriated to discover that the members of his Cabinet immediately formed themselves into competing camps led by Roy Jenkins on one side and Barbara Castle and Tony Benn on the other. A vigorous campaign broke out in which the hard right and the hard left urged rejection of membership whilst the political centre from all parties campaigned in favour. Far from being successful party management, this marked the beginning of the bitter divisions within the Labour movement which led to the party finally splitting six years later with the formation of the SDP in 1981. After Harold's referendum gamble, the Labour Party was unable to win a general election for over twenty years.

In later years, the Eurosceptics created a myth that the public had been deceived in 1975. They suggested that people had been told that the Community was intended to be a free-trade area only without any political commitments. This is wholly without foundation, a total fiction. In fact the arguments in the 1975 debate, like those during the passage of the European Communities Bill three years earlier, almost all turned on the effects on the sovereignty of the United Kingdom as an independent nation.

Margaret Thatcher was one of the leading lights who campaigned vigorously for a vote in favour of British membership and caused a stir on one occasion by campaigning wearing a sweater bearing the flags of all the Community's member states. Other prominent and persuasive supporters were people like Roy Jenkins, Quintin Hailsham and Shirley Williams. Michael Foot, Barbara Castle and Enoch Powell were the best advocates on the other side but they were regarded, not surprisingly, as representing the more extreme elements of both political persuasions, left and right. I was one of the handful of backbench MPs who took an active part in the campaign. I fought on the pro-European side, and in Nottinghamshire only Michael English, the Labour MP for Nottingham West, took part on the other side. All the other Nottinghamshire MPs treated the campaign period as a holiday.

I was a very obscure figure in the national campaign but I have a vivid memory of a meeting in Lewisham Town Hall where two Members from each side of the argument were on the platform. My principal adversary in front of a packed and noisy audience was an MP called Ian Mikardo who was a magnificent left-wing populist campaigner. Even I was riveted to my chair, as I watched Ian – shirt sleeves rolled up – striding up and down the platform haranguing the crowd with his passionate defence of the right of a socialist Britain to run its own affairs free from this capitalist plot.

The media were overwhelmingly in support of the pro-European campaign, which in the days of mass circulation of newspapers made a big difference. The then Bible of the Labour Party, the *Daily Mirror*, was firmly onside. The main opposition came from the *Daily Express*, which was owned by Lord Beaverbrook and still had the symbol of the empire in chains on its masthead.

The *Express* was a widely read newspaper but its campaigning was in vain. The pro-European side was victorious by a majority of two to one. Yet our opponents completely ignored the result – as indeed I would have done if the vote had gone the other way. Tony Benn was one of the first to ignore it and within six months was again vociferously campaigning against European membership. In my opinion, referenda never resolve any difficult issue and merely unsettle the political climate on any subject. The only significant result of the whole episode was that it entrenched the divisions within the Labour Party, politically crippling it for a generation. As it merely confirmed the status quo, the consequences of this referendum were just a small tremor, compared with the earthquake of 2016.

For the Conservatives, though, the major issue after the October election defeat was Ted Heath's leadership. Frankly, he was quite unable to win either the affection or the loyalty of many of his backbenchers and he was largely less than adequate. The real problem was his continued inability to communicate on any personal basis with almost any of his party's members. Ted assumed that the party rules allowed him to continue at will and tried to ignore the mounting pressure for him to submit to a leadership election.

The turning point came in late October 1974, at a very crowded meeting of the backbench 1922 Committee. The redoubtable Kenneth Lewis – who had been so pithily sensible earlier that year on the subject of Heath's attempt to form a coalition government – rose to make another effective intervention. He simply declared that the leader should be told that possession of his office was 'a leasehold, not a freehold'. This received resounding cheers and made a leadership contest inevitable.

The only thing helping Ted Heath was the reluctance of all his former colleagues to stand against him out of feelings of personal loyalty. Willie Whitelaw was the obvious successor and he would have won easily if he had plunged into the contest straight away. However, he and people like Geoffrey Howe and Jim Prior declined to stand until Ted had been knocked out because they were anxious not to be accused of betrayal. Sir Keith Joseph was the obvious candidate for the right of the party but he made a foolish slip in a speech about the cycle of deprivation – 'our human stock is threatened . . . A high and rising proportion of children are being born to mothers least fitted to bring children into the world' – which both reminded the press of his previous controversial references to the 'feckless poor' and demonstrated his complete unsuitability for the job.

I received a telephone call from a prominent Sunday newspaper journalist who was advising Ladbrokes on the book that they were opening according to the new (and not entirely welcome) practice of placing bets on events of this kind. He went through a long list of all the leading contenders and asked for my opinion. When he had stopped throwing names at me I pointed out that there was one name that he had omitted: Margaret Thatcher. He laughed, obviously sharing the almost universal opinion amongst the political pundits that she was not remotely worth considering. I disagreed, suggesting that she might obtain some backing. He immediately offered me very long odds against her himself and I fear that I either failed to take him up on it or placed a very small wager indeed. Three weeks later, Margaret became leader of the Conservative Party.

I was certainly going to vote for Ted, out of pro-European loyalty, but I declined to take any very active part in his campaign. I regarded him as a hopeless candidate and I left it to others to try to persuade him to campaign in a serious way. His most active supporter was Kenneth Baker, who made the mistake of being over-vigorous, concentrating on scoffing at and attacking Margaret Thatcher as someone who could not conceivably ever become prime minister. He paid the penalty by being omitted from Margaret's front bench for the next couple of years.

Ken did, however, persuade me to attend a dinner that Ted Heath was holding for a number of the 1970 intake. I spent much of the evening chatting to Ivan Lawrence, a fellow barrister and the Member for Burton. I was reasonably friendly with Ivan, who complained to me that Ted had always ignored him and never addressed so much as a word to him. Ted was quite hopeless throughout the dinner, remaining churlish, taciturn and difficult. As Ivan and I left, he told me that Ted Heath had still not spoken even one word to him.

Unsurprisingly therefore Margaret easily knocked Ted out after the first round of balloting, but not by enough to win outright. Belatedly, Whitelaw, Howe and Prior stood in the second round and I campaigned for a still-reluctant Geoffrey Howe. We had a very good quality of support – our little campaign team contained many of the brightest and best of my old Cambridge friends and my Nick's Diner companions – but a quite insufficient quantity of votes. Geoffrey was unfortunately an also-ran in the result, together with Jim Prior. In my entire political career I have, alas, rarely voted for the winning candidate in a Conservative leadership election except once on the strange occasion in 1995 when John Major suddenly resigned as prime minister and stood successfully for the leadership in a bizarre contest against John Redwood; and then again for Theresa May on the second ballot in 2016.

Margaret was duly elected. It was not a particularly dramatic or memorable moment for me. I was not shocked, or surprised. I was slightly concerned because I imagined Margaret Thatcher, an acolyte of Keith Joseph, would try to move the party to the right: neither to my taste, nor likely to be successful with the electorate. Like absolutely everyone else, including I suspect Margaret, I had no idea what was to come.

I remained on the front bench as a social security spokesman. My old boss Geoffrey Howe became Shadow Chancellor and my new boss was my old friend Norman Fowler. Norman, who had been ignored by Ted throughout the last four years, was being quite properly promoted: Margaret probably regarded him as 'sound' because he had the backing of her political guru Keith Joseph.

My most prominent activity as a member of Margaret's Opposition front bench was to be the principal spokesman for the party in the parliamentary proceedings on Barbara Castle's Pension Reform Bill. This was Barbara's final attempt to make a lasting mark on events and she was very wedded to the general idea of transforming the state pension scheme by making it more generous and earnings-related. This was popular and attractive as an idea but was wildly ambitious and would have been ruinously expensive if implemented in the way Barbara envisaged, with completely unaffordable financial obligations building up over succeeding years.

Norman Fowler wisely decided to keep out of it as I was already deep into the intricacies of such things and he let me do all the speaking on the subject in debates on the floor of the House and in an enormously lengthy committee stage, with weeks of twice-weekly sessions often involving all-night sittings.

Fortunately, the Minister of State in charge of the bill was a splendid man called Brian O'Malley, the MP for Rotherham, who understood the detail of the bill in a way that Barbara never attempted. Barbara, however, trusted Brian implicitly and since he and I were good friends, he was quite happy to negotiate with me in the background of our ferocious political debates to try to produce an acceptable and workable solution. We did eventually succeed in producing an opt-out scheme and arrangements that, whilst expensive and doomed to be modified substantially, did work for some time afterwards.

On several occasions, I found myself debating opposite Barbara Castle when she insisted on appearing in the Chamber of the House to demonstrate her supposed leadership on the issue. Barbara was a splendid woman and, despite her broad-brush approach to this particular subject, a very formidable debater. Her opening style when starting a speech was always almost excessively sweet and charming reason and she would purr in a rather affected manner, which was not particularly interesting to her opponents. My technique when dealing with her, mainly for my own entertainment, was to try to get her to lose her temper early in any speech, by riling her with my interventions. My favourite approach was to refer to the measure as the 'O'Malley bill' rather than the 'Castle bill', which was a huge embarrassment to Brian and infuriating to Barbara. Once I succeeded in shaking her cool Barbara would then move into her far more impressive and gripping style, spitting passionate red-headed fury, berating me and my backbench supporters for our outrageous suggestions. Fortunately my rather irresponsible approach, which did succeed in bringing the best out of Mrs Castle as a parliamentary performer, did not prove in any way damaging to the sensible progress that we were able to make on the measure.

Brian O'Malley was an immensely talented man and a distinguished Minister of State. Tragically in April 1976, a few months after he had successfully delivered the pensions legislation, he dropped dead at the Despatch Box. He was forty-six years old. I was genuinely very upset by this terrible event, as were all of his many friends on the Labour back benches.

After about three years of becoming ever more specialized as a pensions and social security spokesman and concerned that I might soon be regarded as a one-issue man, I made the rash move of going to see my leader in her office to ask for a change of subject matter. With hindsight, this was reckless folly born of ambition and there was no reason at all why Margaret should not have taken the view that she had plenty of contenders for Shadow ministerial places and if I didn't want the one that I had got she would have no difficulty in replacing me. Fortunately that was not her reaction. She agreed with me firmly saying that I was spending far too much time thinking about how to distribute other people's money and that it was high time I got more engaged in the question of how wealth was created in the first place. She therefore moved me to become a junior spokesman on Department of Trade and Industry matters under the leadership of Sir Keith Joseph. The DTI brief had two junior spokesmen and the other was another old Cambridge friend of mine, Norman Lamont.

I had an interesting but altogether quieter time for the rest of the parliament. Keith was not a great team player and although I got to know him better than I ever had before, we never really meshed as a team. He was one of the very kindest and most intelligent men that I have ever met in politics. But he had hopelessly naive right-wing opinions and was quite hopeless at organizing or administering or campaigning about anything. He was rather indecisive and had a frustrating habit of agreeing a particular political position, then changing his mind the following day when he had spoken to somebody else. He had a brilliant academic and theoretical intellect, but as he was later to demonstrate when he became a Cabinet minister, he was not suited to being in charge of any complex organization.

I became the Shadow of the Minister of State, Alan Williams, a decent and intelligent Member from South Wales. Alan was responsible for the support given to industry through the Industry Act 1975, an amazing piece of legislation put forward by the Labour government. It involved giving enormous grants to private companies in almost every sector of business. This was on top of the much more prominent interventions in politically high-profile sectors like the car industry, with which I was little involved. The huge subsidies mainly served the purpose of enabling British management, which was then exceedingly weak, to avoid having to engage in any serious attempts to change working practices, manning levels or pay levels, any of which might have helped to make the British economy a little more competitive.

Needless to say, all these grants were superficially very popular and thus almost impossible to oppose without getting into difficulty. I would debate them but let them all go through without division in order to avoid attacks on my party for being so reactionary as to appear to believe in 'free-market economics'. In the 1970s this was seen as a dangerously right-wing concept. The grants were particularly difficult to oppose when they were being given to firms in politically marginal constituencies, which was of course exactly where many of the biggest grants were going.

More entertaining was my shadowing of Bob Cryer, who was a very traditional left-winger and concentrated particularly on supporting socialist, co-operative activities that had been formed out of collapsed companies – for example, Meriden Motorcycle Co-operative, which restored the famous name of Triumph after it went bust. I actually made Conservative policy by declaring myself to be totally in favour of the co-operative principle, which was a perfectly acceptable form of business organization so long as the business in question did not need subsidy, soaking up public money. This was quite lively politics because the co-operatives in question were iconic to the left wing of the Labour movement.

My position on co-operatives was actually shared by Jim Callaghan when he became prime minister. Jim decided to sack Bob Cryer from the government. Poor Bob was very indignant at his dismissal. I discovered that he was protesting to Number 10 that no exchange of letters had taken place on the occasion of his departure. Sad to relate, Bob had to admit to me that Jim made it peremptorily clear to him that no such exchange was going to dignify his sacking.

In March 1976 Harold Wilson astonished all his colleagues by suddenly announcing that he was retiring from office. Harold had been surprised to be re-elected in 1974 and he had steadily lost interest in the role. He was particularly disillusioned when, having determined that the benchmark of his success would be to maintain the exchange rate of the pound, this proved completely impossible. He was forced into one of those devaluations to which unsuccessful British governments since the Second World War were driven whenever economic calamity finally descended. He was also said to be increasingly fed up with the problem of managing the Labour Party and the interminable rivalries and divisions between his colleagues.

Mischievous people also joked that he found the domination of his working life by his PA, Marcia Falkender, unendurable.

The best explanation of Harold's retirement that I ever heard was given to me by the Labour MP Charles Morris, who was both a very good minister and quite close to Harold. He believed that Harold was worried that he might suffer the fate of his own father, who had suffered from dementia very early in his life. Apparently Harold began to fear that the same thing was about to happen to him and he therefore took the opportunity of retiring when he was under no pressure to do so, and before anyone detected his early failings. I am sure this story is accurate, because these intimations proved to be tragically true. Within a few years I would occasionally bump into Harold being led around the precincts of Westminster by his devoted wife, Mary. He was by then so badly affected by dementia that he was quite incapable of caring for himself and had to be carefully watched over by his colleagues when he attended the House of Lords where, despite his illness, he took his place almost daily in his last years.

After his resignation, Harold spent his remaining years in the House of Commons as a backbencher writing a number of completely impenetrable and unreadable books under such titles as *The Governance of Britain*. He was a very pleasant man to deal with personally and he occupied a room very close to mine in the Palace. He would write, as I do, smoking cigars, which were a lifelong passion of his. The familiar pipe was purely for presentational purposes and had first appeared when a TV cameraman was trying to get him to do something with his hands that would not interfere with photography. I would scent the waves of expensive Havana smoke coming down the corridor and when I bumped into Harold emerging from his room he would earnestly tell me how many thousand words he had managed to produce that day.

After Harold Wilson's surprise resignation, James Callaghan, the experienced Foreign Secretary and former Chancellor and Home Secretary, won the MPs' ballot to become the Labour Party's new leader. Popular with all parts of the Labour movement, he defeated

Anthony Crosland, Roy Jenkins, Tony Benn, Denis Healey, and finally Michael Foot to take this prize.

A month into Jim Callaghan's premiership I witnessed the worst disorder in the Chamber that I have ever seen in my parliamentary career.

It was late at night and feelings were running high over the Labour government's controversial Aircraft and Shipbuilding Bill. The bill was seeking to nationalize large parts of the UK's aerospace and shipbuilding industries, and the Conservative Opposition was confident it was about to kill it off through the procedural parliamentary means of having it declared to be a 'hybrid bill'. However, when the votes were counted, the government had, to our enormous surprise, won the crucial vote by a majority of one.

It was then alleged that they had in fact won by allowing an MP who had been paired (an MP who has an agreement with another MP intending to vote the other way that neither will vote, allowing them both to be away from the House without it affecting the overall outcome) to go ahead and vote.

When they realized that the vote was theirs, Labour MPs began to sing 'The Red Flag' in defiant delight. A melee then broke out down the middle of the Chamber, involving physical fights between several pairs of MPs. Michael Heseltine, who had been leading for the Opposition, rose to his feet at the Opposition Despatch Box, walked over to the Speaker's Chair, and seized the Mace – the symbol of the royal authority by which Parliament meets, and also of the Speaker's authority. He then swirled about, hugging it in his arms almost as though he was dancing with it. He later claimed that he was displaying it to the government benches to remind them of the sovereignty and dignity of Parliament.

During all of this I was standing at the Bar of the House (the boundary of the Chamber, represented by a white line on the floor), and was rather unhelpfully enjoying the spectacle. One encounter, for which I had a perfect view, leaning on the Serjeant-at-Arms' chair, took place only a few feet away from me. Tom Swain, a stocky and tough veteran coal miner, squared up to Tony Nelson, an elegant younger One Nation Conservative. I knew Tom quite well and I knew that he had recently acquired a magistrates' court conviction of a minor kind for some involvement in a brawl in his native Derbyshire. I watched as he lurched forward and confronted Nelson who was preparing to defend himself with a classic Queensberry Rules stance. Tom swung a most enormous haymaker, which would have felled Tony Nelson if it had hit him. Tom missed, though, by quite a distance. However, he unfortunately caught a very glancing blow to the Serjeant-at-Arms, an elderly officer of the House who was vaguely tottering forward in his ceremonial uniform in a vain attempt to separate the two combatants. If Tom had hit him properly I fear he might have killed the frail old boy.

The Serjeant-at-Arms fell back startled and was caught by sympathetic Members before he hit the floor, which stopped this particular confrontation whilst the rest of the fighting was dying down behind them.

Some newspaper reports suggested afterwards that Tom Swain might have been a little affected by alcohol. The next morning I listened to Tom on the BBC *Today* programme, the only radio interview that I ever heard him give in his life. In his rich Derbyshire accent, he was indignantly protesting his sobriety in carefully chosen words, insisting that everyone knew that he never touched a glass of beer. I smiled as I listened. Like many, I knew perfectly well that his habitual tipple was a double brandy.

The Labour government under Jim Callaghan was steadily losing by-elections with the consequence that Jim rapidly lost his parliamentary majority. In March 1977 Jim Callaghan and David Steel, the affable and popular leader of the Liberal Party, saved the government by forming a so-called Lib–Lab Pact under which the Liberals kept the government in power in exchange for consultation on policy with regular weekly meetings between Labour ministers and Liberal spokesmen.

This 'pact' rapidly became a farce because most Labour Cabinet ministers were not in practice inclined to take very much notice of Liberal advice. A perfectly sensible Liberal spokesman called John Pardoe, for example, once described to me the hopeless impossibility of getting the then Chancellor of the Exchequer Denis Healey to discuss anything seriously with him, and the open rudeness and disdain with which he was often treated.

The government therefore embarked on a steady period of slow death. It was only a matter of time before the Opposition parties would find an issue on which they could all vote together to defeat this limping government, and this opportunity arose when the government abandoned its proposals to devolve power to Scotland, causing the Scottish Nationalists to withdraw their usual support.

The government's eventual defeat was one of the most remarkable parliamentary events that I ever experienced. I spent almost all of that day in the House of Commons and saw a great deal of the activity. It was all made even stranger by the fact that, in the tail end of the miserable and cold so-called 'Winter of Discontent', which had been dominated by strikes in every part of the public sector as years of statutory pay and prices policy finally collapsed, industrial action had reached even into the hushed precincts of the Houses of Parliament. Less high-profile than the lorry drivers, train drivers, nurses, grave-diggers and refuse collectors, but certainly not without impact, all of the Commons catering staff were on strike and no food or drink was being served in the Palace of Westminster. One veteran MP said to me that this could be an unprecedented occasion. If the government was defeated it would not be the first time that a government had fallen in a parliamentary vote of confidence. It would, though, be the first time that this had happened with the entire House of Commons still sober at ten o'clock at night. This proved to be an inaccurate fear as quite a lot of politicians left the House during the evening in order to pack the bars of the surrounding public houses.

All the pundits inside and outside of the House were calculating that the result would be a tie, which would mean that the Speaker would by convention give his casting vote in favour of the government and the Callaghan administration would survive. Everything depended, however, on the Independent and Nationalist Irish MPs who held no strong loyalty to either side.

As a result of my old Whips' Office contacts with MPs on all sides I kept reasonably well in touch with events. I spent many hours in the corridors and bars listening to all the gossip of frenzied groups of MPs. But I was fairly relaxed, and happy to soak up the atmosphere of an entertaining day and evening.

One important vote might have been that of Sir Alfred Broughton, a veteran Labour MP from Yorkshire, who had barely been seen in the House for two or three years as he was gravely ill and believed to be on his deathbed. The Conservatives had refused to pair him because they quite rightly argued that he was no longer an active and genuine Member of Parliament. The Labour Whips' Office wanted to bring Sir Alfred down to the precincts of the Palace of Westminster in an ambulance, which was to be parked in New Palace Yard whilst the whips voted him through.

To his lasting credit, Jim Callaghan, who was a civilized man and feared that the journey might kill Sir Alfred, refused to contemplate this. He vetoed the whips' suggestion and sacrificed one vote. Sir Alfred died a few days later.

My old friend from Mansfield, Don Concannon, was by this point Minister of State for Northern Ireland, where he was popular because of his mining background. He had always very courageously acted as a go-between for the Labour Party with the Republicans. Don was now sent to Armagh to persuade Frank Maguire, the very maverick Member for Fermanagh and South Tyrone, to make one of his rare visits to London to vote in the crucial confidence division.

Maguire was always a diverting colleague. He was the prosperous landlord of the only public house in Armagh that was never bombed throughout the Troubles, which plainly indicated his base of support. Don had told me on several occasions that he knew the pub quite well and had visited it a few times, with safe conduct from Maguire's Republican supporters, although he did have to sit through and join in vigorous singing of Republican songs when he was there. Don also told me that Frank Maguire's wife always objected to his going to London because she feared that he would be in danger there. She knew that there had been bombing outrages in London and she always wanted her husband to stay safely in IRA territory.

On this occasion Don succeeded in fetching the recalcitrant Maguire from his pub to London, but, as was Frank's usual practice, he spent the day in a prolonged session of cheerful and gregarious drinking in Whitehall's bars. He had always been a friendly character and I had been present in Annie's Bar on several occasions when he had insisted on buying a round for all the other MPs and journalists. On the day of the crucial vote members of the government Whips' Office were deputed to keep close to him to make sure that they knew where he was and to ensure his attendance at ten o'clock in the evening for the vote itself. Maguire had a tremendous head for alcohol, which never really seemed to affect him. Loyal government whips struggled to keep up with him, and as each one of them sank at the bar, another would replace him to maintain the close contact.

Frank was insisting, I was told by the Labour whips, that he would only vote with the government if they promised that all the Republicans in the Maze prison would be released immediately thereafter. Meanwhile, the more moderate Nationalist MP Gerry Fitt would only vote for the government if they promised that 'the boys behind the wire' would immediately be given political-prisoner status and privileges. Callaghan refused to authorize either of these conditions but everyone proceeded on the basis that they would both vote against the Unionist parties in the end anyway.

The most remarkable feature of the parliamentary debate, which I listened to standing by the Speaker's Chair, was the closing speech given by Michael Foot, Callaghan's Leader of the House. Facing a packed House expecting a crucial parliamentary oration full of political venom, he very wisely realized that the time had passed for convincing any MP of the merits of the vote. He made a brilliant, entertaining and humorous, even hilarious, speech that was largely a satire of the unlikely combination of parties with which he was threatened.

There was a superb passage in which he expressed his sorrow and concern for young David Steel who, he mockingly suggested, had fallen under the malign influence of 'a lady' – that is, Margaret Thatcher – who was leading him astray. 'I should very much like to know,' he said, 'as I am sure would everybody else, what exactly happened last Thursday night. I do not want to misconstrue anything, but did she send for him or did he send for her – or did they just do it by billet-doux? Cupid has already been unmasked. This is the first time I have ever seen a chief whip who could blush. He has every right to blush. Anybody who was responsible for arranging this most grisly of assignations has a lot to answer for.' And on it went. Scarcely anyone in the Chamber could resist the hilarity of his incisive acerbic address. Only Margaret Thatcher, who had no sense of humour at all, sat stony-faced in her place opposite Foot on the front bench. She was plainly shocked by his speech, and was excessively conscious of the weight of history on her shoulders and the impending moment of triumph that might come in a few minutes.

The Chamber and its surroundings were packed when the time for the vote finally came. Both Whips' Offices were forecasting that it would be a tie. The first division lobby to empty was that which poured out the Conservatives, the Liberals, the Scottish Nationalists and the Ulster Unionists. The first whip who had been acting as a teller on that lobby was a cheery little Labour MP who failed when he re-entered the Chamber to follow the convention of remaining straight-faced, and danced a little jig down the centre of the House arousing victorious cheers of anticipation from the Labour benches.

It transpired that Enoch Powell, who was by now a bitter enemy of the Conservative Party, had himself voted with the Opposition but had used his enormous influence to persuade an Ulster Unionist to stay away and abstain, which meant that the Opposition was one vote short.

I had seen Frank Maguire wander onto the floor of the House after the division bells rang. I had watched Labour whips seize his arms, trying to drag him towards the entrance to the government lobby. He was a huge and powerful man, particularly when in drink, and he simply stood his ground and laughed at them until they had to run away to vote themselves. I have no idea where Gerry Fitt was. At the end of the division, when the tellers emerged back in the Chamber, they did of course announce that the Opposition had a majority of one. The two Northern Irish MPs had, as Maguire later put it, 'abstained in person' and failed to deliver for the government.

Every MP probably marked the government's dramatic defeat in his or her own way. Jim Lester and I went off to Ronnie Scott's, my favourite jazz club in London, where the great American jazz guitar-ist Barney Kessel was performing. There we remained until about two in the morning with Jim and me in a jolly mood until we were startled by a BBC journalist with a microphone. She insisted on recording my reactions to the night's events.

The next morning I listened to the *Today* programme, which was full of very earnest political and philosophical debate about the historic significance of the previous night's vote. The mood of the programme abruptly changed when the presenter suddenly went over to an interview against a background of conversation and drinking in a club between sets. My recorded interview gave cheery but not too ridiculous opinions about my pleasure at the result and my high expectations of better government to come. I was a little concerned but fortunately I detected no adverse reaction to my unorthodox intervention which most of my friends thought had introduced a reassuringly human touch to the otherwise grave analysis. Never again did I allow myself to be interviewed in a jazz club. But it had been a rather exceptional occasion.

A general election was called for 4 May 1979 and the Conservatives were quietly confident that we could win.

Margaret had not been a terribly successful Leader of the Opposition and there had been a lot of muttering amongst the backbenchers who had been surprised by her emergence. When she first became leader she still had a very 'elocution lesson' accent and, in her notori-ous twinset and pearls, a highly conventional way of dressing. But her performance steadily improved as she acquired greater confidence and became more prepared to propound her principles. Unfortunately, in politics presentation matters as much as substance and the trans-formation really only came when a man called Gordon Reece persuaded her to remake her public image. Gordon was a PR man who enjoyed a very sybaritic champagne-based lifestyle which I had occasionally been allowed to enjoy when he had invited me to lunch – presumably to soften me up for a transformation of my own. I cannot imagine how he summoned up the courage to attempt to persuade Margaret to agree to this intrusive interference with her personal appearance but he was astonishingly successful. Her new hairstyle and dress sense engendered a sense of power and she also lowered her voice by an octave which fixed her previous tendency to shriek when provoked in debate. I am the most unobservant of men with no interest in style, but even I noticed that in debate and, in discussion, a new leader of men was emerging.

As a result, by the time that every public service in the country was crippled by industrial action in the 1978–9 Winter of Discontent, a new Margaret was leading the Opposition with enormous vigour.

However, some of the electorate were rather doubtful about the prospects of a Conservative government and most pundits thought it was by no means certain. The Callaghan government was a shambles but his cause was not yet entirely hopeless. Denis Healey had had some success in pulling the country back from economic disaster, helped by the firm discipline of the IMF which had enabled him to persuade the Labour Party to make progress with public spending and borrowing. The public also feared the conflict that a Conservative government might possibly generate with the immensely powerful trade union movement. According to opinion polls the majority of the public believed, quite accurately, that two trade union leaders, Jack Jones and Hugh Scanlon, were the most powerful political figures in the country.

Margaret and the Conservative team therefore fought a vigorous campaign but on a very cautious and low-key platform. There was scarcely any hint of our desire to move towards free-market economics. Jim Prior, our Shadow industrial relations spokesman, led the way in saying that we would, if elected, adopt a 'softly, softly' approach to the trade unions. Our policy proposals were kept as unexciting as possible.

The government proved to be so shattered by recent events, and the Liberals, distracted and undermined by a personal scandal surrounding their former leader Jeremy Thorpe, were so electorally irrelevant, that the election gave Margaret a perfectly satisfactory overall majority and I was comfortably returned in Rushcliffe. The Thatcher years began in an atmosphere of cautious reassurance to the public. I have to admit that the campaign had given the public no hint at all of the tumultuous revolution to come, and we would certainly have been defeated if it had.

8

'Maiden Voyage'

(Herbie Hancock, 1965)

JUNIOR MINISTER

In the last weeks of my career as an Opposition spokesman I had had dinner in the Members' Dining Room with Norman Tebbit. We had both talked about our prospects in the event of a Thatcher government. Norman and I were reasonably confident that our leader might soon be prime minister, and that we might be in government, but we both solemnly agreed that we would only serve as Ministers of State because we could not afford to serve in the lower and less well-paid rank of parliamentary undersecretary. Exchanging intelligence that evening we found that Margaret had promised each of us the middle-ranking roles we sought.

I did not in fact receive my telephone call from the new prime minister until two or three days after polling day. Since I had half expected that she might leave such hopelessly moderate and 'wet' former frontbenchers as Lynda Chalker, Barney Hayhoe and me out of her front bench, I had prepared myself for disappointment and my nerves remained calm. Eventually though, the call came, and Margaret said that she wanted me to go to the Department of Transport, as a parliamentary undersecretary. Very foolishly, I did not murmur my gratitude and consent in the normal way. Involuntarily I said, 'But Margaret, I know nothing at all about the politics of transport.' 'My dear boy, you'll soon pick it up,' she replied, tersely, and slammed down the phone. And so I was appointed to my first departmental office.

It was with wry surprise that Norman and I met at a function shortly afterwards to discover that we had in fact both agreed to serve as parliamentary undersecretaries. Ambition had overcome pride and the financial needs of our families. Happily I was reassured that several new parliamentary undersecretaries had told Margaret that they would not be able to serve for more than a few months unless the salaries – in 1979 parliamentary undersecretaries were paid £9,525 a year, equivalent to £49,400 in 2016 – were raised. Parliamentary and ministerial pay were the only incomes which had been frozen by the Wilson and Callaghan governments under the strict rules of their statutory prices and incomes policies. Almost all other public servants had at least avoided the worst by some contrivance such as a productivity deal at a time of high inflation.

Margaret had always been supported by her wealthy husband, Denis, and, like David Cameron after her, never really understood that some of her backbenchers and junior ministers really needed some money to limit the drop in income they were inflicting on their families compared with a non-political life. They were both averse to the knee-jerk newspaper rage that always greeted any rise in political pay. A few years later I was one of a small group of Cabinet ministers trying to persuade her to agree to a salary rise for MPs. She resisted angrily and then suddenly saw the light. 'Oh, I see,' she said. 'They need to keep up appearances.' On that sound Finchley social-standing basis, she then consented.

As parliamentary undersecretary at the Department of Transport I was serving under my old friend from Cambridge, rival for the Rushcliffe constituency, and former boss from Opposition days, Norman Fowler, who was the new Secretary of State. I know now but did not know then that he had asked for me to be appointed to join him and thus saved my political career. We were the only two ministers in a large department which we were able to lead by ourselves.

At first, Norman was only described as Minister for Transport and, although Margaret had intended him to be treated as a member of the Cabinet, we had difficulty persuading other departments of this. Sometimes he would not see papers from other departments and he also had a row about what kind of government car he was entitled to. Eventually, though, Margaret gave him the full Cabinet minister status he undoubtedly deserved. This all reassured me however that Margaret neither attached great importance to, nor intended to take any great interest in, transport policy.

Lynda Chalker, Barney Hayhoe and a number of other 'wets' had also all made it into government. Now we were all ministers, we were barred from Nick's Diner, so to keep us in touch with party politics, we set up a new dining club, which we called the Amesbury Group after the street in Birmingham where I lived.

There was no induction to becoming a minister, nor anything like it. No one in Downing Street could even tell me where the Department of Transport was. It turned out to be on the fourteenth floor of one of the hideous Marsham Street Towers, the biggest blight on the landscape in central Westminster. Having found my way there and located the main entrance, I made myself known. 'I have just been made a minister here,' I announced, nervously. A young man called Andrew Ramsay approached and, equally nervously, introduced himself as my principal private secretary. I had no idea what a private secretary was, but Andrew presented me to my small team and I steadily got into the world of submissions, meetings and decisions which were to become my normal way of life for most of my political career.

Having spent my Opposition years on pensions and industrial policy, I was almost completely unaware of any policies that we might have had on transport. Fortunately, Norman, who had been shadowing the department before the election, had set out some very radical plans. These were based on the then controversial idea that government should put the needs of the consumer and taxpayer ahead of the needs of the owners and employees of our nationalized industries. We therefore embarked on, amongst other things, the very first privatizations – or, as they were still called back then, denationalizations – in post-war British history. Norman also wanted to deregulate private bus services, and to privatize the National Bus Company, the ports and National Freight, which was then the nationalized owner of about a third of the country's lorries including Pickfords. It is, I think, fair to say that very few members of the public had been aware of any of these proposals – representing the first tentative stirrings of what later became the keystone of Thatcherism, and at this stage neither particularly associated with or championed by Margaret – when they had voted in 1979.

Despite my new and rather formal surroundings I retained the bounding excess of confidence which I had had since I first entered politics, and was eager to set about making some changes. Norman, by contrast, was very much more cautious and took many months to build up the necessary confidence to implement what he wanted. He insisted that I should attend every meeting that he held with either senior officials or interest groups. He also allowed me to participate in every decision, which was fortunate because he was at first unbelievably wary about taking any final decision at all. I became an ally of officials who wanted to know what we were doing and who tried to get me to prevent Norman from finishing apparently conclusive discussions by saying, 'I think that we must take this further at the next meeting.'

Both of us were on a crash course in how to be a minister and I have no doubt that I steadily acquired more caution and Norman steadily acquired more self-confidence until we both filled the role in a substantial and effective way. He produced the radical ideas and I provided the urgent desire to deliver them.

By insisting that I participate in every aspect of what the department did, Norman gave me a tremendously valuable education. I was never confined to ministerial correspondence and adjournment debates, which might have been my fate in a larger department. It has to be said, however, that even compared to my days moonlighting as a barrister during the day, and attending the Commons by night, the workload was immense.

I handled the winding up of second-reading debates and all the endless committee stages of the legislation that we began to pass. In that parliament, the Opposition obstructed all legislation as a matter of course and most standing committees went through all-night sittings. Albert Booth, an amiable but stolid old-fashioned Labour MP, was the Shadow spokesman and he would oppose on the floor of the House and in standing committee every detail of every proposal that came forward, with the eager support of Labour MPs such as John Prescott. They were skilled filibusterers and Albert would express socialist outrage at all our proposals.

For example, we wanted to enable private bus companies to run coach excursions without seeking the permission of the traffic commissioners. It was the custom then for the commissioners to call evidence to demonstrate the need or otherwise for any new journey or route, and the established operators always presented witnesses who would describe their extreme satisfaction with the existing coach trips available. It was very difficult for new operators to get permission to run new routes.

We also insisted on privatizing the National Bus Company including the few long-distance services operated by what became National Express. Much of the Opposition took a vigorously protectionist stance because they feared passengers might be diverted from railway trains if we allowed cheaper buses and coaches on the roads. Albert and his Labour team also made passionate arguments about the mayhem we were about to unleash, because 'cowboy operators' would run dangerous vehicles with unskilled drivers and threadbare tyres, causing death and destruction on a considerable scale.

The same arguments were put forward about the carnage and traffic chaos that would be caused by reckless profit-making buccaneers when we privatized National Freight, which we made an employee-owned company. At a very late stage, horrified departmental officials demanded a meeting and told Norman and me that we would have to drop it. They had calculated that, upon privatization, this loss-making subsidized behemoth might make a profit! We did not agree with their conviction that such private gain could never be permitted. In fact, in due course, the share-owning workforce went on to demand that the management carried out obvious and overdue rationalization and changes to bizarre working practices. Some of the employees eventually became very wealthy. I was told a few years later that the chairman's driver had retired as a tax exile to the Isle of Man.

We had similar difficulties with the ports, which were both expensive and regulated to an extraordinary degree. The real problem was an arrangement called the Dock Labour Scheme which meant that at most ports only registered dock workers were allowed to work, and they could only follow traditional practices in moving cargo.

The registered dock workers were all white with no ethnic minorities permitted and were usually the sons of previous dock workers. Quite a lot of the dockers were actually taxi drivers or working elsewhere and would never take up any assignment in the docks, but they would draw pay because of their registered status as casual employees awaiting work. If any handling company ever went out of business, then any waged employees would have to be given full-time employment by the other employers, even if there was no need for them, so that any financial problems were rapidly spread through the ports. The losses were all paid by the taxpayer and the costs were also borne by exporters and importers. On top of this, the shop stewards were completely resistant to the idea of moving from traditional cargo holds to the rapidly emerging container ships that importers and exporters now wanted to use. Containers required fewer people to put them on and to take them off and, I rather suspected, they were slightly more difficult to pilfer.

This was having a disastrous effect on the competitive nature of the majority of our ports and docks. The old Port of London, for example, was effectively closing down – as I discovered when I visited and saw acres of walls and water with just one or two ships in them. The attitude of the dockers' leaders in London, Liverpool and elsewhere was that it was the government's duty to force ships to come back to their docks in order to provide them with more work. Meanwhile, the one or two non-scheme ports such as Felixstowe were beginning to boom as traffic moved there instead. Long-range trade was also going to places like Rotterdam to be offloaded into smaller lighters to avoid the costs, restrictions and delays of the British ports.

I was more cautious than Norman about the abolition of the Dock Labour Scheme. I confess that I was afraid that we would cause a national dock strike, which would be far more catastrophic than a miners' strike, and therefore unwinnable. With hindsight, I was quite wrong and I probably caused avoidable delay. It was not until 1989 that Norman Fowler, by now Secretary of State for Employment, finally abolished the anachronistic and restrictive Dock Labour Scheme – in the face of fairly minimal industrial action – enabling the revival of previously moribund ports such as Bristol, Tees, Tilbury and Sheerness, and creating thousands of jobs.

The worst problem for our department, though, was British Rail which was operating a nationwide railway system so inefficiently that it and its sandwiches were both a running joke and a byword for poor customer service. Norman and I spent a great deal of time and effort trying to move things forward to a more businesslike railway system that might thrive in a slightly more free-market culture.

The railways were presided over by Sir Peter Parker, an avuncular and well-known establishment figure. He was a perfectly impressive man but he was a classic Hampstead socialist who was best known for having once been a student actor and boyfriend of Shirley Williams. Sir Peter presided strongly over his board and was ever-present in the media. I quickly sensed that he regarded Norman and myself as irritating schoolboys and, although he could influence Norman sometimes, I found him patronizing and a constant obstacle to any change. The other obstacles to change were the union leaders. The long-standing custom was that nothing could be done to change anything on the railways unless they supported it. In particular the formidable Sid Weighell, who as the general secretary of the National Union of Railwaymen was a dominant figure, expected to have a veto on every proposal.

It was our dealings with the railway system that opened my eyes to the extraordinary attitudes within the public sector and the nationalized industries at that time.

For example, it fell to me as the junior minister to explain some changes to Sunday services in Kent. I enquired what public consultation had been carried out about the loss of services, because I was receiving some reaction from local MPs. The railway officials patiently explained to me that a full consultation had taken place. I discovered that they meant that full consultation had taken place with the unions so that the trains could be reduced in the drastic way proposed without any loss of income for any employees. I gained the impression that they regarded my belief that the passengers might be consulted as rather eccentric.

I also tried to argue that we should make better use of our enormous buildings, particularly at the hub stations at our termini in London and the bigger cities. I suggested outside companies could rent accommodation to provide more catering and retail facilities. This was dismissed as an outrageous suggestion. WH Smith appeared to have some ancient right to have a shop on every major station. Otherwise the idea that a public service should be contaminated by profit-making companies seeking to engage in ordinary retail trade was completely unacceptable. It was particularly emphasized to me that if private employers were ever allowed at railway stations there would be a serious risk that they might employ staff who would not be obliged to be members of the National Union of Railwaymen, which of course British Rail and Sid Weighell regarded as impossible.

I was also surprised to find that although the last steam engines had disappeared in the 1970s, all railway engines still had firemen on board alongside the drivers. They were not of course called firemen but were designated trainee drivers. They plainly had the minimum necessary training and were waiting for their turn to become drivers. Some new rolling stock had been ordered, for the London-suburban line between St Pancras and Bedford, which had courageously been designed for single-man operating. British Rail proposed to operate these trains with the usual two men in the cab. Norman and I resisted this for months whilst the new rolling stock stood in sidings with grass growing around the wheels. The trains were eventually brought into service, but we had by then conceded that one driver should be in the cab while another employee could be walking up and down inside the diesel rail sets as a customer guide and conductor.

Some of the board members showed a total disregard for the best of our traditional railway heritage, in the misguided belief that they were modernizing the railways. One of them proudly told me about the demolition of the historic arch at Euston Station which had disappeared a few years earlier. Apparently, he had heard from the department that the arch was about to be listed as a protected structure. He was proud of the fact that he had gathered together a collection of volunteer demolition men who had flattened it in one night before the conservation order could be made. Sadly, the supposed reason for the demolition was later either abandoned or proved unnecessary. However, the board member in question indignantly protested that you could not run a business properly if you had to have regard to the hundreds of listed buildings with which British Rail was lumbered.

Peter Parker and his board were also very keen to make progress towards high-speed trains of the kind which were emerging on the Continent. However, it would have been impossible in Britain at that time to build purpose-built new railways going in a straight line as the French had done: the French had no consultation or planning system to tie them up in knots. As a French minister once innocently explained to me, 'When draining a marsh you do not consult the frogs.' British Rail was therefore working on a new concept: the tilting train. Norman and I and our officials were very cautious about the feasibility of these trains, which were being designed at the old railway workshops in Derby. I knew these workshops well from my old schoolboy trainspotting days. Nonetheless British Rail insisted on publishing a timetable for the introduction of tilting trains on the West Coast main line. Eventually, Norman and I were invited to travel on a trial run of the new stock out of Euston to the North-West to publicize the forthcoming revolution. The train trundled along at a reasonable pace but when it tried to go fast the brakes overheated. We had to sit in a siding at Crewe while the brakes cooled down and then return to London. I well remember keeping a straight face as Norman and Peter Parker explained completely untruthfully to the waiting press that our late arrival had been caused by a quite exceptional signalling problem.

I had no engineering expertise at all but after this debacle I did diffidently suggest that problems such as those of the brakes might be better tackled if someone outside BR engineering at Derby was brought in to give advice. For example, aeroplanes seemed capable of landing at Heathrow under considerable pressure without the brakes overheating. My suggestion was dismissed indignantly. Only British Rail engineers could design British Rail trains and only members of the National Union of Railwaymen could work on the project. The engineering problems were never solved and the whole project was later quietly abandoned and the enormous costs written off.

The only area where we made real progress towards the privatization of the railways was with respect to its hotels. Some of these were magnificent – particularly the Adelphi in Liverpool, a marvellous luxurious old-fashioned Edwardian hotel where I stayed once or twice – but they lost colossal amounts of money at the taxpayers' expense. I can attest from bitter experience that the station hotel in Derby proved to be more austere. All the staff were of course members of the National Union of Railwaymen with, for instance, the waitresses mostly being train drivers' daughters. We caused enormous grief to Peter Parker and his colleagues by moving one or two of these hotels towards private ownership.

Norman and I only managed to make a little progress before we both moved on, but the reforms we began did eventually come to fruition. The Thatcher government never cut public spending on any mainstream public service such as health, education or welfare. Instead, the government's finances were eventually restored to order by privatizing inefficient and heavily subsidized nationalized industries.

My main personal area of responsibility was road-building. Norman had neither the time nor the interest for the details of this. I therefore found time between my meetings with him, my parliamentary obligations and my attendance as Norman's deputy at Cabinet Committees to try to revive the road programme.

Norman pressed me into sharing his enthusiasm for new bypasses which were urgently needed to take traffic out of villages and county towns all over England. There were also many important motorway proposals which were entirely necessary to relieve congestion and costs for business if we were ever to have a modern competitive economy.

It was then fashionable on the left and centre left to be against building roads. To the left, the motor car was an irritating symbol of capitalism and the consumer society. It was also a rival to rail travel which had to be protected at all costs. Noisy lobbies, including some organized on a national scale under the banner of protecting the rural environment and saving everyone from the spread of concrete, opposed with vigour practically every inch of every carriageway that I thought should be constructed in the national interest. They stoutly asserted that there was no need for more road capacity at all, and that the only effect of new roads would be to increase the problems by encouraging more people to buy cars. The best-organized campaigns were put together by an academic from Leeds University who would turn up with huge numbers of his students at every public inquiry in order to obstruct progress towards any conclusion. Some local campaigns became quite violent, particularly over the proposal to build a new Archway road in North London. The police were totally unwilling to maintain order at our public inquiries which they said were a private function beyond their jurisdiction.

I had interminable battles over getting a motorway through to Telford which was a new town that would have collapsed without a proper road. Most importantly the M25 had to be completed around London as only little disjointed sections were then in place.

Our predecessors, Bill Rodgers as Secretary of State and his parliamentary undersecretary John Horam, were both admirable people but neither of them had had any interest in road-building or transport. Bill and John had unfortunately approached the issue by abandoning any scheme if a legal challenge to it was raised. All kinds of obvious schemes were pickled in aspic throughout the country until I insisted that we should press on and fight these legal challenges in court if we were ever to build anything.

Fortunately, I had two splendid officials – Miss Fogarty and Miss Forsyth, I believe, both like archetypal Edwardian headmistresses – who were absolutely delighted that I was so anxious to get their previously moribund roads programme back on track. The two would come bustling into my office with bundles of maps under their arms and sit down eagerly to hear me urge them to make progress and to instruct counsel so that we could steadily get infrastructure investment going again.

I had some difficulties. Another civil servant, June Bridgeman, supposedly in charge of the programme in the South-East, was a very powerful woman who once told me that building roads was in her opinion rather like killing whales. I nonetheless authorized the extension of the M23 from Brighton past Croydon towards central London. Mrs Bridgeman went running to my Secretary of State as soon as I put out my instructions, and persuaded him to abandon it. To this day I mutter under my breath whenever I find myself stuck in the traffic through which one still has to crawl to get out of London to Gatwick or Sussex.

I was also responsible for a plethora of road safety measures and am particularly proud of my contribution to improving the breathalyser law which Barbara Castle had introduced in the previous parliament. This Act had been both ferociously unpopular when first introduced and very badly drafted. The result was that judges had been able to interpret the Act strictly and create various absurd procedural defences to any charge. The legislation had set out in copious detail every step in the process of stopping and interviewing a motorist, including the form of words to be used. Lawyers had been able to run all kinds of technical defences which had led to drunken motorists being acquitted because the police had used the wrong words, put them in the wrong order or committed some other procedural mistake. I was not alone in regarding this as a disgrace. The new law was rapidly gaining popularity as it enforced better behaviour and reduced innocent casualties of drinking and driving.

I now wanted the law to be amended to make it more straightforward and to remove all the technicalities which could be so easily abused. My attempts to do this were thwarted because the parliamentary draftsman who had produced the original bill fiercely advised me that the wording was perfect and could not be improved upon. I eventually resolved this with the help of Leon Brittan, who was then a Minister of State at the Home Office.

At the time, Leon represented the beautiful constituency of Cleveland and Whitby on the north-east coast. I was always rather surprised by this. Leon and John Gummer had been two of the most urbane, sophisticated, and extravagantly metropolitan men I knew, and yet when they ended up with rural seats – Leon in Yorkshire and Gummer in Suffolk – they both became fairly instantly countrified. Gummer took to shooting and wearing tweed, while Leon became a great walker over the moors.

On one particular weekend visit with Gillian to Leon and Diana's home in Yorkshire, he and I tackled the drink-driving problem. As recently practising lawyers we sat side by side on his lawn and drafted a satisfactory alternative to the existing law. The modern enforceable drink-driving law is wholly due to the efforts of Leon and myself as self-appointed amateur parliamentary draftsmen.

My fascinating introduction to the realities of being a minister took place against the backdrop of the most difficult and controversial phase of the Thatcher government's transformation of the British economy. We had been elected on a low-key and unexciting manifesto but Margaret and her closest allies, including Geoffrey Howe, Keith Joseph and Nigel Lawson, wished to embark on major reforms, which the crippled British economy so desperately needed.

This rapidly produced quite a marked division between the liberal radicals and the more cautious consensus Conservative politicians, which became known as a battle between 'wets' and 'dries'. I always described myself as a wet and spoke quite openly to that effect on the rare occasions when a journalist asked someone of my junior rank. However, although undoubtedly a liberal on social policy, I was also a believer, subject to the ability to make progress politically, in market economics. And I still am.

The senior wets belonging to the previous era of Heathite consensus obstructed Margaret on policy grounds, but not only on those grounds. Some of them deeply resented her remarkable emergence first as leader and then prime minister, and frankly thought that she was not up to the job. Margaret gritted her teeth and proceeded by the simple process of steadily dropping her opponents one by one in a series of small reshuffles over the first year or two. This led to the early departure of the irreconcilable Ian Gilmour together with Norman St John-Stevas and others. Eventually she even persuaded Jim Prior to move to the Northern Ireland Department against his better judgement. She rather shocked the political world by replacing him at the Department of Employment with the abrasive Norman Tebbit, who embarked on the first of our drastic reforms to reduce the excessive power of the trade unions and their stranglehold on the British economy.

Margaret's essential ally in all this was William Whitelaw, who became her deputy prime minister. He was a wet, but a fiercely loyal one. He played a key role in keeping all the sensible liberal members of the government and loyal Heathites, meaning all the ministers who shared my political position, onside throughout the steady progress of reform. He was one of the few people who could persuade Margaret to change tack and, on occasion, to modify some proposals. It has to be said, however, that Margaret was not the blind ideologue that her opponents imagined. She understood the realities of democratic parliamentary politics very well indeed. One step backward then two steps forward is often the best way to achieve one's aims.

She did, though, have clear objectives, and she always stuck to them. No later twenty-first-century government would have risked a fraction of the short-term unpopularity we experienced in order to achieve our long-term agenda.

This was nowhere more true than on the government's handling of the macro-economy.

My old boss from Opposition days, Geoffrey Howe, had explained to me before the election that if he became Chancellor he intended to pursue a firm policy of fiscal discipline and tighter monetary policy in order to eliminate inflation and to make room for growth. I agreed with the rationality of this but protested that it would mean 3 million unemployed, and doubted whether that was politically possible. Geoffrey firmly disagreed with my premise that the trade unions would force wage claims so high that unemployment would be inevitable. He said that the unions would see that they had to sacrifice excessive pay claims in order to secure jobs. It would have been very much better if the unions had behaved so responsibly in practice, but unfortunately it soon became clear that they preferred larger pay claims for their members to the creation of new jobs or greater job security.

Matters came to a head with Geoffrey's 1981 Budget, which was introduced at a time of recession and rising unemployment, and was the point at which people realized that the government really was going to deliver the firm, economically dry, free-market Budget that the country needed. Geoffrey caused a shock to many of his Cabinet colleagues when he outlined his Budget to them on the morning before he delivered it to the House. I was not, of course, in Cabinet but I soon heard from Norman that the wets had strongly objected to the cuts in spending and the increases in taxation that Geoffrey felt were necessary to get the economy on track, and some apparently were quite ferocious in their criticisms. Nevertheless Geoffrey went ahead with a Budget which was rational policy but created a political storm. Afterwards, he bumped into me in the House and asked whether I agreed with his Budget. I swallowed hard but had to agree that I did, and I thought then and believe now that he did the right and courageous thing. In my opinion, this was the key turning point that eventually enabled the 'Thatcher revolution' to be such a remarkable success.

After the Budget the government became more unpopular in the country than I recall any government ever being, and it became really quite uncomfortable for any Conservative MP to be out in public. I was content loyally to stick to the line, which I believed was in the national interest, but I became convinced that the government would be destroyed at the next election, whenever it came. I began to worry about whether I would hold my newly carved-out safe seat of Rushcliffe, and even whether the party would survive as a significant parliamentary group.

People now forget and perhaps even downplay how vicious politics was in the 1970s and 1980s. But industrial relations then were extremely tense and sometimes violent. This continued throughout most of the next decade and I became familiar with the ferocious verbal onslaught that even junior ministers would often encounter throughout the Thatcher years. I had to pass through my first picket lines, where I discovered that jostling was inevitable. The word 'scab' was the most popular chant for pickets because, as I discovered, a very large amount of spit could be ejected on the victim whilst the word was being chanted.

It also became near to impossible for Conservative politicians to be heard on some university campuses, the assumption being that Conservatives were capitalist, racist and dangerous. On one occasion I had to be rescued from Swansea campus in a police car across whose bonnet a vociferous protester was lying. On another occasion, I was allowed to address the Conservative Association in I think Manchester or Leeds, but only if I agreed to stop after every paragraph so that a pale-faced student standing at the back of the hall could correct what I was saying. This was counterproductive because it quickly became clear as he spouted his tight-lipped slogans what a complete lunatic this guy was. But I viewed it all as being part of life's rich tapestry and happily for me it was always those accompanying me who managed to get hit by the eggs.

As a junior minister my profile was still low enough that I wasn't often shouted at in the street when I was simply going about my day-to-day life: when I was, any family accompanying me pretended not to notice.

The worsening political atmosphere in the country coincided with a shift to extreme left-wing politics in the Labour Party under the leadership of Michael Foot. Michael was a delightful and benign bibliophile but some of his followers, particularly those in the Militant Tendency, were not. I had conversations in Annie's Bar with moderate old friends in the Labour Party who described the problems they faced. At least one had had his tyres slashed when attending a party meeting in his constituency. Others were being deselected by constituency associations. The militant membership began to call constituency meetings at which they would filibuster into the small hours until the regular membership had all gone home, at which point they would pass extreme motions. A North London MP described to me the growing membership of his local party as trade union after trade union affiliated to the party and sent representatives to its meetings. He was astonished to find branches of the National Union of Mineworkers affiliating themselves to his Islington party. In 1978, Simon Mahon, the Member for Bootle, had ceased to be invited to any meetings by his local party at all and he only discovered that he had been deselected and replaced by a left-wing candidate when he read about the decision in his local newspaper.

Inevitably the Labour Party split, with the so-called Gang of Four breaking away and forming the Social Democratic Party. They were instantly popular as an acceptable alternative to the stern Thatcher government on the one hand and the extreme-left Opposition on the other, and for a time leapt well ahead of both parties in the opinion polls. The Conservatives were often in third place in the polls, with one particularly dire Gallup poll putting the SDP on 50.5 per cent, Labour on 23.5 per cent and the Conservatives on 23 per cent.

However in the later stages of the parliament, the political climate began to improve.

The Labour Party was moving into an isolated and extreme position, adopting policies such as leaving NATO and becoming neutral in the Cold War, leaving the European Union and nationalizing more of the commanding heights of the British economy.

General Galtieri's invasion of the Falkland Islands also obviously made a huge difference to the government's fortunes. The electorate couldn't help but note the contrast between Margaret's decisiveness and Michael Foot's clearly troubled and indecisive position. Galtieri, Foot and, later, Arthur Scargill and Neil Kinnock: Margaret was always very lucky in her political opponents.

I believe, however, that our ultimate extraordinary success in the 1983 general election owed more to the steadily improving state of the economy in response to our firm measures, and the growing sense that whilst those measures had been unpopular at the time, they had probably been necessary and were proving successful. This, more than anything, settled the issue and saw Mrs Thatcher – and me – return to power.

9

'Fever'

(Peggy Lee, 1958)

HEALTH MINISTER

In March 1982 Margaret summoned me to Downing Street. It was my first reshuffle. Like all the other junior ministers in attendance, I didn't know whether I would be sacked or promoted. Margaret invited me to become Minister of State for Health and I eagerly accepted.

Norman Fowler, who was then presiding successfully over the giant Department of Health and Social Security, had asked for me again. Norman's existing health minister, Dr Gerry Vaughan, was a good guy but he was a bit weak and woolly and Norman had no confidence that he would be able to handle the growing controversies in the National Health Service, which were proving to be a nightmare. Norman later confided that his elaborate negotiations to get me moved to Health had 'put Premier League transfers absolutely into the shade'.

Norman wanted to concentrate on the massive welfare reforms he was working on with his social security minister, Tony Newton. He was used to working with me and wanted me there to act as a safe pair of hands in handling the NHS and the health unions. He gave me far more autonomy and discretion than a Minister of State would usually have. Effectively I was the minister with day-to-day responsibility for the NHS for most of the time.

I was – and remain – a fervent believer in the principles of the NHS (which made me slightly surprised that Margaret Thatcher, who was not so sound, had agreed to make me a health minister; I only later discovered how much convincing she had needed). I was delighted to be dealing with issues of such essential importance to the public.

Whilst the crises that surrounded the NHS were tumultuous, I actually rather enjoyed the combative atmosphere. Aneurin Bevan, the chief architect of the NHS, had been right when he said that the Secretary of State for Health would be held personally responsible every time a bedpan was dropped anywhere in England and Wales. I was again forcefully reminded that health care is the most emotional political subject in just about every Western democracy. You can declare war more peacefully than you can reform a health-care system. It will always be like this and the post of minister for health will usually be a political graveyard.

I found myself in the middle of constant rows, both nationally and locally. My approach was to defend myself vigorously and to mount a defence of every change that I was making and against every attack that was made upon me. I rapidly became a much better-known figure in national politics with frequent appearances across the media and on the floor of the House of Commons. I also became the target of the most determined campaigning, sometimes backed up with high levels of public relations spending by every vested interest with a role in the NHS. But although the pressure was intense and the workload enormous, I relished it. For someone of my perhaps unusual temperament, it was exactly what I had come into politics to do.

Most importantly for the future, I steadily formed the view that it was ridiculous that, as a minister, my direct involvement in every difficult decision seemed to be the only way to tackle any crisis or produce any change. The NHS needed reform.

I discovered what life as the health minister was going to be like immediately. Within four days of my entering the department's hideous headquarters at the Elephant and Castle in March 1982, the NHS was plunged into a bitter national strike. By the time it was finally resolved at the end of that year, this strike over pay had become the longest-running strike of the century, overtaking even the miners' strike of 1926.

The dispute had been provoked by the government's move to a

system of strict cash limits for all departments, which was a culture shock to a rudderless NHS accustomed to steadily overspending. Under the previous system, budgets had been inflation-proofed and had changed in response to changes in demand. Norman and I never actually cut the level of spending on health – no British government has ever cut spending on the NHS since it was founded. We increased it in real terms and sought to expand and develop the service through efficiency savings. There was simply no room for the enormous 14 per cent pay claims that the health unions were making without doing damage to the service.

I hasten to add that I played no role at all in provoking the strike which was declared whilst I was still finding my way around the bleak Kafkaesque tower block in which we were housed. I was told that architects regarded it as a classic example of the brutalist style of the 1960s.

The strike was patchy in its intensity because the doctors' union, the British Medical Association, and the Royal College of Nursing did not join it. But it was vigorously pursued by the National Union of Public Employees, led by the redoubtable Rodney Bickerstaffe with whom I got on well personally, and the Confederation of Health Service Employees, led by Albert Spanswick. Some nurses were members of these militant trade unions, however, so in some hospitals clinical services were reduced to emergency treatment only.

Mass picketing had by now become the norm in industrial disputes, and in some parts of the country, particularly London and the North-West, it could be violent and intimidating. The definition of 'emergency admission' allowed through varied from place to place. At many hospitals ambulances with blue lights flashing were stopped by the picket lines. Shop stewards would enter the ambulance to see the patient and hear the description of the problem. They would then give or withhold permission for each patient to be admitted according to their judgement of whether it was an emergency or not.

My own area of Nottinghamshire was as usual quite moderate but it was not free of difficulties. The worst incident in Nottingham occurred when someone refused to stop and drove a car through the picket line. Believing that this was a 'scab' worker 'blacklegging', the pickets smashed the car's windscreen with an iron bar. It transpired that the driver was the worried relative of a patient whom he was trying to visit.

I was plunged first-hand into some of the worst of this when holiday time came around in August. Both Fiona Fowler (Norman's wife) and Gillian were very reluctant to cancel our usual month-long family summer holidays. The holidays, as well as being lovely in themselves, were the only time of year when I could spend time with the children, and we could experience any kind of normal family life. Norman therefore decreed that we should alternate and go for two weeks each. Coincidentally, we had both booked holidays in south-western France, and so we arranged to rendezvous at the airport in Bordeaux where I could pass on the news of my tenure before joining my family on holiday, leaving Norman to go back to London.

Before he had left, Norman had had the bright idea that I should raise morale by making a series of ministerial visits to the 'hotspots' across the country, where the heroic working staff were demoralized by the violent pressure and ostracization that they were facing. This seemed a good idea to me until I began to make these highly publicized and extremely contentious trips. We began reasonably peacefully in Doncaster, but thereafter each visit got livelier than the last as more and more journalists joined in, and the whole thing started to take on a sense of political circus. The week culminated in a visit to a hospital in Liverpool, which was then a very militantly left-wing city. There was confusion about my entrance into the hospital as an attempt was made to get me in by a door avoiding the picket line. The pickets spotted me and streamed across the hospital grounds to waylay my little party as, with many accompanying journalists, I ran towards a small side door. A television crew beat me to the entrance and effectively blocked it. Everyone was trying to film the violent scene which ensued while all I could do was hope that reinforcements would arrive soon to extricate me. I have a splendid photograph to remind me of the experience where I appear to be hugging a police-woman in the middle of a melee in which pickets are reaching over my limited protection and beating me over the head with copies of the Communist newspaper the *Daily Worker*.

I did more national interviews with the media than I had ever done before in which I tried my inexperienced best to maintain a robust but reasonable line. I got into trouble immediately before I was due to fly out to Bordeaux, when someone from the *Daily Telegraph* asked me how long we were prepared to hold out and whether we would go so far as to use the armed forces to keep the NHS running. I portentously declared that we were determined to protect the service by keeping to our position and we ruled nothing out. This was widely reported as a threat to send in the troops which the then Home Secretary Willie Whitelaw stoutly denied when challenged by journalists. My departure on holiday was complicated by the efficiency of my Private Office, who had booked K. Clarke, Minister of Health, through VIP facilities at Heathrow several days in advance. My whereabouts thus well-advertised to anyone interested in such things, I found myself, dressed in relaxed holiday style, being pursued onto the tarmac by a gaggle of six eager photographers, and was saved only by the captain, who refused to allow them onto the plane. Landing at Bordeaux, slightly flustered, I had to inform my disconcerted boss that he would be returning to find that he had to deny that the army were about to enter our hospitals. This was all something of a baptism of fire for me, and certainly helped me develop the pachyderm hide I needed to survive some of the tight spots in which I found myself later in my career.

Despite the rather disastrous hospital tour which almost certainly did not achieve its desired objective of reviving managers' flagging morale, I thought that I managed in the course of the debate surrounding the strike to make the government's position quite respectable. The nurses were the people who had the strongest emotional appeal to the general public and were always positioned prominently in uniform at the front of any picket line. We made a higher offer to the nurses, which was rejected as divisive by the unions, which were dominated by non-nursing members and wished to use the popularity of the nurses to achieve a huge pay rise for all. However, the offer had the desired effect of undermining the unions' appearance of reasonableness, and their resolve. In the end it was war-weariness that finally brought everyone back to the table and enabled us to bring this horrendous dispute to a close.

This was the lively background to my day-to-day work at the department. For Norman and me, arriving at Health in the early 1980s, it felt as if we and the NHS were suddenly in the real world, just coming out of recession, with an icy chill in the financial climate, with cash-limits accounting for the first time, and the politics dominated by allegations of cuts in services. So we had somehow to get hold of this Leviathan and seek to deliver the service, while at the same time trying to reform it. And to get growth in the service delivered out of the money we had available, we had to constrain cost in some way that didn't damage the service.

We had two fundamental problems as we set about this task. One was that there wasn't a management system worth the name. There was next to no management information of any kind, no one knew what the devil we were spending the money on, or how much anything cost. The other was that we could not have a grown-up debate about reforms, because the constant mantra that everything wrong with the NHS was down to Tory cuts drowned out anything sensible we tried to say. In fact, we increased real-term spending every year. But despite this, Michael Meacher, the Shadow Secretary of State for Health, insisted noisily and emotionally that anything below the 4 per cent growth needed to keep up with 'health inflation' was a cut.

The civil servants that I worked with were very capable and professional although horrified by the controversy of the strike. It was their thankless job to try to impose bureaucratic and centralized command and control management on countless district health authorities who all merrily went their own way. However, many of them simply wanted to lead as quiet a life as possible in the permanent maelstrom of health-care politics. There was a beleaguered, 'let's minimize the fuss' feeling underlying everything they did. One official explained to me bluntly that everything depended on getting money out of the Treasury in our spending settlement. His exact words were that 'we always like a Secretary of State who brings back the groceries'. It was also carefully explained to me that my best tactic in handling the

British Medical Association was to make a concession at least once a year that improved its members' pay and terms and conditions. Having recently read *A New Look at Medicine and Politics* by Enoch Powell about his experience as minister for health in which he described his amazement that he was only ever able to talk to any doctor about money and pay – never the reform and improvement of the service as a whole – this was advice I rather recklessly rejected.

I had no personal political advisers at all as a junior minister, and my only arms to pull the levers and my only ears for the mood in the system were the excellent young civil servants in my ministerial Private Office. I also allegedly had clinical advice because of a long-standing agreement with the BMA which stipulated that every meeting I had with my officials had to include one of my medical officers. Some of these medical advisers were very good doctors and some were indeed very helpful, which was fortunate because the obvious intent behind their presence was that they should act as the trade union's eyes and ears to keep the BMA informed of the minister's every intention.

My first Chief Medical Officer, Sir Henry Yellowlees, was quite useless. A well-known and rather pompous public figure, he took no interest at all in the changes that I was making. So far as I could see his only interest was in keeping strict personal control over the patronage he exercised in determining which distinguished medics would receive knighthoods and other honours. He developed a huge filing system to supervise this, and accepted invitations to countless dinner parties in order to form his final personal opinions. Thankfully, Sir Henry retired in 1984 and I was lucky enough to have as his successor Sir Donald Acheson, who was a splendid man: quite quiet, self-effacing but an absolutely dedicated public servant in the pursuit of his own particular interest and expertise in health education. He never attempted, as Sir Henry occasionally did, to obstruct me.

The BMA had had a combative relationship with government from the earliest days of the NHS, even describing Aneurin Bevan as a 'medical Führer' when he first set up the health service. Recently, it had begun to improve its public image by engaging in various health campaigns to demonstrate its care and concern for the public. This may have dispelled its money-grubbing image to the outside world but it did not affect its engagement with ministers.

The BMA's leaders, including the left-wing John Marks and the appropriately named Tony Grabham, took the earliest opportunity to try to intimidate me, as they had done with most of my predecessors and have continued to do with all my successors down to the present day. In one of my earliest conversations with Grabham, a consultant from Northampton who must have had very little time for his clinical practice given the time he spent on union duties, he began to reminisce in an apparently friendly manner about his past victories over former ministers. He seemed to derive particular sadistic pleasure from telling me of the occasion when he had caused Barbara Castle to collapse in tears. I was in no doubt that he was trying to foretell my fate if I resisted his blandishments. I was not deterred, nor ever reduced to tears. Grabham discovered that I had a peculiarly laid-back and stress-free personality and that I was made of sterner stuff. But the fact remains that the BMA was the most ruthless and determined opponent I ever faced in my whole career.

I met many highly impressive doctors during my time in the Department of Health. They would rarely express much fondness or respect for their union leaders. However, I was always left with the strong impression that they felt that this ferociously militant style of representation did serve a useful purpose in that it prevented politicians taking advantage of them. This was a pity, because the effect was to pickle the entire health service in aspic, to the detriment of its employees and patients alike.

By the 1980s the NHS had become the biggest employer in the country. I soon began to say that its only rival in Europe in terms of numbers was the Red Army. I also compared it with the Indian State Railways, which so far as I had ever seen operated a service with no overall direction and management, and relied on all the staff continuing to do exactly the same thing as they had always previously done.

Undoubtedly the overwhelming strength of the NHS was the dedication to the care and treatment of patients that was demonstrated by the vast majority of staff in their daily work. However, this enormous organization quite obviously lacked any coherent system of management. The consensus management which Keith Joseph had imposed and which, as I have already admitted, I helped get through as a government whip, had totally failed. The country was divided up into over 190 district health authorities who all did their own thing with varying degrees of success and attributed to the centre any problems or failings that arose. The machine at the centre tried to help me field all the flak and persistently tried to advise and intervene on all the difficult issues.

The new system of cash limits brought all of this into sharp relief. Some district health authorities found at the end of the year that they had a surplus of money and would rush around trying to find ways of spending it to avoid having their budgets reduced the following year. Others would find that they ran short of cash from about Christmas, and would rush to the newspapers to complain about the 'cuts' they were facing.

Margaret was obsessed with the idea that the underlying problem was that the whole ramshackle service was overmanned. She asked Roy Griffiths, the then managing director and deputy chairman of Sainsbury's, to carry out an inquiry for her into the manning of the NHS but he very sensibly insisted that the inquiry would focus on the overall system of management.

At first, I was annoyed by Roy's appointment. It was announced shortly after my own and although I was never told why this businessman was being appointed to second-guess my ministerial efforts, I strongly suspected it was because my prime minister did not trust me to be sufficiently robust. I rapidly retracted my resistance because he was congenial and his expertise was obviously invaluable. Moreover, we agreed that the complete absence of any sensible structure of management was the heart of the problem.

Roy had no time to interfere with my day-to-day activities because he was still running Sainsbury's. However, he did produce a short and sensible report containing several worthwhile recommendations – for example, that there should be a single individual, a general manager, for each regional and district authority, and for each major hospital, who was responsible and accountable for its effective management – which were steadily implemented. Roy's report also contained one memorable comment, when he pointed out that 'If

Florence Nightingale were carrying her lamp through the corridors of the NHS today she would almost certainly be searching for the people in charge.'

I had never managed anything in my life but I plunged into it with enthusiasm, acquiring a little more skill as I progressed. I had no alternative but to adopt a personalized, centralized approach to driving change and cost control through the system. This involved allocating money and assuming that savings would be made from reform of the services. I introduced a fiercely opposed system of bringing in private providers to bid for cleaning, catering and laundry. I tried to get some rudiments of management information and cost information available, demanding that district health authorities record how many people they employed and how much the services they provided actually cost. I closed run-down and redundant hospitals and insisted on selling off our huge portfolio of empty land and derelict buildings. This enabled us to get a hospital-building programme under way for the first time for many years.

I will admit that I relied mainly on constant meetings with the chairmen of the regional health authorities and some of the difficult district health authorities. I tried to impose my views on these people and on my officials by instruction and sheer willpower. Some officials were very good and very helpful and some of the regional chairmen were powerful allies. Where I had the ability to appoint chairmen of health authorities I got rid of all the useless and hostile ones and replaced them wherever possible with enthusiasts who had some experience of managing private businesses. When I had finally got in post a team of loyal and supportive regional authorities' chairmen, I always described them as my Health Cabinet. I actively sought out volunteers for this public service.

However, I did make some mistakes and my worst was probably my imposition of manpower targets. Inevitably, the wrong people would leave the service and vacancies would become unfillable in key areas whilst excess numbers were retained uselessly elsewhere. But I still believe that my overall approach started to produce a considerable change of culture, as well as significant savings which could go into improving the service.

The one thing that the debate never turned upon, despite all my efforts, was the output of the NHS and the impact on patient care, despite the fact that this actually began steadily to improve.

Those were the days when the general public were rather deferential and unwilling to complain about great institutions like the NHS. I frequently encountered the most dreadful conditions in some of our worst premises and became aware of awful variations in success between different hospitals and different health authorities. Waiting lists were often horrendously long. The system had long been accustomed to a culture where the interests of the patients were not regarded as a very high priority. As a result my daily activities were dominated by controversies about inputs rather than outcomes, and providers rather than consumers – industrial disputes, fights over closures and sales, arguments about the level of public spending and the constant allegation that I was intent on privatizing the service.

Some of the worst controversies were over the closures of old and redundant hospitals. The NHS owned large numbers of hopeless Victorian institutional buildings, many of which were unsuitable to deliver a civilized modern service. My predecessor Gerry Vaughan had taken the political decision that he would never agree to the closure of any hospital, and all such decisions required ministerial approval. I began to close hospitals in a way which had not been done since the service was founded, and became immersed in a constant round of demonstrations and petitions fighting to 'save' clapped-out institutions all over the country.

The most extreme cases were the Victorian workhouses, which had been renamed geriatric hospitals in 1948 and which housed in near-slum conditions wards of comatose and usually demented patients being kept alive in the most basic way. I closed these whenever we were able to build or provide a modern clinical alternative. Each closure was bitterly fought by local residents inspired by the staff who believed that each geriatric hospital was a centre of clinical excellence essential to the strength of their community.

Closely competing with the geriatric hospitals as the most appalling institutions in the whole of the NHS were the Victorian asylums, now termed mental hospitals. The worst were full of chain-smoking, heavily sedated patients in dressing gowns shuffling down the corridors and staring vacantly into space. They were closed, self-perpetuating and grossly overcrowded institutions in which it was almost impossible to provide adequate clinical care. I began to close them with some vigour and to try to give effect to the medical recommendations that we should move over to another ferociously controversial policy – care in the community. This was the policy of treating and caring for mentally ill people in their homes rather than inside institutions, and was widely supported by clinicians as being the more humanitarian, de-stigmatizing and effective approach. It was opposed by some staff who wanted to retain their jobs in the asylums, and became unpopular with the public because of a mixture of underfunding of community care, as health authorities spent the savings from closing the mental hospitals on more popular services like cancer, prejudice against the mentally ill, and media hysteria about the actions of a very small number of seriously ill individuals who should have been committed for public safety.

At one stage I eventually closed a giant mental hospital at Saxondale in my own constituency. This had gone more quietly than most. A strange incident followed because it proved impossible to find out why many of the elderly patients had been admitted in the first place. Some were believed to be the daughters of respectable families who had had them committed in their youth when they had become pregnant outside matrimony. One lady in particular had worked for decades in the kitchens whilst living there. It was impossible to establish whether she was a patient or a member of staff. Eventually the trade union quite rightly succeeded in obtaining a huge award of back pay for her, relating to her de facto employment in the kitchens for which she had apparently only ever received pocket money.

But my most striking memory of a closure was that of a maternity hospital in the Isle of Ely, the constituency of the Liberal MP, writer and broadcaster, Clement Freud. Gerry Vaughan had previously 'saved' this hospital.

When I visited it as part of the consultation process, the building was surrounded by a huge crowd of people, fronted by local journalists and television crews. The crowd mainly comprised women, many of whom had given birth at the hospital and were holding their children in the air. I made my way through the crowd. Inside the building I spoke briefly to Clement who thought the whole thing was hilarious and gave me his private opinion that Gerry had made a terrible mistake in not allowing the place to close. I was then shown around wards which seemed to have surprisingly few mothers in them. I began to form the strong suspicion that the staff were moving some of the patients around ahead of me in order to give the impression that it was much busier than it was. I then had a long interview with the senior obstetrician who gave me his clinical view.

He told me that I should understand that he was never going to agree to deliver a baby in this hospital again. It was dangerous and unsuitable and all his future deliveries would be in the much better facilities in the new hospital nearby. It was my duty to close this hospital. Greatly relieved, I asked him to come outside with me and we could jointly explain that to the journalists and demonstrators. He flatly refused. He said that he had given me his honest and confidential opinion. It was up to me what I did.

Fortified by this, I went outside to face the cameras in front of the milling crowd in order to explain that I would go away to consider carefully all views. A woman strode forward from the crowd and thrust a baby into my arms which she said had been born there. She then vanished. Clutching the baby nervously and hoping I was holding it the right way up I was then interviewed by the local television crew.

I did of course eventually confirm the closure of this hopeless institution and was no doubt reviled locally as a result. But my visit was the first time I met a woman who was later to become a good colleague and friend, Gillian Shephard. Gillian was then the local health authority chairman and had been standing unobtrusively in the crowd, grinning as I addressed the protesters. She had been recommending the closure to ministers for some time.

Even hospital openings could be problematic. When I went to open a new hospital at Cannock in Staffordshire, the police had considerable difficulty in getting me through the huge crowds of demonstrators who were waving placards and chanting to protest at my visit. They were bitterly opposed to the 'cuts' I was making to the NHS, which I found rather startling when we were obviously spending money in Cannock on a very desirable new hospital. In the middle of the rumpus, I was able to make a short speech as I planted a small sapling to commemorate this new growth in the local service. Sadly, the poor tree did not survive for very long. It was almost immediately uprooted from the ground and I saw it borne off on the shoulders of a crowd of demonstrators.

There was one notable occasion on which I had to fight my own prime minister. A strange dispute arose about the future of the old St George's Hospital that stood on Hyde Park Corner. It was an eighteenth-century foundation built on land that had been donated by the Grosvenor family. An attractive building near the park and the Duke of Wellington's house, it was one of the most valuable pieces of real estate in central London. It was completely unsuitable for the delivery of modern health care and I therefore took the decision to close it and to dispose of the land. There was surprisingly little public opposition to this particularly obvious case for closure.

The head of the Grosvenor family and the beneficiary of the huge Grosvenor Estate was the Duke of Westminster, one of the wealthiest men in the United Kingdom. The duke approached Margaret Thatcher full of indignation that the land was not being returned to his family as a gesture to the charitable instincts of his ancestors. The Grosvenor Estate owned a lot of land at the rear of the hospital and the duke's people had developed a very good plan to build a new luxury hotel on the whole site.

I was firmly set on raising the maximum that I could for the NHS from the sale of our old hospital, and was perfectly happy to sell it to the Grosvenor Estate for its market value. But I wasn't prepared to give it to them for nothing. Unfortunately the prime minister was totally persuaded by the duke. Perhaps she had a weakness for the aristocracy, who knows? She instructed me to hand over the site to the Grosvenor Estate gratis, as the duke had requested. I firmly and stubbornly resisted. This led to a considerable tussle between us with the department in total confusion at their conflicting instructions although, as I later discovered, with the key officials firmly on my side. I was outraged by the suggestion that the government should simply give away such an asset, and Margaret was indignant that we should even contemplate offending the duke. With hindsight, I was bound to win if I stuck to my guns as I did, as she would have found a public debate about giving away such a property utterly unwinnable. After a few weeks' deadlock and with considerable bad grace she eventually conceded. The building and the whole site is now the Lanesborough Hotel.

The problems of the buildings were as nothing compared to reforms that took me into direct conflict with the British Medical Association. I first encountered the extreme hostility of which the BMA was capable when I introduced a fairly innocuous measure to put some limits on doctors' ability to prescribe whatever items they wished at public expense, with some fringe GPs being extraordinarily wasteful. The pharmaceutical industry spent as much money on marketing as it did on clinical research. This was a perfectly rational approach given that all the purchasing decisions were made by NHS doctors who did not have to concern themselves about where the money to pay for what they purchased came from, which was of course the taxpayer, nor have any personal regard to the cost. GPs were invited, usually with their families, to conferences in beautiful resorts around the world at which the pharmaceutical companies would promote the virtues of branded products to them. They would then gratefully prescribe the branded products, which were invariably more expensive than the generic equivalent containing the same ingredients and with identical clinical benefits. I would have liked to move to generic prescribing, placing pharmacists under a duty to dispense the cheapest available generic medicine for each prescription, but this would have been a leap too far to be politically possible straight away.

The BMA and the pharmaceutical industry immediately mounted a virulent campaign against me in the national press on the bogus grounds that I was interfering, for political reasons, in the clinical freedom of doctors to prescribe whatever they wished in the interest of their patients. The BMA took out several full-page adverts under the slogan 'don't get sick, get angry'. One of these claimed that the change would create a two-class NHS. Another pictured a doctor trying to prescribe but held down by chains. I stoutly resisted this in the media and in Parliament.

At last, in desperation, several of the pharmaceutical industry's chief executives insisted on a face-to-face meeting with the prime minister. They told her that their companies were major donors to the Conservative Party and demanded that she intervene and overrule her Minister of State so that they could continue to sell whatever they preferred to the NHS.

To her eternal credit, I later heard from her Private Office that Margaret had given them a stern lecture in which she asserted that their donations were general support for the reforming efforts of her Conservative government. Funding was not to be abused for the purpose of obtaining private commercial advantage from the British government and the taxpayer. She sent them away with a flea in their ear and Number 10 officials confirmed that I could proceed exactly as I intended. My list of prohibited products was very small and limited but it was an important breakthrough on beginning to get drug costs in the NHS under some sort of control.

The hostility of the BMA to any change over the decades had also protected the existence of patches of extremely poor working practices. No doubt the whole service was held together by the dedication to the care of patients which was the main source of job satisfaction to the staff. Unfortunately there was no system for replicating the best examples of this hard work and commitment, and no means of measuring comparative costs or performance. I suspected that they varied wildly, but there was no way to demonstrate that: any attempt to obtain estimates of what a particular surgical or medical procedure might cost in an individual hospital only revealed a complete mystery.

The consultants regarded themselves as quite outside the authority of the hospital administrator or anyone else, and decided for themselves what service they would provide. Their individual pay bore no relationship to the quantity or quality of their work. Instead, the service had a system of 'merit awards' which paid the most to the most 'distinguished'. These had been introduced by Aneurin Bevan as a means of buying the profession's consent to the founding of the NHS. He himself said at the time that he had 'stuffed their mouths with gold'.

All consultants in the popular specialties such as orthopaedics boosted their income through private practice where they could. The NHS employed them on what were described as part-time contracts where they allegedly worked 'five-sevenths' of their time in the NHS. In practice, many worked outside for as much time as it took to carry out all the private work they could win.

Particularly in the London teaching hospitals, it was not difficult to find examples of consultants who scarcely ever came in to the NHS hospital that supposedly employed them. Junior doctors would compete for prestigious six-month training appointments in their chosen specialty departments then barely see their consultant, joining with the other junior doctors to carry out all the NHS treatment. If the absent consultant received no complaints, he would give his trainee junior the necessary commendation at the end of the six months so that the junior could apply for his or her next training post.

I had a conversation with one very 'distinguished' and highly paid consultant who apparently never went to his hospital because he was so engaged in his overseas lecture tours and private practice. I had the temerity to ask him how he justified the cost of his salary to his NHS employer. He was not annoyed or fazed by my question but calmly explained that his presence on the payroll of the NHS institution in question was sufficient to give it academic prestige. That was his personal contribution.

Local custom and practice produced astonishing variations up and down the country. I didn't object to local differences per se, but I did object to them being decided by self-interested clinicians who were accountable to no one for the outcomes they produced. In one Lincolnshire district health authority all the orthopaedic consultants agreed that the NHS would not perform the new hip replacement operations which were being introduced. They decided that hip replacements should be private-practice work only. In a hospital in the Home Counties, when I enquired into the enormous waiting lists for surgery, I was told that the local practice was that surgeons would only perform two sessions a week. They flatly refused to move to the more normal practice recommended by their own Royal College of three sessions a week. And at a more mundane level, when I made an elementary enquiry into the costs of ancillary services in Nottingham's two hospitals, I discovered that in one hospital the custom and practice was that one porter would push each trolley bearing a patient through the corridors. In the other, two porters would perform this duty. Everyone was shocked by my suggestion that perhaps the more cost-effective practice should be adopted in both, and no one acted on it.

I even found myself challenging opticians in my championing of the interests of the taxpayer and consumer over those of the providers. Opticians tended to be rather prosperous people who operated in small practices and had a legal monopoly not only of diagnosis and optical treatment but also of the sale of spectacle frames. Aneurin Bevan had chosen a range of frames to be available free on the NHS. Clinical opticians sold all the other frames at a very considerable profit margin, exploiting their monopoly with fixed price levels at all practices. The few successful business people I knew assured me that they always bought their spectacle frames in New York or Hong Kong, where they were a great deal cheaper.

I took up a remarkable suggestion – I cannot remember from whom – that it was time that new NHS frames should be introduced as Bevan's original range remained the only ones available on the NHS over thirty years after their introduction. When I agreed to do this my officials and opticians gathered in my office to display the current range of NHS frames before me. I have no eye for fashion of any kind but it was obvious, even to me, that the frames had been chosen for their stark ugliness which is why only the poor would ever suffer to use them. The one slip that had been made was a wire-rimmed circular variety which John Lennon had popularized so that for a time this style had been adopted on a mass scale by the young. Senior opticians gave me strong advice about the spectacles that I might add to the range. Again, I realized that I was being pressed to choose frames which would perfectly match the existing range in their striking hideousness and would therefore provide no real competition to the opticians' thriving retail trade.

Eventually, I even went so far as to legislate and to scrap the opticians' monopoly on the sale of frames. I did of course retain the exclusive right of clinical practitioners to carry out eye tests, diagnosis and treatment. However, I could never see why the opticians felt they were so uniquely well placed to offer the stylistic advice which individual patients or customers undoubtedly might want as they made the important choice of which frame they should purchase. This change was carried, amidst much controversy, and had extraordinary results. We can now all buy glasses off a rack in any supermarket or from a range of modern optical shops, at competitive prices.

Sadly, this led to one of my few arguments with a delightful Conservative backbencher, Jill Knight, the MP for Edgbaston in Birmingham. Jill was married to an optician and she was my most formidable opponent in the House on this matter, claiming that I was threatening blindness or sight loss for a large section of the population if I proceeded. I liked Jill very much, but I fear that it took a year or two for her to forgive me for all the damage that I had presumably done to her husband's practice.

Much of my effort had to be concentrated on industrial relations and pay bargaining, which were the cause of the very worst conflicts – worse than hospital closures and worse even than trying to restrict doctors' prescribing or other working practices. I quickly discovered that my officials were wrong in advising me to leave this to the long-established process of 'Whitley Councils' in which laypeople supposedly negotiated on behalf of the public to settle the claims. Startlingly unskilled and inexperienced laypeople were guided as members of these councils to give generous pay awards whenever they were demanded.

Increasingly, I personally led the discussions on particular issues, sometimes even on pay. This was certainly not good management practice but I believed it was the best option available. I had always rather enjoyed myself when negotiating settlements as a barrister in my civil practice and I thought myself a tough negotiator compared with the alternatives.

We only ever resolved this absurd pay-bargaining system when, in 1984, we set up an independent Pay Review Body to advise the government on pay for all key grades of staff, on the basis that the government and the trade unions would each submit evidence and then the government would implement the independent recommendations unless exceptional circumstances made it impossible.

Over my two spells in charge of Health, I was also occasionally involved in decisions which had some direct bearing on improvements in patient care.

On one such, a visiting American cardiac surgeon came to see me to complain about the NHS's resistance to his use of angioplasty. He had pioneered this new treatment, which involved injecting a balloon into the artery and then inflating it to stretch the artery and restore the flow of blood. It was, however, being bitterly opposed by British cardiac surgeons, who insisted that the only way of tackling heart disease was the open heart surgery in which they all specialized and which carried a huge risk to the patient. They wanted this suspicious foreign innovation to be banned. I did my best to challenge the resistance to what later became a huge shift in the normal medical procedures.

When I was Secretary of State a Russian doctor suddenly turned up in the United Kingdom with a hospital ship and began to carry out cataract operations on patients on our enormous waiting lists. He moored in Liverpool and performed several operations a day on an almost conveyor-belt system, discharging his patients a few hours after their successful operations. NHS consultants were quite shocked by his methods, since the invariable UK practice was for patients to be kept in hospital for about fourteen days after the operation. The more traditional consultants insisted that the patients had to have their heads held rigid between blocks for most of that time. But thanks to the Russian interloper, I was able to challenge this practice.

Eventually, over the next decades, the most spectacular savings in unit costs were achieved by reducing the entirely unnecessary and indeed often counterproductive recovery periods that we still insisted on. Wards in 1980s hospitals tended to be full of patients who had

had their treatment and were supposedly recuperating, being tended and fed by the nurses. Patients who were actually clinically ill were a tiny minority. It took another twenty years for us to move to the modern practice where about 70 per cent of all surgery is carried out on a day-surgery basis.

There was one key policy about which my boss Norman Fowler felt very strongly, in which he intervened directly to take charge. A new disease called AIDS, caused by the retrovirus HIV, suddenly swept into the Western world and claimed a large number of victims in Britain. The difficulty was that scientific and medical knowledge about this new health risk was initially very limited and no one was certain exactly how it was being transmitted and spread. The AIDS epidemic caused widespread public panic, associated with considerable prejudice amongst those who thought that the disease mainly afflicted people they saw as an underclass of homosexuals and drug addicts who were unfortunately then discriminated against and despised by many people. It gradually became clear that HIV was at least partially transmitted by sexual contact but there was still a great deal of public ignorance about how anyone could protect themselves.

Norman Fowler was deeply committed to running a high-profile campaign to improve public understanding of the disease and of the precautions that could be taken against it. He was particularly insistent that we should emphasize that people of any sexual orientation could contract HIV and that everyone should be taking precautions against it. This became a major government educational campaign with posters, leaflets and other information disseminated across the country. There was a great deal of controversy both inside the government and in the media about this high-profile campaigning on such a sensitive subject. Norman never really succeeded in getting the Scottish Office to agree to equally high-profile campaigning in Scotland because of the sensitivities of their ministers to the perceived prudishness of Scottish opinion. To this day, I have no idea how Norman succeeded in persuading a very reluctant Margaret Thatcher that he should be allowed to launch such a prominent government campaign about a sexually transmitted disease.

I hope that Norman is still proud of what he achieved with his campaign. It had a considerable and beneficial effect on public attitudes and behaviour. In my opinion it is one of the most substantial contributions that Norman made to improving British public health and safety, exposed to such a sudden and frightening threat.

One tragic aspect of the epidemic was because, initially, no one understood that the disease was transmitted by body fluids. Every haemophiliac in the country received frequent blood transfusions from the National Health Service. We acquired the necessary blood from a donation service but also by importing supplies from a wide and not totally reliable range of overseas sources. Very quickly, before our scientists and doctors appreciated that blood supplies needed to be treated to be safe, more than 1,200 haemophiliacs in Britain contracted HIV.

The haemophiliacs who spent the rest of their lives with this disease were eventually given ex-gratia payments by John Major's government. Not surprisingly, they continued and still continue to campaign for more generous compensation for their suffering and to help them with the costs of their illness. When I became the only health minister from that time still prominent in the public eye, these campaigners usually named me in their campaigns, because it improved their prospects of publicity.

In fact, I was not the minister responsible for blood products, which was regarded as a small specialist area of activity and was handled by Simon Glenarthur, a parliamentary undersecretary in the Lords. Simon behaved impeccably throughout the crisis but unfortunately he acted on the medical and scientific advice given to him which was not based on full knowledge of the dangers. Various public inquiries have subsequently been held into the victims' claims, but Simon's reputation has always emerged unscathed as he quite correctly acted conscientiously in the light of the scientific evidence available to him.

Ministerial activity, with its greater pressures and longer working hours, had quite an effect on my daily life including my following of jazz. At first, Roy Gibbons, my allocated government driver, became used to dropping off my red box of ministerial homework at my London home in Kennington before running me on to Ronnie Scott's in Soho after the ten o'clock vote. In my first years as a minister I could stay at Ronnie Scott's into the early hours, sitting at the back of the darkened club and listening quietly to one of my heroes, before going home by taxi and tackling my red box. After a few years of declining regularity, I finally had to admit that I was now too old to survive this crazy way of life. My visits to Ronnie Scott's in later years, whilst always welcome, became very sporadic.

In the early 1980s, though, an additional new enthusiasm began to provide a break from politics at weekends and on the foreign trips and family holidays which Gillian and I so loved.

I had scorned my close friend Martin Suthers' love of birdwatching when I was younger and dismissed it as a very anorak activity that only spoiled a country walk. However, I began firstly to become interested in butterflies, having been attracted on visits to southern France by the wonderful black and white butterfly known as the Scarce Swallowtail. Identifying butterflies is extremely difficult unless one goes on to the mad extent of acquiring a net and killing-bottle and pinning specimens on boards in order to note minor details of their wings and bodies. Fortunately I held back, but I began to notice that the birdlife on holiday was varied and interesting, too, and I became increasingly curious. I therefore bought a handbook of birds with pictures and descriptions and also invested in a pair of binoculars which I proposed to use principally when making my frequent visits to watch first-class cricket at Trent Bridge.

To say that I was a novice when I started would be an understatement. I do recall staying with friends in Cornwall and making a visit to a seal sanctuary on the coast somewhere. With my bright new binoculars, I was distracted by birds and I left Gillian and the others to go down the steep path to the sanctuary whilst I explored the bushes and trees. It was a rather damp day and there was a light drizzle by the time they returned to find me crouching in a ditch, peering at a small bird in a hedge and slowly turning the pages of my book one by one to try to identify it. I think that I had got past the hawks and seagulls but I was making painfully slow progress.

Gillian walked up behind me and said, 'It's a blue tit. We have lots of them in the garden.'

From this very modest beginning, I became as obsessive about birdwatching as I usually am about all my private hobbies and enthusiasms. It eventually led the way to birdwatching around the world with our friends the Suthers on expeditions to mountains, jungles, rainforests, plains and coasts on every continent. Gillian preferred flowers and used to divert our guides from finding birds in forests to taking her off on searches for orchids. We must have been quite a sight – me gazing skywards with the binoculars in search of hawks, and Gillian on her hands and knees with the camera, snapping a small flower in a ditch.

When I try to rationalize my enthusiasm for jazz, cricket, football or birdwatching, I think that the attraction is that I get so absorbed in them that all thoughts of politics, policy or other work vanish from my mind. I gradually added Formula One motor racing to my enthusiasms and became equally absorbed and gripped by that on a worldwide basis. For this, I blame Kenneth Junior. When he was about six, he asked, 'Daddy, can I go to a motor race?' I duly took him to Silverstone, on a Formula One day. I thought I could endure, as a paternal duty, one day of loud noise and men in duffel coats. Almost fifty years later, he and I still go to at least one Grand Prix a year and follow the season together on television. I continue fondly to believe that the combination of birdwatching and Formula One motor racing is a particularly quirky and unusual one – and that it is almost unique to me.

My work at the Department of Health was extremely interesting and enjoyable and there were very many good things about the National Health Service and the congenial, civilized people who worked for it which compensated for the heat of the battle that prevailed at the political level over hospital closures, working practices, and the need to get a grip on costs. It is absolutely clear to me, though, that the changes I fought for began to transform the NHS for the better. There would be riots if we were plunged back now into an NHS that looked as it did in the 1980s.

10

'Nice Work If You Can Get It'

(Thelonious Monk, 1937)

EMPLOYMENT

In September 1985 Margaret finally summoned me to Number 10 to give me a full Cabinet post. Friends had been telling me for some time that she was very reluctant to promote me because I was 'not one of us' which was no doubt a reference to my repeated self-identification as a Tory wet. As I had of course the boundless confidence in my own abilities and achievements common to my trade, my slow progress up the ministerial ladder had been somewhat frustrating, so it was a relief that Margaret had finally found a solution to the problem whilst allaying her concerns about my supposedly moderate centre-ground views.

When I went into her office, Margaret immediately told me that I was to join the Cabinet, but not in a way that I had remotely expected. She was a huge admirer of Lord Young of Graffham, previously known to the world as David Young, a flamboyant businessman who was one of her private friends and advisers. He had also been the successful head of the Manpower Services Commission, a quango responsible for co-ordinating employment and training services, through which he had energetically launched a series of programmes to try to tackle our high levels of unemployment. Margaret told me that she was appointing him to be Secretary of State for Employment. He would, though, need a Cabinet minister in the Commons to handle the lower

House, so Margaret was appointing me as Minister of State with a seat in Cabinet.

I was delighted to be joining the Cabinet at last, although I confess I was puzzled by my joint status. Thinking it over in the car afterwards, however, I quickly rationalized it. David was lively and full of ideas but he had absolutely no parliamentary or political experience. However, he was ideologically sound and a fierce personal defender of Margaret. I on the other hand was still regarded as ideologically dubious. I was clearly intended to provide political skills and an understanding of parliamentary process to the team, and David could be relied upon to keep me under control.

To be fair, Margaret had also hinted that she had been impressed by my high-profile contribution in my previous job. As a battling minister of health, I had both acquired a certain notoriety and had made endless media appearances fighting fires in the health-care system. Margaret would certainly never have objected to the combative approach that I had always adopted towards my critics. Despite our political differences, we shared a rather similar, and robust, debating style. This was probably fortunate, as without it my political career might have stalled irreparably and I would have returned to the Birmingham Bar to endure a quieter if infinitely less interesting career in the law.

David Young and I had not met before, and we both approached our new partnership with slight alarm. On my part there was also the inevitable residual frustration that despite having finally put me in the Cabinet, my leader was clearly not yet sufficiently convinced of my reliability to give me the run of my own department. However, our mutual trepidation vanished almost immediately. We were both rather noisy and gregarious characters and we got on like a house on fire. We also made a great political partnership. David constantly produced brilliant new ideas and I worked hard to deflect him from the madder and less practical ones. Those we kept, I transformed into practical proposals which a government department could be expected to deliver and which we could get through Parliament. We had remarkably few disagreements and the ideological battle that Margaret might have been expecting never occurred. Indeed, we used to joke with each other that when we did disagree he tended to take a rather left-wing view and I would be to his political right.

Our parliamentary undersecretary was Alan Clark, a most unlikely choice for a job in this particular department. He hated the whole idea of the place and privately cast scorn on the 'make work schemes' which he accused David and me of running. He was witty, sardonic and incredibly lazy, rarely coming into the department. As a result he did not really trouble us and I assume that he was mainly concentrating on plotting to persuade the prime minister to give him the job he craved in the Ministry of Defence. Margaret always had a soft spot for him and allowed him to lobby her constantly.

I moved into the office of the former Minister of State, Peter Morrison. I had known Peter in and out of the House of Commons for many years. He was an interesting but rather sad character who had always been a loner and was now steadily developing a serious problem with alcohol. He too was a close friend of Margaret Thatcher to whom he always stayed very loyal politically, inviting her to annual summer holidays on a Scottish island that he owned. Fortunately I was never invited to join Peter on these so-called holidays. He always tried to attract a little group of colleagues to entertain Margaret, who would demonstrate only too clearly that she hated the whole idea of holidays and did not really know why other people enjoyed them.

I discovered from the agreeable young private secretaries that I inherited how curiously Peter had worked. He had made frequent visits to Sheffield where he would spend a portion of each week at the Manpower Services Commission trying to second-guess the unfortunate heads of that organization. When not in Sheffield he worked in the drab department building on Tothill Street, the road running between Parliament Square and St James's Park Tube station. He began work in the afternoon, and proceeded into the evenings and late into the night. His staff had become used to working patiently with him to midnight and beyond as he sipped away at more and more whisky, signing the mountains of letters that the department was issuing in response to MPs' representations about unemployment. His private secretaries had been devoted to him but were plainly delighted that I intended to adopt a more conventional practice of working in the mornings and afternoons, leaving in the evenings with my red box of papers to do at the House of Commons or at home.

More problematic was the fact that my Private Office and most of the departmental officials assumed that I would simply take up Peter's old duties and content myself with the administration of the Manpower Services Commission and routine paperwork. I was alarmed by this because I found that I was expected to take much less responsibility and to be involved in much less policymaking than I had had as the parliamentary undersecretary at Transport, let alone at the Department of Health. I began to stand on my dignity and insisted that I was joint leader of the department, albeit the junior partner. Fortunately David Young entirely agreed. He gave orders that I was to be party to all the decisions that we were taking, and from that moment on we collaborated fully. There was some division of responsibility between us but absolutely no dispute about my role. Looking back I was extremely lucky that at two key junctures in my career I enjoyed such successful working partnerships with Norman Fowler and David Young, who were both prepared to delegate major elements of their ministerial agendas to me.

David and I found being in Cabinet hugely exciting. Cabinet met once a week and sat for a whole morning. Contrary to later popular belief, Margaret Thatcher ran a genuinely collective government in which her many strong departmental ministers insisted on taking a vocal and constructive part. We had a large number of Cabinet Committees where members of the Cabinet, or sometimes their junior ministers, would discuss every and any subject upon which different departments could not agree. Most policy issues were settled at those committee meetings. The full Cabinet only considered the really big issues of the day, or those issues we had not been able to resolve in a Cabinet Committee. I became a member of several Cabinet Committees, including the Economic Affairs Committee where I found myself taking part in serious discussions of macroeconomic policy under the leadership of Nigel Lawson. This proved an extremely good training for later stages of my career.

Cabinet itself was a marvellous experience. There were several important discussions in my first months in my new department, one of the most fascinating of which was the question of building a new Channel crossing. The government wanted to revive the idea of a direct link between the United Kingdom and the Continent, but full Cabinet debate was required to decide the vital issue of whether it should be a tunnel or a bridge.

Most of the Cabinet had assumed that it was perfectly obvious that we should revive the hundred-year-old scheme to build a rail tunnel under the Channel. However, Margaret Thatcher – who hated railways and never travelled on them if she could possibly avoid it – was ferociously opposed. She was convinced that a rail-only tunnel would result in traffic being endlessly held to ransom by the pay and industrial relations claims of the militant railway unions. In 1980 she had appointed a rather bizarre businessman called Ian MacGregor to run the nationalized British Steel which produced inferior steel at excessive prices. Ian, though he had now moved on to the National Coal Board, had convinced Margaret that the best solution would be a bridge, constructed entirely of British steel, over the busiest shipping lane in the world, so that people could drive their own cars over the Channel.

I was not the leading opponent of this madcap Channel Bridge proposal but I was certainly an active participant in debate. Recklessly – for a new boy – I challenged the whole idea of such a structure which would amongst other things have caused a hazard to shipping. The bridge over Chesapeake Bay in the United States was then one of the longest bridges in the world. Fortunately someone produced details of a serious collision between a ship and a pier in the bay, which underlined the dangers of the MacGregor scheme and was a crucial addition to the overwhelming economic arguments against the business case being put together by British Steel.

Margaret always spoke for at least 50 per cent of the time in any Cabinet discussion on any subject in which she was interested. Like every other politician, she always wanted to get her own way. Luckily this was one of those occasions where eventually, after several heated Cabinet discussions, she was persuaded out of her notion and joined with the consensus decision to build a rail-only Channel Tunnel. I think it was the only time that I saw Margaret rather attracted by the notion that French presidents sometimes have of leaving a physical monument of themselves for posterity; in the end she was content that the Channel Tunnel would suffice.

Of course it took many years to build the tunnel and the full story was yet to unfold. It was hugely successful in pure transport terms, but unfortunately the whole project was put in the hands of the construction companies, who cheerily proceeded on the basis that cost was not really an objective and that the government would pick up any bills that piled up. The inevitable result was that the costs of construction and the consequent costs to passengers and freight were far higher than they need have been.

To complete my own Channel Tunnel story, a few years later, I found myself involved again when I was Home Secretary. The Home Office was imposing the most preposterous security costs on the project, which was then close to opening. Incredible debates were taking place about security at the terminals in London, Brussels and Paris. There were endless negotiations about how many British policemen and French policemen were to travel on every train. Futile attempts were being made to insist that French policemen could not carry their guns onto British territory whilst the French insisted that their policemen had to carry a gun at all times. Huge blast-proof concrete barriers were to be constructed at both ends of the tunnel to allow bombs to be removed from trains behind the barriers.

The most ridiculous proposal of all came from the immigration service. My department briefed me to insist that trains should stop when they emerged on the English side of the tunnel. All the passengers should disembark onto a specially constructed platform where their passports would be checked and immigration clearance given before they could all reboard the train and proceed to London. I protested that I had frequently had my passport checked on a train when travelling across European borders, and received staggering advice from my officials that such a practice would be quite deficient in England and particularly unacceptable to our trade unions who represented the immigration officials and really determined policy on these matters.

Suffice to say, I cut through all these nonsensical arguments as rapidly as I could, but by the time I was Home Secretary it was really too late to make any big difference to the project's spiralling costs. The result was high fares, the financial failure of the private company that owned the tunnel, and the survival of the cross-Channel ferries as a cheaper competitive alternative.

The other great event in my first months in Cabinet was the Westland crisis. This was the surreal conclusion of the personal battle between Margaret Thatcher and Michael Heseltine, then Secretary of State for Defence, which led to a famous resignation and an irreparable break between them. Michael was one of the great, commanding political figures of my time and I always admired and sympathized with him. We originally met when he had spoken strikingly and brilliantly at a political meeting in support of my first campaign as the candidate for Rushcliffe many years earlier, and since then I had come to know him very much better.

Nevertheless, on this occasion he made a terrible mistake in elevating to such a point of principle an absurd dispute about the future of a comparatively unimportant insolvent helicopter company which needed to be rescued. Temperament and personal politics were far more significant than any rational arguments in Margaret Thatcher's decision that Westland should be sold to an American owner and Michael's opinion that desperate attempts should be made to find a European buyer.

I sat through all the extraordinary Cabinet meetings in which the two of them fought it out with the remainder of the Cabinet trying to assist. When Margaret and Michael really engaged with each other they had a rather similar style – neither of them would allow the other to finish a sentence without interruption.

I was also at a key Cabinet Committee meeting, chaired by the prime minister, but in which Michael nevertheless successfully persuaded the majority present that he should be given more time in his search for a European purchaser. It did seem to me and to more powerful members of the meeting correct that he should at least be given time to exhaust his efforts. Margaret reluctantly accepted the decision and summed up accordingly, with remarkably bad grace. She threatened us all with a summons back to London for a Saturday

Cabinet meeting as we had failed to settle it that morning. Happily this was not a threat that she actually carried out.

The key Cabinet meeting came in early January 1986 when Margaret confronted Michael with some rules for the future conduct of this very public dispute. She fiercely insisted that he should cease to answer written Parliamentary Questions without first submitting the draft answers to Number 10 for her approval. There was some justice in this previously unheard-of demand. Most of us had guessed that Michael and his team were drafting the various Parliamentary Questions being tabled in the Commons by his supporters and that they were receiving very biased replies favouring his case, which were then widely reported by the media. This was all rather high-wire stuff. Not surprisingly, Michael indignantly refused to accept these humiliating instructions. A ferocious row concluded when a tense and pale Heseltine rose from his place, gathered up his papers, declared that he would have to resign and walked smartly out of a suddenly silent Cabinet Room.

When he had closed the door behind him, complete silence continued to reign in the room where his rather dumbfounded colleagues were sitting. After a few moments, a harassed-looking official put his head around the door and quietly announced to the prime minister that Mr Heseltine appeared to be giving some sort of press conference outside the front door of Number 10. Margaret broke the silence and settled the atmosphere by saying simply, 'Perhaps we should all break to have a cup of tea.'

The entire Cabinet went out for cups of tea and coffee whilst a few people vanished to try to resolve things. After only about ten minutes we were called back to resume the Cabinet meeting. Margaret thereupon announced that George Younger was the new Secretary of State for Defence and the business of the Cabinet continued in the normal way.

There was a very sad sequel to this whole business from my point of view. My friend Leon Brittan, who was then Trade and Industry Secretary, had been persuaded by Margaret to contribute to the furore over Westland by getting one of his officials to leak the legal opinion of the Solicitor General, Patrick Mayhew, about a letter that Michael

Heseltine had written and leaked about the consequences of an American takeover. This leaking of legal advice was totally contrary to every convention of government practice. The then Attorney General, Michael Havers, quite an emotional man, made a tremendous issue about this leak and made it clear that he would resign if no one was held to account for it.

It was perfectly obvious to me and other insiders that Margaret had ordered Leon to instruct one of his officials to leak Patrick's advice to the press. Leon should not have agreed to do so. He later told me that he decided to take the blame without exposing Margaret. The political crisis was such that she would undoubtedly have fallen from office. Indeed, one day at the height of the crisis, she told colleagues that she might not be prime minister by six o'clock that evening. Leon resigned from the Department for Trade and Industry and never sat in the Cabinet again. He told me that Margaret had promised him that she would bring him back into the Cabinet as soon as she could after the dust had settled, but she did not keep her word. Eventually she consoled Leon and no doubt her own conscience by appointing him to be a European Commissioner. There, with Mickey Kantor and Pascal Lamy, he achieved one of the great moments of his career as one of the three people responsible for delivering a vital international trade agreement and creating the World Trade Organization. Leon was a close friend, one of the finest intellects of my Cambridge contemporaries and of the Conservative Party. He was made Home Secretary at a very young age, and it was a great shame that his Cabinet career was curtailed in this absurd way.

The resignations of Michael Heseltine and Leon Brittan took place only a few weeks after David and I had joined the Cabinet. In the weekly meetings in the Cabinet Room we had initially been seated towards the end of the table on the opposite side to the prime minister. As each colleague resigned, we were moved a place to the left. At the beginning of one meeting, I remarked to David that we were moving steadily towards the centre of power in rather unfortunate circumstances.

In order to give respectability to my seat in the Cabinet, which was really due to my partnership with David in the department, I was given the rather nominal title of Paymaster General, one of those British near-sinecures with strange names unrecognizable to foreigners. I had very few actual duties to perform but the most entertaining and pleasant was that I became an ex-officio commissioner of the Royal Hospital Chelsea, the historic home of the revered army veterans known as the Chelsea Pensioners. I had no real responsibilities there, as the hospital was under the command of a retired senior army officer. I did, however, have the agreeable duty of attending various ceremonial occasions at the hospital on festive days. These sometimes involved my turning out on parade alongside the commanding officer in order to review our magnificent pensioners. I tried to enter into the spirit but my lack of military background or temperament was probably only too obvious. I sometimes thought that we made an incongruous couple on a podium or on the march when I was trying to keep step dressed in my grey suit and suede shoes alongside the commanding officer in full dress regalia with braid, ribbons and beautifully polished boots.

Now might be as good a time as any to reveal that these suede shoes were not, and have never been, Hush Puppies. When I was minister for health, diary stories had begun to appear in the papers teasing me about my appearance and in particular my propensity to wear brown suede shoes. This was indeed a habit I had acquired, partly in imitation of my hero Geoffrey Howe, and partly as a reaction to the black jacket, striped trousers and shiny black leather shoes I had been obliged to wear as a barrister. The stories irritated me at first and I almost went back to the shiny black leather. However, I told myself firmly that I was not going to allow the media to force me to change any of my personal foibles. When the newspapers started describing my shoes as Hush Puppies, I again first reacted with indignation. My shoes were handmade by Crockett & Jones in Northamptonshire. However, my attempts to correct journalists on this point were totally unsuccessful and, eventually, since it was doing me no harm at all, I gave up. That I am a wearer of Hush Puppies, though completely untrue, became 'fact' by dint of constant media repetition.

Even without polished shoes, Gillian and I enjoyed our occasional visits to the Royal Hospital because the pensioners were indeed wonderful old men who were only too ready to be engaged in conversation about their remarkable experiences, usually in battle in the First World War. I was told that I was popular with the old boys which they demonstrated by inviting me to join them in their inner sanctum – a bar into which very few outsiders were ever allowed. I would buy beers for the men at my table whilst questioning them about their experiences in Gallipoli and elsewhere and listening to their dramatic tales. Gillian happily joined in with this. She was rightly proud of her mother's family background in the Marines and especially proud of her late grandfather who had fought at Antwerp and Gallipoli and become commander of the Devonport Dockyards after the war.

The Department of Employment's main policy tasks were to reform industrial relations and to tackle unemployment. In previous years, with the country crippled by constant industrial action, the priority had been the former. Now, with unemployment well over 3 million, it was the latter.

At the Manpower Services Commission David had been a pioneer of job training and job-creating programmes. He now set up a Youth Training Scheme for sixteen- and seventeen-year-old school-leavers, and a Community Programme for the long-term unemployed which employed thousands of people in community work, both to be managed by the MSC. These schemes were no doubt full of flaws but they were still a pioneering attempt to give unemployed people some experience and training, and to rehabilitate them into the habits and patterns of work.

Some of the training schemes that I visited were little more than remedial education for young people who had left school without even the basics needed for work. It was good preparation for my later spell at the Education Department to visit schemes in Liverpool where basic numeracy and literacy were being taught to sixteen-year-old boys who appeared to have left after more than ten years of full-time education without the ability to read or count. The schemes also tried to get youngsters into the habit of turning up every day at nine in the morning and not leaving before five in the afternoon, which was a new discipline to most of them.

The schemes were bitterly attacked by our opponents on the grounds that they were not 'real jobs'. The trade unions and the Labour Party ferociously challenged the notion that people on our programmes would not be paid the full rate for employment on unionized terms, despite the fact that this would of course have been unaffordable. Actually, we worked determinedly to try to improve the terms.

David Young, despite being the non-elected partner, was actually more partisan and party political about his policies than I was. He was brilliant at public relations and brought together all our various initiatives under the umbrella brand of 'Action for Jobs'. We developed a full-scale campaign which stretched the limits of the rules on government spending on advertising but which we justified on the grounds that our initiatives were not going to work if unemployed people didn't know about them. We also upset some of our more traditional officials by insisting on publishing a White Paper which did not consist entirely of black text on a white background with just the title and the royal coat of arms on the cover. Shockingly, there was a picture on the cover and some photos inserted at intervals in the text, and it was written to be read by the layman and not just by specialists.

Our officials were actually quite right to suspect that we were trying to advertise the good intentions of our party in government. They also had some cause to suspect our motives in the design of the schemes. I was more interested in the contribution that these programmes could make to returning people to employment. But David was very focused on anything that would get the published unemployment figures down to a level that could be presented as success at the next election. He and his excellent private secretary, Leigh Lewis, were constantly amending the schemes to make them more 'count efficient'. I doggedly persuaded them that this should be combined with improvements to the schemes' real value to people, who badly needed experience to make them more employable in an economy that was steadily returning to growth.

David was also responsible for a particularly valuable innovation, which was the first introduction of an organized structure for vocational qualifications. We introduced a system of National Vocational Qualifications, or NVQs, with various grades set to reflect different levels of attainment. This was a revolution in creating an orderly system of work qualifications, and was a step towards the German system, which we believed to be wholly superior. All subsequent attempts at developing better systems of vocational education and training were based on David Young's pioneering efforts with my modest assistance.

When I had first arrived in the department in 1985, Jim Prior had approached me and strongly recommended that I should resume meeting with a group of personnel management executives that he had put together to help him resolve industrial disputes when he had been Employment Secretary in the late 1970s and early 1980s. This was based on the presumption of the previous decade that the government must always participate in the settlement of any industrial dispute of any size in the public or private sectors. I liked the group of men who comprised this committee and for politeness' sake had regular meetings with them. I have to admit, however, that I never made great use of their advice. I rapidly formed the view that their principal expertise was in calculating the minimum amount that the relevant trade union leadership would expect in settlement of any claim and advising me to offer it carefully in order to buy peace. I was never persuaded that this was the right approach for the government to take in any industrial dispute.

Towards the end of the 1983–7 parliament, I embarked on my only direct contribution to the process of trade union reform which Norman Tebbit had started in 1981. This was my own personal policy proposal. I prepared a Green Paper which proposed that dismissal for refusing to join a closed shop should be unlawful in all circumstances; that union members should be able to challenge a strike that had been called without a proper ballot; and that all union officials including general secretaries should be elected by secret postal vote of all the membership for a set period of office and should be subject to re-election for any further terms. In short, I believed that we had to put an end to the scandalous cases where strikes had been settled on the basis that non-union members should be sacked, that the trade union movement was ready for membership democracy, and that Arthur Scargill should not be able to be president of the NUM for life.

My officials strongly advised me against this, saying that my proposed reforms would create more extreme unions because the membership at large was far more militant than the current leadership who, the officials claimed, actually managed their expectations and restrained them. I had already had quite enough experience of business and the unions to feel that this was nonsense.

I had little difficulty in persuading the relevant Cabinet Committee to agree to my proposal as a pre-election Green Paper and policy commitment. The Labour Party also gave my proposals a reasonably straightforward passage. Neil Kinnock had only just begun the slow process of prising the Labour Party out of the grip of the hard left, and it would take another ten years before his patient reforms and their consequences made the party electable again. He and his colleagues were however aware that fierce opposition to the idea that union leaders should be subject to the democratic process and accountable to their members would be unpopular with the public. It would be a disastrous political stance for them to take. Therefore, because it was still so dominated by the union movement, the Labour Party was obliged to oppose my proposals, but I think it is fair to say that there was a certain amount of going through the motions.

My measures, brought into law by Norman Fowler as Secretary of State for Employment in 1988, almost completed the far more substantial process of reform that had been begun by Norman Tebbit. Norman Tebbit had initiated the long process of removing the extraordinary control which a few trade union 'barons' had exerted over the government, the economy and British political life throughout the 1960s and 1970s, when the country had settled into a form of corporatist, syndicalist rule, totally dominated by mercenary economic pressure groups. The trade unions' power in the private sector underwent a period of continuous decline in the later years of the Thatcher governments and thereafter. However, to this day, the startling role of the union movement in some government departments, the police service, the prison service and other public services continues. Even in the public service, though, I hope that my bill, which was entirely my own idea, has made a modest contribution to the return of more moderate and less politicized industrial relations.

Now that I was in the Cabinet at last, I was allowed to acquire my first special adviser, a politically appointed aide to support me in my work. I accepted a recommendation from someone in Downing Street and was lucky enough to appoint Jonathan Hill, a young man who had been in the public relations industry but was also a serious political thinker with a keen interest in policy. I had never had a political aide before and I had no idea quite how he was supposed to help me. As ever, I devised my own method of working. I closely involved Jonathan in every political and policy issue, as a trusted confidant and critic of my proposals. When I made a decision he would then help to chase the department into implementing it, and advise me on the political and public relations aspects of selling it to the wider public. Like every one of my special advisers he became a good friend and he worked in friendly partnership with me and my Civil Service Private Office. He was an invaluable and trusted companion and stayed with me for a department or two.

Jonathan always told me that he was only doing this for the experience and had no intention of entering politics himself. When he moved on he formed his own public relations company and made a fortune when he sold it. But the bug must have bitten him, because he was later persuaded by the then prime minister, John Major, to come back to Downing Street where he had an equally valuable impact. At the time of writing, he has just resigned as the British-appointed commissioner in the European Commission in Brussels – an extremely difficult task as the appointee of a government divided by civil war over Britain's membership of the European Union. The ill-fated EU referendum has brought the post to an end. Jonathan was brilliant in every role that he filled in a most private and self-effacing way. He was a leading political figure, yet completely unknown outside Westminster because he always maintained a very low profile and took part in no public campaigning at all. He made an excellent and important contribution to every job in government that he ever did, and he remains a good friend.

This was a period of great fortune for me because at around the same time as Jonathan Hill arrived, a young woman called Debbie Sugg joined Hazel Slater in my small constituency staff in Parliament. She has stayed with me for more than thirty years doing my political and constituency work and helping my departmental Private Office organize my diary and the logistics of my hectic life. She is the perfect PA and is a good friend.

Gillian was as pleased as I was. Talking to me about family arrangements had long been a hopeless task and now, with a sense of relief, she started to make any that were supposed to include me through Debbie. Debbie organized me so well that I became both spoilt and incompetent in all things logistical.

I continued to handle the growing volume of constituents' letters and emails in a very old-fashioned way. I still dictate my replies to two ladies in my office who take down my dictation in shorthand and type up letters for my signature. Only ladies of my generation have shorthand.

Like my previous boss Norman Fowler, David Young had absolutely no time for meetings of European Councils of Ministers in Brussels, which British ministers were supposed to attend in order to contribute to the development of European Union-wide policies. I had already attended various transport and health Councils and was becoming familiar with the time-consuming process of international discussion on possible European measures and regulations. Surprisingly, despite my normally rather impatient temperament, I had adjusted to the slow but fascinating pace of these meetings and enjoyed being a regular attender at day-long sessions. The transport and health Councils had actually been something of a waste of time as there was little real business to be transacted at European level. In one extreme case, I wasted a whole day trying to negotiate permits for British lorries. At the time, the common market was very limited, and each country was fiercely protectionist about its lorry drivers. One particularly protectionist rule stated that when a British lorry took goods to, say, Italy, it was not allowed to carry any goods from Italy to France on its way back. This, it was believed, ensured that British lorry drivers would not take Italian lorry drivers' jobs. I spent a day arguing that this was contrary to the principles of the common market, and negotiating permits for British lorries. All the other ministers were terrified of their domestic vested interests and gave no ground, so that by the end of a long day, I had achieved six permits. Of course we subsequently put in place much more sensible arrangements through the single market, which, lamentably, we now look set to leave.

Employment was different. I was now engaged in real political discussions and decisions made by ministers from all the member states.

I began to develop a regular pattern of attendance which continued, at innumerable European meetings, for the rest of my political career. I insisted on going out to Brussels the night before the meeting and staying at my favourite hotel, the Amigo, near to the main square in the old quarter, rather than at the residence of Britain's permanent representative which I found to be a rather boring if ornate bed-and-breakfast stay. I would check into my hotel and then spend the evening having a drink in the medieval square, followed by a meal with my Private Office and an accompanying official in one of the fascinating restaurants in the little streets of the old quarter, serving mussels and chips or some similar traditional Belgian fare.

Before long the UK permanent representative began to join me for these evenings, mainly to try to discover what my approach to the business of my Council would be and to brief me. In later years this became my standard if idiosyncratic way of preparing for Council meetings, and the basis for my close friendship with these Brussels-based Foreign Office officials, particularly Sir John Kerr, who was the distinguished representative when I was conducting negotiations under the Major government. He entered fully into the spirit of lively convivial evenings full of political gossip and chat of all kinds. He was also adept at introducing some element of briefing on the following day's meeting into the proceedings. I strongly suspect that he also always checked that I had read the brief properly before arriving. I am glad to say he would always have found that I had.

Some meetings were held in Luxembourg and there I insisted on travelling a few miles out of the city to a hotel in a small village on the banks of the River Rhine. This was despite the furious and, as it turned out, totally false, advice of the British officials who tried to persuade me that traffic jams would make me late for morning meetings. The food at this hotel was particularly good and the setting in the vineyards on the hills by the banks of the river especially memorable.

The Employment Council meetings were quite significant as Jacques Delors, then the president of the European Commission and a regular attendee, was trying to drive through his own European-wide employment programme aimed at reviving the economies of the Union. Jacques was a very brilliant man but he was a French socialist and his programme was altogether more interventionist than anything that I was happy to contemplate. He also believed that a hugely expensive programme of building long road links across the borders of the Continent was the essential step to reviving member states' economies. I was all in favour of sensible infrastructure spending but this road system was just a populist way of trying to increase support for the EU. I had also never believed, even when I had been a transport minister, that building roads was in itself a direct way of stimulating investment and employment.

As a result, perhaps, I rapidly became one of Jacques Delors' leading critics in the Council. Indeed I think that I became his principal Thatcherite opponent. I also resisted his drives towards more employment regulation when it seemed to impose unnecessary costs and bureaucracy on small and medium-sized employers. I always enjoyed debating and negotiating and I regularly engaged in vigorous discussion, but I realized that I needed some allies in the Council. Indeed, business at Councils of Ministers meetings always involved work inside and outside the room itself, ideally to produce a majority or, failing that, to collect a blocking minority. The aim of the meetings was to achieve consensus and the exercise of the veto was always avoided if possible.

I formed an extremely unlikely Anglo-Irish-Italian alliance with two very able and friendly ministers. One was Ruairi Quinn, the Irish

Labour Party's employment minister. He had had a very left-wing past and had even been known as Ho Chi Quinn in his student activist days. He had actually moved much nearer to market economics since then and became a valuable ally as well as a good friend and excellent company. My other unlikely ally was the colourful and extravagant Italian minister of work, Gianni De Michelis. He too was a capable and powerful friend, although unfortunately his career came to a disastrous end when he was involved in some typical Italian scandal about the placing of contracts for public works in his home city of Venice.

Jacques Delors made his political enmity very plain, but in later years, when I was Chancellor, he discovered that, although unsound on socialist intervention, I was a passionate pro-European. We became good friends and political allies in the world of Maastricht and beyond.

As a result of these Employment Council meetings I soon found myself much better informed about European politics and the tortuous workings of the multinational Union into which the European project had evolved.

Some years later, in late 1989 or early 1990, I was at a European meeting which Helmut Kohl was attending as Chancellor of Germany. One of Helmut's aides was a young German politician whom I had got to know at one or two of the Konrad Adenauer Foundation meetings that I had been going to since I had been a young parliamentary candidate discovering Berlin in the 1960s. He saw me and detached himself from the Chancellor's party and came rushing over in an agitated state. He asked me what on earth the British government was doing. When I asked what he was talking about, he explained in hurried fashion that Margaret Thatcher was making vigorous attempts to block the reunification of Germany. Helmut Kohl was trying to drive this through, with the consent of the other member states, to bring to an end an unhappy period when a separate, finally liberated, East Germany had had a fairly useless government of people compromised by and associated with the former East German regime.

Despite being a British Cabinet minister, I – like most of my colleagues I suspect – was quite unaware that Margaret had taken this position. I was absolutely appalled as I regarded the end of the Cold War and the fall of the Berlin Wall as potentially the most marvellous and exciting event of my lifetime, which I had never expected to live long enough to see. I thought that the reunification of Germany would be a most wonderful historic event and a significant advance for the liberties of mankind.

At the next meeting of the Cabinet I therefore raised the question and asked the prime minister whether it was true that she was opposed to the German Chancellor's proposal for reunification and, if so, why. This set off a most lively discussion, joined by many senior members of the Cabinet, who were apparently equally unaware that such a hard-line stance was being adopted by the British government. It soon became evident that Nicholas Ridley was the only member of the Cabinet who agreed with Margaret's position and she was very hard-pressed to defend it. The discussion was so heated and one-sided that I think it must have played a considerable part in her giving up further attempts at resistance.

Margaret's arguments in Cabinet were based on the assertion that no member state of the European Union could introduce new territory and so many new inhabitants and problems without the consent of all the other members. Germany could not simply enlarge itself as a member state without the most considered negotiation and constitutional process in which all the various problems that this might pose for the United Kingdom and other members ought to be weighed in the balance. In private conversation I agreed with various colleagues that her real motives seemed to be based on some inner instinct grounded in wartime feelings about Germans, which we tended to attribute to her much-loved father, Alderman Roberts.

This was my first strong intimation of the problems arising between Margaret Thatcher and some of her European colleagues which would have a great effect on her previously mildly pro-European views, and on our relationship with our allies in the Union. Helmut Kohl and Margaret Thatcher never really learnt to understand one another. This was a time of great advance in the European Union because, after a period of stale and uneventful progress, it now had formidable figures at its head: Helmut Kohl, François Mitterrand, Jacques Delors – and

Margaret Thatcher. Sadly, from then onwards, Margaret began to drift apart from the other three.

She did, however, personally lead the biggest single leap forward that the European project made at around this time. She was the leading advocate of the creation of a proper single market to replace the old ineffective tariff union known as the Common Market. It was Margaret, inspired by free-market enthusiasm, who drove this through with the Single European Act of 1987.

In her later Eurosceptic years, Margaret tried to disown her leadership of the single-market project and even tried to let it be known that she had been misled and had not properly understood the proposal from the Treasury and the Foreign Office. This was absolute nonsense because she had as ever immersed herself in all the detail and was familiar with every facet of it. I know this because at one point it involved me, as an employment minister, in personal discussions with her about whether health and safety should be included in the single market. She was hesitant about this as she worried about surrendering national control of health and safety legislation. I succeeded in persuading her that it should be included, largely by arguing that our standards were higher than those of almost all our competitors, so that it would be to Britain's advantage if they were all placed under the same obligations as British companies.

My success on this point was rather marred afterwards by the introduction of the Working Time Directive as a European health and safety measure. This over-rigorous directive restricting workers' hours was subject to the qualified majority voting system which Margaret Thatcher had personally insisted should be applied to all single-market regulations. In an early fit of Euroscepticism, the Thatcher government insisted on resisting it as an unnecessary European burden. It was duly carried by a qualified majority against our vote. Later, against legal advice, the government mounted an utterly futile legal challenge. The directive remained thereafter a constant source of controversy despite the fact that in practice the United Kingdom obtained a complete opt-out from its strict application which enabled us to continue with our normal culture of long hours, by supposed agreement between employers and employees.

To avoid excessive regulation, Margaret had appointed her loyal supporter Arthur Cockfield to be the British European Commissioner to preside over single-market measures. The single market is of course responsible for the vast majority of European regulations because universal rules on consumer safety, product quality, food safety and other standards are needed if an open market is to work. The perverse consequence was that Margaret Thatcher and her commissioner presided over the production of an enormous body of European regulation which, in subsequent years, was always attacked by Eurosceptics. In fact, Arthur's regulating, as we had intended, consigned to the dustbin vast volumes of individual nation-state regulation and swept away barriers to trade. The creation of the European single market was probably the biggest single boost to economic modernization, investment, trade and jobs in the UK that the Thatcher revolution produced.

My time as employment minister was interrupted briefly by the general election of 1987. This was one of the easiest elections that I ever fought because our economic policies were finally producing marked success and there was very strong growth in employment, investment and living standards. The Labour Party had meanwhile gone through immense internal battles and trauma and Neil Kinnock had only just begun the reforms that would return the party to electability. Unfortunately Neil had not acquired the political stature with the general public to match Margaret, nor even to conceal the continuing outrageous behaviour of the left wing of his party in industrial disputes and in local government across the country.

Strangely, David Young and others failed to appreciate that we were winning so easily. David had developed a wish to become party chairman despite the fact that that post was held by the formidable Norman Tebbit. He therefore began to lobby Margaret constantly about the failings of our election campaign and the need to take desperate measures to try to rescue any hope of a majority. This caused amazing rows between him and Norman Tebbit. I in the meantime had been sent across the country doing on-the-stump campaigning on behalf of numerous candidates, and appeared at

Central Office only for occasional press conferences. On one such occasion, I startled David in particular by saying that this was quite the easiest election that I had ever fought and that it was quite obvious that we were going to be returned with a substantial majority. David was never persuaded and he continued to annoy Norman and alarm Margaret into various panic measures which they took in the final days of the campaign, fortunately without any harmful consequences.

At one point on my travels, I received an extraordinary message. Margaret had decided that she wanted to see more young faces representing the party on television. She had therefore decided that Nigel Lawson and I should be ordered to have a haircut, and should then be put on the TV screens from time to time. Nigel and I were notorious for being rather lax about such things as haircuts. Male fashion in the late 1980s was fairly hirsute, so our laziness had been reinforced by the hairiness of other respectable people. I think Nigel did as I did and ignored the instruction, even from the prime minister, to go to a barber. I did however make a few more television appearances.

I don't think that I made any real contribution to the sweeping victory that we achieved, which was our just reward for an extremely successful period of government in which Margaret Thatcher had led a near-revolution of our business and economic environment which had restored us to the ranks of successful industrial modern nations. I returned to my duties at the Employment Department fortified by this success, although I would not stay there for very long.

The election had an unfortunate postscript, however. The leadership became hubristic, in particular Margaret Thatcher and Nigel Lawson. Nigel was one of the best qualified Chancellors we had had since the war, and a genuine expert on economic policy. He and Geoffrey Howe were the two heavyweights behind Margaret Thatcher's economic policy success. But Nigel's post-election Budget was a disaster. The economy was growing and he cut taxation and interest rates, basking in the glory of our electoral success, which was indeed largely down to his previous efforts. The Budget was cheered but it set off an economic boom. This inevitably led to overheating and then the eventual crash that caused the recession that was, a few years later, Margaret Thatcher's legacy to John Major.

11

'Work Song'

(Nat Adderley, 1960)

DTI

Two days after Margaret Thatcher won her third successive general election victory on 11 June 1987, I was summoned to Downing Street to participate in the first major reshuffle of her third term. Since a large number of ministers had similarly been summoned to have their fate revealed, Margaret began to run seriously behind time, probably because she was having difficulty with one of the ministers she was sacking. Prime ministers generally find that very few reshuffles run smoothly.

As a consequence about seven or eight ministers, including me, found ourselves twiddling our thumbs together in one of the waiting rooms in Downing Street, where an animated and, in some cases, tense discussion began about what our respective destinations might be. We were particularly intrigued that John Major was there with us. My old friend Norman Fowler had been John's boss at the Department of Health and Social Security for the last two years, and had once told me that I should look out for John as he was the most ambitious man that he had ever met. John was one of the more agitated people present, and the more complacent amongst us had to reassure him that we could all expect some sort of promotion because the unfortunates doomed to be sacked were always the first people summoned. Those of us cheerful enough to be guessing at destinations told him that he was certain to be made chief whip. We soon discovered that Margaret had considerably higher expectations of him – he emerged from his interview with her as Chief Secretary to the Treasury and a new Cabinet minister.

When I finally had my own interview I was pleased to discover that Margaret now proposed to move me to the Department of Trade and Industry. But I was rather disappointed that I was to be kept in harness as the junior partner to David Young, in a role I had come to refer to as 'David's representative on earth'. Nonetheless, I looked forward to a move to another bigger and even more interesting economic department. As at Employment, where I had been Paymaster General, I was again appointed to one of the strange ancient titles that exist in the British machinery of government: as well as being minister for trade and industry I was also now Chancellor of the Duchy of Lancaster.

The duchy was a largely ritual and nominal role and only took up Friday mornings. I would travel to the duchy offices at the northern end of Waterloo Bridge for its council meeting, which was a weekly catch-up on the running of a huge property portfolio which made a very handsome contribution to the income of the royal family. It was always followed by an excellent lunch at a place I came to call Our Duchy Pub. This was in fact the nearby Savoy hotel which stood on the site of the London home of the 2nd Duke of Lancaster, John of Gaunt, the Savoy Palace, destroyed by Wat Tyler's peasant rebels in 1381. The duchy still owned the freehold so we were treated very well, bringing my working week in London to an extremely pleasant end before I headed back to my constituency.

The only serious duty I had was to appoint the sheriffs and the magistrates for those north-western counties which were still duchy territory. The selection of candidates was largely done for me, and carefully vetted. However, the formalities required me to participate in a bizarre ritual in which the Queen formally endorsed my selection by 'pricking' the second name of the three supposed choices with which she was presented, to indicate her approval. This was done alongside the appointment of sheriffs for whom the Home Office was responsible. For those appointments she used a straight bodkin, but when the ceremony reached my sheriff appointments, a bent duchy bodkin was produced. The Queen's grandfather, George V, had apparently disfigured our bodkin when he had angrily stabbed at the parchment because he was so impatient at having to carry out this formality. He had, I was told, been on a shoot at Balmoral at the time and the then Chancellor of the Duchy and Home Secretary had had to tramp over the moors to join him for the ceremony.

This provided a very different experience from that of my day job. The DTI was then an enormous department responsible for numerous nationalized industries and the implementation of such industry policy as existed under the Thatcher government. Business and industry were actually doing extremely well at the time although David and I were rather cautious about the contribution that our particular department was making to that situation. Neither David nor I had much confidence in the interventionist measures of the previous decades, and we had no interest in pumping more subsidy into the system. Indeed we were both rather sceptical about the contribution that any business department could actually make to a successful economy.

It soon became clear to David and me that our predecessor Paul Channon had not made much of a contribution to departmental policy. Our closest officials explained that the permanent secretary, Sir Brian Hayes, had taken most of the key decisions. To be fair, Sir Brian rapidly acknowledged that David and I intended to be very active policymaking ministers indeed and he gracefully and, I think, gratefully retreated to manage the day-to-day affairs of the department on our behalf.

Although there were some superb officials at the DTI, I regret to say that the department itself was one of the weakest that I ever served in. The problem was that all the most senior officials met regularly with the great captains of industry, who were running the country's most successful companies. The best were often tempted away by offers of enormous salary increases from tycoons who recognized their talents, and we were left with those who either did not want to go into business or were not suitable to do so.

The pervading culture was not particularly enterprising. The long-serving officials tended to look back nostalgically to the days of Labour's 'Industrial Strategy' when they had poured out millions of pounds into most sectors of industry and devised interventionist programmes for the future progress of the British economy. I had shadowed that kind of thing when we had been in opposition in the 1970s and neither David nor I felt any yearning to revive it.

David and I divided the department's responsibilities, with each of us explaining and defending the other's policies in our respective Houses of Parliament. I drew the Post Office plus what I described as the 'rust bucket' portfolio – mainly made up of British Steel and British Shipbuilders. My overall view of these three loss-making organizations was that we should control the vast amounts of taxpayers' money that was going into them as subsidy and privatize them as quickly as possible. We could then take a more businesslike approach and turn them into competitive industries making a positive contribution to the British economy. This seemed to be far removed from the department's previous position. Indeed, John Whittingdale, then the former special adviser to a trio of Secretaries of State at the DTI – Norman Tebbit, followed by Leon Brittan and Paul Channon – rather patronizingly told my own special adviser Jonathan Hill that everyone started at the DTI wanting to privatize British Steel, but it was impossible. Within a year or two we proved that rather defeatist position wrong – not, however, without some fairly major battles.

I was not the first minister to discover that Margaret Thatcher quite firmly refused to contemplate any privatization of the Post Office. This was in total contrast to our government's policy in most other areas of state ownership. She would refuse to give a reason to me or anyone else.

At first, our preparations for the privatization of British Steel proceeded reasonably well because the management, led by the formidable Sir Bob Scholey, was very enthusiastic. But a hot strip mill in Scotland soon proved to be an almost insurmountable problem. Ravenscraig in Motherwell was held up in public and political debate as some sort of icon symbolizing the future of the Scottish economy. It was actually depressingly unsuccessful, far too small to be viable, a serious drain on the business, and likely to be totally unattractive to any purchasers. It had only been opened by Harold Macmillan's government as part of his industrial strategy to subsidize investment in depressed regions. They had resolved the problem of whether to put a big new strip mill in Wales or Scotland by opening two smaller units, one in each country.

Of course I favour attracting work and investment to deprived areas. It needs, though, to be good business activity with a secure financial future, not prestige political projects.

The people of Scotland had already developed a deep political hatred of Margaret Thatcher and addressing the Ravenscraig strip mill's future in the face of their belief in its value proved challenging. But what I found when I visited made me question heavily the bizarre notion that Ravenscraig was somehow a lynchpin of the Scottish economy. I certainly did not detect any very great signs that the problems of low productivity, a lack of competitiveness and a shortage of customers were being addressed.

Malcolm Rifkind, a good friend and someone with whom I was normally in close agreement on political subjects, was then the Secretary of State for Scotland. He ferociously opposed any suggestion that British Steel should be privatized, which we all assumed would lead to the closure of the strip mill, because of the impact he feared this would have on the political situation in Scotland. In late 1987 I had several long and difficult face-to-face meetings with Malcolm, accompanied by endless exchanges of letters, where he deployed his debating skills with very great vigour. There was plainly no chance of going ahead if I could not get past his veto.

I eventually succeeded in breaking the deadlock by agreeing that any privatization would include the new company making a binding commitment to continue making steel at Ravenscraig for the first seven years of private ownership, despite its unprofitability. By the time I was next reshuffled and moved on from the DTI, the process was smoothly under way.

Sadly, British Shipbuilders proved far more intractable. I made one or two fact-finding visits to Sunderland, where its main remaining shipyards were. The business was hopelessly loss-making and was receiving continual subsidy. The basic problem was that it had failed to win any orders at all to build new vessels, apart from an order for new ferries placed by a Danish customer. I steadily began to realize that this Dane was unreliable. Nobody seemed to know what he was proposing to use the ferries for and there was little evidence that he had any significant financial backing for his proposed ferry business. The first ship had been completed but the Dane had neither taken delivery nor made any payment. Nevertheless, the policy recommended to me was that we should continue building these ferries, mooring them in the River Wear at public expense until some use could be found for them.

The situation in the shipyards themselves was even more baffling. Huge sums of public money had been invested in the latest technology and equipment to enable the yards to build ships in the most up-to-date fashion. The new equipment was, however, still being manned and operated in strict accordance with traditional working practices. This meant that any given component of a ship had to progress at the traditional pace through the system. The idea that all the equipment could be operating simultaneously with steel plate going through the system in a way that maximized the use of all the machinery at any one time was politely but firmly rejected.

Tradition also apparently demanded that different skills and different processes were located on different sides of the river. The idea that a particular process or set of jobs might be moved from a yard on one bank of the river to another yard on the other bank of the river was completely unacceptable and not to be contemplated. These were only two of the more striking features of the eccentric yet time-honoured practices in this historic shipyard.

I soon decided that it would be quite impossible to float the business and it would take a generation to reform its management. I therefore made very considerable efforts to find a purchaser amongst the more successful shipbuilding companies elsewhere in the world to acquire the business outright. This proved to be a fruitless search.

I had one meeting with some Japanese shipbuilding executives after they had visited the yard and studied the books with a view to possible purchase. They explained to me, with regret, that they had never seen a shipyard anywhere in the world in which so much investment had been made to install the very best of modern shipbuilding machinery. They also explained that they had rarely encountered a shipyard where the engrained management and workforce practices would make the building of any vessels so impossibly expensive. They unfortunately therefore had to back off from any kind of deal.

I reluctantly concluded that the shipyard would have to be closed. After I was reshuffled, my successor Tony Newton understandably balked at this inherited decision and reopened the whole question. But even Tony was eventually driven to accept the inevitability of closure.

I liked Sunderland and its people but it was and remains my opinion that the city could have no serious economic future until the shipyard was closed. Traditional shipbuilding was quite the wrong way to define the future employment of the region: with global overcapacity it had become a low-profit-margin business where the only way to compete was through combining modern methods with either very low labour costs or huge government subsidy. Fortunately the government had attracted investment into nearby Washington from Nissan, the Japanese car manufacturer. The trade unions resented foreigners being allowed to compete with the nationalized monoliths turning out vehicles in the West Midlands and ferociously resisted this plan. Thankfully, they were eventually persuaded and the Nissan works were a huge success, eventually becoming the most productive car-manufacturing plant in Europe. For the young men of Sunderland there were good jobs to be had at Nissan instead of dead-end jobs in moribund shipyards. But for the first few years, Nissan would not recruit anyone over thirty-five, to ensure that their new workforce could be trained in modern industrial methods. It was a tragedy for the older members of the workforce, whose insistence on sticking to an engrained traditional culture had helped to kill off their jobs. When British Shipbuilders eventually closed their Sunderland yards the older men could get no skilled work to replace the jobs of which they had been so proud.

Meanwhile, David Young had taken upon himself the task of privatizing British Leyland, or, as it had been renamed in 1986, Rover Group. This hopelessly union-dominated and loss-making car company, responsible in its time for the Jaguar, Rover, Land Rover, Austin and Mini marques amongst others, had been a millstone around the neck of every British government for many years. To my amazement, he made considerable progress in persuading Ford to buy the company and then hit a totally unexpected snag. Margaret Thatcher was implacably opposed to selling the company to a foreign owner. I remember a conversation in which she explained her instinctive motives for this. She thought that Land Rover particularly was a significantly British institution. She was utterly convinced that the country ladies in headscarves who drove Land Rovers would never understand if a Conservative government sold the manufacturer of their rural vehicle to Americans.

Undaunted, David proceeded to put together a deal to sell British Leyland to British Aerospace. The details were personally finalized by David and Roland Smith, chairman of the recently privatized company. Even when the deal was near to being completed, most DTI officials and certainly my Private Office knew nothing about them.

Once the deal was done, I would have to make a statement in the House of Commons to coincide with David's statement in the House of Lords. Unfortunately, when the day came, the last loose ends had not been settled by the time I had to leave for the Commons. I therefore took with me three versions of the statement. The first draft described what a spectacular deal this was for the taxpayer and the company. The second said that rumours of an impending sale were much exaggerated and I could refute them, while the third said that the final details were being arranged and I would make a further statement on the following day.

Whilst I was on my feet answering Parliamentary Questions my PPS John Taylor dashed to the Lords to see which statement David was giving. He came back to say that David was giving the third version. I therefore repeated this to a rather baffled House and had to return the following day to give the final details of the deal.

Not long afterwards, I had to make a speech in the House of

Commons on another ideological hang-up. The Swiss chocolate company Nestlé had made a takeover bid for Rowntree of York, which was running into ridiculous resistance in the press and amongst certain sections of our backbenchers. In their view, Rowntree was a historic company which, again, should not be purchased by foreigners. My speech vigorously defended the principles of market economics and resisted the nostalgic nationalist protectionism in which people were indulging: 'The British economy benefits from the fact that we are open and welcoming to inward investment. We also benefit greatly from outward investment. The Labour Party can never make up its mind. When there is British investment overseas it says that jobs are being exported, and when there is investment in Britain it says that wicked foreigners are taking over our firms.' There were no competition or other public-interest reasons for intervening and I refused to support government intervention simply on the grounds that the Swiss should not be allowed to buy the peculiar form of chocolate favoured in the British market. Once the deal had gone ahead, Nestlé put considerable investment into the Rowntree enterprise. Although jobs were lost as Nestlé modernized and streamlined production, the company did not fold entirely, as it would have done without this rescue, and instead it became the successful business that it remains to this day.

Looking back, this incident reveals that despite the fact that we had been in office for almost ten years and were well advanced with radical changes to the British economy, we never really succeeded in converting the British public to the virtues of capitalism and market economics. By instinct Britain remained small 'c' conservative, nationalist and reactionary.

The only forward-looking part of the department, which happily came under my remit, was the aerospace industry and the Airbus project. Aircraft building and maintenance was a fascinating modern manufacturing activity in a growing market based on rapid technical change and increased demand for the best of international travel. It had a great prospect before it and we had strong companies like British Aerospace and Rolls-Royce who would benefit from support to provide modern jobs and added value for the indefinite future. I had adamantly opposed subsidizing loss-making and declining industries but I was happy to give limited-term subsidies to these new, growing businesses, which simply needed a bit of investment to become self-sufficient and competitive.

Airbus was a most peculiar project. It was a European Union intergovernmental initiative, devised to create a global competitor to Boeing in the civil air passenger business. I therefore had to attend regular meetings with my opposite numbers from other member states to discuss the project's future. It was all highly politicized, with the manufacturing and design process strictly divided, on an agreed quota basis, between Germany, France, Spain and the United Kingdom. The project was based in Toulouse, where the aircraft were finally assembled, but British Aerospace produced the wings and other designated parts of the aircraft in Bristol. All the governments subsidized their various manufacturers via rather complicated financial instruments.

This seemed to me to be an extraordinary way of organizing anything, let alone an industry hoping to succeed in the global market. I queried why none of the companies involved was under any obligation to tell their national government how profitable or otherwise their particular activities were. Reducing manufacturing costs was in the companies' hands. Some seemed to make more progress than others, but those that did seemed more inclined to keep the savings to cushion their own bottom lines rather than reducing their subsidy.

I soon discovered that my fellow ministers from the other member states regarded the meetings as more social than business occasions. We would have splendid gatherings and go through the motions of reporting and discussing progress. However, there were no discussions of any real substance. Instead, I was expected to enjoy the magnificent lunches and the visits to various factories that were a key part of every gathering.

Despite our good personal relationships, my colleagues began to regard me as something of a pain as I nagged them for more business information and more decision-making at the Council meetings. The Germans eventually decided that I would benefit from a meeting with Franz Josef Strauss, the formidable Bavarian politician who had been the father of the Airbus project and remained the chairman of the Toulouse-based consortium. We had a splendid lunch and a fascinating political discussion. Franz Josef was both brilliant and charming, a man of considerable intellect and eloquence. He patiently explained that the project was not really designed to produce any return for the member-state governments. It was above all a political project aimed at creating modern and sustainable employment for an industrial workforce in Western Europe. Like the Common Agricultural Policy it was designed to produce secure jobs and steady incomes for ordinary citizens of each of our countries so that they might continue to vote for centre-right pro-Western political parties and would not be attracted by socialism or worse coming from the alternative societies to the east of Europe.

As we discussed these issues at length, I put forward my rather more market economics-based view that it should be possible to continue to win political gratitude whilst focusing harder on the attractiveness and profitability of the end product. We were quite plainly not going to persuade one another on this narrow subject. However after a time we moved on to a much wider discussion of the problems facing European democracies, which needed to modernize and raise living standards whilst withstanding the pressures and problems of the Cold War. Franz Josef and I actually got on very well and we found that there was a great deal of agreement between us on the nature of the European project and the development of the sorts of societies which would give European nations a successful, prosperous and influential role in the modern world.

Franz Josef died the following year and I am sorry that this was our only meeting. I would like to have been able to tell him that I had realized that my dreadful capitalist criticisms of the Airbus project were quite wrong. And it was probably fortunate that my ability to influence it turned out to be rather limited. Airbus went from strength to strength, rescuing us from Boeing's monopoly and stimulating competition, which produced whole new ranges of more comfortable and efficient aeroplanes for the rapidly developing international airline business.

Outer space proved to be more difficult. Britain was a member of the European Space Agency (ESA) and we had a growing space industry of our own. On my arrival at the DTI I became the somewhat unlikely minister with responsibility for this sector of our economy.

Despite being something of a petrol head, space travel had never really interested me. I regarded the whole thing as an offbeat and expensive diversion from more serious applications of science and technology on Earth. The high-tech companies and the officials involved were committed and very capable but they had difficulty in keeping me on board. Despite their enthusiasm, I could see no worthwhile future in manned spacecraft exploration of the universe. Nor did I see any great commercial opportunities in rocket launchers. I had a very low-tech understanding and an inner hunch that the only positive financial contribution from all this came in the development of the satellites that went up on the end of the rockets. I thought that both the DTI and the ESA should concentrate on this aspect of space flight.

I found myself in a minority of one in the relevant European Council of Ministers meetings. The French were very keen on launching rockets and for some bizarre reason there was a tiny British stake in the production of their Ariane rocket. I pulled back from this investment as fast as I could. The French minister implored me to visit French Guiana in the hope that I might be starstruck by the excitement of a rocket launch. I didn't go, although I do still regret the fact that I couldn't fit this interesting trip into my diary. It would have provided a chance for some excellent birdwatching of the kind which I later enjoyed on holiday in nearby Guyana, the former British colony.

My fellow European ministers and the Commission remained seized by the ambition to match the Americans and the Russians in putting people into spacecraft. This seemed to me to be a total waste of public money with no scientific point. I flatly rejected the idea and no one was able to move me to give British acquiescence, or investment, to this grandiose folly. The ESA proposal for a manned expedition into space moved slowly towards extinction, until my friend and colleague David Willetts revived it as David Cameron's

Minister of Universities and Science. I still think the idea is fun but bonkers.

We did remain partners in a modified process of running an international space station that circumnavigates the globe. I am not quite sure how I was persuaded that this had any economic importance but it does seem to have played some worthwhile role. Tim Peake has just returned from a popular but expensive trip to this station.

Despite my complete lack of any scientific education or expertise, I was also responsible for the DTI's science and research budget, but I don't think that I did any very great harm. I exercised my role based on my belief that the distribution of funds for science, engineering and medical research should be done by academic peers through the research councils, which I tried to make completely independent.

I believed that such research was essential to our future as a modern advanced industrial economy – a view I still hold. As a consequence I was happy to argue with the Treasury and anybody else for the necessary funds and then steadfastly resisted pork-barrel lobbying from ministers and MPs and policy interference by my officials in how to distribute these funds, sticking implacably to the research councils-based approach in which I made no attempt to interfere. I took part in many Council of Ministers meetings about the distribution of the funds. Of course, I sought to ensure the success of well-founded British bids but I did slightly object to the politicized nature of some of the decisions. Some institutions and projects appeared to have won a permanent place in European programmes despite their apparent lack of success. I tried to challenge one or two examples in Italy but the political lobby from their employees was too strong.

My robust challenging of projects which I thought were financially dubious was, however, nearly responsible for an absolute disaster. The European Centre for Nuclear Science (CERN) was constructing an enormous underground tunnel in Geneva through which a collider would operate in order to discover more about the fundamental nature of protons and nuclei. I gained the impression that we were building it solely so that Europe could claim to have a bigger one than the Americans. The only other clear objective that I could discern

Top On a family holiday, Bridlington, *c.*1950.
Above The shop, Bulwell.

Right In the sea as a boy.

As a youth in the back garden, probably doing my trainspotting books.

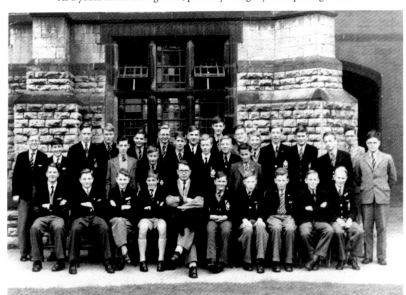

Form IVA, 1953–4.

Cambridge Union with me as chairman. Top, from left: Chris Davis, Alan Watson, John Toulmin, Michael Howard, Peter Fullerton, Ian Binnie and Norman Lamont. Bottom, from left: Mani Ayer, Richard Moore, Dick Taverne, Ken Clarke, Angus Maude, Chris Mason and Oliver Weaver.

At the Despatch Box of the Cambridge Union.

Wedding, 1964. I think Gillian made her own wedding dress.

With Gillian, Ken Junior and Susan.

With Don Concannon (far left) at the 1966 general election count at Mansfield.
Second from right is Reg Strauther, the Liberal candidate whose deposit we tried to save.

Campaigning for Rushcliffe in the 1970 general election with Tony Barber.
My then chairman and champion Norman Beeby is on the right.

Ted Heath's Whips' Office. A gust of wind had caused an entertaining moment.

Addressing the Council of Europe on the OECD Annual Report 1974, wearing a classic Toryboy striped suit.

With the pile of Nottinghamshire 'Yes' votes at the count of the 1975 referendum on joining the EEC. Standing on the right is Jim Lester, later MP for Broxtowe.

Opening a cycle path as
Junior Minister for Transport.

Encountering striking workers
in Liverpool in my first few
weeks as Minister for Health.

In partnership with
David Young at DTI.

Above Margaret Thatcher's cabinet, 1987.
Below With Gillian at the 1990 conference in Bournemouth.

was that we were seeking to discover something called the Higgs boson, a particle whose existence had been theoretically proved but never observed. I was not convinced that the British taxpayer should spend tens of millions of pounds searching for a baffling particle rather than on other science-based research and development. I could not see that any practical value would follow even if we did observe the Higgs boson. I soon discovered that particle physics is a colossally expensive area of research and that it is somewhat wasted on people like myself who do not have the imagination and vision to be excited by the need to discover the nature of matter. It seemed to me that this could easily be left for future generations to discover when they could afford to do so, and I pulled the British out of CERN. My victory lasted for about a week. The outraged scientists immediately rushed to the prime minister to get me overruled. Margaret was inordinately proud of her scientific education. She deplored the fact that most of her political colleagues lacked any scientific training and had old-fashioned humanities degrees. She was always vulnerable to any argument from any scientist who could skilfully deploy the flattering 'only we scientists understand' approach when lobbying her. My department and I received a peremptory instruction from Number 10 to reverse my decision and the whole great project continued to its ultimate triumphant conclusion many years later.

On top of my departmental responsibilities, I was soon given an additional and very worthwhile cross-government role, albeit rather by accident. On the night of the 1987 general election, Margaret had made a public, off-the-cuff remark, saying 'we must do something about those inner cities'. I never had any idea what she actually meant, but if it was the result of any close thought at all, I strongly suspect it was more likely to have been inspired by Margaret's clear aim to win Labour strongholds at the next election. Huge social change and the decline of traditional industries had indeed caused a terrible combination of problems to develop in the heart of many cities. In some particularly disrupted and troubled communities, social unrest had taken the form of serious rioting for the first time in post-war Britain. The middle classes had speeded up their flight to the suburbs and dormitory villages. The worst quarters of several cities were dominated by a combination of unemployment, social breakdown and poverty. The media latched on to Margaret's comment as an indication that she was now determined to tackle the problem.

The only minister who had endeavoured to do so with any vigour in Margaret's first two terms had been Michael Heseltine. He had achieved some remarkable successes in Liverpool, that most difficult and left-behind city, working with community groups on urban regeneration and economic revival. His 1981 report on the future of Merseyside was called *It Took a Riot*, emphasizing the fact that he had only been allowed to take action as a result of the disorder in Toxteth and elsewhere. Margaret now reacted to the press interpretation of her comments and to the threat of future social disorder by deciding that she did indeed have to do something.

I therefore found myself, after about six months of interdepartmental bickering over who would preside over this suddenly prestigious subject, appointed inner-cities minister. Margaret had been clear she wanted me to co-ordinate the actions of the various interested government departments. However no one at Downing Street had any idea precisely what they wanted to happen in the inner cities so I was rather left to make up my own goals and to construct my own approach. I decided that I would try to test my conviction that free-market economics could be combined with social justice.

I had organized a number of 'Inner-City Task Forces' when I was at the Department of Employment. Brian Hutchinson, a senior executive at British American Tobacco, had been seconded to me to help set them up, and we had selected teams of officials from a range of government departments. We initially chose eight areas – North Kensington, North Peckham, Highfields in Leicester, Moss Side in Manchester, St Paul's in Bristol, Chapeltown in Leeds, Handsworth in Birmingham and North Central Middlesbrough – in which our task forces would lead innovative projects to revive the relevant districts. Later we added task forces in Nottingham, Coventry, Doncaster, Hartlepool, Preston, Rochdale, Wolverhampton and Tower Hamlets. Our choices were certainly influenced by the publicity that riots in particular districts had attracted but these areas had all known very considerable depression. With the enthusiastic support of some very eager young officials, we were able to introduce a new level of activity into dealing with the problems, focusing on creating jobs, encouraging training opportunities and stimulating enterprise. For example, development funds were set up in partnership with major clearing banks to help small businesses get access to finance, and a wide range of targeted grants were made to support vocational training in areas from banking to hairdressing for thousands of young people.

Now, with the added clout of Margaret Thatcher's support, I wanted to attract business into these depressed and neglected areas to generate employment opportunities for their residents, particularly their young people. I firmly believed – and still do – that this was the key to turning around the decline and dreadful social breakdown that typified such districts. Sadly, but perhaps unsurprisingly, my team and I soon discovered that effecting change was far from straightforward. The scale of the problems involved was enormous.

A minor but not insignificant irritation was the constant opposition we faced from the Department of Environment. Many of the otherwise excellent officials in that department, some of whom I knew very well after my years as a transport minister sharing their tower blocks in Marsham Street, were acutely aware that their department had always led on so-called urban policy. They therefore inspired their Secretary of State Nick Ridley, an otherwise able departmental minister, to compete with my role and resist some of my innovations.

It seemed to me that the Department of Environment's approach was based far too much on sponsorship of the construction sector. For me, the key was creating jobs, but their focus was on redeveloping infrastructure. I jokingly referred to this as the demolition of old buildings followed by the construction of new ones, but it was broadly what was happening. The problem was that construction did not in itself change the social condition of the people living in the area. It merely resulted in a workforce from more prosperous areas outside the troubled district arriving on the construction site. With the completion of the building work and the return of the workforce to their own areas, the local residents were left just as unemployed, unskilled and poor as they had been before.

I felt very strongly that public works contracts – in the task-force areas only – should require an element of genuinely local employment, backed by the local training needed to ensure the necessary skills. Nick Ridley was more shocked by my non-Conservative approach to tendering and market competition than by almost any of my other policies. But my attempts to introduce such innovations had limited success. Nick was not able to block all my efforts, but I can only recall making a significant difference in a very few cases, primarily Handsworth in Birmingham.

At least as problematic as these Whitehall battles, if not more so, was the opposition we faced in the chosen localities from extreme-left political leaders and the criminal gangs sometimes allied to them. This took even me by considerable surprise. It is still difficult today to persuade younger politicians that such ultra-left-wing extremism existed.

Many of the elected councillors we met believed that they were witnessing the collapse of capitalism that Marx had predicted. They were certainly not going to co-operate with liberal market-based solutions to anything, seeing these as attempts to slow down this inevitable step towards the revolution. Their ideological resistance extended to my attempts to introduce the concept of public–private partnership into urban regeneration, following the successful example of American cities like Baltimore, with some city leaders unable to condone the capitalist profit motive.

Fortunately, the more traditional but enterprising local politicians of Leeds and Birmingham were more prepared to contemplate anything that might bring investment and jobs to their cities. Nowadays, public–private partnership is regarded as a normal, established approach to local economic growth.

Surprisingly, Leicester produced some of the most extreme opposition with its local councillors claiming that I should neither visit the city nor station my officials there unless they were first invited by the city council which 'ruled' it. They were also totally opposed to any employment other than compulsorily unionized public-sector employment. This was an attitude deeply engrained in many areas, perhaps the best example of which was demonstrated at a training programme I visited in Peckham, financed by the government for Lambeth Borough Council. Large numbers of young people were being given rather odd technical training on great quantities of equipment which had been expensively provided for the purpose. Even after my short period of observation, it seemed rather casual and disorganized. I asked one of the trainers what his record was so far of getting young people into jobs at the end of the course. He looked rather shocked by my question. 'We are not into jobs here,' was his pithy reply. This was my first experience of an attitude repeated to me by a left-wing teacher a few years later when I was Education Secretary, who roundly told me that he was not going to produce 'wage slaves for capitalism'.

In some areas the dogmatic pronunciation of left-wing socialist principles was combined with a focus on the enrichment of the municipal leaders. Corruption within councils and the dominance of criminal gangs in the local population were a very serious problem in Knowsley, Lambeth, Southwark and elsewhere. In Liverpool, local government included people who were as much gangsters as political ideologues. Some of the people who described themselves to the local press as the 'community leaders' of St Paul's, Bristol, and Moss Side, Manchester, were in fact leaders of drug-dealing gangs. The lawlessness of those two last districts, which seemed to go unchallenged by their political leadership, was the principal barrier between the normal residents and their hopes for a modicum of prosperity, but the more gullible sections of the media were still quite willing to quote the self-appointed spokesmen as the authentic voice for local opinion resisting my Thatcherite innovations. We kept plugging away but it was like wading through treacle sometimes, and we made limited progress.

There were areas where progress, although difficult, looked more possible. Hartlepool was one of these. It was an isolated north-eastern city whose problems really stemmed from its failure to attract a modern replacement for the declining traditional industries which were the sole basis of the local economy. The place had an attractive and cohesive community and the local leadership were friendly and worthy people, despite their strong left-wing opinions. We had limited numbers of task-force officials there and had difficulty making much progress with economic regeneration. We did make one good break-through by getting a company to set up a ship-refurbishing business which employed some of the neighbourhood's traditional skills, albeit on a modest scale. However, I wish that we could have done more to bring to this solid, overwhelmingly working-class town the economic revival that was being enjoyed by the country as a whole. It was a quite distinct place compared with all the others that we had rather rapidly selected, and gave me a new insight into the strong local spirit of the North-East of England.

I am not sure that we accomplished a great deal in the year or so that I carried this responsibility. I like to think that our experiments, across more than 250 projects in sixteen task-force areas, did however introduce some civil servants, local leaders and local businesses to new ideas of urban regeneration and employment creation that had not been tried before.

One of the responsibilities of the DTI with which I was not involved was the approval of licences for export. I think that David Young approved these but often delegated them to Alan Clark. I gained an insight into our approach when I was asked to step in when both of them were out of the office.

I read an extraordinary application for permission to export to the Soviet Union a particular metal-alloy component that was to be used by the Soviets as the hard point of their intercontinental missiles. I thought that this was an outrageous application and I quickly decided to reject it. My refusal was referred by worried officials to Downing Street. Margaret Thatcher promptly overruled me and permitted the highly secret export to go ahead. At the time I was absolutely amazed but I decided not to make an issue of it.

I assumed that it had been approved – as was often the practice – for purely commercial reasons on the basis that it was in the national interest to promote the economy. I had occasionally heard sensible people arguing that we should not restrict any exports because if British industry did not manufacture and export a product then another Western country would undoubtedly ensure that the order went to its industries.

I was reminded of this sometime later when Alan Clark plunged the government into a dreadful crisis when he permitted the export of machine tools to Iraq, which were fairly obviously for the manufacture of weaponry. This decision and the events around it were eventually referred to a judicial inquiry led by Lord Justice of Appeal Sir Richard Scott. The Scott Inquiry caused amazing problems for the government and for at least two of my colleagues, including William Waldegrave, when it was published in 1996. Although Alan was responsible for the whole debacle I was fairly convinced that he had not been acting completely as a rogue member of the government. Somehow, with his usual skill in getting out of many scrapes, he emerged from Scott as a hero and 'whistleblower' who had blown the lid off a scandal.

Throughout my two-year spell at the DTI I maintained a high parliamentary and media profile, but – thankfully – was not as mired in controversy as I had been at Health. However, the hours I spent at work broken only by sleep at my pad in London and the days that I spent away from my family were much the same. That said, there were many enjoyable parties and dinners at which Gillian joined me, whenever she had the chance. And I certainly tried to help as much as I could as she continued to deal with all our family responsibilities. We kept to our now well-established habit of taking a good break at Christmas with our friends Martin and Pippa Suthers, and escaping for the whole of August to a hired villa in some very rural and untouched part of southern Europe. At weekends, we indulged our mutual interests with visits to Romanesque churches and excursions to stately homes, and continued to take great delight in birdwatching and botany, whether in the English countryside or abroad.

My media notoriety had lent me a certain B-list celebrity, which enabled me to add a few more escapist activities. I became a regular participant in the annual Lords and Commons saloon-car race, which throughout the 1980s was held at Brands Hatch and was sometimes a supporting race on Grand Prix days. I was a keen racing driver, and moderately skilled, but quite unsuccessful. In every sport I ever took up, I would carefully study and practise and learn from those who tried to train me. I would then completely lose my head on the football pitch, the cricket field or the racing circuit and make elementary errors. I usually managed to wind up in the top half of those who finished the race, but never managed to win.

I was already beginning to get a little old for such a hair-raising pastime and it was while I was at the DTI that my racing career came to an end. I was invited to Silverstone to take part as one of the celebrity drivers in a race sponsored by Alfa Romeo, who were hoping to promote a new (and pretty dreadful) four-wheel-drive sporting model. My son Ken came with me and we enjoyed a lively weekend with a collection of celebrities from various walks of life, of whom the most agreeable companions were two snooker players. Unfortunately my performance in the race reached new heights of incompetence.

In practice on the Saturday, I forgot the layout of a course with which I should have been extremely familiar and on my first lap took off at a corner into the gravel, causing considerable damage. I was given a new car for the race itself the next day, but unfortunately it was pouring with rain. At first, I was doing reasonably well and tried to move up the field. Eventually I overestimated myself and went into a spin when trying to overtake, damaging the other car. I then limped on in my own battered vehicle to a rather poor finish. I inflicted thousands of pounds' worth of damage on the three vehicles and no doubt that is why I was never invited to take part in a celebrity race again.

It is possible that some people might draw an analogy between my competitive and occasionally destructive approach to leisure activities and my approach to the various government departments with which I have been involved. But I firmly reject such comparisons.

It is certainly the case, however, that my career so far had given me immense job satisfaction. My only regret was that, after eighteen years in the House of Commons, I had still not been given personal responsibility for a major department. I was keen to finally take charge of something even more demanding than an overpowered racing car.

12

'Now's the Time'

(Charlie Parker, 1945)

HEALTH REFORM AT LAST

My next promotion took me and, I suspect, Margaret Thatcher by surprise.

Empowered and energized by her landslide victory in the 1987 general election, Margaret had decided to embark on the vital question of public-service reform. With Kenneth Baker, her Secretary of State for Education, she had already started to reform the state education system, to try to restore our educational standards to the level required for Britain to thrive in the modern world.

She now felt that it was time to embark on the same kind of radical reform of the National Health Service. She had finally despaired of the firefighting and crises that continued to dominate the political debate in Parliament and in the media.

In that same reshuffle that saw her make John Major Chief Secretary to the Treasury and post me to the DTI, she had moved Norman Fowler, who had been her safe pair of hands at the Department of Health and Social Security for over five years, replacing him with John Moore, a rising star who had made his name in the Treasury. Indeed, Margaret had actually selected John as her favoured successor when she had been forced to abandon Cecil Parkinson, her previous choice, in the wake of the personal scandal that ended his ministerial career. John was Thatcher's newest blue-eyed boy and the media couldn't get enough of him. He had the good looks of a juvenile lead and seemed ideally suited to the emerging fashion for mass-media political presentation. In the first years of his meteoric political rise, he had even been given the nickname Mr Privatization for his work on the denationalization programme.

John was bright and likeable, and had been a very capable junior minister to Nigel Lawson. This new move was very popular with the press – and, at first, with the party. Unfortunately, however, John knew nothing about either health or social security and, as far as I could see, had no views on the subject. He was soon both overwhelmed and unnerved by the sheer scale of the problems he faced and the expectations he had to live up to. His much-anticipated speech at party conference, in which he was billed to make profound statements about the future of the NHS and to outline his great reforms, proved competent but prosaic. The pressure took its toll on him and he had to take a short leave of absence on health grounds. With hindsight it is now clear that he experienced a complete loss of self-confidence and his health suffered.

Margaret was driven to conclude that she had to rescue John from the awful position into which she had plunged him. In July 1988 she suddenly announced that the DHSS was too big a department for one man to handle. This statement both surprised and amused my old friend Norman Fowler, who had been successfully contending with this difficult department through several crisis-torn years. Margaret moved John Moore to a newly created Department of Social Security, where she hoped the less high-profile role would give him time to recover.

As a result, she needed a new Secretary of State for Health and I suspect that, as ever, my friends played some part in persuading her to appoint me. My main claim for eligibility was obviously the fact that I was one of the few members of the government who had been immersed in the problems of the NHS before, and would not have a steep learning curve to deliver the 'reform' that Margaret had promised. I think that Margaret had also finally accepted that I was not a threat to the well-being of her government and that I did indeed share to the full both her taste for radical reform and her readiness to engage in controversy to challenge vested interests.

Our actual conversation when I was summoned to her reshuffle meeting was reasonably short and straightforward. She told me that she would like to move me to be Secretary of State for Health and I told her that I was pleased to accept. I had enjoyed working alongside David Young at the DTI, but I was delighted that, at long last, I was being given a big department of my own. I was also thrilled – if slightly amazed – to be given the chance to go back and implement ideas that I had been thinking about for years, to reform that ramshackle but much-loved service, the NHS. In light of my baptism of fire as health minister three years before, I knew from the start exactly what I wanted to do.

A few days later, John Moore asked me to come to see him for what was obviously intended to be a handover briefing. He told me that Margaret had promised that she would force the Chancellor, Nigel Lawson, to provide tax relief for personal contributions to private health plans. He therefore assured me that improving the finances of the NHS should be fairly straightforward. But I had already been party to a conversation with Margaret in which Nigel Lawson and I had flatly disagreed with her proposal that private health plans should be exempt from personal taxation, and told John as much. I also, to his evident surprise, told him that I did not approve of the American system based on tax relief and private insurance. I think I left him a rather puzzled man. Margaret had obviously persuaded him that this was the great reform that he should deliver in order to demonstrate his statesmanlike qualities.

Sadly, it soon became obvious that John Moore had tried to get back to work too quickly. He could not cope with his ministerial responsibilities at the Department of Social Security and he eventually retired from office and then from Parliament. He completely absented himself from all public life and all political activity thereafter, becoming a silent member of the House of Lords who attended from time to time in order to vote. Fortunately, though, this enabled him to recover his health and he went on to pursue a successful business career.

My immediate difficulty, taking over the Department of Health in July 1988, was that the prime minister had firmly committed herself to radical reform of the NHS in a television interview on *Panorama* the previous January, without giving the slightest indication – and probably with no clear idea – of what these reforms might involve. She had then begun to form a view, with the help of her policy advisers and John Moore. (She had formed a sort of task force of political advisers, among them David Willetts, who had started some work on preparing reforms. While I remained aware of their existence throughout my term as Secretary of State, I never met them and never received any papers from them.) As a result I returned to my old stamping ground of health-care policy with a clear agenda of my own, which was quite different from Margaret's.

Margaret remained privately convinced that the US insurance-based model was the ideal system to follow. Everyone who could afford it would purchase their own health insurance plans, and their insurance companies would then purchase their care. She explained to me at our first one-to-one policy discussion that the government would provide a residual system in which the taxpayer would pay the premiums for that section of the population who could not afford to buy their own insurance, and these premiums would purchase a basic system of essential care at minimum standards.

This was entirely consistent with her view that individual citizens should stand on their own feet and that the state should only step in to help those people who were not fortunate enough to be able to look after themselves. She had a strong view, quite contrary to the overwhelming political fashion of the time, that people should pay for their own health care if they had the resources to do so. Most politicians would proudly proclaim that they relied for all their care on the NHS along with the rest of the population. Margaret told me that she was quite shocked by this, particularly when Cabinet ministers – she singled out Willie Whitelaw – admitted to using the NHS and depending on public support. Nigel Lawson did not get very involved but he and the Treasury encouraged her on the basis that the main objective should be the reduction of the cost of the NHS to the taxpayer.

My whole approach was starkly different. I was (and still am) a strong supporter of the founding principles of the NHS, which I believed should provide treatment free at the point of delivery to every citizen, paid for out of general taxation. I had never had any private insurance myself and regarded it as something of a rip-off. I thought that the American system was quite deplorable as a very high proportion of the population there had no cover of any kind and very poor access to basic services. The insurance-based system meant that there was no incentive to control costs at all as the insurance companies preferred loading the premiums to employers and policy-holders rather than battling with the management of hospitals to get value for money. The Americans paid out a staggering proportion of the highest GDP in the world to finance a system that spectacularly failed to achieve the results that any advanced country should be seeking for its population.

I had continued to follow health policy since I had left the department three years earlier. I had been particularly impressed by an article in *The Economist* by Professor Alain Enthoven who was a health economist at Stanford University, little known in the UK. He advocated setting up a system of purchaser and provider contracting within the health-care system. It was quite straightforward and based on the internal accounting processes that large commercial organizations were beginning to develop.

I was convinced that, instead of one body – the health authority – being responsible for both providing health care and purchasing it, the patient should be supported by his clinical advisers, mainly GPs, who would purchase contracts with NHS hospitals and other providers, based on their judgement of what would produce the best likely outcome for the patient and value for money for the taxpayer. Hospitals and other providers would bid for the contractual right to deliver services to a particular block of patients for a particular set of conditions. Purchasers would aim to obtain the maximum quantity and quality of patient services that finite resources could provide.

The key principles were competition and choice, with the aim of better outcomes for the patient being the fundamental issue in deciding where resources were directed. These principles formed the basis for what became known as the 'internal market' and have, in my opinion, been at the root of every successive development of the

NHS since I introduced them. But first I had to persuade Margaret to let me develop and apply them.

No sooner had my appointment been announced, therefore, than Margaret and I discovered that we flatly disagreed on the reforms I had been appointed to introduce.

I found myself plunged into a series of face-to-face meetings with her in which we engaged in the most robust argument about how to proceed. We had over twenty meetings in all, facing each other across the table in the Cabinet Room at Number 10 with the only other person present being a senior Cabinet Office civil servant, Richard Wilson. He had to listen in to our debates, which were sometimes closer to shouting matches, and subsequently write up the minutes setting out what, so far as he could judge, we had apparently agreed.

Margaret enjoyed a vigorous political argument and I had many debates with her throughout my time in her government. She could be extremely aggressive and sometimes very rude. During one of our many face-to-face rows, for example, she broke off her argument to say, 'There is always one man who talks too much in Cabinet. It used to be Robert Carr, but now it's you.' We had just been ranting at each other and she had been, as she always was, at least as garrulous as me. It seemed to me that she was the last person in a position to make that criticism – the grandest pot ever to call a kettle black.

Our mutual love of combative debate meant, however, that neither of us ever bore any resentment or took it personally. As long as I was prepared to stand by my principles and explain my proposals in detail I was allowed to continue and to return for another round in the ring.

At first, my strategy was to try to close down the debate by asking my officials to prepare mountains of documents in order to bury her in paper. I was certain no one holding the office of prime minister would have the time to take all this on. I seriously underestimated my boss's capacity for work, however. Margaret was a complete workaholic, fascinated by detail, and capable of absorbing it very quickly. I would find that she had read my heaps of material the night before and was ready and able to challenge me on every minute point that I raised in our gladiatorial sessions across the Cabinet table. Her challenges often caused me to work on the weaknesses in my argument and to return, having improved them, for the next meeting. Even then, I did not always win.

The battle with Margaret was often exhausting and took a considerable time. Richard Wilson was absolutely brilliant in his role as neutral recorder and, occasionally, diplomatic arbiter of progress. He would ring my Private Office before I got back from the meeting to inform them of how much progress – or lack of it – he felt had been made. He was also in the habit of marking each exchange on what he described as the Richter scale.

I once complained to Richard about these battles of attrition and asked him whether he had ever experienced anything like it. He told me that I had seen nothing, saying, 'You should have been at the meetings between Margaret and Ken Baker.' Their disagreements had been even more ferocious, it seems.

Margaret challenged me remorselessly on every detail and could be scathing if she thought that I was unsure of what I was saying. However, contrary to popular myth, she could be persuaded by argument. She also realized that she could not move yet another Secretary of State. Just as I was beginning to wonder if it was all worth the hassle and whether I still had stomach for the fight – I enjoy political combat but everyone has their limits – I arrived at a meeting to find that Margaret had done some more reading and now finally appeared to be completely persuaded by my point of view.

A paper was prepared setting out reforms based on my preferred approach. She then personally presented it to a Cabinet meeting, only allowing me to utter a sentence or two, and secured policy approval in about five minutes of cursory discussion. Once we were agreed, she thereafter supported me unflinchingly through the whole embattled process of pushing through these sweeping reforms to the most traditional part of the post-war British welfare state. Only at the very last moment, almost two years later, did she have sudden political doubts.

Securing prime-ministerial agreement to my reforms was, though, only the start. The next stage was getting my department to refine and deliver them. This was a problem from the outset.

The senior officials in the department remained as anxious to appease all their lobby groups and to help their ministers lead a quiet life as they had always been. They were totally peace-loving, totally wedded to the system as it was, and had no appetite for change at all. They would have much preferred to have a Secretary of State who would take all the blows on his chin and concentrate on getting the maximum amount of money out of the Treasury each year to minimize controversy.

So when I returned in triumph from my final, successful meeting with Margaret, my affable permanent secretary, Christopher France, quietly informed me that whilst he understood my enthusiasm for reform, he regrettably did not have any officials who could be released to work on it. They were all too busy engaged on other tasks. This rather amazed me, since I had discovered that the Department of Health employed about 6,000 officials in its central bureaucracy. I was never able to find out exactly what the vast majority of them did.

I therefore had to work around Christopher France and rely on my Private Office to recruit a collection of keen young officials and outsiders who could form a small working group to design, draft and then deliver the system of reform we proposed. My excellent private secretary Andy McKeon devoted himself to the task. We recruited Duncan Nichol, who had been general manager of Mersey Regional Health Authority and had been recommended to me by the authority's keen and supportive chairman, Don Wilson. I also recruited Sheila Masters who had been an accountant in private practice and brought the necessary financial expertise for devising a system for our multibillion-pound budget that had a prospect of succeeding in the way we wanted. Once it was obvious that I was getting my own posse together, Christopher France stepped up and found some people to help, although many were still clearly keeping their heads down and waiting for this madman to leave.

Alongside my posse were my ministers and my special adviser. I had a politically skilled Minister of State, David Mellor, who was at least as tough and belligerent as I was. Tessa Keswick, who I recruited to replace Jonathan Hill, was a highly intelligent aristocratic Scot who became a key political aide battling alongside me and helping to drive the process forward. They soon found themselves at the heart of a controversy which Tessa at one point described as the political equivalent of the Battle of the Somme.

The other Minister of State in the department was the equally excellent, but very different, Virginia Bottomley. Beautiful, elegant and charming, Virginia had a razor-sharp mind and a backbone of steel – as any foes she had soon discovered. I suspected that Virginia and David Mellor couldn't stand the sight of each other. I pretended to be unaware of this and they both remained fiercely loyal to me and to the team.

By this stage in my career I had discovered the necessity of delegating and choosing what you wanted to focus on. So I asked Virginia to take total charge of the other huge area of the department, the community social services delivered by local authorities. She had worked as a social worker herself in her youth, and was a very safe pair of hands who managed, publicly and within the department, the whole policy area without ever troubling me with any items whatsoever. I had an agreement with her that she should warn me if she made a mistake and we were about to face a row that I would need to handle. She provoked no such row and I was able to switch off entirely from the whole matter to concentrate on the political fight of my life.

My parliamentary private secretary in the House of Commons was Philip Oppenheim. This rather brought me up short, because I had entered Parliament with his mother Sally Oppenheim many years before. I realized I was beginning to age. Despite making me feel old, Philip proved a close friend and political confidant who helped me handle the huge amount of parliamentary turmoil that came with the brief.

It also became clear, as we began to prepare for the drafting of a parliamentary bill, that we would need a minister to defend us in the Lords and to argue our case with the peerage, who were being lobbied by all our opponents. Margaret was extremely keen to appoint the young Marquess of Douro to be my junior minister. I knew him to be an entertaining man and I had never fallen out with him, but I thought that his personal style, and the distinct disadvantage of his being a marquess and married to a Prussian princess, made him a totally unsuitable addition in this field of socialist prejudice. I had to have yet more furious rows with the prime minister about this until she reluctantly agreed to appoint Gloria Hooper, a lawyer, former Conservative MEP and since 1985 a life peer. Gloria proved a marvellous advocate for our proposals in the Upper House, where a subtle combination of charm and flattery is always required to get a bill past our ennobled colleagues.

The other relevant junior minister was Edwina Currie, who proved to be a dynamic and efficient parliamentary undersecretary while she lasted. Edwina also carried on a very high-profile public relations exercise of her own, and craved constant exposure in the media and to the outside world. Sadly, this eventually caused me to lose her, but she actually made an invaluable contribution until she fell from favour. Her successor, the lower-key but very capable Roger Freeman, ably handled the detailed debates in the Commons and the day-to-day work of the department.

To my great delight, we were all now housed in Richmond House, a newly refurbished historic building almost opposite Downing Street. It was Norman Fowler who had accidentally managed this escape from the Elephant and Castle. Richmond Terrace had stood derelict with its facade wrapped in plastic sheeting for a very long time, until the Cabinet Office got a major restoration project under way. At some stage, Margaret had noticed the work going on and had enquired what it was for. She had been assured that it was for the Cabinet Office to expand into, and for the Overseas Development Department of the Foreign Office. Margaret was flatly horrified to hear that the Cabinet Office had ambitions to expand and she saw no reason why officials responsible for overseas aid, with clients thousands of miles away, needed offices on the best site in Whitehall. She promptly banned the proposal, causing something of a crisis.

Norman heard of this deadlock and very ingeniously persuaded Margaret that the DHSS needed a base that was nearer to the rest of the government and handier for ministers to vote and participate in Parliament. He thus acquired a magnificent if somewhat tastelessly decorated and reorganized office block with a splendid historic facade.

I was the fortunate inheritor of this headquarters – although the political battle upon which I was now to embark would probably have been more suitably housed in a fortified military stronghold.

I caused a minor upset on moving into these elegant new quarters when I asked about the absence of ashtrays in the ministerial rooms. Shock and horror ran through the building – 'we are the Department of *Health*', etc. – but I insisted on being able to smoke my cigars throughout the many long meetings that were ahead of us. Work was not going to interfere with my personal pleasures. The person most delighted by the arrival of Britain's last ever smoking Health Secretary was Romola Christopherson, the press secretary. She was a veteran Civil Service press officer and the best with whom I ever worked, with a formidable reputation among her colleagues and the press lobby. I was always told, and always suspected, that she was very left wing. This did not affect our professional relations, nor our friendly rapport. Romola was a chain-smoker and happily puffed away alongside me. We were the last upholders of the principle that political controversy is best conducted and controlled in a smoke-filled room. My non-smoking colleagues and officials gave up their protests and endured it.

During the last few months of 1988, my small team of selected officials, my Private Office and my special advisers did a great deal of work to turn my broad ideas into a fully worked up – and practical – policy. Eventually, in January 1989, we were ready to outline our reform plan in detail and publish our White Paper.

Drawing on whizzy then-new video technology, I held a press conference in London which linked in all the chairmen of the regional health authorities and other professional leaders, who had gathered in locations all over the country to watch the presentation. Margaret was absolutely thrilled by this and she commended it to the rest of the Cabinet in a slightly embarrassing way at our next meeting. I sensed that she was naively assuming that we had solved the problem of selling my proposals to the nation. After Cabinet I therefore took her to one side and told her that this was in fact going to be the beginning of a titanic battle: political blood would flow in the gutters before we would be able to put our proposals into practice. At first, she was slightly incredulous, but I explained that it was as if we had taken out the British Medical Association's tablets of stone and smashed them on the pavement in front of their Tavistock House headquarters.

We did indeed face absolutely formidable and ferocious opposition as we tried to implement our reforms over the next two years. The only supportive medical body was the newly founded Royal College of GPs, headed by modern and reformist officers. The other royal colleges sat icily on the fence. The so-called Royal College of Nursing, which was actually a trade union, behaved reasonably despite being opposed to the changes. The BMA, which was also actually a trade union, though it didn't like the term, engaged in completely manic highly publicized opposition both to my proposals, and to me personally, for the remainder of my time in office. If truth be told, we were foes of old from my first stint at Health, and both eager to join battle again.

The whole fight was made worse by the unavoidable coincidence of the negotiation of a new contract for GPs. I had inherited from my predecessor John Moore a commitment to negotiate such a contract, but he had got no further than making the commitment. The negotiations themselves – and I have no idea what John had intended to achieve through them – had to be carried out by me. On the other side of the table, the BMA had dreams of a large increase in expenditure on general practice, directed at raising the pay of their members and meeting their long-standing ambition to relieve GPs of their contractual commitment to twenty-four-hour responsibility for their patients. I was determined to keep the costs of the new contract as near as possible to the existing planned total. I intended to concentrate on changes that would link rewards more closely to hard work and experience and give some incentives to those who introduced new services and hit high standards of performance.

The position of GPs within the service was in any event somewhat ambiguous. GPs had always been private-sector providers of services to the NHS with their costs reimbursed and their pay settled by contract. They bought drugs and equipment and the taxpayer paid for whatever they purchased. The predictable result was huge out-of-control expenditure. They also were each left largely to themselves to decide the pattern of practice they provided and the extent of the effort that they put into it.

Recklessly, I decided to overrule advice and to take the key part in conducting negotiations on the new contract myself. My confrontations between Michael Wilson, the chairman of their practitioners' committee, and myself became extremely combative. I had enjoyed negotiating as a lawyer and I was heavily influenced by my recollection of official attitudes to dealings with the BMA, which were largely that this was a group that had to be appeased, and the case then had to be made to the Treasury for meeting any costs. This was very far from my approach. I was deliberately belligerent at times and one of my techniques was to pretend to lose my temper at key points in what were inevitably long and acrimonious sessions.

At a key moment, I negotiated through the night, with myself and one or two officials on one side of the table and the BMA GP negotiating committee on the other. Finally we agreed on a settlement that the service could afford. We shook hands and the committee left. A few moments later an ashen-faced press officer came back to tell me that what they were saying to the waiting journalists bore no relation to what they had just agreed with me. The negotiating committee was insisting on going to a ballot of all their membership despite the fact that they had just shaken hands. One of the most difficult concessions that I had wrung from them had been an agreement that they would publicly commend the settlement to their members: a ballot would simply become an enquiry to the GPs as to whether they wished to vote for more money. I insisted on sticking to our bargain.

It is worth noting that I never had difficulties as bad as this in my negotiations with the National Union of Public Employees, the Confederation of Health Service Employees, or any of the traditional trade unions. When I shook hands with the traditional left-wing union officials they would always go out and tell their membership that they had settled and order an end to the dispute.

Carelessly I added to our difficulties in the presentation of the new contract, linked to work and performance, by making a silly joke in an after-dinner speech. At the Royal College dinner, trying to make a witty remark that would encourage GPs to desist from linking every change to the question of pay, I said that 'I do wish that the most suspicious of our GPs would stop feeling nervously for their wallets every time that I mention the word "reform".' This was reported to the world in a variety of forms, including that I had said that doctors were falling off their loaded wallets and so on. This was far from the only time in my career when a weak piece of black humour got me into quite unnecessary trouble, when I was already up to my neck in controversy.

It would be tedious to set out the blow-by-blow detail of the press and television interviews, the exchanges and the media reports that dominated the headlines from then on. Suffice to say that the BMA succeeded in scaring and confusing people – including elderly and vulnerable patients – with insinuations and untruths. One of the BMA's final moves was to launch a nationwide poster campaign with the theme that the NHS was 'underfunded, undermined and under threat'. One poster showed a driverless steamroller with the caption 'Mrs Thatcher's plans for the NHS'. Another carried a caption which read 'What do you call a man who ignores medical advice? Mr Clarke.'

Opinion polls confirmed that my proposals were both misunderstood and deeply unpopular with the general public throughout the whole debate. This was, in my experience, true of just about every policy that the Thatcher government ever had – but in those days we argued our case, pushed on, and ignored the opinion polls until general elections drew near. One of the joys of serving under Margaret Thatcher was that she never read newspapers (her bullish press secretary Bernard Ingham gave her a carefully selected digest each day, leaving out most of the unfriendly bits) and ignored opinion polls. Arguments between Margaret and a colleague, however ferocious, turned on whether a proposal was in the public interest, and whether it would serve the national good. This was rightly called 'conviction politics' and at least I was a politician with some convictions, even if they did not always coincide exactly with hers. This is alas a sad contrast with the conduct of business in the twenty-first century.

I actually rather enjoyed the whole controversy while it lasted. My even temperament has always served me well at such times, although I now realize that my personality is rather different from others'. Compared with most politicians, I must seem so far laid-back as to be horizontal. But I had come into politics to try to change things for the better and the arguments got the adrenaline flowing and sustained my enthusiasm. The BMA had always personally vilified the minister involved in any changes – it was their traditional tactic. Lloyd George had been excoriated for introducing 'panel doctors'. As I have already related, Nye Bevan had been denounced as a 'medical Führer' for creating the NHS. Barbara Castle was reduced to tears. I reflected that some of them had survived politically.

Sadly, Gillian found it harder to bear and always suffered a lot at times when I was under fire. And our daughter Susan was then a student nurse, which could have made her life very difficult. Thankfully, her hospital helped her to try to keep the press away.

In May 1989, there was a parliamentary by-election in the Vale of Glamorgan in South Wales. It had been a Conservative seat held with a small majority by the popular previous incumbent, Raymond Gower, who had sadly died. It now became the focus of political opposition to the reforms. The Labour Party and the local doctors fought the whole campaign on the subject. Their literature and their speeches emphasized, quite untruthfully, that patients would be obliged to pay a fee in order to see their GP if my reforms went ahead. We lost the by-election to the Labour Party's John Smith (not the subsequent leader), who won with a 14 per cent swing.

The most bizarre incident was when the left-wing *Daily Mirror* ran a front-page story saying that my reforms would cause GPs to strike elderly patients off their lists in order to improve their performance statistics. I publicly refuted this claim immediately, describing it as both completely irrational and completely wrong. The newspaper was then owned by the colourful multimillionaire Robert Maxwell, who had been a Labour MP and was now such a major donor to the Labour Party that he practically owned that too. I had got to know him quite well over the years and had always found him a most engaging rogue with whom I had been on perfectly pleasant personal terms. It seemed to me that he was quite obviously a crook, but he was never prosecuted. In those days the prosecuting authorities were not up to taking on a very wealthy prominent public figure, however notorious he might be.

Following my angry denunciation of his newspaper's story, I was faced with the extraordinary threat that the Mirror newspaper group would sue me for defamation. Robert was used to silencing his critics through intimidatory writs of this kind. I soon received a telephone call from him. In a grim, but false-friendly tone, Robert explained to me that I had traduced the reputation of the award-winning journalist who had written the story and that he felt that he would be obliged to protect her reputation and that of his newspaper by suing me. At one point he pointed out to me the financial risks involved in litigation of this kind. 'The costs involved would be of little consequence to me, my dear boy, but you would be betting the ranch.' He kindly offered to drop the litigation as long as I published a full and abject apology. Rashly, and feeling a certain amount of alarm, I robustly refused to do so and repeated my assertion that it was nonsense to claim that the elderly were about to lose access to general practice medicine. I never heard anything more about the threatened litigation apart from the reports of its impending commencement which appeared for a day or two in the press.

Later, after Robert Maxwell's mysterious death falling off the back of his yacht at a time when he was facing imminent scandal, it emerged that he had left over 150 writs for defamation outstanding because he had never pressed any of them to a court hearing. They were simply the way in which he had been accustomed to defend his reputation against quite regular insinuations of dishonesty appearing in the media.

Labour's Robin Cook led the official political opposition. He was the most redoubtable and aggressive Shadow spokesman that I ever faced, and the only one during my ministerial career with whom I was quite unable to establish any friendly personal relationship. He was a Rottweiler of a debater and we fought many stormy battles. (Ironically, he eventually became something of a friend in later years when amongst other things I strongly supported him in his principled stand against Tony Blair's invasion of Iraq.)

Robin's arguments were initially based on the usual assertion that the government was hell-bent on 'privatizing' the NHS. This was a claim that had first been levied against Keith Joseph almost ten years earlier and was an assertion that the Labour Party has continued to make hysterically against every one of my Conservative successors – as well as some of their own ministers – thereafter. As I have already described, I did in fact begin the process of outsourcing some services to private contractors when I was Minister of State. These reforms would certainly, I hoped, enable the principle of outsourcing to be developed further, but I was still passionately committed to the founding principles of the NHS. It is worth noting that the practice of outsourcing services was only taken forward on any significant scale some years later by Blair's Labour government.

Another frequent allegation made by Robin Cook – and most of my medical and journalistic critics – was that we were introducing the American system of financing health care into the United Kingdom. This well-worn assertion bore no relationship whatever to what I was actually proposing, and I found it rather ironic given that I had put up such fierce resistance to the idea to my prime minister, who had indeed been attracted to moving to the American model when she had first appointed me.

Yet another major and rather bizarre argument was about the principle of 'medical audit' which I had put into my reforms. This was denounced as political interference with the clinical independence of professional people – a dictatorial threat to medical freedoms. Nowadays, I never meet any clinician who does not regard clinical audit as a routine and essential process of monitoring performance and outputs.

One of the key things that I built into the reforms was a proposed system of implementation that would win the more reform-minded practising clinicians to my side and persuade the more enlightened to seek the intended benefits and take ownership of the reforms.

We recommended that in the reformed structure of the NHS, each hospital's management would be able to choose to move to the status of a 'self-governing hospital' outside the control of the local health authority. Self-governing hospitals would then be providers who would bid for contracts from purchasers and seek to deliver their services. They would of course wish to compete on the basis of the quality of their services and not just on the price, since this would be the basis on which purchasers would be awarding their contracts.

My team debated at length the name we should give to these self-governing organizations. I think I personally proposed the title NHS Trusts. This was rather meaningless as there were to be no trustees of these bodies, nor any trust deeds. It was, however, a reassuring-sounding brand name, and a very satisfactory number of the more go-ahead hospitals did eventually opt for this NHS Trust status which in the end became universal.

I also proposed, for the same reason, the idea that GP practices could opt to become GP fund-holding practices, that is, they could become purchasers in their own right of services for all their patients. They would of course have to be given a strict budget within which they would be expected to stay when placing their contracts. I rather unsubtly proposed that if they underspent, they would be allowed to keep the savings themselves. Again, this eventually became one of my most successful innovations as all the better GP practices steadily began to opt for fund-holding status. My own constituency had acquired a very good set of general practitioners because of its attractive rural and suburban nature. I think that all but one of the practices in Rushcliffe constituency eventually took on the fund-holding role.

The result, as my successors discovered, was that the hospitals and GP practices that volunteered to become trusts and fund-holding practices sought to run them in the most successful way possible. They had a definite stake in demonstrating the success of the change that they had volunteered to take on themselves.

This approach proved a very successful alternative to the BMA's fall-back position. When it became obvious that I was going to push ahead, they had urged that my proposals should be introduced on a trial basis in a small select area of the country to be agreed with them. Undoubtedly, had I accepted this enticing compromise, the BMA would have found an area where the doctors could be relied upon to make the whole trial an abysmal failure. I was certain that this was their motive.

An additional blazing controversy erupted in the middle of my programme of NHS reform when in the summer of 1989 I found myself dealing with a nationwide ambulance strike. The trade unions representing non-clinical employees had all submitted an enormous 14 per cent pay claim for an increase well above the rate of inflation. I had known that there was trouble brewing when the Cabinet had approved, despite my vigorous protests, a very generous settlement for the London Underground drivers a few months before. The drivers in the London ambulance service then tended to move backwards and forwards between being Tube drivers and ambulance drivers according to the terms and conditions of each service at any given time.

When the time came for the health pay claims to be pressed the ambulance men held one of the first ballots. Rather to the union leaders' surprise they voted for a strike in support of an 11 per cent pay claim (against inflation rates of under 5 per cent in 1988 and under 8 per cent in 1989), which soon went ahead.

I knew that my health-authority budgets could not possibly afford such an enormous claim. I was also certain that any award won by the ambulance men would create an expectation of similar pay increases for all the other so-called ancillary workers in the health service, which would have produced an enormous, and quite un-affordable, pay bill. I therefore determinedly rejected the claim and found myself having to fight the strike. This soon became the most passionate political battle, knocking even my health reforms out of the headlines while it lasted, and I followed my usual practice of constant public appearances to argue my case.

The intensity of the strike itself varied across the country according to the militancy of the local branches. London, Liverpool and parts of the North-West of England were as usual the centres of adamant militant industrial action. Huge picket lines formed at most ambulance stations in these areas, which were also occupied by many members of staff. They posed for photographs, suggesting to journalists that they were eager to be at work were it not for my obstinacy. In fact, they were occupying the ambulance stations in order to make sure that we could not use our own ambulances.

The unions had promised that they would maintain an emergency service so that no lives would be put at risk. After many weeks of the strike the newspaper coverage began to grow a little less friendly to the strikers when an enterprising journalist discovered that the most militant of the stations were not even honouring this promise. The first dent in public support for the strike occurred when someone discovered that an ambulance station had decided not to respond to a serious shooting incident in London on the bizarre grounds that they were not satisfied from the incoming phone call that this was an emergency.

I was obliged to get the government to make army ambulances available for emergencies. There was some initial resistance from the top brass. At one point, Tom King, Secretary of State for Defence, Lord Ferrers (six feet seven), who was then a Home Office minister, and another very tall man in uniform marched themselves down Whitehall from the MOD to put me right. Having startled my staff as they strode three abreast down the corridor, they arrived in my office and announced in stentorian tones that I was not going to be allowed to use 'our boys' to sort out my dispute. They were all far too busy. Fortunately, they were persuaded to change their minds and the army, as one might expect, responded extremely well. At one point I was assured that the army ambulance staff were rather enjoying the process, because at last they were receiving training with real casualties. They regarded this as a great improvement on their prac-tice drills which involved volunteers playing the role of the injured with tomato sauce daubed upon them, instead of blood and gore. In my office in Richmond Terrace we got into the habit of going to the window whenever we heard a siren on the street below to see whether the ambulance was 'one of ours' or not.

Somehow the National Union of Public Employees managed to lock away their sternly militant leader, Rodney Bickerstaffe – with whom I was actually on very friendly terms – for the duration of the dispute. Instead, the union official who most often represented the senior ambulance drivers in public was Roger Poole. This was a smart move. Roger Poole was a charming man with a delightful West Country accent, who always made out that all his members wanted was to get back to the negotiating table. 'Come on, Ken, why don't we just get together, sit down and sort this out,' was his beguiling plea. In practice all our regular contact with the union leadership made it clear that the only thing they would accept at any negotiating table was full settlement of their original claim.

As the bitter dispute dragged on for weeks and weeks, Margaret became a little concerned about its dramatically high profile. I was only too aware myself of being the most unpopular member of the Thatcher government, and by extension the most unpopular man in the country. I had started having to detach myself from my family when we went out and about together, so that they didn't have to take the brunt of the abuse that members of the public would occasionally hurl at me.

At one point, my old friend Ken Baker approached me, saying that Margaret had asked him to see if he could offer me any helpful advice. We had a rather frostier conversation than usual because, as I explained to him, the only advice that he appeared to be offering was that I should follow the course that he had taken a few months before in settling a teachers' strike at the Department of Education. As far as I could see, this so-called settlement had been arrived at by Ken cheerily offering to give the teachers the pay increase they were demanding in full.

I decided to take a different approach to resolving the strike. I widened the issue from being simply about pay, introducing an element of reform and improvement of the service to the public. The line that I now adopted in my negotiation was that I would pay a higher settlement to those drivers who would agree to be trained as medical ancillaries. At that time, none of the drivers had paramedical training and some of them barely had training in first aid. The union resolutely resisted my offer on demarcation grounds, asserting that it was not part of a driver's job to provide care or treatment for any sick or injured people they picked up.

When I was explaining my stance, making the point that ambulance drivers regularly moved backwards and forwards to jobs driving lorries or Underground trains, a journalist alleged that I had dismissed the ambulance men as 'mere drivers'. The 'mere' was the journalist's own addition, of course, but the furore that was whipped up around my apparent sneering dismissal of these caring health workers caused a particularly bad few days of publicity.

The strike lasted for six months, until the unions finally realized that I was not going to give in. Many of the strikers had become financially hard-pressed because the unions could not afford to maintain full strike pay and the Thatcher government had abolished the old practice of paying unemployment benefit to workers on strike. I considered this a good thing. By this time the iron had entered my soul in relation to strikes. I had decided that the only way to protect the country from constant industrial action was to leave strikers feeling that it had not been worth it. The traditional approach of ensuring strikers went back to work cheerful and content simply encouraged any rational person to strike again the following year. In the run-up to the Winter of Discontent, a person would have been an idiot not to vote to strike, because it always led to more money. With considerable reluctance on the unions' part, the whole ambulance dispute was eventually settled in February 1990 with a more reasonable 9 per cent increase, with additional pay for those who successfully retrained as paramedics, so that, where possible, they could stabilize the patients and reduce the risks before transporting them to the hospital.

I could now turn my wholehearted attention back to the wider NHS reforms. Or so I thought. Just as the legislation needed to implement my reforms was completing its passage through Parliament in June 1990, Margaret Thatcher suddenly got it into her head that she wanted to postpone implementation until after the next general election – which was likely to be in 1992. I discovered that she had come up with this idea during a conversation with Charlie Haughey, the then prime minister of the Republic of Ireland, and an old scoundrel. He had apparently persuaded her that it was impossible to win a democratic election campaign if the government upset the doctors. She imparted this advice to me and yet another stand-off ensued.

Eventually a meeting was arranged between the prime minister and me. Again we were to be ranged round the Cabinet table, but this time she was to be accompanied by about half a dozen of her most valued senior businessmen who advised her from time to time on policy. The leading figure amongst them was a man called David Wolfson whom she particularly trusted. She hoped that they would persuade me, from their experience, of the folly of proceeding with these changes in the face of such hostility.

I attended with four or five members of my own little group. I decided that the atmosphere would be improved if experts on the NHS such as Duncan Nichol and Sheila Masters explained to the assembled businessmen what the whole thing was actually about.

Unfortunately, this tactic did not completely succeed. My little team of experts were of course somewhat overawed by a meeting at the Cabinet table facing the redoubtable Mrs Thatcher. They gave a rather feeble and tongue-tied presentation of what we were doing which was neither very confident nor persuasive in its form. On the other side of the table, Margaret's businessmen seemed equally uncomfortable. Most of them knew nothing at all about the management of a health-care business and they were most reluctant to intervene in any discussion. I suspect that several of them privately agreed with me, and had been bullied by Margaret into attending. Inevitably, the meeting soon reverted to the old gladiatorial slanging match between Margaret Thatcher and me, this time with an embarrassed audience.

I am not at all sure that I persuaded her on this occasion. It did, however, become quite clear to Margaret that I was not going to give way and she probably guessed that she would be faced with my resignation if she persisted in ordering the postponement of the reforms. I was convinced that we had to fight the next election with the reforms already in place, so that the absurdity of allegations about fees for visiting a GP, and other such claims, would be only too clear. If we postponed them, our critics would be free to make the wildest allegations about the threats that the reforms would pose, and they would never be implemented even if we survived the campaign. Reluctantly, she allowed the reform process to continue.

The next general election actually took place in 1992 after I had moved to the Department of Education and Margaret had left office. The Labour Party did indeed try to use the NHS as one of the principal campaigning issues. But the usually formidable Robin Cook completely blew it in the first days of the campaign. He lit upon a supposed example of a young girl in Kent who had been refused treatment for glue ear because of my NHS reforms. However, her mother immediately appeared in public to refute the accuracy of the account that Labour had given, via the girl's father. The whole thing foundered in an absurd public battle about exactly what had or had not happened in the case of 'Jennifer's Ear', and the NHS reforms vanished from the media and from the election debate for the remainder of the campaign, which John Major succeeded in winning on totally different issues.

To complete the story of NHS reforms, when Tony Blair eventually took office in 1997 he had no particular policy on the NHS at all. He seemed to imagine that the NHS would thrive simply because there was now a Labour government. He decided that Health Secretary was a suitable post in which to install a left-winger and appointed the amiable Frank Dobson. Frank did indeed try to reverse the reforms we had implemented, but he was stoutly resisted by a lot of the medical profession, including many otherwise left-wing practitioners, who were now persuaded that the purchaser–provider divide was working well. Indeed, I was told that some leading Labour activists in the medical world had tried to persuade Tony before the election to drop his commitment to repeal the changes.

Frank did very little damage in his time in charge of health care, except that he unfortunately abolished GP fund-holding which was beginning to work extremely well. The principle of the purchaser–provider split remained, however, with the quality of the commissioning and purchasing decisions the principal problem area in successful implementation. Frank was removed after a little over two years and persuaded to fight an unsuccessful campaign against Ken Livingstone to become mayor of London. Thereafter Tony Blair appointed

Secretaries of State who implemented and refined my reforms with considerable zeal. I greatly admired Alan Milburn in particular, who used to make speeches about his proposed reforms which, I liked to tease him, were identical to the speeches that I used to make. I was also able to tell him privately that he had gone much further in implementing the reforms and introducing private-sector participation than I could ever have done as a Conservative minister.

Health care continues to be the most bitter and controversial policy area in Britain, as in every other democracy in the Western world. The subject is emotional, full of competing interest groups, and of huge public importance. Obamacare has dominated an American presidency. In the Cameron government, first Andrew Lansley and then Jeremy Hunt faced the full force of the BMA's venom. It will probably always be thus.

Ironically, as is usual in the world of politics, the inevitable process of ministerial changes and reshuffles meant that none of my original team of ministers stayed in office long enough to take part in the actual implementation of our reforms.

Firstly, Edwina Currie's insatiable and normally effective desire for publicity embroiled her in a scandal and led to her fall from office even before we had published our White Paper. Edwina was a very prominent public figure, with an amazing ability to capture headlines on all kinds of subjects including her own ministerial field of public health and health education. One weekend in December 1988, she went too far. She summoned the entire press corps to Derby for an announcement on her 'Keep Warm, Keep Well' campaign, where she and her husband were engaged in some sort of DIY activity, possibly insulating a wall. When they arrived she suddenly changed the subject, and memorably and spectacularly declared that most British eggs were infected with salmonella. This caused a ferocious controversy between Edwina, on the one hand, and the agricultural and farming lobby on the other. The cause of British farming was enthusiastically taken up by several of our nastier backbenchers who hated Edwina Currie for her assertive feminism and who even, in one or two cases, added a tinge of anti-Semitism in for good measure.

Neither Margaret nor I wished to lose Edwina Currie and I had several conversations with the prime minister about how to save her. At one point John Wakeham, then Leader of the House of Commons, joined me in trying to persuade Edwina to modify her original statement. It was simply inaccurate to claim that the majority of British eggs had salmonella because the true figure was nearer to 40 per cent. Unfortunately we completely failed to move Edwina with our suggestion that she should correct her statement to say that 'too many' British eggs were infected with salmonella rather than 'most', and to substitute, in a mildly apologetic way, the true figure for her original claim. This could have been combined with some advice that eggs should preferably be hard-boiled or handled with care. Edwina most resolutely adopted the old line that politicians should never apologize and never explain, and stuck to her guns. She became particularly indignant when I instructed her to stop giving any more interviews on the subject. This was well-intentioned advice because with each repetition of her remark she was digging deeper into the hole in which she found herself.

Margaret resisted the demands for her dismissal for two weeks. Eventually she decided that she could not face the 1922 Committee with Edwina in post. Very foolishly, I allowed myself to be persuaded by the prime minister to give Edwina the news that Margaret wanted her to resign. Edwina was, not surprisingly, shattered by this news and resigned with the greatest reluctance. Unfortunately, for many years thereafter she believed that I had contributed to her dismissal. I am glad to say that our mutual friends eventually managed to convince her that I had in fact made considerable efforts to save her political career and that I had worked with Margaret Thatcher for as long as the prime minister was able to withstand the storm to keep Edwina in the job which she had been doing very well.

The next blow came in October 1989 in the middle of the ambulance drivers' strike when Margaret Thatcher decided that she had to move David Mellor away from Health because she needed him to take responsibility for broadcasting, culture and the arts in the Home Office. David was indeed the minister with the most expertise on this subject in the whole government. She called me early one morning at my flat to give me this news. I was outraged and indignant because

David had been a very good friend and partner in office and he was also invaluable in defending our reforms as robustly as I did. My powers of argument during that telephone conversation were somewhat inhibited by the fact that I had jumped out of the bath to answer the telephone. I did not feel my usual confident self as I stood there naked and dripping wet. I lost the argument, Margaret slammed down the phone and David was fortunately eventually replaced by another excellent junior minister, Stephen Dorrell, who had an equally well-informed, but somewhat quieter, approach to political discussion.

The final blow came in November 1990 when Margaret eventually reshuffled me away from the Department of Health myself. This came a few days after the resignation of Geoffrey Howe, which triggered Margaret's eventual fall from office a few weeks later. During this interval she had to make some consequential changes, which also involved me.

I protested vigorously against my proposed move. I argued that having gone through the political fire to produce these reforms, I should be allowed to be there on the day when we 'pressed the button' so that I could oversee the unfolding of the whole new revolution. I told her that if the thing went pear-shaped, she could dismiss me. She assured me that she would indeed dismiss me in that eventuality. But she still insisted that I now move to become Secretary of State for Education.

In desperation, I asked her who was to be the new Health Secretary. She told me that it would be William Waldegrave. Joyfully, I pointed out that no one was more suitable to become Education Secretary. Firstly he was an outstanding intellect and political figure and his arrival in the Cabinet was much overdue. He was also such an educated and erudite man that the world of education was entirely suited to him. 'My dear boy,' she said, 'I could not appoint an Etonian to be Secretary of State for Education!' This killer argument reduced me to silence and ended my time presiding over the reform of the health service. 'Prime Minister,' I conceded, 'you leave me a very amazed man.'

I later discovered that Margaret had told William several times after his appointment that she would not object if, upon reflection, he decided to drop my health reforms altogether. Margaret Thatcher was a brilliant politician, but she was also rather a popular pragmatist. She was never the ideological 'Thatcherite' as advertised. Fortunately, William was as radical a reformer as I was and he began to implement my reforms rather skilfully.

It remains my opinion that the reforms I introduced into the NHS were a turning point in the successful operation of our health-care system. Of course, the actual design of the changes was riddled with problems because we had had to introduce it all in such a hurry and implement it all so quickly, because of the constraints of the electoral timetable and my determination to have it in place before polling day arrived. All kinds of refinements and improvements have been made by my successors, but the essentials of the purchaser–provider divide and the use of competition and choice to drive up standards have remained. The policy was driven forward determinedly by every one of Tony Blair's Health Secretaries after Frank Dobson's removal, and further reforms by Andrew Lansley were an attempt to bring back the GP participation that I had always intended in the purchasing and commissioning part of the process.

I am also convinced that the old centralized bureaucratic NHS would not have survived if we had not introduced a more business-like, accountable and competitive approach to the service based above all else on outcomes for patients and on responding to changing patients' needs. My spells first as Minister of State and then as Secretary of State in the Department of Health were the most exciting and controversial of my political life. And the reforms that I pushed through were amongst the most important that I was ever involved in.

Looking back, I do still wonder how I managed to keep sane and happy throughout tumultuous times such as these years in the Health Department. Obviously, I regularly escaped to cricket matches at Trent Bridge or the Oval, football matches at Nottingham Forest or Notts County, and to jazz clubs or concerts of various kinds. Overwhelmingly, however, I think it was the fact that I continued to have such a happy family life with Gillian and the children to fall back on. Of course, they did lead lives of their own as well. Gillian became a very enthusiastic and expert maker of patchwork quilts. She had begun by making traditional quilts as bedcovers for all the family's beds and for friends, and then moved on to make ever more advanced and elaborate wall hangings of various kinds. These were all hand-stitched, and involved hours of meticulous needlework. She reached her pinnacle in 1988, when at a prestigious exhibition she was awarded a national championship known as the crystal vase. My son Ken pursued his career as an information technology expert with one of the major banks, and Sue greatly enjoyed her nursing career which eventually evolved into nursing management. By this time, they were both married.

Only once did political controversy intrude on one of our sacrosanct August family escapes. This was shortly after I had been appointed Secretary of State for Health and we were holidaying in Galicia, in north-west Spain. In between birdwatching and tourism, I sat on a headland on the coast near the little village of Sanjenjo, writing down my great thoughts on GP fund-holding and other future health reforms. In my absence, the acting leaders of the Royal College of Nursing decided to demand a meeting with me to discuss some undefined problem of nurse employment. I refused to return home on their command, not least because I knew that the general secretary of the union was himself away on a long holiday in Asia. There was also no particular issue upon which I needed to have any discussions with the RCN.

The nursing leaders won a splendid amount of front-page publicity during the press 'silly season' by insisting that I was the 'missing minister' who should be searched for and returned. At one point they staged an appearance at a London airport carrying 'wanted man' posters and asking holidaymakers to join in the search.

We were as usual holidaying somewhere where we could not be telephoned. (On the odd occasions when we holidayed somewhere that I could not credibly claim had no telephone, I would deliberately leave my Private Office with a plausibly inaccurate number on which to contact me.) Brilliantly but unfortunately, my Private Office on this occasion discovered the telephone number of a local peasant woman who lived in a cottage near to ours. Most evenings she would walk over to our house to say that '*La señora Flora ha llamado*' ('Mrs Flora has called'). This would cause me to walk back to my neighbour's cottage with her to telephone la señora Flora (Flora Goldhill in my Private Office) and resist her attempts to persuade me to return.

(One of the small but important reforms that I found time to get through Parliament whilst I was Secretary of State was the creation of the Human Fertility and Embryology Authority (HFEA). This body was designed to remove from dreadful uninformed parliamentary and political debate the difficult ethical questions that arise in the fields of fertilization, abortion and embryology research. I helped to ensure that 'la señora Flora' was appointed as the first chief executive of the HFEA, which she managed very successfully. Years later I joined in a political alliance with Frank Dobbs to rescue it from the quango cull launched by the Cameron government in its first year. It had initially been tabled for abolition simply to make up the numbers of quangos disposed of.)

Towards the end of the holiday I was discovered by a *Daily Mail* reporter. The *Daily Mail* had been interviewing all my friends and relatives at home and had acquired one of Gillian's postcards, with the postmark Sanjenjo. The reporter agreed to leave me alone if I would pose for a photograph with him as evidence of his triumph. He wanted the photograph in a bar or on the beach but I hated beaches and I did not want a photograph above a story describing me boozing in the bars of Spain whilst starving nurses awaited my return. I did eventually go back a few days early, leaving the department to arrange for my car to be driven back for me to London (Gillian never learnt to drive). Gillian and the family still managed to enjoy the holiday and remained reasonably resilient to yet another wild controversy erupting around me at home which I presume they tried to shut out of their minds.

Their acceptance of the bizarre political controversies that formed the background of our lives and the support that my family gave me was the bedrock upon which my political career was always founded.

13

'Wham Bam Thank You Ma'am'

(Charles Mingus, 1962)

THE THATCHER EXPERIENCE

With all respect to the other leaders and friends under whom I served, Margaret Thatcher was the best prime minister I ever worked with. Her government achieved more, and made a bigger difference to the state of the country, than any other post-war government, with the possible exception of Clement Attlee's. Margaret took office at a time when the country was in a state of economic collapse and social crisis, and suffering a tremendous loss of national self-confidence. She led her government to create an entrepreneurial market-based economy that could be both competitive and successful. She restored our influence in the wider world, and our ability to affect events and protect our interests. The policies she pursued were already privately supported by many other Conservatives, but before she took office had been regarded as politically impossible in the face of public opinion. I always said that she gave us, her colleagues, the courage of our convictions, and she enabled us to apply them as never before.

Almost every policy our government came up with was unpopular with the public when we first proposed it, and we were always languishing in the opinion polls except in the run-up to the general elections. Margaret affected to ignore public opinion. It was conviction politics that we were practising: every minister decided on the right thing to do and then argued their case. In the 1990s Tony Blair was to introduce the very different style of populist politics which we still practise today.

Despite Margaret's determination to dominate every political conversation, and contrary to the widespread view being encouraged by the popular TV satire *Spitting Image*, she ran a collective government. Cabinet meetings took a whole morning every Thursday and Cabinet Committees were allowed to operate effective collective decision-making in every field. Although Margaret would speak for at least half of any Cabinet meeting and was a poor chairman on that account, she did let other ministers express their views and could be prevailed upon to change her mind or even, occasionally, be overruled.

Margaret's aggressive style of man-management was less commendable. My own relationship with her can only be described as robust, but it was not only me. She constantly argued with her colleagues, sometimes being unpleasant and even rude. She enjoyed passionate political argument, however, and never bore malice so long as her interlocutor did not take offence. I always said that serving in her government was great fun as long as you were able to stand the hassle. And she could be very winning.

I was a junior minister in the Department of Health at the time of the Falklands War in 1982. Margaret had put a fleet to sea in response to Argentina's invasion and occupation of the islands. The campaign became politically very controversial once Michael Foot changed his initial pro-war position and became ever more vehemently opposed.

At one point Margaret accepted advice that she should have a meeting with a small group of Ministers of State in order to make us feel included, at this time of national crisis, and to give us more up-to-date information on the campaign. Most of those present, standing in a large semicircle around our leader, were typically deferential and fairly silent. Tim Raison, who was then a junior Home Office minister, and I were the only two who expressed our doubts about the whole invasion plan. I said that I understood the legitimacy of the use of force to react to an armed invasion of our territory. However, weren't we taking a terrible risk because it only needed one submarine to sink our aircraft carrier and then all would be lost? (I did know from insider gossip that the Argentinians had several German-built submarines and we had no idea where they were.) She strode over to me and jabbed me firmly in the chest, saying, 'Politics is about taking risks, my dear boy.' Patronizing perhaps, but I was entirely won over.

Only once or twice did Margaret reveal to me a rare insight into her softer skills. I was taking part in a meeting with her and several others. I was arguing a case, but, unusually for me, I began to feel rather fed up and no doubt was looking forlorn. I was quietly thinking to myself that there were many easier ways to make a living. Margaret suddenly paused and leant towards me as I was sitting in an armchair in her small room. She tapped me on the knee and said very quietly, 'I am sorry to have to talk to you like this, Kenneth, but it is my job, you know,' reinforcing my loyalty for weeks to come. She always called me Kenneth, never Ken – unless I had annoyed her, in which case she would revert to the rather patronizing 'my dear boy'.

Gillian was granted no such insight. Margaret always gave every appearance of viewing her, and the wives of her other Cabinet ministers, as irritating inconveniences. Greeting us as we entered a drinks party, for example, Margaret would chat to me quite happily. With an 'Ah, hello my dear' she would then turn to Gillian, seize her hand and pull it past her, propelling Gillian onwards and into the room. There was no attempt to engage or get to know her.

Margaret's vital partner in implementing all our policies through constant political battles on many fronts was her deputy, William Whitelaw. Willie was a most tremendously loyal man. He was very much a One Nation Conservative by instinct and he was a much more liberal politician than Margaret in many of his personal convictions. Unlike all the other senior 'wets' in her Cabinet, however, he doggedly gave her his wholehearted support and endeavoured to influence others to stick with her. Willie was a bluff and straightforward traditional country squire Tory from the Borders. He was not intellectually brilliant, but nor was he stupid – and he had a tremendous amount of common sense and cunning.

I saw his style at closest range shortly after entering the Cabinet when I became a member of the Star Chamber, as we called the

Cabinet Committee set up to resolve differences between spending ministers and the Treasury in each year's public spending round. The dissenting Cabinet minister would be summoned to appear before this committee, chaired by Willie Whitelaw, where he would be questioned alongside a Treasury minister. I had obviously been recruited because I had previously practised as a barrister. My task was to study the brief carefully and then to soften up the departmental minister by cross-examining him, which I would do from the position of someone who agreed with the Treasury instincts of tight control on public spending. Willie would chair the Star Chamber meetings benignly, but he had a set of brilliant techniques for handling dissenters.

Willie would take the recalcitrant colleague to one side for a private conversation at a suitable moment. With the slightly weaker ones, he would pretend to lose his temper, which was one of his favourite tricks, and he would denounce them for displaying a lack of team spirit and co-operation on a scale that – he would declare – he had never seen before in his career. His victims would recoil before this completely feigned rage and he would get his way.

With more robust colleagues, he adopted the arm-around-the-shoulder approach and deployed the best of his considerable charm. He would express complete understanding of the departmental problems and assert how much he would love to help if he possibly could. He would beseech the colleague to move a little as a personal favour to help him out of his difficult position. By this means, he could cunningly cajole hapless ministers who arrived each year determined to get what they believed to be necessary for their department, to back down.

Willie must have used all these techniques and many more on Margaret herself. She in turn must have realized how affected were Willie's occasional protestations that he was only a simple man and could not be expected to understand all the complexities of the clever arguments being bandied about. She was, however, clever enough herself to accept that his advice was not only extremely wise but was also coming from a genuine supporter and friend who knew how to help her out of a serious difficulty. Willie was the only member of the Cabinet who could almost always talk her out of even her most determined and impetuous positions. Thatcher was cognizant of her debt to him when she infamously said, with accidental wit, 'Every prime minister needs a Willie.'

The miners' strike of 1984–5 lasted an entire year and was the bitterest industrial dispute in Britain's history. It was also the biggest social crisis of my political lifetime. It generated many of the myths about Margaret's supposed ideological approach to politics and it dominated her second term in office, as Arthur Scargill, the firebrand president of the National Union of Mineworkers, used violent and militant campaigning to try to bring down the elected government as he had done a decade earlier when Ted Heath was in office. Scargill was pursuing the claim that no pit should be closed on economic grounds. All pits should remain open until the last seam was exhausted, no matter how expensive they were to mine. Even Communist Poland could never have accepted these absurd demands.

By the 1980s the coal mines in the United Kingdom were hopelessly redundant and uneconomic, and the continued scale of production and subsidy was causing high energy costs and great damage to the economy. It was also a desperately old-fashioned industry as coal could not be safely or economically extracted from the deep mineshafts that were necessary in Britain. This state of affairs had been recognized long before Margaret Thatcher came to power. The majority of our coal mines had been closed years earlier, mostly when the admirable Alf Robens, a former Labour Cabinet minister, had been chairman of the National Coal Board under Harold Macmillan, Alec Douglas-Home and Harold Wilson. Margaret was merely presiding over the latter stages of the process.

Parts of Nottinghamshire were very tense during the months of the strike. Miners there refused to strike and continued to work because Scargill had ignored the union's constitution and called a strike without first balloting the membership. The old animosity and rivalry between the miners of Yorkshire and Nottinghamshire, which dated back to the days of the breakaway Spencer Union before the Second World War, was revived as huge numbers of violent pickets and policemen from other counties moved into the area. (In 1985 the Nottinghamshire miners broke away from the NUM again and formed their own new Union of Democratic Mineworkers.) I had every sympathy with the miners of Nottinghamshire, having seen at first-hand during my childhood, and in the industrial-accident cases that I took on as a barrister in Birmingham, what mining was really like for its workforce. It was a dreadful job. I did not share the sentimental view of coal mining that was so prevalent in the Home Counties and among the chattering classes of North London.

North Nottinghamshire was particularly tense as I saw for myself when I drove over to do a speaking engagement in Mansfield. There were huge numbers of police around and at one point I even had to pass through a police checkpoint at which they stopped and quizzed everyone heading into the town. Fortunately, physical injury was quite rare although one man, David Jones, died when picketing at Ollerton Colliery.

By this time, there was only one operating mine left in my constituency, at Cotgrave, where production continued. There, pickets arrived from Kent and policemen arrived from Essex and they confronted each other on the village roads throughout the day. My constituents, however, avoided them all by walking over the fields to the colliery, and work at Cotgrave was never interrupted.

The strike was a dramatic moment in modern British history and it has divided opinion ever since. It has been romanticized by the left as a heroic workers' fight against the cruelties of capitalism. In my view it was a blatant bid by Arthur Scargill to use militant action to topple a democratically elected government. The mass pickets were organized with military efficiency, paid a day's allowance by the union which was not far off what they would have earned from a working shift, and bussed to vulnerable targets in the power-generating system in an attempt to close them down. Soviet money helped to finance the campaign, donated supposedly by the coal miners of the USSR as an expression of solidarity.

Every minister who knew anything about the coal industry had been bracing themselves for a showdown. In Thatcher's first term in government, Scargill had launched a national strike based on a pay claim. Nottinghamshire miners had joined that strike because all of the NUM had been balloted and everyone loyally backed the majority. Some of my collier constituents had told me the size of the award that they were expecting to settle for, so it was with some surprise, to them and me, that the government yielded to a higher figure. Power stations at the time had low stocks of coal on site and could not get additional fuel through the picket lines.

After this capitulation, Margaret had insisted that both the government and the Coal Board prepare for the next time. When the decisive strike began in March 1984 there were therefore mountains of coal heaped on the site of the giant, coal-fired Ratcliffe-on-Soar power station in my constituency, which experienced some picketing but was never remotely threatened with closure. And the most absurd mistake that Scargill made was to launch the campaign in the spring instead of waiting for winter when demand for coal would have been so much higher.

Of course the long strike was a cruel event and caused great hardship to many miners, and their communities. Families were divided, friendships broken and communities embittered for years to come. Public opinion was emotional and polarized across the country. I strongly believed, however, that a liberal democracy could not allow itself to be derailed by the violent force of a politicized trade union. That is why moderate One Nation Conservative ministers like me never wavered in our support for our policy. Indeed, it was led by the Energy Secretary, Peter Walker, who was as 'wet' as I was.

The year-long strike created a period of intense social conflict across the country. If the government had capitulated to the miners, it would undoubtedly have fallen from power and Britain's political and social culture would be very different today. Instead, the eventual collapse of the strike was a turning point in the development of the British economy and the modernization of its industrial relations. The most difficult problems arose later, in the 1990s, when the Coal Board failed to win contracts for tenders for power generating and the final modern pits closed. We tried to mitigate the consequences of these closures with extremely generous redundancy payments for the older mine workers, and, gradually, my own county of

Nottinghamshire and other parts of the country, especially in the South, developed a more diversified and forward-looking economy.

Our post-industrial problems were not confined to coal mining, however. We had to rationalize a great number of other old-fashioned heavy industries, a process I became directly responsible for during my time at the DTI. The eighteenth- and nineteenth-century-style foundries which had existed all over the Black Country when I had practised at the Bar (and from which I had unfortunately derived a considerable income because of the injuries caused by the regular explosions and other incidents with molten metal) were equally redundant and had either to go or be modernized. Car manufacturing and other industries were in a parlous state, either in public ownership or supported by public subsidy, because of the power of militant trade unions which resisted all modernization of products – which were useless and out of date – and of production and working practices. The Thatcher government's approach to these problems – standing up to the unions and privatizing where possible – was a necessary step to modernizing the British economy. I believed that then, and I believe it now.

We also had to deal with the public utilities and public services. These had been nationalized in such a way that during the 1960s they had taken the form of syndicalist workers' control. As a result, by the 1980s, they were expensive, inefficient and delivering a poor level of service to most of their customers, patients or pupils.

The privatizations of the great businesses providing electricity, gas and water were extremely unpopular with the general public at the time, but they too led to a transformation in the delivery of these services.

In her third term, Margaret switched emphasis to a new agenda of radical reform of public services and of education and health in particular, using Kenneth Baker and me to lead the reforms and backing us both once we had convinced her of what we wanted. In fact, in many ways she was actually not too far from my own principles of combining free markets with a social conscience and social reform.

Over the past twenty years absurd myths have built up about the Thatcher era on both sides of the political divide. Few people following politics felt neutral about her. To many on the right, Margaret Thatcher became a goddess: a dynamic heroic reformer who swept all before her with her ideological enthusiasm. In particular, right-wing nationalists, who emerged as Eurosceptics in the 1990s, persuaded themselves that they were defending Margaret's true legacy. To much of the left, she became a callous dictator who crushed the working class and destroyed British industry, and a symbol of everything that was hateful about those who backed the rich and the powerful against the oppressed. Unfortunately, the Labour Party succeeded in persuading many people who were too young to have any direct memory of her government – or, crucially, the mess that had preceded it – to accept this particular version of events.

One of the particularly pervasive myths that developed about Margaret Thatcher was that she was an ideologue who based her judgements on deeply held philosophical convictions. The truth was that she was more pragmatic, and less ideological, than either the right or the left have made her out. It is true that Keith Joseph had firmed up her belief in free-market economics in principle. However, she never reduced overall public spending. She always worried when her monetarist Chancellors wanted to raise interest rates, and always hoped to find other ways of reducing inflation, which was the great bogeyman of the 1980s. She was as intelligent and sharp as any of her colleagues, but was inspired not by some great new creed but by the traditional Tory values of hard work, thrift and meritocracy.

I have always said that the beginning of the decline of Mrs Thatcher's formidable rule was when her more sycophantic followers began to persuade her that she had somehow invented a new ideology called 'Thatcherism'. She in fact led a very pro-European and socially liberal government. And she was very much more successful when she was a practical and pragmatic politician of force and vision.

The difficulties Margaret Thatcher had in her first years with the senior wets in the Cabinet were largely personal, rather than political or ideological. Although people like Jim Prior and Ian Gilmour were friends with whom I had some political sympathy, they deeply resented the fact that this woman had improbably emerged to lead the party. They were unable to respect the authority of her office and frequently conspired against her, particularly after the 1981 Budget. She dealt with their insubordination by the simple technique of sacking them from the government one after another – Norman St John-Stevas, Ian Gilmour, Christopher Soames and others – in her early reshuffles. But she actually replaced them with younger wets including – eventually – me. The political balance of her Cabinet was the same at the end of her term of office as it had been in the beginning. The difference was that people like John Gummer, Ken Baker and me never once doubted her authority as prime minister and could be relied upon to work loyally as part of her team.

Margaret's pragmatism and her tendency to take her first decisions based on her middle-class provincial instincts meant that she could be persuaded, by the right people with the right motives, to apply her considerable mind to great problems and reach a more balanced and sensible view in due course. She was always, as prime ministers have to be, intensely political and highly sensitive to the problems of party opinion and party management.

One of the best examples of this was the 'Right to Buy' policy for tenants of council houses, which was in later years viewed as the epitome of Thatcherism. She was actually instinctively opposed to this policy at first, and its advocates within the government had considerable difficulty in persuading her to adopt it. She was, of course, wholly in favour of owner occupation. In the conversations that I witnessed, however, she always insisted that 'our people' (which was how she always described Middle England Conservatives) would be angry if council tenants were allowed to buy their houses at a generous discount when they had to pay the full market price. It was only after many colleagues urged her to adopt the policy by making comparisons with the sitting tenant's discount when a tenant bought a property from a landlord that she reluctantly gave way. It was an immediate success and of course she warmly embraced it when she realized how effective it was in spreading the principle of property-owning democracy in which she fervently believed.

The other pervasive myth about the Thatcher era was that Margaret was a Eurosceptic. The Thatcher government was in fact very pro-European for most of its life. I have already described how Margaret took an active role in the pro-European campaign during Harold Wilson's 1975 referendum. She never questioned our membership of the European Union throughout her whole period of office. Indeed, she took a very active and leading role within the Union as she, Helmut Kohl of Germany, François Mitterrand of France, and Jacques Delors of the European Commission surged forward in the development of the European project. The single market was a Thatcher initiative to which she was very strongly committed and for the success of which she was personally responsible.

In the latter years, after a period of attrition, Margaret did become ever more cautious about Europe. I think that the root of the problem was the lack of any warm personal relationship between her and Kohl, Mitterrand or Delors. I suspect that they hated her robust style, and her stubbornness: her rather pointless battle over the British budget contribution to the EU caused more political ill will than the financial gains were worth. I suspect too that these three great Continentals treated her in a rather patronizing way and may even have lacked respect for a female leader. This all led to growing difficulties, firstly over her attitude to German reunification, and then over the steps towards European currency reform. Margaret had never been an enthusiast for the European currency and became steadily more hostile to the direction in which events were moving.

This hostility was a contributory factor to her eventual fall, although it was far from being the most important cause. Geoffrey Howe and Nigel Lawson, then her Foreign Secretary and Chancellor respectively, became increasingly irked by her refusal to contemplate any steps towards membership of the so-called Exchange Rate Mechanism (ERM). Geoffrey was an enthusiastic supporter of the whole European project. Nigel was more cautious but he was determined to avoid the problems of volatile exchange rates and loose monetary policy which had plunged the whole of the continent of Europe into crisis in the 1970s, and which had contributed to the hyperinflation that we had inherited when we took office.

Matters began to come to a head over a European summit in Madrid in June 1989. I discovered soon afterwards from insiders that both Geoffrey and Nigel had threatened Margaret with their resignation if she maintained her adamant, outspoken refusal even to contemplate British membership of the ERM. Support for membership had been the position of almost the entire Cabinet, apart from Nicholas Ridley, and I had even heard Norman Tebbit trying to urge potential membership upon her. She had to concede to them that our policy should be that we would join the ERM 'when the time was right'. That still meant 'never' to her.

Unfortunately, the threat of resignation totally destroyed Margaret's personal relationship with Geoffrey and Nigel. These were the two men upon whom she had relied more than any other to drive and deliver the economic reforms of the 1980s which had successfully transformed the British economy. Margaret had appointed them as successive Chancellors and wholeheartedly backed them although she did not share all their beliefs: for political reasons she was always very hesitant about the use of dramatically high interest rates as a weapon to control the money supply and bring down hyperinflation, which had reached a record-breaking height of 25 per cent per annum in 1981.

After their ultimatum to her over her attitude to the ERM, she lost all confidence in both of them, leading to the inevitable break.

Nigel's resignation a few months later in October 1989 was forced by Margaret Thatcher's increasing reliance on the advice of an eccentric economist called Alan Walters. Walters was regarded by many as a not particularly distinguished economist. To Nigel's great annoyance and embarrassment, he made frequent public statements of his unfashionable economic views, with which Margaret politically agreed. Finally Margaret announced that she was bringing Alan Walters into Number 10 as her personal economic adviser. She was astonished by Nigel Lawson's refusal to accept this. She told me that at one point she had urged him not to resign because he was on the point of becoming the longest-serving Chancellor since the war. She apparently assumed that this would persuade him not to leave, but Nigel was not interested in such statistics and he vehemently resigned, to be replaced by John Major. Ironically, John immediately insisted that we should join the ERM and she was obliged to concede. John came to regret that decision.

As for Geoffrey, he and Margaret had never had a good personal relationship and, after Madrid, she lost all faith in him. Four weeks after his threat of resignation, she infuriated him by moving him from the Foreign Office to the much less important position of Leader of the House, which he regretted accepting from the outset. She fobbed him off with the title of deputy prime minister to ease the blow, but he soon found that this was meaningless, not least as Bernard Ingham made it clear to the world that the title signified nothing, and was merely a token gesture to try to heal the wounds. Margaret had always found Geoffrey's rather quiet and hangdog style of political argument irritating compared with the more combative styles of Willie Whitelaw, Nigel Lawson, Ken Baker and others, including me. From then on she treated him with open contempt in front of Cabinet colleagues to an ever increasing and embarrassing extent.

She also made the mistake, from the point of view of her own position, of promoting John Major to fill these key vacancies in her government, first as Foreign Secretary to replace Geoffrey in July 1989 and then as Chancellor to replace Nigel in October 1989. She was always particularly impressed by colleagues who had triumphed over poor and disadvantaged backgrounds, embodying the qualities of the meritocratic society that she so much wished to create. She had decided that John Major was now to be her successor, having been disappointed first in Cecil Parkinson and then in John Moore, and she promoted him accordingly. John certainly was the shining example of social mobility and political talent in which she believed. Unfortunately, she was wrong in her belief that she would be able to dominate him and that he would operate as a kind of lapdog heir apparent. She did not take long to discover after her fall that he was made of much sterner stuff and had very strong political views of his own.

These events exemplify the period when Margaret began to lose her previously impeccable political instincts and was increasingly running a personalized autocratic style of government. She shocked everyone at a Cabinet meeting by loudly responding to some procedural quibble raised by Geoffrey about the business of the House of Commons by saying, 'Why do I have to do everything in this government myself?' I am sure that I was not the only person present silently thinking that the whole problem was that she *was* trying to do everything herself.

This all coincided with the disastrous implementation of Margaret's decision to abolish the domestic rating system which financed local government and replace it with a new tax called the community charge. She had got it into her head that her problems with extreme left-wing local government, which had undoubtedly dogged her throughout her time in government, were due mainly to the fact that such a large proportion of the population did not pay any taxation directly towards the cost of local government policies because they were not householders. She was therefore proposing a flat-rate tax to be levied at a level determined locally on every member of the population. This was quickly – and unsurprisingly – dubbed the poll tax.

Margaret drove this absurd proposal through the government machine without any regard to the advice of dissenting colleagues and without any proper use of the Cabinet system. She had increasingly begun to develop policies in little ad hoc groups appointed by her for particular purposes. She put huge pressure on a small group of young and ambitious ministers on the edge of the Cabinet to sit with her in a Cabinet Committee set up for the purpose of developing her pet project. She desperately tried to coerce other members of her government to join with her. Nigel Lawson, as her Chancellor up until his resignation in 1989, was openly contemptuous of the proposal and correctly argued that it would be quite impossible to collect efficiently and was also socially unfair and politically dangerous. I personally was invited to one of the meetings of her Cabinet Committee when I was Health Secretary. I attended one meeting only and was never invited again because I insisted on asking difficult questions, and on challenging answers when they did not resolve my considerable doubts. No doubt others underwent the same experience.

The poll tax was driven through and introduced first in Scotland, where it had catastrophic long-term political consequences for the Conservative Party, and then in England where it produced fierce resistance and, in the spring of 1990, some of the worst riots in memory.

These composite growing problems came to a head during a Cabinet meeting on 1 November 1990 where Margaret chose to behave in a quite appallingly offensive manner towards Geoffrey Howe, who was again telling the Cabinet the business of the House for the following week. She reduced everyone to an embarrassed silence. Shortly after the meeting Geoffrey resigned and set in train the course of events that ended Margaret's political career.

I had been in the Chamber during a key incident only a couple of days previously that should have given me warning that things were going badly wrong. Margaret had had another of her difficult European meetings in Rome where she had again clashed with Kohl and Mitterrand. The press had suggested in advance of the meeting that she was squaring for a fight. Alarmed by these rumours, I therefore sat on the front bench about four seats away from the prime minister to hear her report back from the summit in a statement to the House. She actually delivered a perfectly anodyne statement which the Foreign Office had no doubt persuaded her to read. She did, however, give vent to her pent-up frustration in a very lively and impromptu way when answering questions on the statement from both sides.

She had begun to be persuaded by some of her friends that the other Europeans were intent on some federalist European plot. She expressed her feelings about this in response to a fairly bland question from one of our backbenchers. She gave a description of what she would accept, and then went on in fine and stirring style to conjure up the danger of other Europeans wanting a new super-national structure, in which the Commission would be the government, the European Parliament would be the equivalent of the House of Commons and the Council of Ministers would be the Upper House. She would say 'no' to this, she said. Then, in a magnificent declamatory style, she proclaimed, 'No! No! No!'

I sat there rather admiring the tremendous hubris and style of all this, and actually thought that this was Margaret at her most amazing and theatrical. However, I later learnt that Geoffrey Howe and several other pro-Europeans had been deeply upset by her outburst. It was at this moment that Geoffrey decided that he did not wish to stay in the government any longer.

After publicly announcing that he had given Margaret his resignation on the evening following the dreadful Cabinet meeting, Geoffrey Howe decided that he was going to make a resignation speech on the floor of the House. On 13 November, nearly two weeks later, I dutifully attended a very crowded House to listen to his statement, and I again found myself sitting only three or four seats away from the prime minister. As a friend and colleague of Geoffrey, I thought that this would be a sad occasion, but I did not expect anything very dramatic. Knowing the extreme reasonableness of Geoffrey's personality, I assumed that he would merely express his regret at feeling obliged to leave the government and his pleasure that he had had the privilege of serving under Margaret, make a few tributes to her as a leader and to the achievements of our government, and then give a statement of continuing loyalty to the Conservative cause. His speech could not have been further removed from this conventional courtesy.

It took only a few sentences to realize that Geoffrey was making a carefully crafted and brilliant attack on the prime minister with a view to expressing his rage and destroying her credibility. He delivered the speech in his usual clear crisp way, with a reasonably light tone. I sat as silent and startled as every other MP in the House, all of us looking at Margaret, who was staring pale and straight-faced ahead. I could almost feel the knife wounds in her back being inflicted by Geoffrey's clipped phrases. His joke about being sent to the wicket as a batsman and finding his bat had been broken by the team captain caused the most amusement, but it was nervous laughter on our side of the House. Everyone present felt that something historic was happening.

I had spotted Michael Heseltine standing and listening to the speech from behind the Speaker's Chair. He left abruptly at the end when Geoffrey sat down. On the back benches since his dramatic resignation over Westland in 1986, Michael had for some considerable time been allowing the newspapers to speculate about his ultimate and open ambition to succeed Margaret. I said to my ministerial neighbour that Michael Heseltine now had no choice but to put in a leadership bid if he was to retain any credibility.

Before Geoffrey's devastating resignation speech, it had never crossed my mind that the Thatcher government would fail to go on until its term expired in 1992. I was fairly resigned to the fact that Margaret would lead us to the next election and that business would proceed as usual. I was also fairly resigned to the probability that we would finally be defeated at that election. Geoffrey's speech dramatically and immediately changed all that.

In its wild and controversial aftermath, some of Margaret's more unscrupulous friends ran a story in the newspapers that Geoffrey's remarkable speech, quite out of character for such an easy-going and often low-key personality, had been written by his wife, Elspeth. I could see where this theory came from, because Margaret and Elspeth had certainly hated each other for many years. There was an icy correctness to any brief exchange that might take place between them. However, I was assured by Geoffrey – with vehemence, because he was angered by the story – and by Anthony Teasdale, his political adviser at the time, that this story was quite untrue. Another suggestion, attributed to Margaret herself, was apparently that Nigel Lawson and Peter Jenkins, a prominent commentator on the *Independent*, had written the speech for Geoffrey. Anthony, who later became a close political adviser to me when I was Chancellor of the Exchequer, told me that it was in fact he who had assisted Geoffrey with his Commons speech. Elspeth's attitude towards the text had been rather circumspect, and neither Nigel Lawson not Peter Jenkins had been involved in any way. Anthony, however, confirmed that the great bulk of the speech was very much Geoffrey's own work, in which he had given clear and sharp expression to the months, if not years, of inner tension, the 'tragic conflict of loyalties' as he described it, that had been boiling up 'for perhaps too long'. Geoffrey had asked Anthony to suggest some wording, especially on Europe, and to join him the evening before it was delivered to finesse the language. It was as they were watching the prime minister's Guildhall House speech on the news, where she implausibly used a series of cricketing metaphors and declared 'the bowling's going to get hit all round the ground' that

Geoffrey said that, ' . . . but the problem is that the captain has already broken the team's bats before the match.' The idea of broken bats was then incorporated into the text, as a response to Margaret's cricketing foray, and they continued to work into the early hours on a speech that was to change the history of the country.

The most startling revelation that Anthony shared with me, which I kept completely secret for many years, was that Richard Ryder, a Treasury minister, who had once been Margaret's political secretary and who became, a few weeks later, the government chief whip under John Major, had participated in the writing of Geoffrey's resignation letter and commented in detail on his speech. Richard's involvement underlined how much Margaret's behaviour had finally shaken the support of her previously loyal followers. Richard was a close friend of Geoffrey, but he would never have acted in this way if he had not suffered a lack of confidence in Margaret's leadership himself, and it was a telling indicator of how bad things had become.

Thereafter events moved rapidly to the inevitable conclusion. Within nine days, Margaret Thatcher was out of office.

The morning after Geoffrey's speech, Wednesday 14 November, Michael Heseltine did indeed throw his hat into the ring, prompting the first serious leadership election within the Conservative Party since 1975.

Margaret's candidacy was nominated by her Foreign Secretary, Douglas Hurd, and seconded by her new Chancellor, John Major. However, between the opening of nominations on 14 November and the ballot six days later on 20 November, she actually took little personal part in the campaigning in the House of Commons, despite the fact that the only electorate was going to be Tory MPs. In fact she flew off to a summit in Paris on 18 November, only to return after the results of the first ballot had been announced. I think she assumed that her authority would be sufficient to command the loyalty that she had begun to take for granted. That is the only possible explanation for her decision to place her campaigning in the hands of, amongst others, Peter Morrison, who was an amiable man but did little actual work and was not known personally by many MPs. When, in the middle of one afternoon, I visited Peter Morrison in his office in the House of Commons to consult him on a possible approach, I was not too surprised to find that he was soundly asleep after an overindulgent lunch. He did not seem particularly interested in campaigning activity or proposals when he roused himself for a brief conversation. I undertook a little campaigning myself by talking to the younger MPs whom I knew personally, but nothing more.

Although I kept large quantities of paper throughout my career, I didn't – and still don't – write diaries. However, conscious of the extreme febrility of these days, I did keep a diary of sorts between 16 and 22 November. What follows is based on those diaries.

On the night of Friday 16 November, my good friend David Trippier, then a junior minister in the Department of Health, came to Nottingham to address my annual constituency dinner dance and stayed overnight with me and Gillian. We sat up late into the night drinking brandy and putting the world to rights. David was vehemently and passionately pro-Michael Heseltine. He was also eloquent in his opposition to the community charge, which he insisted was going to lead to his certain defeat at the next election. David confirmed what Spencer Batiste, a loyal and sensible backbencher, had said to me earlier in the week: that the party was unelectable in the North with Margaret Thatcher as leader.

My conversations with David and Spencer reinforced my growing opinion that Margaret Thatcher was not going to be elected on the first ballot. Ministers and backbenchers of previously impeccable loyalty were now rapidly deserting her.

I conducted all my conversations over the next days on the basis that a hung result in the first ballot seemed likely.

On Sunday 18 November a number of journalists rang me at home in Nottingham to discuss the prospects of this. Trevor Kavanagh of the *Sun* revealed to me that Norman Tebbit had told him that he, Norman, would step down from any contest if I was a candidate. Norman had been making favourable references to me and John Major for some weeks. I knew that John was a favoured successor of Margaret Thatcher and Norman Tebbit, but Trevor Kavanagh's remark made me decide to explore further.

There was a great deal of confusion through the day with Margaret talking of referenda on the European Community and the single market. I was slightly reassured when I read the *Sunday Telegraph* to see that she had wrapped up her references to another referendum and tried to reassure John Gummer when he rang up to express his own irritation. Later Peter Jenkins of the *Independent* told me that her private briefing on referenda was much stronger than any of her public statements. I seriously began to wonder whether I was doing the right thing in supporting Margaret. I had hoped that Geoffrey Howe's resignation had brought us all back to our senses on the referendum issue, but apparently not.

I also thought that the tone of the personal attacks being made on Michael Heseltine on the prime minister's behalf were wholly counterproductive and doing great harm to the party.

The next day, Monday 19 November, I headed down to London. That evening I had a long discussion with Norman Tebbit in my room in the House of Commons. It was a friendly conversation during which we delicately moved towards what we both knew we were talking about. The conversation began on the basis that we both hoped the prime minister would win the first ballot, in which case there would be nothing to talk about. If Michael Heseltine won on the first ballot, there was also nothing to talk about. We agreed, though, that a hung ballot seemed likely. We also virtually agreed that the prime minister would have to stand down if she failed to get through on the first ballot. We briefly discussed the merits and demerits of Douglas Hurd and John Major as candidates. We then talked about each other's prospects.

Norman said that he had all but decided that he could add nothing to the prime minister's vote and was minded not to run. He was, he said, prepared to consider supporting me. In the most diplomatic way, we eventually arrived at the situation where he was asking for a key place in the government as the prize for his support, which he had not yet decided to offer. He thought the idea of being a genuine deputy prime minister, without departmental responsibilities, was quite attractive, although he explained, I am sure honestly, the heavy financial problems that would pose for him.

Norman was plainly interested in returning to government and plainly also saw himself as a kingmaker. I was inclined to agree: it would have been very difficult for anyone to run successfully without the 80–100 votes that he might be able to deliver. However, I was never certain that Norman was wholly trustworthy in any given conversation. I also thought (rightly, as it turned out) he favoured John Major. So this little dance would only become relevant if, for some reason, John Major was not a candidate.

I then spoke about the prospects with John Wakeham, who was now the Energy Secretary, and John Gummer, then Secretary of State for Agriculture, Fisheries and Food. Like Norman Tebbit and me, they were campaigning for the prime minister and hoped we would win on the first ballot. But they shared my fear that she was not going to make it. As former whips, we suspected that MPs were being untruthful about their voting intentions and that those around Thatcher were being over-optimistic. We therefore discussed whether she should stand down if she didn't win the first ballot, and if so, how it should be done. We all agreed that she could not go on to a second ballot without damaging the authority of the government and splitting the party.

The problem was that Margaret, in Paris with Douglas Hurd, was quite out of touch with events.

John Wakeham explained to us that Margaret's entourage had discussed it all with her already. It had been agreed that, in the event of a hung result, she would emerge onto the steps of the Paris Embassy and give a brief statement, saying that she would fight on. She had been persuaded, John Wakeham told me, not to underline it too heavily with 'one vote is enough' type remarks (in other words, one is a good enough majority). We would then ensure sufficient show of support for her in Westminster to get her back to London with dignity, so that the next steps could be seriously discussed with the 'men in grey suits'. John Wakeham hoped that Denis Thatcher and their daughter Carol might discuss the matter with Margaret and prepare her for the possibility of stepping down, before she saw any colleagues.

The result was declared at 6.30 in the evening of Tuesday 20 November, by Cranley Onslow, chairman of the 1922 Committee. It was the disaster we had feared. She had both clearly won, and clearly lost. Or put another way, she had neither won decisively, nor lost decisively. She had beaten Michael Heseltine by fifty-two votes, without obtaining the 15 per cent margin over him necessary to win on the first ballot. But, rather to my surprise, she was only four votes short of this crucial threshold. (I later checked and discovered that every member of her Cabinet had loyally voted for her in this first ballot.)

I immediately plunged into TV appearances in support of the prime minister. I spent the day doing countless interviews amid scenes of excited mayhem on the Green outside the House with my last appearance, on *Newsnight*, coming between 10.30 p.m. and midnight. Throughout, I gave a vigorous defence of Margaret's position and her result, as part of the plan agreed with John Wakeham to get her back from Paris with dignity and with no sign of doubts or erosion of support at home. We thought that she could then give a dignified and proud announcement of her decision to step down of her own accord and not under any apparent pressure. I later discovered that five Cabinet ministers – Chris Patten, Norman Lamont, Malcolm Rifkind, Tony Newton and William Waldegrave – had been searching for me, unsuccessfully, wanting me to join them for a meeting at Tristan Garel-Jones's house. Tristan was a very effective government whip, said to be the inspiration for the fictional Machiavelli, Francis Urquhart, in *House of Cards*. But I only heard about this, and the agreement made there, the following afternoon. They had decided that it would be for the best if Margaret were to release Douglas Hurd and John Major from their obligations to support her so that they could stand.

I also later discovered that in Paris Douglas Hurd had been put under pressure to sign the prime minister's nomination papers to go through to the second ballot. He had declined, on the basis that they should return to England to talk about this with colleagues first.

The following morning, Wednesday 21 November, I took a large number of telephone calls in my office from other ministers, including John MacGregor, who had been asked by John Wakeham to ring round the Cabinet to find out our views. I told John in strong terms that I believed that the prime minister should step down. I also told him that I would not support her any longer. I believed that a further contest between her and Michael Heseltine would split the party hopelessly. I also told John that she should release Douglas Hurd and John Major and allow them to stand. When I asked him whether I was the only one expressing that view, he replied that I was by no means the only one. I later spoke to John Gummer, who entirely shared my view. He told me that John MacGregor's survey had shown that twelve members of the Cabinet were against her standing and seven in favour. Much later it transpired that 12:7 was wrong. John MacGregor had not bothered to consult Douglas Hurd and John Major, mistakenly assuming that they were in favour of her going on. The true count was therefore 14:5. The five in favour included David Hunt, Secretary of State for Wales, who was in Tokyo and completely out of touch. He had merely sent protestations of loyalty and support.

By this time, we all thought that 'the men in grey suits' were going to persuade her to step down when they saw her shortly after she returned from Paris.

I was therefore astonished to hear at about 3 p.m. that the prime minister had declared that she was fighting on. I learned later that the 'men in grey suits' meeting had been a fiasco. Cranley Onslow, the chair of the 1922 Committee, had given ambiguous advice and no opinion. John MacGregor, the Leader of the House, had failed to report the results of his Cabinet survey because he did not want to give them in front of Cranley Onslow – the party's most senior back-bencher but still a backbencher. Kenneth Baker, the party chairman, had given sycophantic advice, telling her she had the best chance of defeating Michael Heseltine. Norman Tebbit, there in his capacity as a senior and influential backbencher and Margaret's chief plotter, had taken charge of events with vigorous advice that she should fight on and destroy the Heseltine campaign.

That afternoon, I received a telephone call from Peter Morrison, who surprisingly thanked me for campaigning for Margaret the night before. But when he asked me whether I would continue to support her, I told him I would definitely not be campaigning any further and that I would probably not support her in the second ballot. Norman Fowler later told me Margaret and her close entourage had been considering asking me to become her campaign manager until that phone call. Shortly thereafter – and much to his surprise, since no one had actually asked him to do it – John Wakeham was announced as her campaign manager.

I went into the Chamber to listen to the prime minister's statement on the Paris summit. I was sitting on the front bench, staring in front of me, not listening to the words, still quite amazed by the decision Margaret had taken to fight on, and by her calm and confident demeanour. I caught the eye of Norman Lamont who was standing on the Opposition side behind the Chair and we raised eyebrows and pulled faces at each other. Kenneth Baker who was sitting nearby congratulated me on my appearance on *Newsnight* and seemed put out when I told him vehemently that I would not be going on *Newsnight* again to campaign for the cause. Then, I caught the eye of Chris Patten, who was standing behind the Speaker's Chair, and we nodded to each other to go out for a discussion. In the corridor behind the Chair, Chris and I rapidly discovered that we were in complete agreement. We were joined by Norman Lamont, whose views were equally strong. For the remainder of that evening until midnight, I was in almost constant conversation with Cabinet ministers in the Cabinet corridor.

We learned that each Cabinet minister was to be invited to give their opinion individually in a five-minute interview in the prime minister's room. I was offered the first appointment at 6.15 p.m. I assumed I was the first because of my conversation with Peter Morrison, although it might have been because I was available, or the first in the alphabet. I discussed the situation with other Cabinet members who were all gathering in anxious little groups in each other's rooms. We all agreed that we would give our forthright opinions and rather steeled each other on. After all, John Wakeham had asked us to be totally candid.

I was indeed the first minister to go in, although I was a little delayed because I had to follow Francis Maude, then a backbench MP who had simply turned up in the hope of an audience with the prime minister. He had duly been given an interview and, stout Thatcher loyalist that he was, he had told her that she was going to be defeated and must stand down.

Margaret's mood was still calm and confident and we had a very friendly but robust conversation. She tried to cheer me up and jog me out of my pessimism by talking about what could be achieved by a better-organized campaign than the disastrous one that had been conducted so far. I refused to be cheered up. I described the proposed campaign as a charge of the Light Brigade. I was quite sure that support was moving away from her very quickly. By refusing to stand down and release Douglas and John Major, in order to allow them to run, she was giving the leadership to Michael Heseltine who, in my opinion, would win easily. I refused to promise her my support. I advised her to release Douglas and John, and to give the party the choice they were obviously demanding.

But Margaret insisted that she had to stay on. She was the only person who could lead the successful resolution of the aftermath of the Gulf War, which was liberating Kuwait from Saddam Hussein's invasion, and the recovery of the economy from recession. 'After that,' she said, 'you can all sort out between yourselves who is going to take over from me.' I was not persuadable.

Margaret was visibly shaken by my attitude and advice. She said I was defeatist. I agreed that I was, but added that I was realistic. I told her that I had already met Alan Clark, one of her most right-wing and devoted loyalists, who was convinced that she was about to be routed. Alan had indeed just told Chris Patten and me that, and had agreed that I could quote him in my support.

I left the interview to join a room full of Cabinet ministers, and some parliamentary private secretaries. A little row of white faces asked whether I really had told her what I thought. I assured them that I had and urged them to do the same. From later accounts I think most of them did, with more or less candour. Some she tried to bully. The later ones found her rather misty-eyed.

Some may wonder what evidence I had for my conviction that Margaret would have been defeated after the first ballot. Throughout those feverish days, I campaigned in the House of Commons and was closely in touch with many MPs. The atmosphere in the House after the ballot result was extraordinary. Some Tories were shocked, many saddened. Others were almost jubilant in their hopes that she might go. It confirmed my view that MPs would think that their loyalty to her was discharged by her failure to win the first ballot outright, and that they would then turn to Heseltine. I heard that Hal Miller, the MP for Bromsgrove, knew sixteen MPs who had voted for Margaret on the first ballot, and who had already told him they were voting for Heseltine on the second. Four MPs had appeared on Central TV declaring their intention to switch to Heseltine in the second ballot. Alan Clark, who had correctly predicted Heseltine's vote within two votes on the first ballot, thought she would get no more than ninety votes on the second, out of a possible 372. This would have been a devastating humiliation. I did not meet a single person who thought she could win a second ballot. Norman Tebbit, whom I did not talk to in the aftermath of the first ballot, must have been almost alone in his conviction that she could.

There was continual toing and froing for hours, with ministers crowded into the Cabinet corridor. Chris Patten and I asked for a Cabinet meeting to be called at 11 p.m. that night. Kenneth Baker was particularly evasive about this, while John Wakeham advocated leaving it for the morning. Chris and I both insisted that we would raise Margaret's position at the following morning's Cabinet meeting if it was not resolved overnight. We both told John Wakeham and Alastair Goodlad – the deputy chief whip, who appeared to be keeping an eye on us – that we would resign if she did not step down.

Chris and I also agreed that neither of us could possibly stand as candidates if our resignations forced her to go. There would have been 'blood on our hands' and we would not have been forgiven. It was essential to persuade Douglas and John to abandon their apparent commitment to support Margaret.

Alastair Goodlad and I went to get Douglas Hurd out of a dinner being held in one of the Commons dining rooms. We huddled in a corner and explained what was happening. As Chris had previously explained to me, as well as promising to support the prime minister,

Douglas and John Major had agreed that neither would stand against the other. Douglas now said that he and John wanted their friends to take soundings to discover which of them had the best chance of winning. It was quite impossible in the time available for anyone to give them reliable advice on that score, as Alastair and I explained. The little group of Cabinet ministers we had been talking with had all agreed to a suggestion which Michael Jopling – a former chief whip and now an influential Tory grandee – had first put to me at lunchtime: that both should stand in friendly contest, in response to pressure, to offer the party the wide choice that it plainly wanted. Douglas was happy with this and happy with the idea of an 11 p.m. Cabinet meeting, if we could get John to agree.

About an hour later Alastair and I rang John Major. He had been out of London since 16 November as a result of an operation to have his wisdom teeth removed. He still sounded unwell over the phone. He told us that the nomination papers for Margaret's candidacy were being sent to him for his signature, although the press and public had been informed by Number 10 that he had already signed them. I strongly advised him not to sign but he admitted that he really had promised to do so. On the important point of his own candidature, he was fairly receptive to the idea that Douglas and he should both stand in a contest that was demonstrably friendly. I told him that if they did not stand and if the prime minister stayed, we were giving the government to Michael Heseltine. Interestingly, John asked me whether I really thought a Heseltine government would be a particular disaster. In normal circumstances I would have agreed with him, and said as much. But if he won this way he would appear to have hijacked the party and the subsequent recriminations would make it almost impossible for the party – and the government – to reunite. John was eventually persuaded that both he and Douglas probably ought to run.

At 11 p.m., the proposed late-night Cabinet meeting was finally abandoned. This was because John Wakeham told me, and he and Peter Morrison told others, that Margaret had more or less decided to step down and was going home to sleep on it. Chris Patten and I were very suspicious and said so. I later discovered that the whips had devised a Number 10 plan to rush in her nomination papers, not yet delivered to Cranley Onslow, who as chairman of the 1922 Committee ran any leadership election, because of fears that Chris and I might resign overnight.

By the end of that evening, with Gillian, who had had to go to the concert for which we had tickets on her own and now rejoined me in the Commons, I was drinking wine with Norman Lamont. He made a vigorous effort to persuade me to nominate John Major and not to support Douglas Hurd, as he knew I intended. I was not convinced. I genuinely admired John, but I thought that Douglas was much closer to my views on Europe than John was, and I preferred Douglas's cool head in a crisis. Ironically – and much to my surprise – the other Eurofanatic in the Cabinet, John Gummer, was later persuaded to nominate John Major.

Before leaving the flat for the Cabinet meeting at 9 a.m. the following morning, Thursday 22 November, I told Gillian that I intended to resign if I found the prime minister had decided to fight on. She quite agreed it was the right thing to do. I knew perfectly well that that would end her candidature, and would probably end my ministerial career as well. I arrived just before the meeting was due to start, having been delayed in traffic. I instantly checked that other views had not changed overnight and was relieved when John Wakeham told me that she had decided to go.

The Cabinet meeting was tense and emotional. It began with the prime minister reading a prepared statement announcing her intention to go. She was weeping profusely and for a few moments was quite unable to read the statement without breaking down. Someone suggested that the Lord Chancellor, James Mackay, might read it for her. However, she was able to recover enough to read it, although she was still very tearful. Thereafter she recovered further and seemed reasonably bright. After tributes had been paid she asked, not unfairly, that we might refrain from any over-sentimental shows of sympathy. She found business more helpful than sympathy and went on with the meeting's agenda, handling the decision to send more troops to the Gulf with calm and confidence.

Before the Cabinet dispersed and left Number 10, the announcement had been made to the public.

Every member of the Cabinet was genuinely deeply saddened by the whole occasion. As I had told her at my interview the night before, I believed that every member of the Cabinet had voted for her in the first ballot. One of the amazing things about the whole affair was that the entire Cabinet had stood together and many had campaigned together on her behalf throughout, until the first ballot. That Cabinet had now driven her from office. But we had, however, acted as candid friends and had at least given her the frank and truthful advice which she had lacked, on too many occasions in the past, from her closest entourage.

That afternoon, I sat in the House and heard her give the most amazing speech opposing the motion of no confidence, put forward by Neil Kinnock, which was roundly defeated. It was a triumphant performance.

That Saturday I wrote to the prime minister, as I assume every member of the Cabinet did. I sent the letter of course, so no longer have it, but, so far as I can remember, this is what I said:

I think that you knew that you had lost when I had my interview with you last Wednesday. I formed the opinion that you had decided to go down fighting, rather than to surrender. I believe that your performance in the House in the afternoon gave you the magnificent end to your premiership that you were looking for.

I gave you my advice and acted as I did because I genuinely believed that you would face humiliating defeat if you had persevered to the second ballot. You would have handed the premiership to Michael Heseltine. The party must now make a choice between Douglas Hurd and John Major, which I am sure is the choice they wanted.

I will always be proud to have served in the government of one of the greatest prime ministers of this century, and I am grateful to you for allowing me to serve in it. We will continue the work.

When nominations for the second ballot closed on 22 November 1990, papers had been received from Michael Heseltine, John Major and Douglas Hurd.

When Margaret fell I had almost immediately decided that I would not run as a candidate myself. I had had such high exposure in recent years that I had already suffered the frequent media references to my being a possible future leader of the party, usually the kiss of death to any rising politician's career. Moreover, my recent history at Health had made me far too unpopular to make a run. The timing was simply impossible; the dust from my battles with the medical trade unions was not going to settle for some time.

As I have said, I was not against the idea of Michael Heseltine becoming prime minister at some point. However, I was convinced that if he won this leadership election the Conservative Party would inevitably split, and all hope of our remaining the natural governing party of the country would be destroyed. Michael was an exhilarating and controversial figure who aroused very strong feelings in all wings of the party. He had deprived Margaret of a decisive majority in the first ballot. But the man who had been forced to wield the knife was not the right man to inherit the throne. Had I known how quickly the Conservative Party was going to take up internal civil war, and with what enthusiasm, I might have taken a different view. I regret that I never did have the opportunity of seeing exactly what kind of prime minister Michael would have made if events had ever favoured him.

I had thought John Major would be a contender for the leadership from the moment in 1987 when Norman Fowler had warned me that John was the most ambitious man he had ever met. I very much liked and admired John, but felt that he had not yet acquired enough ministerial experience at a senior level to be prime minister. Probably because he had joined the Cabinet so much later than me, I somewhat patronizingly judged that he could wait a few years to be tested before possibly emerging later.

My old friend and colleague Douglas Hurd was so likeable that he had no enemies. He had a quite brilliant mind and very considerable ability. He was a particularly skilful diplomat and I was certain that he would apply a soothing leadership to an overexcited and divided party, which we would need to carry us to the next election with any prospect of success. I therefore joined his campaign team.

Douglas was the oldest of the candidates so I attracted some sarcastic remarks about 'young cardinals voting for old popes'. But my choice was based on my estimation of Douglas's considerable political and diplomatic skills and not my personal position. (I did have a conversation a couple of years later with the *Financial Times* political journalist Philip Stephens, who reminded me that he had once asked who I would be prepared to serve under, should Margaret fall. Apparently, I had replied 'John Major or Chris Patten.' Philip jokily asked why I had then in fact voted for Douglas Hurd. My reply was 'So did Chris Patten!')

The campaign that swiftly formed itself around Douglas was an excellent collection of friends led by younger members of the Cabinet. Most were close followers of Chris Patten who was effectively the leader of the campaign with others eagerly taking part. Our candidate worked hard and could be persuaded to meet people that he scarcely knew to try to win support. But he never demonstrated any real enjoyment of the debate.

Douglas did, however, contribute greatly to the atmosphere of perfect friendliness between all three camps. Everybody involved in the election campaign had agreed that there was to be no animosity and no negative campaigning, and that we were to present to the public an image of a united party undertaking a civilized process of freely choosing its next leader. John Major was particularly co-operative in maintaining this atmosphere. I had several cheerful conversations with him in the corridors of the House where we exchanged news from our respective camps and talked hopefully about the outcome whoever won.

What I had not anticipated was how vigorously Margaret Thatcher and her intimate followers would throw their weight behind John. A very strong team of Thatcher worshippers, led by Norman Tebbit, lobbied every right-wing member of the parliamentary party who remained loyal to Margaret to support John Major as her anointed successor.

In conversation with friends and journalists I expressed some surprise at this turn of events. It seemed to me that John Major was obviously the most left-wing Conservative of the trio, slightly shading Douglas Hurd for that title. Michael Heseltine had excellent qualities but was undoubtedly rather more right wing and mainstream Conservative than either of them. I suspect that my isolated opinion stemmed from the fact that I had got to know John rather better in recent years than most of the other politicians and commentators involved.

In the ballot on 27 November, John had an easy triumph thanks to the Thatcherite block of support that he attracted on top of his more natural supporters. Although strictly speaking a third ballot was needed as he was two votes short of an absolute majority, Michael Heseltine and Douglas Hurd immediately withdrew in John's favour. I thereby maintained my record of never having voted for a successful candidate in a Conservative leadership election.

Unfortunately, the opportunity to restore party unity that his success presented was completely undermined by Margaret's sad misjudgement that he would somehow be her poodle in office. This was a grave mistake and John was angered when she gave a comment to the newspapers explaining that while she might not be pulling the levers any more she would be a 'good back-seat driver'. Relations between the two rapidly deteriorated when John firmly took the wheel himself. Thereafter, Margaret's bitterness about her fall from office became ever more all-consuming and she spent most of John's term in office plotting against him and stirring up hostility amongst that faction of the party whom she could still influence. This appalling behaviour was a very great shame, not only for her reputation but also for John's ability to govern the country.

It was a desperately sad end to Margaret Thatcher's remarkable and brilliant career. Her greatest error had been to try to stay in office for too long. In modern politics, it is most unwise for any politician to seek to head a government for more than ten years. I describe this as the 'maximum permitted dose for adults'. Thereafter hubris, loss of judgement and loss of authority take hold. Margaret had held a very pleasant dinner for her Cabinet colleagues to celebrate her tenth anniversary as prime minister. With the wisdom of hindsight, she should have followed Harold Wilson's precedent and startled us all at that gathering by telling us of her intention to resign in the near future and asking us to begin the necessary process to produce her successor. If she had taken that course, her career would have ended on a glittering high and her reputation would have been completely assured and almost unblemished. Sadly, she continued, in an atmosphere where even loyal colleagues like me became resigned to the increasingly unhappy thought that we were doomed to serve under Margaret's faltering leadership until our inevitable defeat at the next general election.

14

'Off Minor'

(Thelonious Monk, 1952)

JOHN MAJOR

John was a modest and self-effacing man whose mild demeanour masked the fact that he actually had a steely backbone and was a man of great principle and purpose. The most noticeable change that he introduced was a reversion to a quite spectacularly co-operative and collective form of government. Margaret's government had always had a collective nature but this had steadily been weakened in her last two or three years as she had quarrelled with more and more of her colleagues and become more determinedly authoritarian.

Now, Cabinet meetings suddenly became open-ended, wide-ranging discussions of every feature of policy. The atmosphere was utterly transformed. John was obviously prepared to engage at considerable length in efforts to produce truly consensus conclusions on most major issues. Some commentators picked this up and quite accurately described the new Cabinet as a 'Cabinet of chums' because we worked in such a friendly and mutually supportive way.

We all genuinely found the new style of Cabinet debate enjoyable and stimulating. But there was a downside to this approach, mainly the fact that John was most reluctant to make a decision that over-ruled the opinion of any minority within the Cabinet. Throughout his premiership, he always retained an optimistic belief that with enough time for discussion it would always be possible to reach a consensus with which everybody would be truly pleased. He was always searching for a 'form of words' with which to frame a conclusion so as to bring in every strand of opinion.

This was indeed a very desirable objective but it sometimes involved a very long discussion. It became seriously problematic that Cabinet could not reach a conclusion in one meeting on any subject. Also, Cabinet discussions were always in danger of extending beyond the morning allocated to them and into the lunch hour and on. This would not have been a serious matter except that it had the embarrassing side effect of suggesting to political journalists the existence of some internal crisis. Even John's closest colleagues, like Chris Patten and myself, tried to persuade him to curtail the discussions to a modest extent. We also tried to encourage him to reach a conclusive summary of the discussion and a decision even when one or two colleagues were still in a tiny and outnumbered minority. Unfortunately, we were only moderately successful.

This, though, was a minor feature of an otherwise wholly refreshing and successful period of innovation in the conduct of government business, which lasted for the whole of the eighteen-month period leading up to the 1992 general election.

One of the only moments of minor drama in that first Major Cabinet was a wholly ridiculous one. My seat in this Cabinet was always opposite the prime minister and alongside Michael Heseltine. On one occasion, Michael was engaged in a vigorous political argument, with John and me ranged against him. Throughout the meeting, officials entered periodically to hand little handwritten notes to the prime minister. He threw these across to me and I read them before folding them and passing them to Peter Brooke, then Secretary of State for Northern Ireland. Michael became increasingly agitated by this and plainly began to suspect that some briefing was being supplied as part of a concerted campaign against his views. On about the fourth or fifth occasion he snatched a note thrown to me in order to intercept it. He opened it and read 'England 175 for 4'. It was the Test match score in a game being avidly followed by three cricket fanatics. Michael, who could scarcely understand the difference between football and cricket and had no interest whatever in any kind of sport, reacted with a look of disbelief and obviously decided that he was dealing with lunatics.

After the 1992 election, John made the mistake of bringing into the Cabinet more of his bitter right-wing opponents. Again it was all part of his sunny temperament, which led him to believe that any group of people could be induced to compromise and reach consensus in a properly conducted discussion. Sadly, he underestimated the vehemence and passion of some of our hard-line colleagues, whose promotion was eventually to bring this initial period of happy and united Cabinet government to an end.

Under the new leadership, the government's unpopularity slowly eased, although we were still trailing in the polls, so that John was obliged to delay the general election to almost the last possible moment. By the time Parliament was dissolved in March 1992, most ministers were resigned to the inevitable defeat, and saw only a faint chance that the government would survive. I was mildly more optimistic than that when we began the campaign but even I was quite startled by John's singular triumph in achieving real movement in the polls. His whole presentation is best described as 'Thatcherism with a human face'. Winning his own parliamentary majority in those circumstances was probably the pinnacle of John's career.

A few things were responsible for the Conservative victory. Firstly, John Smith, the Shadow Chancellor, was allowed to produce a draft Budget for a putative Labour government, which he set out in the early days of the campaign. Our government was already raising public expenditure to an extent that alarmed people like me, who had orthodox economic opinions. John Smith calmly proposed further large increases in public spending, to be financed by quite significant increases in taxation. This package proved extremely unpopular with the electorate.

Second, Neil Kinnock, the Leader of the Opposition, despite having successfully reformed the Labour Party and moving it very much nearer to electability, still had difficulties with a recalcitrant left wing who were distrusted by many opinion-formers. Neil's public style was pleasant and engaging, but also extremely garrulous. Neil was the right man to reform the Labour Party after its ultra-left-wing years, but the wrong candidate to be prospective prime minister in the eyes of the wider public.

Neil brought these doubts about his leadership qualities to an extraordinary climax at an election rally held in Sheffield shortly before the election. This was a televised occasion with a massive 11,000-strong audience of party faithful assembled before a platform of Shadow Cabinet members. Unfortunately the atmosphere of the gathering carried everyone away and it turned into a public orgy of triumphalism and hubris. Neil himself laid on an embarrassing performance, leading the audience in football-match-style chants of 'We're all right,' and rejoicing in an inevitable victory at the polls.

My campaigning style then involved as much door-to-door canvassing as I could possibly manage, together with evening public meetings. I didn't see the broadcast of the rally myself but the following morning I heard all about it from almost every householder who came to the door, each one keen to express their rage and indignation at what they had seen.

John Major, meanwhile, in reaction to the fierceness of the campaign, had the inspired idea of reverting to a very personal style of campaigning. He had always been relaxed and human in interviews. Now, he adopted the old political tradition of standing on a soapbox at crowded meetings in town centres, addressing genuine gatherings of the general public surrounded by the inevitable television cameras and journalists. Hard-left objectors sometimes attended these little events and subjected John to unattractive abuse, which TV viewers seemed to come to associate with the Labour Party. These, in my opinion, were the three most striking features of a campaign in which sympathy slowly built up for the new prime minister while doubts about Labour's readiness to govern grew.

Unfortunately, significant sections of the Labour Party and the media drew different conclusions. The *Sun* newspaper carried a ridiculous headline claiming that it was 'The *Sun* Wot Won It' on the Saturday after the poll. Many moderate Labour politicians could not believe that they had failed to defeat a government that had only recently been so unpopular. They too – wrongly, in my opinion – attributed their crushing disappointment to ferocious journalistic attacks from the right-wing press, which had caused them, understandably, many personal wounds.

I do not believe that the *Sun* or the other tabloids had any significant effect on public opinion at all during that campaign. From 1992 onwards far too many of the political class became obsessed with the power of the newspapers and the media context of campaigning, in a way that has had a most undesirable effect on political campaigning ever since. The further reforms of the Labour Party carried out by Tony Blair, Gordon Brown and Peter Mandelson were very desirable in themselves, and certainly made Labour a more modern and democratic party. But the instincts driving these reforms – the belief in the power of public relations and constant press campaigning, provoked by the traumatic shock of the 1992 election result – were wrong. However, the result was undoubtedly that the right wing of the Conservative Party became similarly convinced that the Murdoch press and the right-wing tabloids should be constantly courted in everything that the party and the government did.

The irony is that the favourite cause of the newspaper proprietors and their minions played no part at all in the 1992 campaign. John Major had negotiated the Maastricht Treaty with the leaders of the other member states of the European Union shortly before the election. He had drawn up his negotiating position after a long collective discussion involving most Cabinet ministers. We had all agreed that we would support the treaty proposed so long as Britain was allowed the option of 'not necessarily' participating in the creation of the single currency and the Social Chapter. John succeeded in negotiating these opt-outs and was greeted as a hero by his colleagues and most of his opponents when he returned with the eventual bargain. Even extreme Eurosceptics like Teddy Taylor MP publicly congratulated him on what he had achieved. The Maastricht Treaty was not exposed to any significant opposition during the 1992 election and scarcely featured in the campaign. This was to prove a dramatic contrast with the atmosphere once we were returned to our ministerial duties at the beginning of the next parliament.

The 1992 election was a turning point in the affairs of the Conservative Party. Before then, the party had been a broad right-of-centre coalition of well-disciplined parliamentarians and members, which had succeeded in becoming the natural governing party in the country, where the middle ground of opinion was usually in the centre right. The Conservatives had been in office for the vast majority of my lifetime punctuated only by three periods of Labour government. After 1992, it would take twenty-three years before we were again able to win an overall majority in a general election, in 2015.

It was the result of a complicated combination of circumstances which contrived to make the party increasingly more right wing and less attractive to a broad range of opinion, particularly in Scotland and the North of England. While the party moved right, the general public, in my opinion, did not move significantly at any stage after 1992, although political attitudes did of course gradually adjust to the irreversible consequences of a changing world and the modernizing of the country that had finally been achieved.

The rather abrupt change in Conservative politics had its roots in the deeply traumatic fall of Margaret Thatcher. The inevitable division, resentment and desire for revenge that followed her political demise had a lasting effect on the internal culture of the party.

Another crucial factor was that all the major political parties began to lose their ability to attract a large volunteer membership. Modern technology, mass travel and a vast range of entertainment possibilities had transformed society, and the general public was now much less likely to join voluntary bodies and associations. Institutions like the Women's Institute, the British Legion and the Scouts and Guides felt the effects of this as much as the political parties did. When I had first been adopted as the candidate for Rushcliffe in the 1960s, my constituency association had thousands of members, including hundreds of Young Conservatives, in several branches. Every village had its own Conservative Association which raised funds through dances, drinks parties and other social events. There were frequent political meetings and people were used to attending them. Many members became campaigning volunteers and played an active role in both national and local election campaigns. By the early 1990s, the membership in my constituency and in constituencies throughout the country was dwindling and ageing. At this point, this smaller membership still contained a good representative sample of Middle England. However, the proportion of people with more zealous opinions steadily increased. Younger recruits became rarer and the age profile of my association and every other Conservative Association in the country grew ever older.

Happily, my local association remained a very reasonable bunch of people and I still had many friends in it with whom I had been campaigning for decades. But from my speaking engagements in other MPs' constituencies I became aware that some associations were very diminished indeed, and dominated by rather reactionary right-wing older people who were no longer very representative of the Conservative vote at large. This trend got steadily worse over the next decades.

These constituency associations were solely responsible for the selection of parliamentary candidates. Most continued to do a reasonably good job as a huge number of the ablest people were attracted by the idea of taking part in national politics. Nevertheless the political centre of gravity of the parliamentary party began to swing to the right after the 1992 election and in a more pronounced way thereafter.

The third principal influence on the Conservative Party at this time was the changing nature of political reporting and campaigning. This in turn was being accelerated by some important changes in the ownership of the right-wing newspapers, which between them accounted for the majority of the national circulation.

Rupert Murdoch, the Australian-born media magnate, had become a British newspaper proprietor in the late 1960s and some of his influence had been beneficial. He had modernized the style of his newspapers, moving them away from their stuffy traditional format in line with the post-1960s changes in society. He had launched the *Sun* as a tabloid newspaper produced with some skill and professionalism. In 1986, he had challenged the Fleet Street trade unions and succeeded in breaking the closed shop that had dominated the industry and maintained ludicrously expensive working practices for decades.

But throughout the 1980s, under its editor Kelvin MacKenzie, Murdoch's *Sun* became an ever more raucous populist right-wing publication. Kelvin combined topless pin-ups and celebrity gossip with outspoken right-wing comment. I did not share his political opinions but I got on with him reasonably well. He once explained to me with some vehemence that he was following an editorial policy which he believed gave voice to the views of his working-class audience for the first time. The man working on the track for the Ford motor company at Dagenham was the man whose opinions he was trying to circulate.

Margaret had been very attracted by Rupert Murdoch's vigorous right-wing approach and his denunciations of the Labour Party. When he had bid in 1981 to acquire *The Times* and the *Sunday Times* to give a broadsheet respectability to his growing British base, she had intervened and supported him strongly. John Biffen, as the brand-new Secretary of State for Trade, had been the minister responsible for ensuring the tests of competition, avoidance of concentration of ownership and other rules were applied to such bids. Her personal break with her hitherto loyal supporter came when she bullied him into setting aside his own doubts, taking a flexible view of his statutory duties and awarding the newspapers to Rupert.

Rupert Murdoch did appoint some excellent people: in addition to Kelvin MacKenzie, he appointed Andrew Neil to be a brilliantly successful editor of the *Sunday Times* through the 1980s and early 1990s, boosting that paper's circulation and standing to become one of our leading broadsheets. But, despite his protestations to the contrary, Rupert took a vigorous interventionist line on the editorial and political line of his newspapers. Notwithstanding his undoubted intellectual ability, his views were rather simplistic and he insisted that his newspapers reported the news and campaigned in a way which promoted these views.

Andrew tried to introduce me to Rupert Murdoch. I am sure the intention was to help me in my political career and to see whether

Rupert would be interested in supporting my progress. I am afraid that his efforts were unsuccessful as Rupert and I had limited personal exchanges at the drinks party and dinners that I attended with him for a short time. Instead, Mr Murdoch and I rapidly confirmed that we were deeply unsympathetic politically and that neither found the other congenial company.

Even more significant for the Conservative Party than the increasing influence of Rupert Murdoch, was the Berry family's sale of the *Daily Telegraph* in 1986. Under the Berry ownership, and under a series of magnificent editors including Bill Deedes, the *Telegraph* had been a sound traditional newspaper and the voice of Conservative Middle England. Accurately described as 'the voice of the Tory Party at prayer', it had had a huge and loyal readership amongst committed Conservative Party supporters including a very large circulation in my own constituency. In 1986 it had been sold to the Canadian media magnate Conrad Black. Conrad was a somewhat notorious character whose increasingly controversial profile in Canada had been part of the inspiration for his moving his base to the United Kingdom. I got to know him over the next few years and, although he was undoubtedly a scoundrel, I always found him rather engaging before he finally went to prison in the United States.

I first met Conrad through my special adviser Tessa Keswick and her husband Henry. Tessa hadn't been with me long before going out of her way to introduce me to Conrad at a private meeting, in which she urged him to support my ultimate progress to become leader of the Conservative Party. I was somewhat taken aback by this, and thought it a rather startling move but I happily engaged in the conversation. Tessa was obviously rather persuasive with Mr Black, as he seemed quite tempted by the idea. He did, however, make it absolutely clear that he would only support a hard-line Eurosceptic and that the condition for his support would be a U-turn on my part on Britain's membership of the European Union.

As I got to know Conrad better it became quite clear to me that his main motive in purchasing the *Telegraph* titles had been to launch a campaign to ensure that the United Kingdom left the European Union and became a member of the North American Free Trade

Area. Indeed, I once spoke against him in a public debate on this very proposition. Not surprisingly he was not able to persuade me. Conrad Black pursued his aim, however. Eventually he eased out his first excellent editor of the daily newspaper, the pro-European Max Hastings, and replaced him with Charles Moore who quickly assembled a team of journalists to pursue the anti-European aspects of Conrad's political agenda with great enthusiasm and skill.

Finally, the *Daily Mail* was a hugely successful middle-of-the-market right-wing newspaper. In 1992, its rather passive owner Lord Rothermere replaced its excellent editor of twenty years, the pro-European David English, with the equally brilliant but more populist and anti-European Paul Dacre, who remains the paper's editor in 2016. Dacre produced a strident but very readable newspaper that commanded a massive circulation exceeding any other publication apart from the tabloids. He also took the always-robust newspaper even more to the right with a strong anti-European flavour.

Through the 1980s and 1990s the style of newspaper reporting moved, by appropriate degrees according to the role in the market of the particular title, to a much more vigorous, constantly campaigning mode. Political reporting incorporated the celebrity culture that was sweeping the country, so that the personalities and private lives of a few leading political figures became an essential ingredient through which all news was filtered. News and comment mixed as never before. Only the BBC, the *Financial Times* and, surprisingly, Murdoch's Sky News remained immune to the changes.

It did not take long for both major parties' political campaigning to adjust to what was now believed and feared by many leading politicians to be the dominant influence in the country. Tony Blair was so convinced that media power had robbed the Labour Party of its otherwise inevitable victory in 1992 that he altered the whole style of his party, first in opposition and then in government, surrounding himself with popular journalists and public relations figures, led by the redoubtable Alastair Campbell, a former editor of the left-wing tabloid *Daily Mirror*. He changed the whole nature of political debate and the public presentation of government as soon as he had the chance.

*

This, then, was the background for the newly re-elected Conservative government in 1992. We had a healthy parliamentary majority, but a parliamentary party that was bitterly divided between the old mainstream (of which I was a part) and a large new and noisy faction of extreme anti-European campaigners. When the legislation came forward to ratify John Major's previously perceived triumph of the Maastricht Treaty, the proceedings coincided with a referendum in Denmark which had rejected it. Combined with our crash out of the ERM and the simmering resentment about Margaret Thatcher's fall, this was the final ingredient in the toxic mix that provoked the emergence of fierce opposition to the treaty from a section of the parliamentary party. The previously unexceptionable and uncommented-upon Maastricht Treaty became the key element in a ferocious civil war that dominated John Major's government and made party management almost impossible. The ferocity of the internal disagreements and their prominence in political debate steadily made the government ever less popular and ever less credible, making its ultimate electoral defeat inevitable.

15

'School Days'

(Dizzy Gillespie, 1951)

EDUCATION

In November 1990, John Major was ascendant and triumphant, newly anointed as leader of the party and our fresh-start prime minister. He very quickly telephoned me, asking me to continue as Secretary of State for Education. I had expected this, but others in the defeated Hurd camp were less optimistic. I spent much of the rest of that day reassuring them that John Major was quite happy to 'take prisoners' from our ranks.

I then turned seriously to the business of being a reforming Education Secretary. Margaret Thatcher had moved me to the department before her fall from power. She wanted to cool down the wild controversy over at the Department of Health but she plainly wanted me to warm up the level of political activity at the Department of Education. As Education Secretary, Ken Baker had initiated radical legislation to introduce self-government to state schools – to be called 'grant-maintained schools' and 'city technology colleges' – a national system of regular testing of all pupils, and a national curriculum. However, in the eighteen months since he had been reshuffled away from the department, his reforms seemed to have lost all momentum. John MacGregor had presided over the department in an exceptionally calm and inactive way even for someone of his measured temperament. I was once told that, many years later, he had had to be reminded that he had once had a spell at Education: it had momentarily slipped his memory. John had a very distinguished political career but he was certainly not an activist in this particular portfolio.

Margaret had therefore stressed how much she wanted me to get on with her government's reforms. Until this conversation, I had not realized, despite working with her for so many years, how much she had hated her time as Ted Heath's Secretary of State for Education. She apparently had had a very dominant permanent secretary with whom she had obviously been at war most of the time. She now bitterly denounced the department's left-wing tendencies and gave me dire warnings of the obstruction that I should expect.

Margaret's warnings might have been infused with an element of personal retrospective animosity, but they soon turned out to be not very far from the truth. The officials in the Department for Education were friendly, agreeable people, but the whole culture there was totally hostile to the Baker reforms and resistant to any further implementation of them.

I am a great believer in and defender of the non-political Civil Service, and a great fan of the many hard-working and talented civil servants with whom I have worked over a long career. I deeply object to the growth in the number of politically appointed advisers, who are exempt from the requirements on civil servants to be appointed on merit, to behave with impartiality and objectivity, and to act so as to retain the confidence of future governments of a different political complexion. Many of these so-called special advisers are not nearly so expert as they think they are and simply magnify the political faults of their ministers. Any suggestion that the top posts in the Civil Service should be politicized is, to me, deeply suspect. However, this fine British tradition of a non-political Civil Service only works so long as the civil servants accept that their role within it is not to determine policy, but rather to advise, warn and deliver.

The dominant personality in the Department for Education was a very able senior civil servant called Nick Stuart. An intelligent and articulate man, Nick took the lead in presenting every argument to me. The permanent secretary, John Caines, was more self-effacing. I had by this time got into my own way of running a department and, as usual,

I treated it as an enjoyable debating society. However, I had longer and more argumentative meetings with Nick Stuart and the officials in Education, and encountered more straightforward political opposition to my views from them, than in any other single department.

The constant debates with departmental officials were terrific fun but implementing policy could be like wading through treacle. Nick and others insisted on regarding the principles behind Ken Baker's 1988 Education Reform Act, which had legislated for the national curriculum and Standard Assessment Tests (SATs), and given schools the ability to 'opt out' of local authority control, as essentially experimental in nature. John MacGregor, Ken Baker's successor and my predecessor, appeared to have been satisfied with the official line that the limited implementation Ken Baker had managed before moving on in July 1989 should be considered 'trials', and that these trials should continue for a few more years so that they could be evaluated before any question of extending them nationally was considered. This was exactly the approach that the BMA, in its more conciliatory moments, had tried to persuade me to take at the Department of Health. Now, at endless long meetings, I argued my case for rapid implementation of Ken Baker's education reforms as vigorously as the officials argued theirs for trials, equivocations and delays. I insisted on concluding the meetings by giving my final decisions point by point. Even so, I soon found that I had to keep closely in touch with each topic to find out whether anything very significant was being done to implement those decisions.

Reforming the education system was important not because I wanted to kick teachers, most of whom were – and are – pleasant and hard-working people. It was important because the system within which the teachers were working was too often failing children and their parents. The system had developed in such a way that it prioritized the needs of the professionals working within it over those of pupils or their parents. Moreover, there were unacceptable variations in outcomes which no one was measuring properly, and for which no one was being held accountable. As I had done at Health when Margaret and others had been so keen on private health insurance, I quickly repudiated the right wing's preferred solution of vouchers and instead got on with introducing measurement, accountability, openness and choice.

Underpinning everything that I wished to do, and everything Ken Baker had intended, was the desire to restore and raise standards of educational attainment in the country. Amazingly, there were many people who did not regard this as the principal aim of education policy. One of my first meetings with officials at the department was about the controversial new GCSE exams, which had recently been introduced to replace O levels. There was considerable controversy about whether or not the new examination had, as most members of the public believed, lowered educational standards. The officials assured me and my team that the GCSE had raised standards but it became clear in later years that this was not the case. Arguments about standards were at the heart of the continual policy battles between me and my officials. I steadily came to realize that one of the clear aims of those who took a more progressive view was to avoid excessive judgement of pupils' attainment or the prompting of any sense of failure amongst those who either did not or could not achieve high academic standards. GCSEs survived, but there was later an attempt to get rid of A levels and replace them with a similar broad-brush appraisal system. I did dig my heels in and resolutely defended A levels as the 'gold standard' of our educational system.

I am sure that the intelligent and highly motivated people who disagreed with me were convinced that I was an old-fashioned reactionary going back to a notion of education that was thoroughly outdated. I had no illusions at all about returning to some lost golden age of traditional academic teaching. But I was convinced that the rapidly changing nature of society required higher standards in basic academic subjects as well as artistic and cultural creation. We needed to keep pace with the technological and scientific advances of our time. We needed to aspire to the standards that were being achieved by some of our rivals in the world including emerging competitors in Asia such as Singapore and China. I was quite convinced that we faced a danger of producing future generations of school-leavers who would be inadequately prepared for all the pressures of the modern world.

I had of course been educated myself in a very traditional way at an excellent school which I have already described as having been something of an academic sweatshop. I had arrived there, and later at Cambridge University, because I was good at taking exams. I was, though, only too aware that most of the people outside the educational world with whom I discussed these things were very prone to take as their model whatever school system they themselves had come through. Even people who had hated their school seemed to regard any subsequent changes unfavourably. I consciously tried to avoid succumbing to this tendency myself. I shared the widespread misgiving that educational standards had somehow dropped in the country over the previous ten to twenty years, but I also realized there was no clear evidence for this. I did, however, firmly believe that we should develop a system that would succeed in stretching all pupils to the limit of their individual abilities, and in maximizing every pupil's opportunities to improve their quality of life.

I felt that the introduction of regular testing was one of the most important elements of Ken's package. The actual progress of individual pupils and the evaluation of that progress school by school was at this time still a matter completely closed to the outside world. Most parents had no idea whether their children's school was doing well or badly in comparison with similar schools in the neighbourhood, let alone elsewhere. Their natural inclination was to feel loyal to their children's school, and thus not to question the abilities of the staff to bring out the best in their pupils.

Particularly problematic was a tendency to assume that any failure on the part of individual schools was entirely attributable to the social make-up of the local area. In the poorer parts of cities, the most appalling outcomes were automatically blamed on the deprivation of the neighbourhood. Conversely, success was always attributed to the school and not to its intake. In middle-class areas, some schools were quite content to coast along without the slightest thought as to whether they were actually adding significantly to the efforts of their pupils' supportive parents.

The teaching unions, though, were totally opposed to the idea of formal testing of pupils in any way. And the department agreed with

the NUT and the other unions on almost every feature of policy.
Astonishingly, this included the introduction of pupil testing via SATs,
despite the fact that these had been passed some two years earlier.
Unions and officials seemed to believe that it was utterly outrageous
that any school should be accountable to the outside world for the
results of its teaching, even to the point of resisting my argument
that parents should at least be informed of their children's actual level
of attainment. I was told authoritatively that testing was elitist and
would divide pupils by revealing the differences in attainment between
them. It was seen as part of a defunct Victorian academic tradition
which post-1960s education theory rejected. Children should neither
be tested nor pressed too hard in any way, lest they be discouraged
by a sense of failure. Despite exhortations to refer to the new Statutory
Assessment Tests only by their acronym 'SATs', I soon began to take
a certain grim pleasure in talking regularly in public about the introduction of 'testing'.

I very strongly insisted that we were going to proceed both with
the introduction of the compulsory SATs, as provided for in Ken
Baker's 1988 Act, and, further, with publishing the results for every
school. I thereby created the so-called league tables, which we
published for the first time in 1991 and which have dominated the
education world ever after. Encouraged by my special adviser Tessa
Keswick, who had moved with me from the Department of Health,
I insisted that schools in disadvantaged areas could quite sensibly
explain why their results were not as good as those of schools in leafy
suburbs. Most members of the public would understand the difficulties facing teachers in deprived areas. What the results rapidly began
to show, of course, was that some inner-city schools did spectacularly
better than others, and that some got better results than weaker
schools in much wealthier areas. The whole exercise proved to be
one of the strongest stimuli to incentivizing schools to pay attention
to their pupils' progress.

Before he left the department, Ken Baker had also set in train the
implementation of his proposed national curriculum, another essential feature of his reforms. Until now, there had been no uniformity
or consistency in what was taught in our country's primary and

secondary schools. I shared Ken's conviction that there were some key banks of knowledge which every pupil needed to acquire. It was quite ridiculous to pretend that literacy, numeracy, a knowledge of history and a basic knowledge of the sciences were not crucial priorities in the education of every child, but this was in fact the situation in the most eccentric of our state schools, and in a very large number of institutions they were not given adequate regard. The schools that had been worst affected by the absurd fashions and anti-academic bias of the 1960s had developed some quite extraordinary curricula.

Ken Baker had had the same trouble getting his reforms through Parliament that I had faced at Health and had made various concessions. In particular he had accepted that politicians should not be allowed to dictate the actual content of the curriculum. Our left-wing critics assumed that left to themselves Conservative ministers would produce a diet for the country's children of laissez-faire capitalism and right-wing elitism, imparted via military-style teaching methods. Ken had been obliged to concede that the detailed content of his curricula should be drafted by committees of experts drawn from a wide background, who would produce recommendations for the Secretary of State.

I suspect that the department had packed these committees with members with very strong fashionable left-wing biases. The civil servants had also provided the secretariats for each committee and had therefore drafted the actual reports. I was absolutely astonished by some of the proposals.

The curricula recommended to me included no requirement of any kind for any pupil to be given any knowledge of the essential facts. Any suggestion of facts to be understood and memorized was dismissed as 'rote learning'. When I insisted that part of the point of education was to enable pupils to acquire the body of knowledge in each subject that had been built up over the generations, I was accused of wanting to return to the days of blackboard and chalk. The point, apparently, was not to fill little heads with any facts but to enable them to acquire a sympathy with the subject at their own pace, and to develop their own personalities and approach to any problems.

I have always had a particular interest in both British and global history. I was presented with a proposed history curriculum which required no teaching of any historical facts of any kind. The pupils were instead to be given a feeling for various stages of mainly British history, and to be taught to empathize in particular with the working class in their historic struggles. When I tried to insist that some essential elements of key events and dramatic occasions should be included I was dismissed, both inside the department and at outside meetings with teachers and experts, as wanting to return to old-fashioned 'Kings and Battles' history. They only composed a comparatively small part of the narrative of events that I thought should be included, but no king and no battle was going to intrude into the educational establishment's proposed curriculum.

Similarly, the geography curriculum recommended to me mainly concentrated on teaching how capitalism was destroying the environment and contained no factual education into the nature, topography or economy of any particular part of the globe. I was scorned for wanting to return to Victorian 'Capes and Bays' geography lessons. I had a particularly entertaining meeting with a room full of geography teachers held in Church House where the claims from the floor became ever more ludicrous and the very notion of teaching where other nations were and how lives were lived there was derided.

English literature appeared to play no very important part in the English curriculum. One of my opponents angrily asserted to me that it was quite wrong to include in the teaching of literature the work of 'dead white males', regardless of any literary quality which conventional wisdom might ascribe to any of them. To such critics Shakespeare was obviously a reactionary and even Byron must have been a Tory.

The officials had high hopes that I might appreciate the music curriculum because it did mention jazz which is my own enthusiastic musical preference. There was indeed one reference to jazz in the draft curriculum, as a black man's music from America derived from the music of slaves – white men like Benny Goodman and Stan Getz had, to my horror, been overlooked. However, there was no mention at all of any European classical music. The curriculum instead made frequent references to the then fashionable West Indian reggae music, which I quite enjoyed myself but which I did not believe should be made so dominant in a curriculum which should introduce pupils to a wide range of musical forms.

In short, I encountered the worst and most extreme examples of the 1960s alternative culture which seemed still to attract many of the leading figures in the closed world of educational policymaking and teacher training.

Alongside these skirmishes over SATs and the national curriculum, the main business of implementing our education reforms consisted of my attempts to achieve a huge increase in the number of schools gaining independent status as grant-maintained schools or city technology colleges. This policy had been Ken Baker's method of enabling the more ambitious and go-ahead governors and head teachers to achieve independence from the usually stifling and inhibiting control of their local education authorities, and gain more control over their own affairs. Almost all local education authorities were completely controlled by their large numbers of education officials who sought to impose precisely the anti-academic 1960s culture which the government was trying to reverse. I strongly approved of Ken's policy – which like others had been entirely suspended under my predecessor – and I wanted to resume the conversion of as many schools as possible to independent status. I wanted standards and norms to be set nationally, but delivery to be determined locally with accountability to the general public for results.

Many head teachers were only too anxious to free themselves from the unwelcome local authority control under which they found themselves. Unfortunately, another concession Ken Baker had been obliged to concede to the House of Lords during the passage of his legislation was that any change of status would be subject to a ballot of the parents of the school's current pupils.

This gave the local authorities an important weapon in their bitter fights to retain ideological control of all the schools in their patch. Some authorities devoted very considerable resources to the campaigns that ensued, causing consternation amongst parents who found themselves inundated with sometimes totally unscrupulous arguments about the supposedly nefarious motives of the governors and head teachers who wanted to change the status of their schools. Some governing bodies were reluctant to apply for grant-maintained status, fearing that if their application was ultimately unsuccessful they would face reprisals from the local authority. In my own area, Nottinghamshire County Council regularly argued that any change in status would lead to substantial cuts in the budget for the school in question. This was in fact the very opposite of the truth, because we had built financial incentives into the transition to help grant-maintained schools or city technology colleges build up their own support services.

The outcome was that only a very few schools escaped local authority control whilst the Conservatives were in office. This problem was only resolved a few years later by Tony Blair who, under guidance from his extremely astute adviser, the former political journalist Andrew Adonis, accelerated the process, partly by rebranding our city technology colleges as 'academies'. This produced a permanent beneficial change and the steady movement of schools away from the old political controls into a more open and competitive world.

No changes in the education world are uncontroversial, but perhaps my most lastingly controversial reform as Secretary of State for Education was my introduction of a truly independent inspectorate to advise on and monitor standards in all schools across the country.

I had inherited the body known as HM Inspectorate of Schools, which came with an excellent reputation. To my great disappointment, however, I soon discovered that it carried out almost no inspections. Most schools could expect to be inspected once every forty years and consequently very many schoolteachers could go throughout their entire careers without ever being involved in an inspection. Perhaps the paucity of inspections was no bad thing though, since I also discovered that the inspectorate entirely shared the outlook and culture of my departmental officials.

Instead of carrying out inspections, the inspectorate provided me with so-called expert advice on policy. Attempts were made to persuade me that advice had some additional authority if it came from the inspector rather than from the department, but I rapidly realized that the two sets of advice were strikingly similar, and that this was just another hugely conservative restraint on anything that I wished to do.

In frustration, I created a wholly new inspectorate called the Office for Standards in Education, which became known as OFSTED. Its main duty was to carry out regular inspections of every school across the country, through which it would assess the quality of education being offered and the standard achieved. I also charged it to make its inspection reports publicly available. The creation of OFSTED resulted in another enormous leap forward in the general public's knowledge and understanding of what was happening in local schools. This in turn increased parents' ability to identify which school might be best for their children, as well as providing greater evidence about what sort of teaching techniques actually worked.

I very much wanted to bring in an outside expert adviser to be chief executive of the new inspectorate, someone who shared my outlook on the desirability of raising standards of academic performance and outcomes for pupils. My special adviser Tessa Keswick was particularly enthusiastic about this policy change and introduced me to Chris Woodhead, a blunt advocate of traditional teaching methods who she felt would be a very suitable candidate. I was impressed by Chris, but felt that he might be a little too abrasive to lead a brand-new organization and instead appointed Stewart Sutherland, then Vice Chancellor of the University of London. Stewart brilliantly shepherded OFSTED into being and was Chief Inspector from 1990–2, at which point my successor at the department, John Patten, appointed Chris to succeed him.

Both were terrifically successful appointments. Unfortunately, many of the teaching profession were extremely hostile to this public examination of the quality of their achievements, and to their new accountability. A sense of near-paranoia and victimhood reared its head the moment anyone made any attempt to discuss or influence the way in which teaching was delivered. I met far too many teachers who were overexcited and agitated about the whole idea of finding themselves subjected to an inspection by OFSTED, and debate raged throughout my time and thereafter about the very existence of such a system. I continue to believe that the introduction of regular inspections had an extremely desirable effect in persuading teachers to pay more attention to the quality of their work. OFSTED remained a powerful force in the education world for many years, although, unfortunately, the influence of the teaching unions was too great for some of my Labour successors and eventually they appointed chief executives who were much more sympathetic to the educational culture that I had tried to reform.

The Secretary of State was also responsible for higher education. As an ever-increasing proportion of school-leavers began to go on to higher education, the universities and polytechnics were also in need of reform.

Inevitably, many of my arguments were about funding – of institutions and of students. I was constantly frustrated by the old-fashioned and reactionary attitudes of far too many of the vice chancellors and governing bodies of our universities. In all too many cases, the vice chancellorships were filled by distinguished but unworldly academics who often regarded their role as honorary, and engaged only to a very limited extent in the actual management of their universities.

I spent a great deal of time trying to persuade vice chancellors and governing bodies to look for additional sources of funding. Some of the more go-ahead amongst them responded to this very well and some were already doing it without ministerial encouragement. A few had also developed links with local businesses and used these as a source of support and additional funding for particular faculties. I constantly emphasized the desirability of close links between the relevant departments of universities and the business world, which could – and indeed did – stimulate a great deal of innovation, and often generated new commercial activity in pioneering fields.

I made some progress but still frequently encountered the fiercest resistance. The more left-wing academics were extremely hostile to the idea that universities should obtain any resources from private funds, seeing any hint of moneymaking as corrosive of the ideal of the ivory tower. During my short time at the department, shifting opinion on this proved remarkably difficult. It was years before many universities eventually moved to a more American-style culture whereby funds were solicited from alumni and links formed with business sponsors as a fairly regular feature of higher education.

At that time, higher education was divided into two distinct categories – universities and polytechnics – which I found utterly bizarre. Polytechnics had originally been intended to be more vocational and business-oriented than traditional universities, with a wider range of students, including part-time students acquiring degrees in the course of their working careers. These were admirable aims, but they were sadly accompanied by a prevailing view that polytechnics were of lower status than conventional universities, precisely because they were tainted by their connections with the real outside world of business and work.

Even more bizarrely, the academics and lecturers in the polytechnics shared this view. They were obsessed with a feeling that they were looked down upon both by the traditional academic world and by the wider public. This was a wholly unnecessary persecution complex because there was substantial overlap in standards between the two kinds of institution. The best of the polytechnics achieved much higher academic standards than the worst of the traditional universities. Hatfield Polytechnic, Trent Polytechnic and others had very much better faculties than some of the weaker universities which diplomacy constrains me from naming.

There was also a quite absurd distinction in the way the two types of higher-education institution related to ministers and the department. They had two completely separate systems of funding which were administered on quite different policy bases. Polytechnics were subjected to a system of inspection and quality control whereas universities were entirely exempt from any outside accountability. Apart from anything else, the separation of the two categories of higher education was wasteful and inefficient in its administration.

Unsurprisingly, I was quite exasperated by this ludicrous arrangement and I declared the abolition of this division as a matter of policy. In any other Western country, all these higher-education institutions would have been described as universities. In future, therefore, they would all be universities, and they would all be dealt with by government on the same basis.

There were some problems with this which I was never quite able to resolve. Before announcing the new policy, I had been assured by many heads of polytechnics that they would not abandon their more technical, engineering and business-oriented cultures. Unfortunately, the lure of the status of academia led several institutions to renege on this. Contrary to my guidance and to the assurances that I had received, several of the newly designated universities decided to open up rather second-rate arts faculties in the belief that this would give them a greater veneer of respectability in the wider world.

I was also put under enormous pressure to designate other colleges of various types as universities. Colleges of rather lower academic levels, including some that were really further-education colleges providing a few degree courses, lobbied their MPs to support their claims to be given university status. I resisted all these, sometimes to the deep disappointment of backbench Conservative colleagues who had been persuaded to join in local campaigns of this kind. Unfortunately, some of my successors gave way to this kind of lobbying so that the category of university did acquire one or two rather fringe additions in later years.

Overall, however, this policy was a great and lasting success and I am happy to say that no one has contemplated trying to revert to the system I had inherited.

Further education was an area in which I also tried to take a close interest during my time as Education Secretary. It has become a cliché to describe further education as the 'Cinderella service' of the education world. It is of vital importance to all those who do not achieve enough at school, allowing them to prepare themselves for the world of work or to make a last attempt to enter university. Several Education Secretaries have tried to improve its status and performance over the years. David Young and I had already done our best to introduce some substance into this area with our introduction of vocational qualifications when we were at the Department for Employment.

The difficulty was that most local education authorities, who were responsible for the FE colleges, regarded them as fairly unimportant and many gave much higher priority to school sixth forms which regarded the colleges as their rivals and competitors. After considering the subject for quite some time, I finally decided to take all the FE colleges completely out of local authority control and to give them independent publicly owned status as autonomous institutions. I believed that the best directors and staff might leap at the opportunity to make their courses better and more relevant to the wider world than they had previously been allowed to.

Fortunately I succeeded. Whereas Ken Baker's attempts to give schools more autonomy and to remove them from the dead hand of local government had been staged and delayed, and indeed the process of moving to academy status is still controversial twenty years later, I simply legislated to give the FE colleges autonomous status in one fell swoop.

The legislation attracted some political controversy but it was surprisingly muted. Perhaps this was because the colleges did not matter to the local councils, or perhaps it was the advocacy of the best FE college principals to their MPs. The Labour Party went through the motions but as the 1992 election approached they did not block the proposal. Indeed, every parliament ends with negotiation through the Whips' Offices of both sides of the House about which outstanding pieces of legislation should be allowed to go through to royal assent and which the departing government should drop. The Labour Party allowed my further-education proposals to go through. I strongly suspect that my Shadow ministerial team were quietly sympathetic to the proposals I was making so long as the Conservative Party was allowed to take the blame. This, too, has been kept in place by subsequent governments and I'm constantly assured by further-education principals that it was a significant stage in our development of the full range of post-school and adult education.

My time at the Department of Education – and before it at Health – had been years of perpetual high-profile conflict and controversy while I did public battle with a wide variety of vociferous and popular lobbies in the world of health and education. I know many colleagues who have found it very difficult to withstand the stress of a political career of this kind.

I have already observed that I have a remarkably calm temperament, have the hide of a pachyderm and positively enjoy controversy. It makes me feel that what I'm engaged in is important and actually matters. A long, quiet, uncontroversial tenure of office in any department would have had a more depressing effect upon me than the constant stimulus that I derived from political battles for causes which I, mistakenly or otherwise, firmly believed in.

Unfortunately, Gillian's temperament was quite different. She enjoyed aspects of ministerial life and remained unreservedly supportive of my turbulent political career. She got pleasure from political life in the constituency and our involvement with events. But crisis and criticism always hurt her and as the years went on she found it more and more difficult to deal with. She became really quite distressed about the insults that were thrown in my direction during my time at Health and Education.

In later years, when I was Chancellor of the Exchequer, she began to find it even more arduous. Whilst insults, abuse and attacks bounced off me, she was wounded by some of the exchanges in the Maastricht era. At one stage I decided that it would improve her general well-being if she no longer read the rabidly Eurosceptic daily news as reported and commented upon in the *Daily Telegraph*. I unilaterally changed the newspaper delivery to our house in Nottingham so that she thereafter received the *Independent* and the *Guardian*. Thankfully, this did cheer her up a bit.

I couldn't stop her from listening to the radio though. Gillian made an angry and distressed call to the BBC after the comedian Jeremy Hardy had said that there were still some things that made life worthwhile – 'birdsong in the spring . . . and the prospect of seeing Kenneth Clarke go to his grave'.

Gillian's way of protecting herself, and me, was to refuse the many requests from journalists to discuss our personal life, whether for the purpose of better understanding me, or to write some kind of profile of Gillian herself. 'I believe,' she wrote to one, 'that our private and personal life should remain so – a haven, perhaps, in the hurly-burly of political life. As such it is to be guarded and protected.' In making the same point to another she said that our private and personal life is 'a sanctuary and refuge which is closed to all but family and our closest friends. Attempts to examine and analyse personal relationships, especially marriages, are, to my mind, akin to pulling up plants to make sure that the roots are doing well.' Gillian was also conscious that any personal details, once recorded, were available to all commentators who 'can, and usually will, put a hostile twist to suit their own theses'. She also never wanted to lay herself open to the charge of being happy to use the press when it suited her, but unhappy when it turned on her: her solution was not to engage at all.

I was obviously influenced during my too-short time at Education, and indeed throughout my life, by my own background as a spectacular beneficiary of the meritocracy of the grammar-school system. I knew how fortunate I had been to arrive in Nottingham in the early 1950s when someone of my background could enjoy such opportunities. By the time I was Secretary of State for Education, the then MP for Nottingham North, Graham Allen, a man I liked and quite admired, assured me that Bulwell had the lowest level of university entrance of any similar area in England. I'm not a man given to nostalgia and I had no desire at all to return future generations to the rather grim atmosphere of post-war England which was as cruel to those unable to take advantage of its opportunities as it was kind to those lucky enough to be given them. I was, however, driven on by a desire to make the life chances of future generations as good as we possibly could. I continue to hope that my grandchildren's generation will find themselves living in a much fairer and more open society than those of my parents' generation, and my own. The underlying principles of the reforms devised by Ken Baker and given impetus by me have never been reversed by any successor of any political party so far. I hope that that will continue.

16

'You're Under Arrest'

(Miles Davis, 1985)

HOME SECRETARY

On the morning of 10 April 1992, re-elected with the biggest popular vote ever received by any British prime minister, John Major summoned me to Number 10. He told me rather solemnly that he wanted me to become Home Secretary, saying 'It is time for you to hold one of the great offices of state.' I was thrilled and accepted without hesitation and – rather matching his solemn tone – I expressed my gratitude and loyalty. I did not ask at the time and indeed never discovered why he had dismissed his previous Home Secretary from the government, bringing Kenneth Baker's ministerial career to a rather surprising and abrupt end. Ken Baker was a salesman with a serious interest in policy and a driving ambition, and was a very congenial colleague. He must have been rather shocked at being dropped. In 1997 he went up to the Lords, from where he continued to take an interest in education policy and promote good ideas like his university technical colleges.

This next move in my much-reshuffled ministerial career took me to an enormous – and hideous – concrete fortress opposite St James's Park Tube station in Petty France, the headquarters of the Home Office. The office was as bleak inside as it was out, but it did indeed house a vast and powerful organization.

The Home Office at that time had a huge and eclectic range of powers, many dating from when it was first established, in 1782, to deal with domestic, as opposed to foreign, affairs. Its core responsibilities were the police, the prison service, MI5 and immigration, but it also had countless other responsibilities that sat rather oddly with its main focus.

For example, I found that my most problematic responsibility, in my short fourteen months there, was for horse racing and gambling. Far too much of my time was occupied in trying to reconcile the competing interests of the owners of racecourses, the owners of racehorses, the bookmakers and the government-owned betting organization known as the Tote, which since 1976 had been chaired by an old confidant of Margaret Thatcher, the engaging but eccentric Woodrow Wyatt. All these interest groups hated one another with deep bitterness and were constantly bringing me proposals to gain an advantage over the others. It came to a head when I discovered that one of my duties as Home Secretary was to settle the annual negotiations about the size of the levy which the betting interests were obliged by law to pay to subsidize the sport upon which they then so heavily depended.

My other responsibilities were considerably more significant. I was most heavily engaged in attempting to start the reform of the police. In my relations with the police and fire service generally, I was ably assisted by my splendid minister in the Lords, Earl Ferrers. Robin Ferrers was a wonderfully old-fashioned and very charming hereditary peer. He was one of the very few working peers who really was a descendant of a medieval military family that had won its title in armour on the battlefield, unlike the generality of hereditary peers who were usually the descendants of Victorian entrepreneurs who had bought their titles from Gladstone or Disraeli. Robin carried out all the more symbolic duties of the day-to-day minister for the police service: his galvanizing visits to units all over the country, designed to show interest and encourage, had an inspirational effect on morale.

As well as being responsible for national policing policy, for some peculiar reason the Home Secretary was also personally responsible for the Metropolitan Police, acting as its police authority. I soon realized, however, that I was as powerless as the county councillors and magistrates who made up the largely useless local police authorities across the country. Only four officials helped me with the Met and they usually advised me that there was nothing that I could actually do to influence the activities of the force for which I was nominally responsible. Its commissioner, the most senior police officer in the country, who regarded everything the force did as his personal operational responsibility, led the Met. The only serious decision that I managed to take in this regard was to exercise my right to appoint a new commissioner when Peter Imbert, the man I inherited, retired. I infuriated some members of the Met by appointing Paul Condon, who had been a vigorous and reforming leader as chief constable of Kent. Resented as an outsider at first, he went on to take serious and much-needed steps to reduce corruption and improve performance, until he had an unfortunate disagreement with my eventual successor, Jack Straw.

Being Home Secretary gave me my first direct contact with the important work of the intelligence services. MI5 is responsible for the UK's internal security, which was then dominated by the continued violent insurrection in Ulster. MI5 was then led by Stella Rimington, a very capable and personable woman. Both Stella and her ex-husband John Rimington were from Nottingham, and he had been school captain during my time at Nottingham High School. Several years earlier when I had been at the Department for Employment I had been amazed to discover that John had become head of the Health and Safety Commission. I found him rather stuffy and he did not improve my opinion of that very tricky quango. By this point, Stella and John were long separated and she and I had a considerably more cordial relationship.

Nevertheless, I was never persuaded that MI5 regarded my role as much more than formal and nominal. It is in the very nature of secret services that they live in a closed world, keeping all information to themselves except when it is essential to share it. They are also obliged, in the public interest, to engage in some lawful but unusual and unconventional activities. This does not make them the most open and forthcoming organization in their dealings with their supposed political boss.

When I was first appointed I had a conversation with the most distinguished of my predecessors in this office, Roy Jenkins. His only comment on MI5 was to warn me to treat them with care and to say that I would never really discover what they were up to. His tenure had covered the period in which the then prime minister Harold Wilson had become convinced to the point of paranoia that MI5 were spying on him and seeking to undermine him. Although it was a most unreliable account, a later memoir published by a maverick former member of the service seemed – to some limited degree – to support that Wilsonian fear.

MI5 were friendly enough when I insisted that I should be kept better informed about what they were doing but I was never left with the impression that I would be allowed to know very much about anything except their more spectacular operations and their successes, which were occasionally presented to me in order to reassure me. This was not necessary: I knew they had a difficult task, and that they were quite essential in our fight against the IRA in Ireland and on the mainland, in which they were achieving considerable success. I simply wanted them to be more open and accountable. I did make a point of refusing to sign some of the huge numbers of warrants which were presented to me to authorize surveillance and other covert activity against various individuals, to establish that I was not going to rubber-stamp every operation, but I never made as much progress as I intended in establishing proper accountability for their more unconventional activities.

The prison service was another world of its own. By the early 1990s we had a problem-ridden and deplorable prison service with far too many overcrowded, ancient and unsuitable jails. The whole service was dominated by a very strong and reactionary trade union, the Prison Officers' Association (POA). The POA regarded itself – correctly – as a powerful and independent body and I soon realized that many of our prisons were managed at the dictate of the local POA leadership, rather than by the governor.

I was greatly assisted in my dealings with the prison service by my Minister of State Peter Lloyd, an old friend. Peter, a quiet, diplomatic and determined man, had been chairman of the Cambridge University Conservative Association in my first term at Cambridge and I soon learnt to trust him entirely with day-to-day responsibility for that difficult service. As I had done with Virginia Bottomley and social services at Health, I simply said to Peter that the prison service was his to get on with, but that if we were about to have a monumental row, he should tell me. Then we could sit down and work out together what to do and what to say. In the meantime, it took an enormous load off my own desk.

In this job, monumental rows were almost inevitable. The career of my predecessor but one, David Waddington, had been entirely destroyed by a dreadful riot at Strangeways Prison in Manchester which had lasted twenty-five days, caused two fatalities and cost tens of millions of pounds. David had bitterly complained to me at the time that his officials had not allowed him to play any part in managing the riot and he had really only known what was happening day-to-day by reading the newspapers.

It was obvious from my visits to prisons that conditions in some of them were still so poor that the risk of violence and rioting was ever present. I was extremely lucky on that front. Only once during my time did prisoners burst out of a prison roof, camp themselves in the open air and threaten a riot. The press and the TV crews gathering outside rapidly exacerbated the situation. I found myself in a ferocious argument with my veteran private secretary, Colin Walters, about my wish to get directly involved in managing the incident. Senior officials had forbidden him even to tell me where the emergency command headquarters was located, while I was firmly insisting that I wanted to drive down there to speak to the command team (wherever they might be) when news came through that heavy rain had begun falling on the prison. The potential rioters became so drenched and dispirited that they went quietly back inside through the hole in the roof, and the riot was averted. Nevertheless, it did seem slightly odd that civil servants expected ministers to meekly take responsibility and, if necessary, the blame, for the management of such incidents whilst allowing us no role whatsoever in the decision-making.

Immigration was another potential nightmare and I insisted on appointing my friend and former parliamentary private secretary

Charles Wardle to handle it. There were constant problems with immigration cases and policies.

Campaigns about immigration decisions would often come from the hard-right tabloid press and also from the ultra-liberal left-wing broadsheets with support from predictable members of the public.

One of the odder cases involved an application for asylum from a very corrupt former office-holder from Nigeria who had fled his country and wanted to settle in the UK. My old friend Lynda Chalker, now a junior minister at the Foreign Office, encouraged me to reject the claim, believing that it would damage relations with the Nigerian government if this notoriously corrupt man was allowed to settle comfortably in England. The problem was that his wife was already living in London and his daughters were attending a very expensive and well-known British public school. He was living in a very comfortable flat in Paris but now wished to rejoin his family in London.

I tried to support the immigration service in treating his application for political asylum as coming from someone trying to escape from legitimate criminal justice, which would have meant that we refused him. The *Guardian* newspaper, supported by predictable lobbies, made a tremendous fuss about our heartless decision. Accounts appeared of his escaping his enemies in Nigeria in a small boat. His mortification at being separated from his wife and children and left stranded and solitary in France was underlined. My officials tried to get me to follow their long-standing policy of never commenting to the media about the details of individual cases. I respected the need to preserve the confidentiality and privacy of individual harrowing claims, but I tried to get this principle abandoned in the case of someone who was using publicity to promote a totally misleading and untruthful account of his circumstances. Charles and I maintained this line for as long as we could, but I seem to recall that the legal processes of appeal eventually enabled this multimillionaire to move to join his family in the country of his choice.

But we managed to keep things reasonably under control and immigration was not in my time the crisis-ridden and poisonous subject of public debate that it became again in later years. I only intervened occasionally when there was any press controversy over rather startlingly liberal decisions by my immigration officials, apparently based on their assumption that immigration could not really be controlled in the world of modern travel. I was firmly of the view that public xenophobia should not be needlessly stirred.

The army of officials who helped me to preside over this mare's nest of challenging issues were both high-powered and high quality, but the department had the most distinctive – and old-fashioned – culture of any government department in which I ever served. It was intensely hierarchical. Everything had to go through the permanent secretary Clive Whitmore, who ran the department. My usual debating-society approach was not only frowned upon, but effectively prohibited. Only very senior officials were ever allowed into my room for the policy meetings that filled the day. The permanent secretary was usually the only official to speak at such meetings, suffering very occasional short interventions from the most senior of his colleagues. Eventually I discovered from my Private Office that Sir Clive exercised the right to set out the department's advice based on his personal opinion. Every one of the relevant senior colleagues might have disagreed with him at previous internal meetings, but they would then sit at my table and remain almost silent while he alone debated with me.

It was only through the services of my excellent Private Office and my own little team of junior officials that I could begin to penetrate this and make some progress. My first private secretary, Colin Walters, was quite a veteran in the post and on good terms with both me and with the permanent secretary. This was helpful: every good private secretary is able to act as a kind of double agent. Colin would brief me on what Clive was really up to and wanted to achieve. No doubt he also briefed Clive on what I was really up to and wanted to achieve. I had, of course, taken with me to the Home Office my keen and activist special adviser, Tessa Keswick, and together with my Private Office, she was a close ally.

However things really took off when my Private Office took on an unexpected and very reformed quality of its own. Colin Walters decided to move to Australia and was replaced by the formidable Joan MacNaughton. Joan was a very purposeful and forceful woman with strong opinions. She and I got on extremely well although I probably had more flare-ups and rows with her than with any other public servant I ever worked with. I usually have a reserve of personal good manners and diplomacy with which to handle difficulties but once – uniquely amongst my private secretaries – she did storm out of a meeting with me, slamming the door behind her. Joan's advice was always very good and her firm opinions were often quite right. She was a determined feminist and she succeeded, with my passive consent, in assembling the first all-female Private Office that I had ever had. I always took the view that we should accelerate the promotion of a proper proportion of women as quickly as possible: whenever I had the chance, in every department in which I served, I gave preference to a female candidate if she and a rival male contender were of equal ability. In the Home Office, I gave Joan her head and she assembled around me a very able and very supportive group of intelligent young women who acted as my eyes and ears in the department.

Once I managed to deal directly with officials other than the permanent secretary, I discovered that the department in fact had a great deal of high-level intellectual and managerial talent in its ranks. Unfortunately, though, the whole culture was still very resistant to change. Change was unwelcome and even when eventually accepted, it was implemented extremely slowly. A great deal of the advice I received implied that everything was under control and did not need much disturbance or any particularly spectacular innovation. This was not totally suitable advice to give to someone of my political reforming temperament.

Alongside private secretaries and special advisers, one of the most ever-present people in a minister's life is their driver. Roy Gibbons was first allocated to me when I had become a junior transport minister in 1979 and had driven me ever since. As my official driver, Roy, a very agreeable man, spent most of the day with me and, like all the experienced government drivers, he was well up to speed with all the political gossip and intrigue in Whitehall. He was excellent company and the two of us got on very well.

When I reached the Home Office, this great department of state insisted that the Home Secretary was always driven by a police driver and escorted by police security. I protested, but I was assured that, because of my responsibilities for the anti-terrorism policies protecting the country against the IRA, these security arrangements were essential. I therefore acquired a police driver and escort every time I travelled anywhere, whether for public duties or privately. This required the construction of a hut in the garden of our house in Nottingham so that a collection of firearms could be kept there, accompanied at all times by rotating shifts of police officers. It also meant that Gillian and I were put under pressure, to which we eventually succumbed, to leave our flat in Kennington because the police officers would have had to stand outside all the time to guard it. We moved instead into a very superior official residence in South Eaton Place in Belgravia.

A temporary snag arose when we discovered that the Treasury was attempting to move Norman Lamont and his wife Rosemary into the same residence, because yet another attempt was being made to maintain and improve the security of the Chancellor's normal residence at 11 Downing Street. Gillian and I got on perfectly well with the Lamonts as friends but neither couple was very keen on sharing the large house, and there was undoubtedly a disagreement about which floor would be taken by which family because the upstairs was markedly superior to the ground floor. I had one very keen and efficient official whose main job seemed to be to handle all the logistics of South Eaton Place. She was splendidly proprietorial about this Home Office residence and fiercely indignant about the Treasury's efforts to intrude. Exchanges of memos written in an almost comic parody of Civil Service prose failed to resolve the stand-off between these two great offices of state. Finally my Home Office champion decided that possession was nine-tenths of the law and arranged for Gillian and me to move in to the whole place, from where we defied the Treasury with our de facto occupation. The Treasury backed down.

These arrangements no doubt were a way of giving me complete security but they were also a dreadful nuisance. I'm inclined to think that they were also partly to ensure that the Association of Chief Police Officers and the senior ranks of the police service were kept fully aware of the Home Secretary's political intentions. This unworthy suspicion was no doubt extremely unfair to the friendly policemen who worked with me and who were always perfectly agreeable travelling companions. The combination of danger money, overtime and anti-social hours payments meant that they had one of the best-paid jobs in Whitehall.

The inconveniences were various. My police protection insisted that I sat in the back of the car. I would have much preferred to sit in the front passenger seat alongside the driver but I was assured that it was essential for security for my armed escort to sit there instead. I suspected that he sat there because of the superior legroom but my entreaties were overruled. My successor, Michael Howard, successfully overcame this rule by claiming that he suffered from travel sickness in the back of a car but I never thought of that wheeze. The other minor irritation was the habit of my police drivers of speeding excessively at all times even when we were not late – or indeed even running ahead of time. I succeeded in overruling their insistence, when driving Gillian and me to do the weekly shop in my own constituency car, that they park in disabled parking places or on the pavement right outside the door to the shop. They insisted that this too was necessary for security but the practice was – quite rightly – losing me votes by the minute. I eventually persuaded them to allow me to shop in Sainsbury's and to take the appalling risk of walking a few yards from the car park to the door.

But the fact that they had to share all my private activities and that everything had to be arranged in advance with them was a major inconvenience. They always sat at a separate table in restaurants but, early on, made it clear that they preferred good restaurants to the curry houses that I occasionally frequented. They quite liked football but several of them would have preferred more rugby. And they hated birdwatching, hardly surprising given that they were generally very unsuitably dressed for treks across wet grassland or into woods.

They also escorted me on foreign visits, both public and private, again with a varying level of enthusiasm. I visited Peru as part of our attempts to improve co-operation with the reforming but autocratic government of President Fujimori, whom I met to discuss ways of tackling the supply of and demand for illegal drugs. In preparation for the trip, one of my police officers read a book about Peru in which he discovered that it was largely controlled by a cruel and fanatical terrorist organization called Shining Path. He came to me in a state of panic, explaining that our visit was quite impossible. Peru was far too dangerous. I insisted that we had a good chance of being safe in the capital city of Lima so long as we kept to the right places, and that the Foreign Office had assured me that my proposed add-on birdwatching trip to the Ballestas Islands on the coast was perfectly safe. Reluctantly, I was allowed to go, accompanied by my nervous escort. It was an interesting and useful trip. The birdwatching in the Ballestas Islands was a great success, although the bemused British police officer did not seem able to engage with the pleasure of bouncing in a small boat round guano-covered islands which attracted the seabirds but which he realized were essentially the droppings of seagulls.

While I was in Peru the leader of Shining Path, Abimael Guzmán, was arrested. It turned out that he had been visiting a girlfriend who lived very near to the ambassador's Residence where we were staying and his arrest was the beginning of the end for Shining Path. I found Fujimori impressive and congenial, despite his fearsome reputation and alleged corruption, and our discussions did indeed pave the way for future co-operation.

As Home Secretary I was responsible for the provision of police protection to all present and past politicians believed to be at personal risk from IRA terrorism. There were too many of these and I had the difficult task of trying to persuade a number of eminent former ministers that their protection should come to an end. Ministers, in my experience, divide into two categories on police protection. Some are delighted to have it and like to keep an armed driver who can act as a valet and carrier of golf clubs. Others find the constant presence a considerable nuisance and cannot wait to get rid of it. One former Labour Secretary of State for Northern Ireland, who had left office many years previously, always protested that he was still at risk and would make provocative speeches in the House of Lords on the subject of the Republican threat if ever we threatened to remove his protection. The former prime minister Sir Alec Douglas-Home, on the other hand, could not be persuaded by me or anyone else to have police protection and lived quite alone in a huge house in the Scottish Borders.

I am firmly in the category of those who found the whole experience of protection an irritant. I abandoned my police protection on the day that I left the Home Office and I never had police driving me or camped out in my garden ever again.

The Shadow spokesman I found myself facing across the floor of the House was a rising young star of the Labour Party called Tony Blair. He was congenial and extremely bright, and he soon proved to be the most politically skilled Shadow minister that I ever faced. He had no interest at all in criminal justice policy or the police and prison service and he did not take much trouble to get involved in the detail. He was instead very absorbed in promoting himself and his friends, and in the final transformation of the Labour Party into an electable left-of-centre organization. Supported by Gordon Brown and Peter Mandelson he had embarked on a clever public relations exercise to capture, first the party, and then the modern centre left.

The high point of Tony Blair's political campaigning came in 1993, when he first adopted a brilliantly meaningless slogan which had all the right nuances for both the right and left of centre. Pledging to be 'tough on crime, tough on the causes of crime', he committed the Labour Party to be sterner than its soft left image in dealing with criminals, but sympathetic and reformist in tackling the social causes of criminal behaviour. Gordon Brown always told me and indeed everyone else that it was his phrase. But no matter who thought it up, Tony used it brilliantly.

Tony, Gordon and Peter had all studied new campaigning techniques developed by the Clinton camp on the other side of the Atlantic. This included a PR doctrine known as triangulation which held that a progressive party must not allow itself to be outflanked by the right on the populist right-wing causes such as law and order. When Blair's Labour Party was in government, this principle was fully applied. Foreign policy remained suitably warlike, for example, and Tony appointed Home Secretaries who applied tough law-and-order policies in line with the editorials in the right-wing tabloid newspapers.

Tony Blair's tenure in the role of Shadow Home Secretary gave him a much bigger platform to engage in the wider political debate nationally. On my own departmental front, he was a quite challenging if occasional critic of our policy. On most other political issues, however, we soon discovered that there was very little between us and I always regarded him as a One Nation Conservative who admired Margaret Thatcher and had somehow wound up in the Labour Party because his wife was a left-wing political activist and he had an innate distaste for the old Tory tradition.

In later years, after the Conservative Party moved to the right, I came to be regarded as very liberal on all matters of law and order. By the time I arrived at the Ministry of Justice under David Cameron it was anticipated that I would be an ultra-liberal Justice Secretary. However, this was not my reputation when I was at the Home Office. Not only had I been a very controversial minister under Margaret Thatcher, but I was also not as liberal as most of my predecessors. Ken Baker had been fairly moderate, and Margaret had always had ultra-liberal Home Secretaries in Willie Whitelaw and Douglas Hurd. I remembered Willie, usually hugely popular with the party faithful, being booed at a Conservative Party conference because of the liberal content of his speech on law and order, which had determinedly resisted the reintroduction of hanging and flogging.

I was in fact very liberal, but I had inherited from Ken Baker some measures that went too far even for me, some of which had been handed to him in turn by Douglas Hurd. In particular, I immediately found myself confronted by controversy over two pieces of legislation that had just been introduced by the Criminal Justice Act 1991, on unit fines, and on the relevance of previous convictions to the sentencing of criminals.

The unit-fine measure had been designed to fit the admirable principle that any financial punishment should bear some relationship to the prosperity of the accused. It was certainly reasonable to argue that a financial sum that might be trivial to a wealthy person could be crushing to a poor one. Unfortunately the legislation applied an extremely mechanical and artificial approach to the level of fines to be imposed, not only for crimes but for the vast number of motoring offences for which fines are the usual penalty.

Magistrates began to apply the new rules in the most pedantic way so that people believed to be very wealthy found that they were being fined thousands of pounds for speeding and other motoring offences. Other people, believed to be penniless, were being given minute penalties for the same offences. Some magistrates' benches seemed to apply no sense of proportionality when imposing their fines. Not surprisingly, this caused outrage.

The real practical problem was that magistrates' courts had no efficient means of checking the income and assets of the people before them for minor matters. The assertions of the motorist or other accused usually had to be accepted. A man who boasted of his income would be shocked by an enormous penalty, while anyone asserting that they had no income escaped almost scot-free. There was no practical or affordable way of getting around this.

Initially, I defended the scheme but I also anxiously began to have discussions with officials about how to reform it. I eventually despaired after a series of useless meetings with the leaders of the Magistrates Association. These were a formidable collection of ladies who simply asserted to me in schoolmistress style how the system worked, and made it quite clear that they were not inclined to flex the way they were implementing it to make its outcomes more sensible.

Having dutifully defended the collective decision of my government for a few weeks, I eventually did as elegant a U-turn as I could manage and calmly gave a statement in which I explained that I had decided to abolish the system and replace it with something more open to the exercise of common sense. Gillian was furious with me as she had been loyally defending unit fines on my behalf at constituency meetings. I tried to explain that loyal backbench MPs were left looking equally foolish whenever a government did a volte-face. She was not placated.

The equally problematic legislation I inherited on sentencing introduced a new sentencing rule that the sentencing of criminals was to have no regard to the offender's previous convictions. Ken Baker had been pursuing the very worthy aim of reducing the prison population. There were at the time only about 45,000 people in our prisons (about half of today's prison population) but this exceeded the capacity of the buildings. I always took the view that prison was the best and only effective penalty for a serious criminal. But I also believed that it was a mistake to fill up the prisons with minor offenders or with people who were really social problems, albeit often very unpleasant individuals, including those who had offended under the influence of drugs, mental illness or other difficulties best tackled in some other setting.

I had not noticed this piece of sentencing legislation when it went through Parliament: I had been buried in the affairs of another department. Now that I did notice it, the lawyer in me was outraged, as were many judges and members of the public. I was traditional enough to believe that it was highly relevant to sentencing to know whether the person in the dock was a first offender or someone with many previous convictions. In fact, my own view was that this was one of the most relevant features of any case in determining how long the penalty should be for the protection of the public.

As with unit fines, I first defended the government policy then performed a U-turn, attempting to be as matter of fact as possible. All governments sometimes have to make U-turns in the face of parliamentary and public opinion. It remains my view that this should be done plainly and brazenly but with as much elegance and acknowledgement of error as possible.

In other ways, though, I embarked on what would have been liberal changes in the prison service. Home Secretaries can have considerable influence on the judges' sentencing policy to reduce excessive and unnecessary prison population, and I now tried to exert that influence. I also wanted to improve prison management, by bringing in stronger and more effective management systems from outside the service. When Douglas Hurd had been Home Secretary he had been persuaded to experiment with contracting-out the building and operation of a new prison to the private sector. In all honesty, my officials would have preferred for me to stop this experiment but I am glad to say that the first privately operated prison opened during my time at the Home Office. I intended to introduce more private-sector prisons as comparators and competitors with the public-service prisons, but I did not stay long enough to be able to put this into effect. Nearly twenty years later, I had the opportunity to revisit this policy as Justice Secretary, by which time some progress had been made by some of my Labour successors.

It was also always my hope that I would manage to close down some of our oldest and more dreadful jails. No one had closed one in living memory. I now informed my officials that I wanted to start with the dungeons at Lancaster Castle, the oldest premises still in use. I accepted that the prison installation in the castle had been extensively modernized but it seemed symbolic that we were still using a facility hundreds of years old. The local authority was keen to co-operate as it wished to turn the castle into a tourist facility. Unfortunately I moved on before I had time to close a single institution. Eventually, as Justice Secretary, I was finally able to achieve the triumph – in my own opinion at least – of closing our last medieval prison facility.

I arrived at the Home Office expecting to stay there for the whole of the parliament. If I had done so, I would have embarked on major reform of both the prisons and the police service – and no doubt would have had some glorious battles with both the Prison Officers' Association and the Police Federation. As it was, I had the time to identify the problems, decide on some solutions, and encounter fierce initial resistance before events moved me on.

In the early 1990s the police service was, in a phrase first used publicly by me and repeated by others in subsequent years, the 'last great unreformed Victorian public service'. It was still organized on very nineteenth-century lines. Each of our many local police forces had its own ineffective local police authority but was actually run by a chief constable. Underneath the chief constable, and constructed along the lines of a Victorian army, was a vast hierarchy of unnecessary ranks – all attempts at delayering had been resisted – each of whom reported upwards to the rank above. At the bottom were the police constables, who made up the great majority of the employees.

Anyone recruited into the police service was obliged by tradition to start work as a constable. There was a little accelerated promotion for a few graduates but the police culture largely insisted that every senior officer should have made his or her way up through the hierarchy.

The service also had a generous but very complicated pay structure which was in no way related to performance. Indeed nothing in either the promotion structure or the day-to-day organization of the county police forces was related to performance. The collection of data on key matters like detection rates and levels of public satisfaction was extremely patchy. Crime statistics were particularly unreliable and were collected on a completely different basis from force to force with the methodologies being chosen to produce the results required. Nottinghamshire, for example, always reported a staggering level of crime because the force cleverly charged many suspects with a multitude of alternative offences and then counted each offence charged as a separate crime. The National Crime Survey, conducted as a poll of random members of the public, was more reliable than the police reporting numbers and was the only set of statistics to which I ever paid any attention.

The most difficult problem was the absurd breaking up of a comparatively small country into such a large number of different forces – over forty of them. Courageous governments had attempted amalgamations in the past and I had witnessed at close hand as a lawyer the difficulties involved in producing a West Midlands police force out of the old Birmingham city and Coventry and Warwickshire forces. The pattern that I inherited in 1992, however, still produced a patchwork of responsibilities with huge inconsistency in the performance of neighbouring forces. Communication and co-operation between the police forces was of very variable quality and the whole thing needed rationalization.

It was yet another public service focused more on the needs of those working within it than on those of the public it supposedly served. I decided on the outlines of my reforms fairly quickly. First, I wanted to stop police forces from being minor branches of the local government service. The councillors appointed to them were not always the strongest local elected politicians, and many police authority members regarded their service as an honorary thing involving a few not very informative committee meetings and some rather enjoyable dinners and county functions. Second, I wanted to redesign the management of the service in line with modern practice: I could see no point in having levels of responsibility and ranks that were merely imitations of the way in which a nineteenth-century army might have been organized. I wanted a smaller number of officers, each with clear responsibilities and clear accountability. Third, I wanted to reform remuneration to make sure that an individual's pay was dependent not only on seniority but had some regard to performance. I also wanted the whole service to be more accountable to the general public, with much more attention paid to measures of performance such as conviction rates and public satisfaction. And finally, I wanted to rationalize the huge number of forces and create a more sensible national structure.

To help me on the issues of pay, rank, structure and responsibilities, I approached Pat Sheehy, the colourful and autocratic head of British American Tobacco. My first contacts with BAT had been a few years earlier when Pat had very kindly loaned me Brian Hutchinson, one of his senior executives with experience of public affairs and sponsorship of good causes, to be a leading light in my Inner-City Task Forces. I knew Pat was both an excellent chief executive of a successful giant company and very public-spirited man. He willingly accepted my invitation.

However, Pat actually had a very difficult time taking evidence and preparing his report. He was followed by police cars when travelling in his own car and he told me of several occasions when he had felt personally intimidated by the hostility which individual police officers went out of their way to display towards him. Nevertheless, he carried out a careful inquiry with typical determination and came up with some strong recommendations for change, which he felt was long overdue. He did indeed propose some reform of the ranks including the complete abolition of the rank of superintendent. He also made some extremely strong recommendations on the linking of pay to performance.

It was almost impossible to get any agreement to any of this from the department, the police service or my political colleagues. The Home Office believed that my principal source of advice should be the Association of Chief Police Officers (ACPO). This was a huge club of the senior officers which held regular gatherings at a so-called staff college in a well-appointed country house. The dinners at the staff college, like police mess dinners held in the county forces, were highly entertaining, particularly if one had a reasonable head for a drink. The annual dinner was an extraordinary affair where, after a good meal, every chief constable and every guest had to wait for the name of their county to be declared and then stand on their seat and sing some suitable song of local connection. I certainly swayed on a chair once or twice singing 'Robin Hood' with officers from my part of the world. The chief constables kindly praised my efforts but I plainly could not compete with Willie Whitelaw's legendary 'D'ye Ken John Peel?'

Despite the many individual chief officers who tried to be helpful and who were not hostile to my proposals, the advice I received from ACPO was always extremely conservative and resistant to any substantial change or interference. The quality of chief constables varied enormously. There were a significant number of really outstanding ambitious and reforming leaders. There was also a large collection of very pleasant but unimpressive people who did not have the intellectual or managerial ability to make any useful contribution in their role.

I was always impressed by Her Majesty's Inspectorate of Constabulary, which, unlike the inspectorate I had abolished at the Department of Education, carried out a very useful function in applying real pressure for improvement of service delivery in the weakest of the local services, in a field where the difference in performance between the best and the worst was quite extraordinary. Ironically, though, this inspectorate – unlike the one I had abolished at Education – was not treated by the Home Office as a major source of policy advice and could not weigh in helpfully on behalf of my proposed reforms.

The most formidable opposition to change came from the Police Federation, the service's trade union. This was a most bizarre and powerful institution which dominated relations between the police and politicians at both national and local level. Policemen who were elected to the federation were allowed to become full-time union officials on full pay for whatever rank they had attained without ever carrying out any more police duties. Many of them appeared to have very undemanding jobs and were still being promoted to senior ranks, commanding good public-sector salaries and very attractive pensions. Locally, the Police Federation representatives could dominate the service and have an enormous influence on the chief constable. The public was actually financing a large organization giving very secure and sheltered jobs to people who then exercised huge sway over such vital matters as the allocation of duties and overtime, as well as protecting their members against any disciplinary procedure or accountability for their performance.

My dealings with the Police Federation never advanced very far, although to be fair the national leadership did try to greet me in a friendly way. They explained that I had acquired something of a 'Rottweiler' reputation in my previous roles. They therefore gave me at our first meeting a symbolic offering of how they would like to regard me, and placed a cuddly teddy bear in my hand as a peace offering.

I was never very keen to attend their frequent gatherings and soon discovered that if one did agree to speak to a Police Federation conference it was wise to insist on a morning slot. Policing was quite a hard-drinking occupation. In my one and only speech to an afternoon session, I suggested that I was contemplating altering the burden of proof for disciplinary charges against serving police officers from the criminal standard of 'beyond reasonable doubt' to the civil standard of 'on the balance of probabilities'. This attracted a burst of barracking. Some of them regarded even this move to a standard applied by most other employers as outrageous.

All the proposals in the Sheehy Report caused consternation and great hostility amongst all the trade unions involved. The Police Federation organized a rally at Wembley Stadium, attended by tens of thousands of police officers. The perfectly sensible proposal to abolish the rank of superintendent was strongly opposed by the Superintendents' Association, a trade union whose sole role in life was to represent officers of this rank. My hints at amalgamation of forces were also greeted with horror. Unfortunately this was the kind of issue that aroused every kind of parochial loyalty amongst local government politicians and many activist constituency MPs.

However ACPO, the Police Federation and the other unions were all spared the ordeal of implementing my reforms by my sudden removal in yet another reshuffle. Just a year after his election triumph in April 1992, this was really forced on John Major by the fallout from Black Wednesday, which I describe in detail in the next chapter. My proposed White Paper on police reform was also consigned to the scrap heap by the reshuffle. This was designed to redirect police efforts away from easy targets – whether 'helping old ladies across the road' or persecuting motorists (a famous hotelier's wife was apprehended in her bath for not paying a parking fine) – towards more serious crimes, that were certainly harder to deal with but rather more necessary for the public good. The first draft of the paper produced by the department's officials was weak, and designed to protect the police from such demanding objectives. I gave it to my special adviser, Tessa Keswick, who immediately set to, renaming the paper *Protecting the public and solving crime* and placing these two objectives at the top of the agenda rather than well towards the bottom. My officials were furious, but I stood firm and the White Paper stood, at least until I moved on and my successor Michael Howard was persuaded to drop the reforms.

The only legislation affecting the police service that I had managed to pass by this point was the removal from police authorities of magistrates' representatives, and the reduction of local authority nominees. I have to say that in later years I did not notice that my reforms made any very significant difference.

Also less effective than I would have liked was the legislation I passed to better protect society against money-laundering and other financial crimes. I have always believed that the British criminal justice system is quite hopeless at enforcing the law on white-collar crime such as fraud. It is far too complicated for the police service, who prefer to deal with more straightforward offences such as burglary and assault. But it is a hugely lucrative criminal activity and, sadly, had become quite an important part of the profitability of a lot of the banking and financial services industry. London had undoubtedly become the safest and best place for any dictator, oligarch or corrupt political leader to place his or her ill-gotten gains. I introduced a system obliging banks and others to report suspicious transactions so that they could be investigated. This unfortunately was turned into rather a bureaucratic and ineffective exercise affecting most ordinary bank customers. Almost a quarter of a century later I found myself, as a Cabinet Office minister and as Justice Secretary, urging more enforcement measures to try to rid London of its deserved reputation as the money-laundering capital of the world.

When I became Chancellor of the Exchequer and Michael Howard succeeded me at the Home Office, he took a totally different approach. He became a law-and-order populist, concentrating on longer sentences for all criminals, more police officers, and punitive short sharp shock treatment of young offenders. He also sought to make himself a reputation as a crusader against crime and played to the gallery of right-wing tabloid journalists with considerable enthusiasm. A succession of Home Secretaries followed suit. The result was that over the next decades the prison population soared, all meaningful reform in the department ended, the Sheehy Report was abandoned and senior policemen found their every wish complied with so long as it won good headlines in the popular press. In my opinion this was a terrible mistake, but my new role would at least afford me the opportunity to block Michael's insatiable demands for more public spending on his department and on the police service in particular. This had its entertaining side and Michael and I, as ever, remained friends.

17

'Out to Lunch!'
(Eric Dolphy, 1964)

BLACK WEDNESDAY TO MAASTRICHT

In the happy, early months of John Major's 'Cabinet of chums', I was of course involved in the whole range of government activity as the Home Secretary, a member of key Cabinet Committees and a high-profile public figure in the celebrity culture now infecting politics. This led to my being present on a day of huge consequence for British politics, for my friends, and for my own political career – though not, contrary to popular belief, for Britain's economy.

Wednesday 16 September 1992 was a day of such drama that it quickly acquired its own name. Black Wednesday, the day of sterling's crash out of the European Exchange Rate Mechanism (ERM), completely destroyed the Major administration's authority and provoked a crisis which nearly brought down the government.

John Major had finally persuaded Margaret Thatcher that we should join the ERM when he had been her Chancellor, and Britain had formally joined in October 1990. It meant that we were committed to keeping the pound's exchange rate with the German Deutschmark (DM) within certain limits. This had actually been very useful to Norman Lamont, who became Chancellor in November 1990, as he began to try to get us out of the recession, because it increased confidence in the currency and made it easier to reduce inflation and interest rates. In the 1992 general election the Conservative Party had made quite a feature of our commitment to this stable exchange rate as the fundamental feature of our proposed economic policy. Unfortunately, John Major and Chris Patten had so far believed this propaganda that they had persuaded Norman Lamont to sign up to a significant increase in public spending as part of our election manifesto, and this caused quite excessive increases in public borrowing after we were returned to power. By September 1992 this was leading to growing pressure on the exchange rate, and shrewd financiers like George Soros began to eye sterling as a vulnerable target in which a considerable amount of money could be made by anticipating a devaluation.

Black Wednesday began quite quietly for me when I was asked to attend a meeting to be chaired by the prime minister at 9.30 a.m. The meeting was to be held at Admiralty House where John and Norma Major were living temporarily while Number 10 was being refurbished. We were, I was told, going to discuss contingency plans for the forthcoming French referendum on the ratification of the Maastricht Treaty, presumably with a view to considering possible implications and government reactions to a result either way.

Gathered in Admiralty House, a small group of senior ministers talked in a desultory way about the French referendum for a few moments. My opposite number, the French interior minister, was responsible for the conduct of the referendum and he had assured me that the government was going to win. Rather cynically, I felt that he had been able to predict this with some confidence about a week before polling day. The French government was able occasionally to exert a certain amount of indirect influence on the results declared from the French overseas territories if it was felt that the result was going to be tight on the mainland.

It became clear that the prime minister's mind was not really on this particular subject and within less than half an hour we were joined by the Chancellor of the Exchequer, Norman Lamont, and officials from the Treasury and the Bank of England. The meeting rapidly switched focus to a strong run on the pound which had started that morning and which the Bank of England had been trying to guard against by buying up sterling using our reserves. This run on the pound threatened to send sterling's value against the DM below its ERM 'floor'. Only five days earlier, John Major had committed himself strongly and personally to defending the pound at its existing rate.

Apart from the prime minister and the Chancellor, the assembled company now included the Foreign Secretary Douglas Hurd, Michael Heseltine, the governor of the Bank of England Robin Leigh-Pemberton, the permanent secretary of the Treasury Terry Burns, the head of the prime minister's Policy Unit Sarah Hogg, the chief whip Richard Ryder, and me.

Those who had arrived from the Treasury were in a state of intense panic. They insisted that the Cabinet ministers present agree to a rise in interest rates because we had already spent at least £10 billion of the country's reserves that morning, and the flow was continuing. We were really given little choice and it only took five minutes of discussion for us to agree. It later transpired that the run had really started the previous afternoon. Sarah Hogg was afterwards quite scathing about the lack of overnight preparation that the Treasury and the Bank of England had made for that morning's market opening.

This decision made, and in what turned out to be the first of several journeys backwards and forwards that day, Douglas, Michael and I returned to our government cars and our departments. At 11 a.m., Norman Lamont, as agreed, put up interest rates from 10 per cent to 12 per cent.

By 12.30 p.m. we were all back at Admiralty House for a second meeting with the same cast list. Panic and tension prevailed and a strong attempt was made by Terry Burns and Robin Leigh-Pemberton to bounce us all into agreeing that the United Kingdom should leave the ERM within the next fifteen minutes. They argued that we were losing £20 million from the reserves each minute and that the flow was likely to continue until the pound devalued. The ministers from outside this policy area – Douglas, Michael and I – refused to be bounced in this way, on a subject we had just been told about. Instead, fairly quickly, and led by Michael and me, we agreed to make one more effort to restore stability through a deliberately dramatic increase in interest rates by another 3 per cent, to 15 per cent, and then to leave the ERM if it became clear after about half an hour's trading that it had not worked. The Chancellor and the governor were extremely unenthusiastic about a further rise in rates, which they regarded as unlikely to work, while Treasury officials were furious that we were being allowed to interfere. Douglas, Michael and I insisted, however. We believed that the government would lose all credibility with the public and with our European partners if we were not seen to be going to the limit in defence of our economic policy of keeping within the ERM exchange-rate band. The figure of 3 per cent was simply plucked out of the air by Norman Lamont.

We also agreed that our meeting should be followed by telephone calls from John Major to German Chancellor Helmut Kohl, French prime minister Pierre Bérégovoy and other European figures, and from Robin Leigh-Pemberton to his fellow central bankers. This seemed to me to be hopelessly belated. John and Robin should have been in steady personal contact with these key figures both before the crisis and as soon as it had begun.

At 2.15 p.m., as agreed, Norman Lamont raised interest rates to 15 per cent. It was the first time ever the UK had raised interest rates twice in one day.

I left Admiralty House once more, but as soon as I took my seat in the car, my driver, who had been listening to the radio, turned around and said, 'It hasn't worked, sir.' The financial commentators were reporting that despite the rise, the markets had not abated in their determination to force a devaluation of the pound. Not surprisingly, this had become apparent immediately.

Nevertheless, it did not seem to provoke any reaction in Downing Street and the Treasury until we were all summoned back again for a third meeting at 3.30 p.m. Douglas, Michael, Richard Ryder and I were asked to wait in a pleasant sunny room because the Chancellor and governor were not yet ready for us. We four discussed the situation in a perfectly friendly way and were in a relaxed and joking mood. There was really no alternative because, stuck in our antechamber at Admiralty House, with no radio, TV, market screens, ticker tape or information source of any kind, we were the most out of touch people in London. The only route of escape from our cloistered ignorance was through the gauntlet of waiting photographers. Having no desire to provide any more minor public entertainment than we already had, or to add to the growing sense of crisis, we remained where we were.

At 5 p.m. we finally went in to see the Chancellor and the governor. It was clear that there was absolutely no choice at that point but to take the decision to suspend our membership of the ERM. The only policy issue we discussed was the interest-rate level that should be set after we had announced our departure. Michael Heseltine and I were both very anxious to remove the 15 per cent rate which we felt would act as a quite unnecessary brake on the economy the next day. We both pressed for the rate to be returned to 10 per cent first thing in the morning. Norman Lamont resisted this with considerable vigour. The deputy governor of the Bank, Eddie George, had joined us by this time and he voiced considerable distress that non-Treasury ministers were trying to intervene in decisions about interest rates in this way. I actually rather agreed with Eddie and would have preferred to have had an independent Bank of England in charge of the whole matter, assuming that we could find a governor with the necessary capacity. Robin Leigh-Pemberton was a pleasant but not very forceful country gentleman who had been appointed by Margaret Thatcher for precisely those qualities: she had hoped to control him. After a rather fierce exchange we settled at a return to 12 per cent in the morning, to be reviewed again after we had the results of the French referendum.

The announcement of the decision to leave the ERM was then complicated to a ridiculous degree by the advice of Foreign Office lawyers. Douglas dutifully insisted, based on their advice, that no formal decision could be announced until we had gone through the process laid down by the European treaties. This required the appropriate Treasury official, Nigel Wicks, to go immediately to Brussels to attend a meeting of the EU Monetary Committee and obtain their consent for our decision. The Treasury also insisted that the Chancellor could not possibly make any public statements until the formal announcement had been made to the markets – which was going to be sometime in the course of the evening or the night, once Nigel Wicks had ticked his box in Brussels. Michael and I protested that this was absurd. The government's reputation was going up in flames outside our room and apparently no senior member of the government who had been involved in the decision could give a word of explanation.

The formal statement was indeed delayed and Nigel Wicks made his pointless visit to Brussels. Meanwhile Norman Lamont was reluctantly persuaded to go out into the courtyard below to give a terse two-minute explanation of what we were contemplating. This interview was repeated frequently on television thereafter with the Chancellor looking taut and terrified in dreadful half-lighting with his then special adviser David Cameron standing gloomily behind him. An even more bizarre decision was then made that the party chairman, because he was not a government minister, could perhaps give interviews. The unfortunate Norman Fowler was summoned for a sketchy briefing on a subject that was totally new to him, and then tasked with the impossible job of going out, at a moment of intense political drama, to explain and defend our position in bland and meaningless terms.

The atmosphere amongst both politicians and officials throughout the late afternoon and evening was generally quite calm, clear and amiable, albeit in a slightly unreal way. A small cheer even went up when Norman Fowler arrived: at that point he was the answer to a maiden's prayer. This rather unlikely climate was the inevitable result of the fact that events had taken decisions completely out of our hands. At one point, I resorted to black humour, remarking that I had never been in a government with absolutely no economic policy before. Sadly, this was only too accurate. More than any other aspect of our economic policy, our membership of the ERM had been emphasized as a guarantee of stability and a signal of our determination to reduce inflation. We were now a government with its economic middle stump flying through the air.

The next two months were a period of ferocious crisis, which nearly brought down the Conservative government.

Not surprisingly, the press the following morning was every bit as bad as the government deserved. Michael Heseltine and I were the two most active ministers giving interviews, defending the Chancellor's position robustly and trying to hold on to the government's authority. Everybody else seemed to try to vanish.

Actual policy was discussed rather feebly at the Cabinet meeting that Thursday morning. None of our colleagues seemed to have any strong views on what to do or say: instead they simply appeared to agree to what had happened. Norman Lamont and I together firmly insisted that, to hold our short-term political and economic position, we must say that our policy remained 'to rejoin the ERM as soon as conditions permit'. Michael Howard, a convinced Eurosceptic, strongly resisted this and only gave in because he was in a minority of one at the table and he was personally loyal to Norman Lamont. The truth, as Norman and I agreed later, was that we were never likely to rejoin the ERM, but we felt it would be ill-advised to abandon entirely the only semblance of a policy that we had at this point.

John, Norman, Douglas, Michael and I met again at Admiralty House on the Sunday to manage the government's reaction to the French referendum result. This proved to be a non-event – remarkably the French interior minister's forecast had proved to be correct, although the majority declared was not very impressive.

By this time the media coverage of the situation was manic and I was being declared the bookies' favourite to succeed Norman Lamont as Chancellor. I felt very little attraction to the prospect, although I would have loved to have been offered the job when the government had been formed six months earlier.

By the time Parliament reassembled from its summer recess in the middle of October the pressure on the government was extreme, and tensions were running high.

On Friday 16 October, for example, I was one of seven ministers at a stormy and somewhat farcical meeting of EDX, the Cabinet Committee that considered public expenditure. Five ministers believed that the public spending remit that had been agreed by the Cabinet in July, before Black Wednesday, could not now be delivered. Michael Heseltine and I argued strongly that Norman Lamont, in his attempt to deliver a responsible Budget, and because of his inability to get his colleagues to agree to cuts in public expenditure, was cutting capital expenditure too deeply. Infrastructure spending was a vital part of our return to economic growth and should not be cut simply because buildings, unlike people working in the public sector, did not have the vote. When Michael and I raised the possibility of an increase in income tax alongside a package of spending cuts, the debate became quite heated. Eventually Norman lost his temper and swept out of the room slamming the door behind him, leaving his concerned colleagues to abandon the meeting.

The problems, though, extended well beyond economic policy. The beginnings of a backbench rebellion against the Maastricht Treaty had already been quietly stirring in the months leading up to Black Wednesday. The treaty, which John Major had negotiated and signed just before the 1992 general election, provided for the creation of the single currency, setting out the convergence criteria which member states would need to meet in order to join it; and the development of the 'pillar structure' for the European Union, which set limits on the powers of the EU in relation to foreign policy and criminal justice. Its Social Chapter set out broad policy objectives for improving living and working conditions in member states. When John Major had negotiated it, together with opt-outs for the UK from necessarily joining the single currency and from the Social Chapter, he had been hailed as a hero, even by hard-line Eurosceptics. Now, the many on the right wing of the Conservative Party, in anti-European fury, turned to a form of isolationist nationalism which became known as Euroscepticism, with the Maastricht Treaty as its focus. The ERM crisis had put a match to the dry tinder of resentment that backbench and grass-roots Conservatives continued to feel about the fall of Margaret Thatcher two years earlier. Adding to this was an extraordinary turn of events in the coal-mining industry.

I had been present in early October at a Cabinet Committee meeting, chaired by the prime minister, with Michael Heseltine there as president of the Board of Trade, the traditional and rather gran-diose title he had taken for himself when appointed Secretary of State for the Department of Trade and Industry. Heseltine calmly told us that the Coal Board had failed to land a contract with the National Grid to provide them with power. The recently privatized National Grid wanted to replace coal with gas. As a result he was about to announce the closure of thirty-one coal mines with the loss of 30,000 jobs, representing more than half of Britain's remaining coal miners. Michael stated this in a very matter-of-fact way, and plainly regarded it as a perfectly normal commercial event. I guessed that most of these collieries would be in counties like Nottinghamshire, and that we would be making redundant the miners who had refused to take part in Arthur Scargill's strike just a few years ago. This would be enormously controversial and I insisted we should discuss it properly. The Labour Party and the left had always had a sentimental attachment to coal mining, regarding the miner as the embodiment of all that was most admirable in the culture of the British working man. The right regarded the 'working miners' as heroes who had saved the Thatcher government and the country by refusing to bow to violence and intimidation. There would be cross-party horror at these closures. I firmly expressed my view that this announcement would cause outrage and would require extremely skilful political handling, but I do not think that the message was totally taken on board.

Michael went ahead with his announcement on 13 October 1992, unleashing a pitch of fury from all sides, including from very many Conservative supporters angry that the miners who had defied Scargill were being betrayed. By the following Sunday, the small group of ministers, including me, who had been summoned to discuss the issue at Number 10 agreed that we must have a complete change of policy or at least the presentation of the policy. Without this we had little chance of avoiding defeat in the House the following week.

On the Monday, 19 October, Michael Heseltine finally made the statement to the House that he should have made in the first place. I stayed in the House all that afternoon and evening to judge the mood of the party and I have to say that I had never known our Members to be in a worse state of total rage and despair. I spoke to Michael Jopling, an MP since 1964 and a former chief whip, who agreed. Neither of us could remember backbench feeling ever being anything like this.

Every Conservative MP's constituency association seemed to be in turmoil because of their feelings towards the 'working miners'. But, more fundamentally, a combination of Black Wednesday, the coal closures and the impending legislation for the ratification of the Maastricht Treaty had shattered the Conservative Party's normal tribal unity. There was unprecedented animosity and anger in discussions between our MPs, fuelled by the resentment of Margaret Thatcher's supporters, who were giving vent to feelings that they had kept contained since her fall. I am quite convinced that Margaret was in touch with quite a lot of them, encouraged by her closest aides, and was feeding this frenzy.

The party needed rallying. Shocked, I spoke to John Major, urging him to make himself more publicly visible and to come out fighting. He assured me that he would appear on television soon. I was quite convinced that I was doing more television and radio interviews to try to put our case and rally the party than the rest of the government put together. I suspected that one or two colleagues were keeping their heads down in order to prepare themselves for any possible change of leadership in the near future.

From this point on, a vicious, destructive battle quickly began, centred on the unlikely subject of the Maastricht Treaty, the negotiation for which had seen John Major achieve such a popular and triumphant success only a few months before. Then, he had been praised by hard-line Eurosceptics for his skill in achieving opt-outs on the single currency and the Social Chapter, Margaret Thatcher had said that she was 'thrilled for John' and the treaty had not featured at all in the general election campaign. But Black Wednesday had opened the Eurosceptic floodgates. From then on, the Maastricht Treaty became a symbol, a proxy and a focal point for Eurosceptic, right-wing, anti-John Major passion. The unending splenetic debates that raged around the treaty were not about its detailed substance – with which everyone had been happy a few months earlier – but about implacable opposition to Europe and to John's premiership. The life of the government began to be dominated and slowly poisoned by highly publicized fratricide which was fought out on the floor of the House of Commons. Holding court behind the lines in the House of Lords, injecting the poison and stiffening wobbly rebels to become more and more impossible, was Margaret. The proceedings on the bill to ratify the treaty made the debates on the 1975 European Communities Bill seem like a picnic, and it was extremely hard for John personally.

After our conversation in the House on the night of Michael Heseltine's statement on coal, I next saw the prime minister on the morning of Wednesday 21 October. He was much more cheerful than he had been on Monday, after a successful appearance in the House that afternoon and on television the day before. I congratulated him and urged him to repeat the performance. However, later that day John Patten rang me to tell me that he was sure that the prime minister was thinking of resigning. He had spoken to Robert Fellowes, the Queen's private secretary, who hinted that if the Queen was asked by her prime minister for a dissolution, she would refuse. She did not want a repeat of 1974, when she had allowed Ted Heath to call an election because his government did not know what else to do about the miners' strike.

John and I then discussed the Norman Lamont position – a topic I had also discussed with Norman Fowler two days earlier. Norman Lamont had reacted to the savage and unfair attacks upon him after Black Wednesday by withdrawing from public life and refusing to appear on the TV or radio. Norman Fowler and I had agreed that as Norman Lamont would not defend himself he was becoming quite indefensible and that he really would have to leave the Treasury. Norman Fowler had said that he would pass on our advice to the prime minister.

John Patten and I now also agreed that Norman Lamont should go, but that we would both back John Major through this crisis in which we believed he was being most unfairly attacked.

The following day, Thursday 22 October, I had a meeting with the prime minister before that morning's Cabinet. John looked wretched and was obviously deeply upset. At such times his complexion became so grey that he looked almost ghostly, quite apart from his sad and dejected demeanour. Unfortunately this physical reaction to crisis was eventually taken up by the same puppet-based political satire that had portrayed Margaret Thatcher as an unstable bully. *Spitting Image* started to parody John Major as a grey, virtually invisible, and very boring man. At this pre-Cabinet meeting, John told me that he thought he had only a fifty-fifty chance of surviving the Maastricht debates, and that Douglas Hurd might have to resign too. He was determined, however, to leave a Conservative government behind him if he was forced to go, and wanted me to remain. He urged me to keep on with my public appearances but to stay out of the worst trouble. Trying very hard to cheer him up and to raise his spirits, I told him that I thought the odds of him being forced out were only one in ten.

The Cabinet that followed was awful, one of the worst that I ever attended. The atmosphere was febrile. The majority persuaded the minority that we must press on with the ratification of the treaty. Peter Lilley was particularly difficult and he openly quarrelled with Tristan Garel-Jones, who was deputizing for Douglas Hurd. John Gummer, David Hunt, Virginia Bottomley and William Waldegrave were very robustly on my side in arguing for pressing on.

The next day, Friday 23 October, the prime minister telephoned me, sounding much better and more confident. He knew that I was going to give yet another interview on *Channel 4 News* that evening and wanted to brief me.

The atmosphere did not really calm down. Then, at the weekend, Norman Tebbit came out with an almost hysterical attack on the prime minister and the whole crisis was wound up again. Reports surfaced in the press that John Major was threatening to hold a general election, or, alternatively, to force a leadership election, if he was pushed too far on Maastricht.

By the time of the next Cabinet meeting the following Thursday, John Major had made it quite clear that he was going to fight the Euro rebels, and was putting forward a substantive motion at the end of the procedural so-called 'paving' debate on the Maastricht Treaty the following Wednesday, 4 November. A defeat on this obscurely worded motion would effectively be a parliamentary veto on ratifying the treaty. Untypically, John would not allow any real discussion of his decision. Richard Ryder as chief whip made it clear that the Whips' Office thought it likely that we would lose a Labour amendment deferring discussion of the whole issue indefinitely. Using the 'not tonight' analogy, Richard described this as the Josephine amendment. If it had been passed it would have killed, on a technicality, any prospect of ever ratifying the treaty.

John overrode a few feeble doubts, expressed by Peter Lilley and Michael Howard. He made it quite clear to the assembled Cabinet, as he had made clear to me a week earlier, that if he was defeated over Maastricht he was determined that the Conservative government should remain in power. But he was determined to go ahead with the paving motion even if there was a risk of being defeated: so far as the Euro rebels were concerned he talked of 'a line in the sand'. I did not take much part in the discussion but I firmly approved of the position to which he had committed himself.

The early days of the following week involved frantic discussions in the corridors of the House of Commons in the run-up to Wednesday's key votes. In fact I played little direct part in the intensive lobbying and whipping of backbench MPs. My Home Office diary was crowded and I was also spending a huge amount of time attending EDX meetings. John Major was also trying to keep me out of the firing line on Maastricht. He and Michael Heseltine, though, worked tirelessly to convince wavering MPs.

I began to believe that John's reason for keeping me away from the front line was so that I could succeed him if he fell. In fact, my friends in the House – Jim Lester, Philip Oppenheim my PPS, Charles Wardle, John Patten and Peter Luff as well as Tessa Keswick my special adviser – had all been urging me to prepare for a leadership campaign in the event of John's defeat. I genuinely believed – and had told them all as much – that the idea was ridiculous. If John had to resign and was replaced by another pro-EU and pro-Maastricht leader, that new leader would merely face even worse bitterness and chaos. And I had always felt, and Gillian had always kept me true to this feeling, that I could not lead the Conservative Party if I had to disown or put on ice my European enthusiasms.

I had made my position quite clear in the endless media interviews I had given. In particular, I had vigorously defended the prime minister on the BBC's *Panorama* programme, first advocating the ratification of Maastricht and then being drawn into being very critical of Margaret Thatcher and her zealot supporters.

The night before the key parliamentary votes I was at a presidential election party at the American Embassy. Bill Clinton beat George Bush but the conversation at the party was all about the British crisis. The overwhelming majority of the politicians and journalists that I spoke to there thought that the government would be defeated the following day.

On Wednesday 4 November, about half an hour before the 10 p.m. votes, I was sitting in my room with Tristan Garel-Jones discussing our fate. He confirmed what I had been hearing repeatedly that day. The whips were now sure that we would lose the second vote – the substantive motion, not the amendment – by four votes. Tristan had been a brilliant deputy chief whip for many years. No one had a better feel than he did for the swings of mood and the general state of the Conservative parliamentary party. Tristan said that though the whipping operation had been the best that he had ever known there were just too many rebels and the vote could not be won. He told me that Douglas Hurd would definitely resign, partly to protect John Major. John would go on to a vote of confidence the following day.

We talked for a full half-hour but I still could not quite accept Tristan's view. I offered him a bet that the government would win, which he declined on the basis that he could not properly bet against the government.

An hour later, the government had won both votes – the vote on the Labour delaying amendment, and the vote on the government's paving motion. There was hysteria and rejoicing on the government side, in which I participated. Afterwards, over champagne with the whips in their office, I heard the worrying news that we had won over two rebels in the short interval between the two votes by telling them that the third reading of the bill would not be held until after the second Danish referendum on the Maastricht Treaty, to be held in May 1993. John Major assured me that he had had to do it. The whips had told him that the majority of six on the first vote indicated we did not have the votes to win the second. If we had lost the second we would never have been able to ratify the treaty at all.

To me this concession was something of a setback as it made our position too dependent on the Danes. In reality, the degree of fili-bustering to which the government had to submit, because it did not have a majority for any 'guillotine' motion to timetable debate, would probably have prevented the third reading being reached before the Danish vote in any case. And in the event, the Danish referendum was a disastrous rejection of the treaty, increasing even further the intensity of the British Maastricht debate.

*

These critical weeks between Black Wednesday on 16 September and the Maastricht votes on 4 November were the beginning of a period of prolonged agony for the Conservative parliamentary party and in particular for John Major. The poison that had been injected into the party as the Maastricht debates dragged on and on never drained. John correctly realized that most of his enemies were personally hostile to him, and in conversation he would angrily denounce the *Daily Telegraph* and one of its journalists, Simon Heffer, in particular, for hating him. John never lost his sensitivity to even mild personal attack and at times he obviously suffered some mental agonies. I always thought that it was a tragedy that he did not really enjoy his period as prime minister, as every politician ought to enjoy the peak of his career, even in the middle of the inevitable daily hassle and frequent crises and controversies.

Later, Norman Lamont and I agreed and continue to agree that Black Wednesday had had momentous political consequences but scarcely any economic effect. The whole idea of the Exchange Rate Mechanism had been a reaction to the obsession with exchange rate changes a decade before. It was in reality a wholly unnecessary precondition of membership of any future single currency. Currencies were now floating in global markets and governments could no longer control those rates by buying or selling their own currency because of the mountainous piles of money involved. In the event, we had not had to draw too greatly on the reserves. Interest rates were back to their pre-Black Wednesday levels within a day. It was not 'Black Wednesday' nor – as the Eurosceptics sometimes dubbed it – 'White Wednesday'. It did not start the economic recovery: the recovery had started before then. It was an incident of no direct economic consequence. However, because we had placed such an emphasis on our membership of the ERM, so foolishly with hindsight, in the 1992 election campaign, it appeared to leave the government without an economic policy. Politically, in a matter of hours it had completely discredited the government and turned the mood of the country against John Major. Perhaps more significantly it marked the beginning of a fierce Conservative civil war over Europe, a war which played itself out over the Maastricht Treaty and damaged the party for decades to come.

18

'Money Jungle'

(Duke Ellington with Mingus and Roach, 1963)

CHANCELLOR

After Black Wednesday, Norman Lamont was politically crippled as Chancellor but he endeavoured to carry on. I was one of many political colleagues who tried to support John Major's noble – though, I thought, doomed – determination to keep Norman in office. I thought that Norman's share of the blame for Black Wednesday was quite slight. Much more culpable were Margaret Thatcher and Nigel Lawson, for their mistakes in the aftermath of the 1987 election, and John Major and Chris Patten for the very costly Conservative manifesto of 1992. John and Chris had bullied Norman into letting them make unaffordable public spending promises in the campaign which in my opinion had not in practice won us any votes. In most general elections, electors do not take detailed election promises very seriously but instead make their judgements on overall mood and personalities. It would have been an injustice for Norman to have to carry the can, particularly as he had been making some progress towards getting Britain out of recession. John very honourably kept to this view through torrid months of press and political pressure, hoping that Norman would recover his reputation.

This proved to be impossible. The political class and the media would not deal with Norman on any basis except as the central figure in the debacle. He tried to make some quite witty remarks about 'singing in the bath' to brush off the criticisms, but these just produced synthetic outrage. He found himself unable to talk publicly about economic policy except in terms of post-mortems of Black Wednesday.

Norman turned therefore, unwisely, to a complete withdrawal from public debate. This meant that the government had no economic spokesman and I became one of the Cabinet ministers who now found themselves fielding questions about economic policy. Eventually, in May 1993, John steeled himself to remove Norman from the Treasury, offering him instead the post of Secretary of State for the Environment. If Norman had accepted this, he could have continued with a serious political career. Not surprisingly, however, he was so angry about this public demotion, and so bitter about what he felt was a personal betrayal by a man whom he had helped to become leader, that he angrily resigned with the potent phrase that John's government gave the impression of being 'in office but not in power'. Privately, I agreed with this.

There were few members of the Cabinet who could easily be moved to become Chancellor. The obvious candidates were John MacGregor or me, although Norman Fowler later confided in me that John had also flirted with the idea of Michael Howard. The press had been mischievously touting me as favourite for some time, but I was genuinely taken by surprise to find myself rescued from my mounting conflicts with the police by being appointed Chancellor, with a new home in 11 Downing Street. John would later tell me that with hindsight he would have done better to have appointed either the more rumbustious Chris Patten or me to the Treasury from the start.

I arrived at the grimy and semi-derelict Treasury building on King Charles Street – a pale imitation of the neighbouring Foreign Office building it was supposed to match – to be greeted by Michael Portillo, whom I had inherited as my chief secretary – the number two ministerial job in the department. We posed briefly for a photograph on the front step, which made us both look rather like two nightclub bouncers when it was published the next day.

I had not previously known Michael very well and had been slightly inclined to dismiss him as a right-wing ideologue. However, I quickly developed an excellent working relationship with him and he proved to be an invaluable ally in my determination to make serious reductions in public spending. In Cabinet, though, he was the leading hard-line Eurosceptic plotter and campaigner. He mellowed a lot in later years and I now quite admire him.

My special advisers, Tessa Keswick and David Ruffley, were anxious to join me in this surprising turn in my responsibilities. This led to a slightly embarrassing incident. One of Norman Lamont's former special advisers came to see me and diffidently asked whether he might stay in his job. I had known David Cameron a little and was very impressed by him. Unfortunately, I had to explain that I was limited to a maximum of two special advisers, a limit of which I strongly approved – there were already beginning to be too many, and some – not mine – had a tendency to leak and brief the press, particularly against pro-European colleagues. I was not prepared to turn away either of my existing able and loyal advisers and so had to turn away David. I did though make a call to my old friend Michael Howard who had just become Home Secretary and was looking for a special adviser. Michael took up the suggestion with alacrity and David's career went on from strength to strength thereafter.

My new principal private secretary was a young man called Jeremy Heywood. I soon discovered though that Jeremy's youthful appearance, and his slightly unconventional habits of dress – such as always wearing short-sleeved shirts under his suit – belied his ability. He was a high-powered and very intelligent workaholic and we got on extremely well in the short time we worked together. And we were still friends when I encountered him nearly twenty years later, when he was David Cameron's Cabinet Secretary.

Contrary to some comments made in the press at the time, I was not a complete novice to economic policy and I had some very strong opinions about it. I had been a member of the so-called Star Chamber which controlled public expenditure in Margaret Thatcher's government since the early 1980s, and of its successor, EDX, under John Major. I had watched and learnt from Willie Whitelaw's remarkable performance in chairing the Star Chamber, when he had bullied, charmed or wheedled Secretaries of State into making concessions and reaching agreement with the chief secretary of the day.

I had also served on the extremely powerful Economic Policy Committee of the Thatcher Cabinet throughout my time at Employment and Industry. This had given me many opportunities to get close to economic discussion and policymaking from the inside, as Cabinet Committees were serious political debating forums at that time. I had also wound up Budget debates in the House of Commons several times during the life of the Thatcher government.

The role of Chancellor ranged widely across the whole of government, with important domestic, European and international responsibilities. At home, I was now responsible for the whole of macroeconomic policy – including all tax and spending and interest-rate decisions – and for many aspects of microeconomic policy.

The economy I inherited was in a weak stage of recovery. Inflationary pressures had reduced enough for Norman Lamont to have made some interest-rate reductions, the economy was beginning to respond to this monetary stimulus and the cycle was beginning to turn. However, as Black Wednesday had shown, the recovery was extremely feeble and was unlikely to be sustained without some much firmer measures.

Over the next four years I set out to reverse the fiscal irresponsibility of the period running up to the 1992 election. Following a budget surplus in 1987–8 spending had risen in most departments by about 10 per cent a year. Meanwhile, due to a marked slowdown in the economy together with Nigel Lawson's tax reductions, revenue declined considerably. By 1993 public borrowing was over £50 billion a year, or just over 7 per cent of GDP – rather higher than when we had gone to the International Monetary Fund in the mid-1970s and certainly considered a great deal in those days. It did not reach this level again until 2009–10 when it rose to over 10 per cent of GDP. In 2015–16 the figure was 4 per cent.

As a right-of-centre politician believing in market economics, my approach was extremely orthodox, and followed the broad principles that had been set out by Geoffrey Howe and Nigel Lawson. Fiscal policy (i.e. decisions on tax and spending) had to be disciplined, keeping public expenditure at an affordable level. It was not usually the right weapon to use to stimulate economic growth. The control of inflation and the prevention of economic overheating were the principal objectives of monetary policy (i.e. decisions on interest rates). At one stage I coined the phrase that there should be 'no return to boom and bust', which later came to be associated with Gordon Brown. I did not mean that we should, or could, avoid such economic cycles. I meant that monetary policy should be deployed so that interest rates were raised in time to cool any overheating bubble and to take the top off the boom, then lowered when the economy was cooling and going into recession so as to raise the bottom of the bust.

Political pressures, felt most intensely by every Chancellor's next-door-neighbour at Number 10, had prevented both Nigel Lawson and Norman Lamont from sticking to their principles. Prime ministers are more attuned to the political consequences of policy, and to the exigencies of party management, than they are to long-term economic goals. That is an inevitable problem for any Chancellor. I was stubbornly determined though to apply sound principles throughout. In this regard, it was undoubtedly helpful to me that John Major had already sacked one Chancellor of the Exchequer – in my opinion the maximum permitted limit for any prime minister. I had observed Roy Jenkins enjoy a similar period of semi-unsackability as Harold Wilson's Chancellor in the late 1960s, after Harold had already sacked James Callaghan from the post following the devaluation crisis. This had left Roy in a strong position to resist any pressure from Harold to try to buy votes.

Fortunately, John and I began the prime minister–Chancellor relationship already good friends, and we maintained this through very regular contact, including informal meetings in Downing Street once or twice a week. This is not to say that John was not nervous about some of my more robust moves over the next four years. I am sure that, after some of our conversations, we went back to our respective offices with me muttering that the prime minister appeared to have lost all recollection of his time running the Treasury, and with him telling his staff that I appeared to have lost all my political judgement. He had to be extremely sensitive to political events, while I had to be equally sensitive to economic reality. But ultimately we worked together in the classic way recommended by Harold Wilson when he said that the duty of the prime minister is to 'advise and to warn' the Chancellor, without trying to second-guess him. I paid proper regard to his opinions on economic policy. He in his turn never attempted to overrule me.

John also solidly supported me in Cabinet whenever I was challenged. For my part, I was John's most determined ally in the battles within the Conservative Party over Maastricht which dominated our daily political lives. Our relationship could not have offered a greater contrast to that of our successors, Tony Blair and Gordon Brown. I would confidently have predicted that any government so deeply divided at the top would have collapsed. How they managed to maintain their modus vivendi for quite such a long time completely baffles me.

Other than on the crucial issue of interest rates, there are only two occasions on which I recall John expressing dismay. The first was over attempts to host the Olympic Games in Britain. The second was over the proposal to replace the ageing royal yacht *Britannia*.

I was against supporting our attempts to host the Olympic Games, first in Manchester and then in Birmingham. I thought these two provincial cities had little chance unless we joined with particular enthusiasm in the International Olympic Committee's then custom of bribery on a monstrous scale. Despite being a great sporting enthusiast, I also felt strongly that we should not inflict upon ourselves the costs of building huge stadiums or the security problems of running such a circus. I withdrew my opposition on the basis of the strictest undertakings from my relevant colleagues that no bribes of any kind would be offered by the British team negotiating our bids. I also reluctantly allowed a new velodrome to be built in Manchester as the modest cost would be taken straight out of our small existing sports budget. The whole thing fizzled out, with only a handful of votes cast for us on each occasion, presumably because we did not make the usual and expected offers.

I adamantly refused, though, to contemplate spending £60 million of public money on anything as nineteenth century as a royal yacht at a time when we were cutting back on public spending. I thought that the public reaction would be very negative, and difficult to manage, with every lobbyist citing the yacht when complaining about constraints in their areas. I was also unpersuaded that the yacht made any practical difference to our export performance, which was the only serious argument of any practical kind used in its favour.

I was led to understand that the Queen was quite distressed by the prospect of our failure to provide this facility for her and her family. I am a great enthusiast for the Queen, and as monarchist as most other British politicians. However, I differ in one respect. Most politicians are so in awe of the royal family that expressions of displeasure from the Palace about issues bearing directly on the family can usually produce quite significant policy shifts. Eventually, faced with the distress of my colleagues and their eager belief that recommissioning the yacht would arouse an electorally advantageous patriotic fervour, I gave way. Nothing had been done to enact the decision by the time of the 1997 election, however, and my successor, Gordon Brown, obviously took the same hair-shirted attitude as I did, so that the British royal family no longer has the royal yacht that their ancestors were accustomed to enjoy.

We did not, when I became Chancellor, have an independent Bank of England. Interest-rate decisions were made not by the Bank, but by the Chancellor. I had advocated an independent Bank, as had every Conservative Chancellor since 1979, bar one. Unfortunately, that one was John Major, who was as adamant as Margaret Thatcher had always been that interest rates should be set by a politician and could not possibly be trusted to a powerful independent body like the Bank. As a result, the very patrician Robin Leigh-Pemberton, for a brief time, then his successor as governor of the Bank of England, the jovial Eddie George, were confined to giving me advice – courteous and gentlemanly on Robin's part and robust and analytical on Eddie's – while the decisions remained mine.

Responsibility for the sensitive subject of interest rates left me dangerously politically exposed and I rapidly made some changes. Norman Lamont had introduced monthly meetings for Treasury ministers and senior officials to discuss monetary policy with the governor and chief economist of the Bank. Without consulting anyone, I announced that the minutes of these meetings would henceforth be published. This meant that the advice of officials and of the governor would be publicly revealed for the first time.

After a while I became annoyed that not enough notice was being taken of the minutes – journalists and economic commentators appeared to assume they were bogus public relations documents that did not reflect any actual discussion and I could not persuade any of them that they were accurate minutes of real meetings. This was resolved the first time I decided to reduce interest rates by twenty-five basis points (a quarter of 1 per cent). Eddie and his stern chief economist, Mervyn King, both disagreed. The published disagreement attracted wide press attention – a split between the Chancellor and the governor on any point, however trivial, was newsworthy. The minutes were taken seriously thereafter, particularly whenever disagreements emerged, and the meetings, which became known as 'The Ken and Eddie Show', became a popular feature in public debate on the economy. The governor of the Bank – previously an obscure mandarin – also became a prominent public figure, as governors have remained ever since.

I was delighted, because my whole point had been to try to develop a more informed and intelligent debate in serious circles about the decisions that I was taking.

Once I had implemented this change, I was also able to argue furiously with the prime minister that I could not totally disregard the advice I was receiving for political reasons without terrible political consequences. (Prime ministers are always tempted to demand interest-rate cuts before difficult party conferences and the like.) This was particularly useful when I needed to raise interest rates. No one had done this since before John had become Chancellor several years earlier, and John had always rejected any suggestion from Norman Lamont that interest rates should move in any direction but downwards. My attitude to monetary policy was that, just as taxes sometimes had to be raised and sometimes lowered, so too did interest rates, depending on the level of demand and activity in the economy.

In September 1994, the first time I decided to raise interest rates by fifty basis points (one half of 1 per cent) from 5.125 per cent to 5.625 per cent, with the agreement of Eddie George, John Major expressed very considerable distress at the prospect which he thought would be politically hugely unpopular. He implored me to drop the idea and got very excited. The only concession that I made to calm him down was to hold a press conference to announce the measure. This rather over-the-top way of announcing the move seemed to go reasonably well and this fairly inconsequential small movement in rates passed by without any difficulty.

In both monetary and fiscal policy I clearly and repeatedly set out the principles I intended to follow.

I eagerly embraced the inflation target of 1 per cent to 4 per cent which Norman Lamont had announced after Black Wednesday – one of the best and most significant decisions he had taken as Chancellor. Inflation had risen to 9.5 per cent in 1990 but by 1992 was back at 3.7 per cent. It remained between 1 per cent and 4 per cent throughout my time as Chancellor.

I explained regularly that I would try to sail between the twin dangers of overheating on the one hand and economic recession on the other, by using monetary policy to control growth and demand. I stuck to those principles quite firmly throughout my four years as Chancellor, sometimes raising interest rates but happily more often being able to reduce them.

I also set out my principles for the control of fiscal policy – tax and spending. I declared that I would seek to achieve a balanced budget over the economic cycle. The aim was to run a surplus of tax revenue over public spending during periods of growth, but to permit a deficit to whatever extent was necessary, whenever the economy looked at risk of a downturn.

In addition to a balanced budget, my declared objectives were to satisfy the Maastricht criteria of an annual deficit of no more than 3 per cent of GDP and a national debt of no more than 60 per cent of GDP. I took pleasure in declaring my aim of compliance with these objectives partly to tease our increasingly rabid Eurosceptic back-benchers. These were of course the criteria that would have to be complied with by any nation wishing to join the eventual single European currency. I did also defend them on the basis that they amounted to no more than fiscal common sense for any policymaker of centre-right convictions.

I also declared that my aim was to bring down the level of total public expenditure to no more than 40 per cent of GDP in any one year. This was criticized by more right-wing backbenchers as a feeble aim for a 'small state' party, but the small state for its own sake was an ideological objective that I did not share. John Redwood attempted to demonstrate that we should aim for a much lower figure, but the policies he advocated to achieve this seemed largely to be made up of accounting devices rather than anything more substantial. I in fact believed that it would be a very tall order to oblige my spending department colleagues to get down to my own perfectly reasonable recommended levels, and so it proved to be.

More prosaically, I gave several speeches in which I said that my overriding role as Chancellor should be to make it easier for a businessman in the Midlands to run his business successfully and to generate jobs and earnings. In the end, that had to be the test.

These simple goals that I set for myself were very orthodox liberal policies. The difficulty was that most Chancellors before me had been prevented from achieving very similar objectives by political pressures and vote-winning hopes.

Armed with these basic principles, I embarked on my Budgets.

Each Budget I presented was the culmination of a period of extremely hard work over the preceding six months. Norman Lamont had decided that he would move the date of the Budget to November each year, away from the traditional spring delivery. This meant that Budgets would for the first time involve a combination of tax changes and public-sector spending plans, presented in the context of overall fiscal and monetary policy. Since Norman sadly did not survive long enough in office to deliver a November Budget and Gordon Brown abandoned this very sensible approach, I am the only Chancellor of the Exchequer to have delivered a huge all-embracing Budget at this time of year.

The whole process was organized by my excellent private secretaries, first Jeremy Heywood, and then, after about twelve months, Nicholas Macpherson, who later became permanent secretary of the Treasury and a personal friend. With the help of a high-powered Private Office, they organized a long and elaborate process of preparatory meetings and papers that culminated in Budget day.

The process began inauspiciously. Some senior Treasury officials, led by their impressive permanent secretary, Terry Burns, had become somewhat over-obsessed with the new concept of computer modelling of the economy. They insisted that we began every series of Budget preparation meetings with a presentation of the analyses and forecasts prepared for me by the officials responsible for modelling the UK economy. At the time, there was a fashionable notion that it was possible to produce a comprehensive computer model of the behaviour of the economy. This was then supposed to produce a perfect blueprint of the way in which policy should be loosened or tightened. In my usual low-tech way, I thought this was nonsense, and based on a naive belief that history would repeat itself. It might be possible one day, but it certainly was not in the mid-1990s. I rather dutifully sat through these presentations and analyses without allowing them to affect my judgement. I opined that policymakers were always taken by surprise by the causes of the next recession and that the only thing we could be certain of was that they would not be the same as the causes of the last one.

The Treasury's computer model was filled with data from the 1980s so it constantly predicted that every time growth ticked up a little we were about to enter a period of unsustainable cost–push wage inflation. When officials used the computer model to insist that we were heading for a bout of aggressive wage rises, I would take the trouble to check this assertion by ringing up one or two chief executives of major British companies and asking them whether wage demands were currently a problem. I was always advised that this was not a particular difficulty and I ignored the computer's predictions.

I certainly did not reject or ignore the advice and opinions of my officials on all matters. Intellectually, the Treasury was the most impressive government department in which I ever served, and Terry

Burns gave it splendid informal but formidable leadership. I encouraged constant debate and, in striking contrast to my experience at the Home Office, everybody eagerly joined in and vigorously argued their case. The youngest person present, sometimes a recent graduate, would openly argue with the permanent secretary in front of me, or challenge his or my own opinions. I definitely took all the decisions, and often made up my mind quite quickly, but I was also genuinely influenced by the better arguments I heard. (Terry Burns used to say that he would run down the corridor when a crisis broke, so that he could get to my room and start arguing with me before I had begun to decide what to do.) But there was always a slightly unworldly element to the discussions. I used to compare it to high table at an Oxbridge college. Everyone there was brilliant intellectually, and full of ideas, but most of them were devoid of any practical experience of running anything.

To prepare for the spending half of each Budget, and in partnership with Michael Portillo, I reviewed public spending through a rather ingenious process.

At the end of weeks of discussion with my officials, I agreed a total target for public spending for the next three financial years. My practice was to take this figure to Cabinet in the summer and achieve firm Cabinet agreement to the overall total for the negotiations to follow. It was usually fairly easy to gain unanimous consent at this point, because most departmental ministers were convinced that the spending total's effects would not be borne by them, after they had defended their case. Thereafter, every minister became aware that if they were to succeed in obtaining more than the sum we thought right for their department, then greater savings would have to be found from another department. More significantly, once any individual minister had reached a satisfactory agreement with Michael Portillo and me, they became the fiercest opponents of any attempt by a colleague to win concessions against us. This was for the obvious reason that they wanted to avoid at all costs their settlement being reopened to pay for another colleague's largesse.

Michael handled almost all the initial face-to-face negotiations with spending ministers, mastering the brief and debating policy objectives and the detail of administration in each and every area. His negotiating skills were such that he successfully reached settlements in many cases. The only services I identified as priority areas in which we would always increase spending were health, education and the police.

For those ministers who held out against Michael's attempts to negotiate, there was the EDX Committee, comprising of Michael and a number of Cabinet members who had already settled – allies all. As Chancellor, I chaired the meetings and was both judge and a member of the hostile jury that confronted a spending minister trying to argue his or her case. Michael starred in the prosecutorial role. Neither one of us was able to emulate Willie's performance but success rates for appellants were very low.

A really determined and infuriated colleague had the right to appeal against the judgement of EDX by taking their case to a meeting of the full Cabinet. This was of course a completely futile endeavour because their arguments would inevitably be presented in the middle of a crowded Cabinet agenda. The unfortunate minister would also be appealing to Cabinet colleagues all determined to hold on to their settlements, and therefore disinclined to grant the appellant funds that Michael and I might then try to recover from them by reopening their settlements. Only one minister ever succeeded and that was Virginia Bottomley when she was Health Secretary. She regularly held out all the way to Cabinet, and John Major and I used to see her right with an extra £100 million or so.

I discovered quite a lot about the character of several of my colleagues, all of whom I thought I knew well, during these endless spending rounds each year. Some of the most right-wing 'small state' ministers were the most spendthrift in their own departmental portfolios and the most over-influenced by their officials. Some ministers were weak, and easy to bully into going further than even we felt sensible. Occasionally in these cases we would hold back from taking cuts we might have won because of our own political judgement of the likely consequences. Some ministers devised effective and forceful techniques of their own.

Douglas Hurd at the Foreign Office was quite the most entertaining colleague to deal with. I greatly admired Douglas, who was a classic and natural Foreign Secretary of great distinction. He seemed born to the role. His spending limits were almost a matter of light entertainment for Michael and me because the sums involved were tiny compared with the massive budgets of the great public services. His officials were totally resistant to making any concessions at all and adopted the usual practice of suggesting that the only possible cuts to be made were in the most vital parts of their service, involving the closure of embassies in the most sensitive capital cities in the world, or the failure to maintain the Commonwealth Institute's ceiling, which was likely, they claimed, to collapse any day and kill a party of unsuspecting visitors.

Douglas eventually insisted on dealing with me personally. One or other of us would cross the Bridge of Sighs, the overhead covered footbridge linking the Treasury building with the magnificent imperial Foreign Office, then have a rather pointless discussion.

I would arrive fully briefed with pages of material, breakdowns of spending figures and subjects that I wished to raise. Douglas would arrive with nothing and would discuss generalities about foreign policy and sensitivities in some areas of the world. He genuinely told me that he was surprised that I expected to talk about figures at such discussions. He took the view that we each had bookkeepers buried somewhere in our departments who sorted these things out. He always succeeded in resisting me, and usually resorted to approaching the prime minister, saying that I was about to bring his government's entire foreign policy to a grinding and disastrous halt. Like all prime ministers, John got deeply involved in foreign affairs and frequently insisted that I should stop troubling Douglas in this way.

Even Margaret Thatcher, who had hated the Foreign Office when she was prime minister – she saw it as full of grand diplomats who had gone native and were far too fond of compromise – once came to its aid. She was now touring the world doing speaking engagements and always stayed with her entourage at the British ambassador's Residence. We were trying to sell off the more extravagant of these mansions. Like her, I had stayed at the marvellous but decayed old colonial house in Bangkok with its dilapidated extensive gardens, now surrounded by skyscrapers and worth millions. When Margaret heard that we proposed to sell off the gardens for development she was outraged and told me that I was a philistine with no regard for our imperial heritage. I retreated and settled for selling a strip on the road frontage only.

Michael Howard, my successor at the Home Office, had a different, more aggressive technique. I was only able to get any savings out of him because of my first-hand knowledge of the department and my confident conviction that it was overstaffed, badly organized and extravagant.

The Home Office official representations usually annoyed me because the civil servants there held the police, the courts and to some extent the fire service, in far higher esteem than they did the immigration service. They were always terrified of offending their 'customers' in what they regarded as their key areas. Instead, they would offer the most substantial reductions in the manning and expenditure of the immigration service. Many of them regarded attempts to control immigration as almost futile in practice, and the service was viewed as an irritating fringe activity to the grander parts of their work. I thought the immigration service had one of the most challenging and difficult tasks of all Home Office services and I simply resisted attempts to blame me for imposing onto it financial constraints which I believed would do substantial political and social damage. However, I was not always successful enough in this effort to spread Home Office savings more evenly.

Michael meanwhile was anxious to reinforce his political reputation as a martinet. Law and order formed the basis of his ambitions to succeed John Major. I always allowed him a modest increase in police numbers. He always wanted more. He devised a technique, which I managed to control, of preparing in advance to win a standing ovation at the Conservative Party conference every autumn. The conference was always a formidable challenge for any Home Secretary, who had to confront and impress some very right-wing grass-roots enthusiasts. Michael always attempted to announce a popular and impressively bigger increase in police numbers for the coming year than I had agreed. He yearned to be able to claim to be the minister who put more 'bobbies on the beat' each year. I soon realized that I had to obtain a draft of his speech before he delivered it and engage in more arguments, bringing in John Major, to stop him from making commitments which we were quite unable to pay for.

The colleague who got most distressed about her spending settlement was the otherwise excellent Gillian Shephard, when she was Secretary of State for Education. I was a great admirer and friend of Gillian, who was then one of the most likeable people in political life and a very able minister. Unfortunately, she got personally involved and was very upset when the Treasury team insisted on controlling her budget, or at least she contrived to appear to be so. She had very poor personal relations with Michael Portillo, who usually enraged her. I have never been over-endowed with diplomatic skills but I tried very hard to discuss matters with Gillian in a friendly and civilized manner and to reassure and calm her down without giving way. In some years, her distress led her to share her feelings about the impossible behaviour of her Treasury colleagues with a fair number of Conservative backbenchers, which then generated unhelpful publicity around our negotiations. Michael and I were never persuaded to desist from getting what we believed to be sensible, but I do suspect that she achieved some success in limiting our raids on her budget. To my relief, our friendship was not damaged by this, although she must have been sticking pins in my effigy at the time.

Throughout my four years as Chancellor, events forced us to continue to reduce public spending. Michael Portillo was promoted to Secretary of State for Employment and was followed as chief secretary by Jonathan Aitken who was, with respect, less effective. John Major and I had only agreed to appoint him to give me a fierce Eurosceptic as my Cabinet partner in order to appease the Maastricht rebels. Jonathan, the great hope of the Tory right, proved to be rather too kind-hearted and laid-back for the job. Within a year, he had resigned and left the government armed with 'the simple sword of truth and the trusty shield of British fair play' in a libel action he initiated, after the collapse of which he was charged with perjury and perverting the course of justice, for which he eventually went to prison. Jonathan was in turn succeeded by William Waldegrave, who had asked John Major for the job. William was a brilliant intellectual, very competent and a good friend. But he did not have my combative and aggressive approach to the task.

Nonetheless, we achieved big reductions in public expenditure, at a level that had not been seen for many years. The Thatcher governments had never cut spending on the public services at all; indeed it had increased steadily throughout the 1980s. The fiscal position of her governments had largely been improved through privatization, which had taken off taxpayers' backs the ridiculous levels of subsidy they had been providing to every loss-making nationalized industry.

The tax decisions taken for each Budget were considered over a period of months in significant detail. I would quite early on have to make a provisional decision about how much revenue I needed to raise. A variety of ways of doing this would then be prepared and presented to me. Eventually this became a process of studying a list and eliminating options, until we had our final proposals.

I was entirely fixed on tightening fiscal policy, and alongside the strict public spending negotiations that I was inflicting on my Cabinet colleagues, I was quite certain that I needed to raise government revenue. I was probably the last Chancellor for whom this was a straightforward political possibility. I regularly explained that taxes would undoubtedly need to be raised, as I had inherited a fiscal crisis. This was not a particularly popular position, but it did not cause the hysterical reaction that is now customary. In later years, beginning with right-wing Republicans in the United States, the idea spread that no elected politician should ever raise taxation that might affect the general public. I regarded this as rather a simplistic notion.

On arrival at the Treasury, I was slightly embarrassed by some of the statements that had been made by my colleagues in the course of the 1992 general election campaign. Apparently John Major had promised in a speech that he would reduce taxes year by year if he was re-elected. Fortunately, I discovered that this reckless remark had not formed any part of our written election manifesto. Within two weeks of taking office, I therefore asserted that I would only regard myself as bound by commitments made in the published manifesto

– which, in common I suspect with the vast majority of my Cabinet and parliamentary colleagues, I had actually never read – and not by stray remarks that might have been made in obscure meetings during the pressure of campaigning. My exact phrase was that I did not feel bound by stray remarks thrown out at a public meeting 'on a wet Wednesday evening in Dudley'. This caused contrived fury in Dudley with the local press apparently denouncing me as having said that it was perfectly all right for politicians to tell lies when they were in that town. I ignored this rather wild parody of my views.

From the outset I made a policy decision that I would not raise taxation on the generality of business. I was also not going to raise taxation on personal incomes, because I thought that low marginal taxation on earnings was an incentive to economic activity. I therefore targeted taxes on spending.

I did realize, though, that a Budget which only raised taxes and didn't lower any would be more difficult to sell. I therefore set myself the ambition of simplifying and reducing the burden of income tax with the eventual aim of producing a standard rate of 20 per cent and a higher rate of 40 per cent. As a simple political tactic, I twice reduced the basic rate of income tax by one pence, from 25 per cent to 24 per cent and then 23 per cent, in order to move towards my 20 per cent target. This gave me a popular sub-headline to offset the announcements of tax rises. I also wanted to raise the threshold at which low earners were subject to income tax at all, because I believed that that had been allowed to drift far too low. John Major was never keen on raising thresholds, expressing the opinion that 'it seemed to cost a lot' and 'was not worth any votes'.

I believed that the pain of increased taxation would be eased if it was distributed among a reasonably wide variety of different sources. I repeatedly quoted in discussions in the office my favourite saying of Louis XIV's finance minister, Jean-Baptiste Colbert: 'The art of taxation consists in so plucking the goose as to obtain the largest amount of feathers with the least possible amount of hissing.' I therefore decided to invent a few new taxes.

Customs and Excise were particularly thrilled to have a Chancellor who was trying to invent new taxes for them to collect. We looked at all kinds of innovative suggestions, including a then Irish novelty of a tax on plastic bags, which my officials and I eventually rejected as being almost unenforceable.

In the end, I went for an Air Passenger Tax and an Insurance Premium Tax. I chose the former because, at that time, only the better-off flew in aeroplanes and aviation was the only industry that paid no duty at all on its fuel. I favoured the latter because certain retailers of white goods and other consumer goods were offering bargain prices for their products, which were subject to VAT, and then selling the vast majority of their customers almost worthless and grotesquely overpriced insurance guarantee policies which were free of all tax and boosted their profit margins. I introduced both taxes at modest levels in my first Budget in 1993, and, in due course, turned them into reasonable earners.

I was also persuaded by my friend John Gummer who, as Secretary of State for the Environment, was becoming a green enthusiast, to introduce a Landfill Tax in 1996. This was to reduce local authorities' excessive use of landfill, which was both environmentally damaging and a blight on the landscape, and to induce the authorities to use more environmentally friendly methods of waste disposal. John persuaded me to allocate the proceeds of this tax to grants for environmentally friendly measures, which was a huge boost to conservation organizations. I needed some persuading to forgo the money, but as I was extremely enthusiastic birdwatcher and something of a conservationist myself, John eventually prevailed.

I was horrified to discover that the 1992 written manifesto included an embarrassing commitment to curtail inheritance tax. I regarded this tax as a very valuable source of public revenue – taxpayers offer least objection to being penalised when they are dead. Their potential heirs might be annoyed by the tax, but only reasonably large estates ever paid it. I could see no point in giving up this revenue and I certainly did not wish to preside over the recreation of a rentier class of the Bertie Wooster kind. I was reinforced in this view by my private secretary, Nick Macpherson, who had carried out an extensive study of the tax on first entering the Treasury and had come to hold a very favourable opinion of it. I never made a clear public pronouncement of my views. Instead, I only ever made small token increases in the inheritance tax threshold, accompanied by rather exaggerated descriptions of my moves. I also 'forgot' another silly pledge in the 1992 manifesto to abolish stamp duty on share transactions, ignoring dire warnings from the City that London would be destroyed as a financial centre if I did not remove this burden.

I was also determined to move towards the abolition of tax relief on mortgage interest. In my opinion, the madness of the housing market and the obsession of the British middle classes with the value of their houses was one of the principal causes of the continuous instability of the post-war UK economy, as purchasers overcommitted themselves to mortgage debt and drove house prices to ever higher levels in periodic housing booms. I saw no purpose in subsidizing such reckless behaviour by relieving the interest charges of tax. I therefore began the process of cutting the tax relief. The process was not quite complete when we left office and I am glad to say that Gordon Brown polished off the residue of this ridiculous relief almost as soon as he succeeded me.

Another move I made was to abolish the married couples' allowance, which seemed to me to be pure social engineering, and ineffective at that. The tax system should not be used to tell people how to organize their private lives, and £150 was anyway unlikely to influence a couple's decision to marry or not. George Osborne later tried to resist fairly strong political pressure in the coalition government to reinstate this allowance and was forced to bring in a feeble substitute.

When Tessa Keswick left to run a think tank in 1995, I was persuaded to take on Edward Troup as an expert special adviser on tax policy. Edward had been a tax partner at the law firm Simmons & Simmons where his very successful practice had consisted in devising ingenious but entirely legal tax-avoidance arrangements for high-net-worth individuals. He now began to advise me and Treasury officials on every tax proposal we put forward, proving to be a quite brilliant poacher turned gamekeeper. Every time we produced a marvellous new scheme for raising revenue in a sensible way, or for closing a tax-avoidance loophole, Edward would explain how any skilful accountant could exploit or get around it. Through my remaining time in office he served the public interest by shooting down many suggestions that would otherwise have provided a very steady income for his fellow professionals. Years later, in 2004, he was recruited by the Treasury as a civil servant. As I write, he occupies an extremely senior position as executive chair and permanent secretary of Her Majesty's Revenue and Customs.

To the utter consternation of the Treasury mandarins, I wrote my own paper while on holiday in 1993, about my philosophy on the micro 'Economics Ministry' issues that I wanted to tackle. I was as committed to liberal free-market policies as Nigel Lawson had been, and sought to reinvigorate the privatization programme, for example by putting the student-loan book up for sale. This idea proved so far ahead of its time that it was not implemented until some years later. I also felt the Treasury could do much more to promote growth. My experience at Employment, Trade and Industry and Transport had been that the Treasury often opposed sensible policies in this area for narrow theological reasons which made little sense. And so I worked closely with my financial secretary, Stephen Dorrell, and other like-minded ministers to introduce policies to encourage investment, such as making greater use of private finance in the design, build and operation of infrastructure. I also increased Family Credit, the main in-work benefit, to raise take-home pay and therefore the incentive to work, while at the same time increasing conditionality in the benefit system, so that a life on welfare became less attractive. This approach rapidly became the consensus across the political spectrum and when the Labour government was elected in 1997 it sought to intervene in the same areas but on a larger scale. Sadly, a lot of money was wasted in the process as Gordon Brown announced ever more elaborate schemes such as the New Deal and new tax credits. Sometimes in politics less is more.

In British political history, there is nothing so dead and forgotten as old Budgets. They are a spectacular pantomime on the day that a Chancellor delivers them. They usually cause huge political controversy. Their actual contents – the culmination of months of hard, important and battling work on tax and spending plans – are virtually forgotten within six months of their delivery, and a long and detailed narrative account of my four Budgets would be a tedious challenge to any reader of these memoirs. At the time, though, they mattered hugely.

I treated the delivery of the Budget as a fun day in the House of Commons and on television and a reward for the year's hard work. I was quite determined to enjoy every minute of every occasion. I therefore waved Gladstone's old red 'Budget box' above my head for the photographers with considerable vigour, accompanied by Gillian and by my junior ministers on the steps of Downing Street. Sometimes I rather battered the historic old box, and Gordon Brown later saved it for posterity by introducing a new one for his and future Budgets.

There was a long-standing convention, again going back to Gladstone, that a Chancellor giving his Budget speech was the only MP ever allowed to drink an alcoholic refreshment in the Chamber, in order to sustain his energies through the ordeal. I insisted on making my own tradition that my parliamentary private secretary should ensure that a good glass of whisky was on the Despatch Box when I delivered my Budgets. My usual whisky was from the Western Isles, but I specified the Glenfarclas distillery in Aberdeenshire after I made a ministerial visit there in the spring of 1994. Some of my parliamentary aides understood the strength of whisky and others did not, so there was always a degree of uncertainty with the first sip. Sometimes I would feel that I had been provided with a somewhat weak and watery mixture. Angela Knight provided me with a tumbler of neat Scotch which would have made me totally inebriated if I had got through it all. I usually succeeded in creating a fair degree of amusement by my obvious interest in pausing occasionally, at suitable moments, to have a sip of my whisky, during a speech which generally took something over one hour to deliver.

It is an irony that the Scotsman who succeeded me abandoned the whisky-drinking and ended the tradition.

I had an extremely good speech-writer, Mridul Hegde, who was surprised that I took little interest in altering the details of her text. The reason was that it was extremely important that it was technically accurate. Input to the speech came from the experts in each area and Mridul was perfectly capable of turning their contributions into everyday English. I would freely depart from the text from time to time when actually delivering it in the Chamber, but I was careful to ensure that any extempore or personal remarks contained nothing that was market sensitive or likely to mislead accountants.

I never took a close interest in the contents of the *Financial Statement and Budget Report*, better known as the Red Book, which was prepared by my officials. The Red Book was then regarded as the key detailed analysis of the Budget measures which had to be studied by every economic and financial expert in business and journalism. It was published when the Chancellor sat down at the end of his speech. Journalists were allowed to look at it in the morning, before the speech, but only if they stayed in a locked room in the Treasury without telephones until being released along with the Red Book itself when the Chancellor sat down. I used to read the various drafts as they advanced, but I took it to be an objective and factual laying out by specialists for specialists of the details of every measure. It never occurred to me to interfere with it. I would occasionally challenge some assertion that I thought was fanciful and I would occasionally have a meeting. However, the text would only be changed if I succeeded by argument in persuading officials that some particular feature of their analysis was either wrong or overly confident.

I discovered that this approach was quite unusual and officials did sometimes suggest that I might intervene more. It was explained to me that the Treasury would give me their objective expert advice on the likely figures for growth, inflation, public borrowing and so on. However, they also said that in the end the figures 'were your figures, Chancellor' and implied that it was not unusual for ministers to substitute their own when they seriously wanted to do so. I regarded this suggestion as outrageous and never acted upon it. Unfortunately it seems to me that the changing of estimates and forecasts became habitual after I left office, and I certainly found Gordon Brown's Red Books pretty useless when it came to preparing my contribution to economic debates over subsequent years.

Some conventions I abandoned. It had been traditional for the

Chancellor to begin the Budget speech by giving a long and detailed analysis of the state of the economy. This was because it was believed that no actual tax proposals could be publicly announced before the London markets had closed. I regarded this as old-fashioned. We were moving to a system of global electronic trading so that the closing of the London market no longer had any particular practical relevance. This change spared me and my audience from the ordeal of lengthy, boring and mostly pointless analyses, killing time at the beginning of the speech, in the vein of the lectures Nigel Lawson used to give about the virtues of the various methods of measuring the money supply when such ideas had been fashionable.

Somewhat reluctantly, I was persuaded that every tax change still had to be announced in the Budget. Some of these were very technical changes to obscure provisions that were being used for tax avoidance or evasion and which had to be closed as part of the permanent battle between the discipline of the Revenue and the ingenuity of professional accountants. My speeches would therefore occasionally include paragraphs that were entirely incomprehensible to any ordinary human being. When I delivered these paragraphs to an uncomprehending House of Commons, there was always some backbencher who would try to signal his specialist knowledge by nodding sagely as though he understood the deep policy implications of what was being said. Sometimes I thought that only about half a dozen people in the whole country would know what the text really meant.

All four of my Budget speeches went down remarkably well. The most spectacular was my first, in November 1993. This speech actually represented quite a formidable change of policy, but it was perhaps the enthusiasm of my delivery and the novelty of my appearance after the sad misfortunes of my predecessor that gave it momentum. The buzz in the House felt extremely good as I sailed through the speech and I was amazed when I sat down to find myself surrounded by the cheers of my colleagues and the energetic waving of order papers. I remember thinking that they obviously had not listened to a single word, as I had just raised the tax burden by more than any single Budget since 1945. My cheery presentation – and a rather neat trick

Top With the 'A' Team, 1992 election. Ken Baker, Ken Clarke, John Major, Chris Patten, Michael Heseltine, Douglas Hurd and Norman Lamont. *Above left* The Treasury. *Above right* With Gillian at Dorneywood. I think we staged this photo as a joke, trying to look like stately-home residents. Gillian couldn't play a note.

Breaking all office rules after a gruelling press conference in 1994.

'The Ken and Eddie Show'. Sitting opposite, Governor of the Bank of England Eddie George with Treasury officials. Nick Macpherson, my private secretary and later permanent secretary to the Treasury on my left. Note the ashtrays.

With Gillian and
the red box,
Budget Day, 1995.

With John Major
at the 1996
Conservative Party
conference.

With John Major
at Kitty O'Shea's,
Dublin, December
1996. On the far
right is David
Davis, then the
very Eurosceptic
Minister for
Europe.

Top Announcing the 2001 Leadership bid. Amongst the throng are John Bercow, Graham Bright, David Curry, Jim Lester, Anthony Steen and Ann Widdecombe.

Above A special edition of BBC *Question Time* with all the candidates in the 2005 leadership election. From left: Michael Ancram, Ken Clarke, David Davis, David Dimbleby, Iain Duncan Smith and Michael Portillo.

OPPOSITE PAGE *Top* With Ken Junior at Monza. I am waving a trophy. It was one of the few times BAR ever got on the podium; *Middle left* Presenting a jazz programme on BBC Radio Nottingham; *Middle right* With saxophone and genuine saxophonist, Graeme Radcliffe; *Bottom* Motor racing at Brands Hatch.

Top left Trying on the infamous brown suede shoes at Crockett & Jones.
Top right With John Major at Trent Bridge Cricket Ground.
Above With Roy Gibbons, my government driver.

OPPOSITE PAGE *Top left* Leading my fellow coalition ministers into the
rose garden at Number 10. From the back: Philip Hammond, David Laws,
Nick Clegg, Gus O'Donnell and Ken Clarke. *Top right* Lord High Chancellor.
Bottom With David Cameron in the Cabinet Room.

With Baroness Warsi at the inauguration of Pope Francis.

With Gillian, Ken Junior and Susan after receiving the Companion of Honour from the Queen.

at the end in which I suggested I might have to raise VAT on such items as children's clothes and food, only to reveal that in fact our public-expenditure discipline meant that I would not – had sugared the pill sufficiently to win the day.

The flattest Budget speech that I ever delivered came in 1994 when I spoke the day after a very late and extremely bad-tempered sitting in the House on the European Communities (Finance) Bill, which I describe in Chapter 20. This was at one of the many fevered heights of the Maastricht ratification crisis, with a threat of leadership challenges and open Eurosceptic rebellion. I had wound up the debate the night before and in the end the government had won the vote, but eight rebels who had refused to vote with the government had had the whip withdrawn. As a vigorous pro-European and as Chancellor, I had greatly enjoyed winding up in front of a packed and noisy House and I think I gave a rather effective and entertaining speech.

This second Budget was a solid second instalment of policies to pull the country further away from financial crisis and build the foundations for healthy sustainable economic recovery. I needed to raise yet more taxation. I was announcing another tight squeeze on public spending. I had some solid announcements to make on measures to incentivize lower-paid employment. And I had a package of measures to encourage risk investment and venture capital. The difficulty was that everybody, including me, had had too much excitement and stayed up far too late the night before. I was not tired, and thought I delivered my Budget speech with my usual panache, but perhaps I did not have my usual attentive audience. As the speech went on, I noticed that Michael Heseltine was fairly solidly asleep near to me on the front bench and I suspect that quite a proportion of my audience gently nodded off at some stage or another. Fortunately, this did not seem to affect the political reception of the measures I proposed, and I survived the experience. But there were none of the favourable diary pieces about my delivery of my financial message to the nation that I had come to enjoy.

One big problem I had inherited from Norman Lamont's last Budget was the imposition of VAT on domestic heating fuel, to be introduced in two stages over the next two years, which had proved extremely unpopular. I was left having to implement this tax, against which there was a fierce campaign. In my 1993 Budget I had got it through by dint of a compensation scheme to help those worst affected by it. This year, with feelings running high, it became obvious during the passage of the Budget Resolutions the week after my Budget speech that we faced a potentially major backbench rebellion.

Personally, I could see no reason for any of the various political exemptions from VAT that had been made over the years, and I tried to persuade my backbench colleagues not to try to defeat the increase. Some very able and sensible backbenchers were hostile to the measure and dubious about the need to stick to our commitment to this second instalment. However I knew my goose was cooked when Teddy Taylor, one of the 'whipless eight' who had rebelled on the EU Budget and become overnight celebrities, suddenly turned up in the Chamber. VAT on fuel was a subject about which he knew little and on which he had always previously supported the government. Teddy now stood up and made a rambling speech about how VAT was a European tax and this Commons debate was all a sham anyway and these things were all decided at the behest of Brussels. He appeared to have found some farcical anti-European reason for voting against us. It later transpired that the whipless eight, now nine, who were now working together as a caucus to cause mayhem, had met that afternoon and agreed to act and vote as a block against us. All except Nick Budgen and I think Michael Carttiss, who was abroad, did so, ensuring that we suffered the embarrassment of a defeat on the finance bill, and a loss of revenue.

I insisted on recovering this lost money by introducing amendments to raise the taxation of alcohol and tobacco beyond my original intention. My colleagues, including even the Scottish ones lobbied by the whisky industry, dutifully obliged and gave me the revenue.

I was actually extremely unhappy about having to raise tobacco and alcohol taxes, because I thought that Chancellors over the years had raised these 'sin taxes' to quite ridiculous levels. It was part of the English Puritan tradition that we had very heavy duties on such wicked things as smoking and drinking, but it was beginning to damage the industries concerned. I regularly tried to lobby the finance ministers of other countries to ease discriminatory taxes against Scotch whisky, as this was at the time the country's second most valuable export. I was always greeted by the argument that duty in the relevant country was very much less than that in the United Kingdom. In order to strengthen my position, I eventually responded to this by becoming the first Chancellor for a hundred years to reduce, by some admittedly tiny amount, the duty on Scotch whisky.

As a lifelong smoker, I was also aware that British duty on tobacco was very high. The cigar importers would come to see me and complain that half of all British cigar smokers bought their cigars whilst travelling abroad – a proposition I could believe, as that had been my own invariable practice for many years. I was also concerned that the main beneficiaries of this high taxation were professional smugglers, who enjoyed a higher profit margin on tobacco than they did on cannabis as they smuggled huge lorryloads of product through our ports. I was worried that we would start seeing declining revenues from this tax as an ever greater proportion of the population bought smuggled products.

However, the campaign about the health risks of tobacco smoking was forcefully under way. Perfectly reasonable lobbies pressed me every year to raise the tax on tobacco and it was the only popular tax increase that was available to me. I resigned myself to the fact that, because I was a smoker, it would be quite impossible for me to stop raising tax on tobacco. I would be condemned and derided if I did.

I was finally induced to move when I discovered that the biggest selling brand of 'roll your own' tobacco in the country was Drum, a Dutch product, which I was told had never legally been imported into the UK. I was assured, though, that university students would never use any other brand. I therefore daringly froze the duty on roll your own tobacco in my 1995 Budget. It caused minimal fuss but I was never brave enough to do it again.

My final Budget in 1996 was accompanied by a particularly unusual crisis. Throughout my period of office, we had adhered very strictly to the long-standing convention of absolute secrecy about every

Budget measure. I strongly approved of this rule because advance knowledge of tax measures was market sensitive and scoundrels would have been able to make money by acting promptly on advance information. It was regarded as an extremely serious disciplinary offence for anyone to trail the Budget and I had never had any problem with leaks of any kind despite the involvement of hundreds of Treasury officials at various stages each year. This convention was quite wrongly abandoned by Gordon Brown as soon as he took office, with his press secretary, Charlie Whelan, briefing selected journalists in the Red Lion pub in Whitehall the night before his first Budget. The convention collapsed, never to be restored.

The evening before my last Budget, I was just leaving the Palace after my traditional pre-Budget audience with the Queen when I was suddenly told by my panic-stricken private secretary, Nick Macpherson, that the *Daily Mirror* had the text of my Budget speech, and were proposing to print it in the following morning's paper, some hours before I rose in the House. Apparently there was an industrial dispute at the secure printing firm which printed copies of the Budget papers, which had hitherto been totally sound. Some militant striker had decided to further the cause of the dispute by giving the *Daily Mirror* a copy of the full text.

The *Mirror*, fearing that they were the victim of a hoax by their arch rivals, the *Sun*, had grown suspicious. One of their journalists had therefore rung the Treasury Press Office and had read out passages from the speech over the telephone to a horrified press officer, who realized that they did indeed have an authentic version.

Every senior official in the department was wildly excited by this threat and Nick found himself inundated by phone calls from people making suggestions, some sensible and some not, about what we should do in this unprecedented crisis. These even included a proposal that we should cancel the Budget speech due the following day and begin work on an alternative Budget, which we might deliver later, with different measures that had been kept confidential.

As it was about 7 p.m. by this time, my reaction was to announce that I was going to have a curry at the Pimlico Tandoori with Nick and a couple of other people from my Private Office. I suggested that, by the time we returned, someone should have found me a specialist lawyer to advise as to whether we had any means of stopping publication. I enjoyed a decent curry and appropriate measures were taken. To cut a long story short, our lawyer eventually made a late-evening visit to a judge at his home and obtained the necessary injunction to stop the *Daily Mirror* carrying out their threat. I delivered my Budget speech the following day in the usual way.

During my period of office, the economy steadily grew, unemployment fell, living standards rose and inflation was low. My aim had always been to produce steady growth with low inflation – to me, the holy grail of economic policy. No British Chancellor since the war had achieved this, because even those with a sound feel for policy had been buffeted off course by political pressures. I doggedly stuck to my principles and could not be deterred. I doubt whether this was solely responsible for the economic recovery, but it certainly seemed to do no harm.

In my more ambitious moments in later years I would claim that I had been the most successful Chancellor of the Exchequer since 1945. Given that Chancellors can be judged objectively on the performance of the economy rather more than other ministers can, I could possibly maintain a good debating case for that with a reasonably straight face. Be that as it may, the political climate in my own immediate policy area became extremely benign. By the time we got to the general election of 1997, the economy was the only subject upon which the government was miles ahead in the opinion polls. Unfortunately, the political world was obsessed with other issues, mainly divisions over Europe and scandals within the Conservative Party. However, Tony Blair and Gordon Brown very wisely fought their campaign on the basis that they had no intention of changing my economic policy in any single feature.

19

'The Nearness of You'

(Sarah Vaughan, 1955)

EUROPE AND THE EURO

Then, as now, the UK's domestic political and economic debate was firmly dominated by the politics and economics of Europe. As Chancellor I became the UK's member of the EU Economic and Financial Affairs Council – always known as ECOFIN – and attended its monthly meetings in Brussels and other European capitals. Our principal activity during my term in office was the development of the rules for the single currency for which the Maastricht Treaty had paved the way.

I firmly believed that the single market, whose creation had been led by Thatcher's government in the 1980s, would function better if it had a single means of exchange between those economies which were sufficiently convergent to compete with each other. A single market achieves its best results in terms of growth, investment and jobs if there is free movement of goods, services, capital and labour within it. If a free market is financed by separate national currencies freely floating against each other on the global currency markets, then there are unnecessary costs and distortions on trade as currencies rise and fall in value. The creation of a single currency, however, is a hugely complex process involving the creation of a single central bank and an elaborate set of rules for fiscal discipline, financial regulation and many other matters. It is also only possible for countries to share a single currency if their economies are sufficiently convergent for each country to be able to compete and survive. ECOFIN therefore had the most enormous agenda before it, of setting out the principles and rules by which a single currency could eventually be run. Unfortunately Black Wednesday had scotched any chance of Britain joining the single currency in the near future but that did not mean that the Chancellor, the Treasury and the Bank of England were not vital participants in negotiating its overall structures. I think that the ECOFIN of the time did a very good job of setting out these important structures. Sadly, our successors made a complete mess of implementing the project when the euro actually launched, ignoring all our carefully negotiated rules and causing enormous economic problems for the eurozone.

I also believed in the underlying political objectives of the single-currency project, which had been designed to bind the EU's member states more closely together.

I found that my views were shared by every minister at every ECOFIN meeting I attended. Almost all the member state governments were also publicly committed to the idea. But in Britain and Denmark political controversy was strong and our governments were wavering under pressure. Fortunately the Danish minister, Marianne Jelved, and I were as pro-European as our fellow finance ministers, so the purpose of the meetings remained firmly unanimous.

I had been attending Councils of Ministers since 1979 when I had been a junior transport minister. Despite the slow, tortuous processes by which Councils crawled towards their decisions over endless meetings, I always thoroughly enjoyed them. I have always been a European enthusiast and I took pleasure in the politics, the diplomacy, the intrigue and the personal relationships that were key in the inevitably convoluted network required to bind together large numbers of democratically elected governments from diverse sovereign states.

From transport and health to employment and trade and industry, the Councils I attended had all been fascinating. As I mentioned in Chapter 10, the Employment and Social Affairs Council had been particularly interesting because of my especially strenuous battle against the efforts of Jacques Delors, the president of the European Commission, to develop the Social Chapter – a new area of EU activity relating mainly to workers' rights – and to launch a costly infrastructure programme. Because Jacques was basically a French socialist, his approach to regulation and public spending was in stark contrast to my own. When I arrived at ECOFIN, Jacques finally discovered that I was a fervent pro-European in favour of the single market and the single currency. Thereafter we became comfortable friends. Gillian, who came with me to the less formal gatherings, always got on well with his wife, Marie.

ECOFIN meetings were, of all the Council meetings I ever attended, the most significant, the most productive, and the most fun. Formal meetings were often theatrical public performances necessitating lengthy and tedious speeches, partly aimed at our disparate domestic audiences, and partly staking out ground for discussion and compromise later in the day. The so-called informal meetings, held twice a year, were usually in some splendid location in the country holding the rotating presidency, and ministers were encouraged to attend with their spouses. The more relaxed discussions between social functions were often where the real business was concluded.

There was a certain amount of competitive hospitality involved in the informal meetings. The finest occasion in an impressive field was when Dr Theo Waigel, the jovial centre-right German minister of finance who became known as the father of the euro, took us to a splendid lakeside resort in his native Bavaria. Gillian, who was as enthusiastic as I was about both the European project and foreign travel, greatly enjoyed the company of the other ministers' spouses and the opportunities to see some of the great places of Europe. Unlike me, she spoke good French and German. She did the tourism whilst I did the work.

Unlike any other Council of Ministers that I attended before or since, ECOFIN proved to be an extremely friendly club. This was partly due to the remarkable continuity in office of almost all the finance ministers around the table. We soon became a close-knit group with easy working relationships and the ability to work together to settle, in a professional way promoting our various national interests, the extremely complex issues that arose – in particular the construction of the proposed single currency.

I had some splendid colleagues, both amongst the ministers themselves and also amongst the central-bank governors and senior Treasury and finance ministry officials who attended from every member state. The dominant members of ECOFIN through this period were Theo Waigel, and Hans Tietmeyer, formerly permanent secretary of the German finance ministry and then president of the German central bank, the Bundesbank. Waigel was a cheerful, bouncy, rotund Bavarian and Tietmeyer was a dry, formal, very intelligent banker. Tietmeyer possibly played an even more key role in the creation of the euro than did Waigel. He was a strong defender of the orthodoxy of his great institution and I believe his instincts were to protect the Deutschmark and not to hand power to a European central bank through a new multinational currency. However, he was a very close friend of German Chancellor Helmut Kohl and had obviously been persuaded to promote the project to which his friend was so devoted. Kohl himself had little understanding of or interest in economic policy. Tietmeyer was the brain and the technocrat who steered German policy towards what he believed were workable proposals. Theo Waigel could hold his own with Tietmeyer, or anybody else for that matter, and essentially they were a very strong German partnership.

The most dominant central banker besides Tietmeyer was Jean-Claude Trichet, who would go on to succeed Jacques de Larosière as governor of the Banque de France in September 1993. He was a dynamic personality whose fluent advocacy could impress his extremely sensible views on any meeting.

I was particularly close to two ministers whom I had first got to know when we had been employment ministers together. They had both followed the same path as myself from employment to finance. Jean-Claude Juncker of Luxembourg, then that country's finance minister, was a brilliant backroom fixer who used his position as the representative of the smallest and least significant state, with a population of less than 500,000, to act as the broker in pursuit of the common European cause – and of Luxembourg's – in almost every difficult situation. It was typical of him that shortly after I became Chancellor he skilfully negotiated his way to becoming both prime minister and finance minister of his country – positions he then held for the next almost twenty years. My old friend Ruairi 'Ho Chi' Quinn of Ireland was also once more an unlikely ally.

National officials were more prominent than usual in ECOFIN's processes. Officials from member states had been so nervous of their political bosses handling economic affairs in Brussels that a parallel official committee had been given a formal role. This so-called EU monetary committee – the self-same committee that we had had to consult before we could announce our withdrawal from the ERM on Black Wednesday – discussed the agenda in advance, and then participated in our ministerial meetings through the presence of their chosen chairman. Fortunately, in my time, the chairmanship was soon taken by Nigel Wicks, a quite brilliant British Treasury official with whom I worked closely and whose judgement I greatly respected. Nigel and I would often furiously debate details of economic policy or the possible structures of the new currency but he was as committed a supporter of the single currency as I was and we enjoyed working together as a partnership.

Nigel's hold on his chairmanship was confirmed by the way in which he would occasionally openly disagree with me at ministerial meetings. I had no difficulty with this myself and I was quite happy to debate and try to thrash out problems with him as he acted on behalf of his committee. Ministers and officials from the other member states were obviously astonished that I gave a civil servant such liberty. His opposite numbers were firmly convinced that he had to represent them because of his freedom to put forward their views fearlessly, sometimes in the face of the opinion of his political master. I, however, thought that his and their opinions were always worth listening to.

We finance ministers also attended the main EU Heads of Government meetings alongside our own prime ministers and foreign ministers – the famous European Council summit meetings – whenever the single currency was being debated. This innovation was a wise precaution as a few of the prime ministers involved knew nothing at all about economic policy. This gave rise to some entertaining problems. Several foreign ministers and some of the great political leaders resented the attendance of their better-informed colleagues and competitors. François Mitterrand in particular was so deeply insulted by the whole thing that he would ostentatiously walk out, leaving a deputy in his place, whenever the people whom he contemptuously described as the 'bookkeepers' were present.

These tensions came to their greatest height at an informal gathering in a splendid palace with beautiful views somewhere in the middle of Tuscany. We bookkeepers had taken part in the first day or two of discussions and had then had meetings of our own. However, the key moment in any European Council is the last morning meeting when a rapid discussion takes place of the so-called final communiqué, or the conclusions of the meeting. This communiqué enshrines within it key decisions that afterwards bind all the governments present. John Major was extremely good at thinking and acting quickly to get the results he wanted from these communiqués, but the members of the bookkeepers' union were always as one in our concern about what might be decided if we were excluded. For this reason we had been involved in this final session at every previous meeting I had attended. However on this occasion, the Italian foreign ministry contrived on the last morning to set up only two seats for each member state. The Italians plainly intended to exclude finance ministers from the room, along with all officials. We gathered in an angry huddle on the splendid terrace outside the meeting room. I solved the problem satisfactorily by seizing a terrace chair and carrying it into the meeting, followed swiftly by a procession of similarly armed colleagues. We all settled ourselves down alongside our prime ministers and in this way de facto forced our attendance.

John Major was, understandably, always seeking opportunities to demonstrate to the media that he could get his way in Europe. This sometimes had unfortunate consequences. Douglas Hurd and I always went with John to the Heads of Government meetings and we were startled to discover in the aeroplane on the way to one such meeting that he intended to block the appointment of the proposed next president of the European Commission. The usual fix had been arranged, led by Kohl and Mitterrand, and the presumed successor to Jacques Delors was to be the then prime minister of Belgium, Jean-Luc Dehaene. The unfortunate Belgian was certainly a very enthusiastic pro-European likely to be very receptive to the ideas of Chancellor Kohl, but he was otherwise a perfectly excellent politician.

John was completely undeterred by our mild protests over his plan, and he proceeded at the meeting to make a tremendous show of exercising his veto. There was absolutely no way in which this could be overridden so he did indeed force a rapid change of course on his fellow Heads of Government. The problem was that this enabled Jean-Claude Juncker of Luxembourg to plan behind the scenes to move his prime minister Jacques Santer into the role. Santer was duly appointed, supported by John Major. He was a fairly weak and ineffective man and provided the Commission with very poor leadership for some years to come. Jean-Claude Juncker, meanwhile, conveniently slipped into the role, for which he was eminently well-suited, of prime minister of Luxembourg.

My attendance at ECOFIN and Heads of Government meetings, and the role that I played in them, was obviously a constant source of merciless controversy in British domestic politics and a central feature of the absurd civil war that had now broken out within the Conservative Party about the European Union and the supposed conspiracy to undermine our national sovereignty by creating a 'superstate' in Brussels. This was the dominant feature of politics and debate in the British media and Parliament over the period of my Chancellorship, and was an issue in which I enthusiastically engaged.

The heat of the debate was particularly enhanced by the fact that the *Daily Telegraph* had appointed as its European correspondent a man called Boris Johnson.

Conrad Black, the newspaper's rascally but very intelligent Canadian owner, was fiercely opposed to British membership of the European Union – he was still fixated with the idea that Britain should join the North American Free Trade Agreement – and exerted ferocious and authoritarian control over the paper in order to promote his Euroscepticism. Boris was an engaging and colourful character who was obviously set on a political career. He had not so far made much progress in his young life so he was, it seemed, determined to build a national reputation in the political world through his reports from Brussels.

Boris buzzed around and reported back on every ECOFIN meeting I attended in Brussels and elsewhere. He fervently followed the desired policy line of his proprietor and would attend the bars, receptions and surroundings of our meetings composing savage reports for his readers back home about the wicked progress of our conspiracy to undermine and destroy the national identity of the United Kingdom. I enjoyed his company and admired his intellect. I made vain attempts to persuade him to modify his reports, to no avail. The difficulty was that, in my opinion, they were often nearer to fiction than reality. He was, however, quite oblivious to my vehement complaints that he had on occasion filed reports attributing views to me which I did not hold and which I was supposed to have given to the Council on subjects which had never been mentioned on the actual agenda of that day. No doubt his proprietor and his readership loved his improved account of the way in which the single-currency project and the European project in general were progressing with my fervent support. One or two of my ministerial colleagues, and particularly the growing number of ferocious Eurosceptics that John Major insisted on appointing to his Cabinet in an attempt to appease them, agreed with Boris's views. In their opinion, I should simply be vetoing the single currency and making sure that every proposed decision about it was not only blocked but wrecked on behalf of the British government. They were unfortunately quite correct in believing that I was ignoring this position and was instead making a positive contribution to the development of what became, after we had left office, the euro.

It was probably fortunate that most people in Britain were unaware that, quite early in my period as Chancellor, I had saved the whole single European currency project from destruction. This at least was the opinion of several of my Continental colleagues. Jean-Claude Trichet, then chairman of the officials' committee and later president of the European Central Bank, repeatedly credited me with saving the euro in public political gatherings, which happily were usually held outside Britain.

The British had exited the Exchange Rate Mechanism on Wednesday 16 September 1992 after failing to control our fiscal policy adequately to keep the value of sterling within the range permitted by the mechanism. By July 1993, less than twelve months later, the French were facing the same problem. The franc was coming under intense pressure to devalue and go outside the permitted band against the Deutschmark and other currencies.

This led to a crisis meeting of finance ministers and central-bank governors in Brussels, chaired by the Belgian finance minister Philippe Maystadt, which went on into the night. I was present, accompanied by Nigel Wicks and others, although as Britain was no longer a member of the ERM I was essentially just an interested observer.

At the first formal gathering I spoke up in favour of a deal the French and German ministers had cooked up in advance. This proposed that Germany and the Netherlands should be relieved of their obligations to stay within the bands of the ERM and as strong currencies be allowed to float upwards in order to relieve the other weaker currencies under pressure. Unfortunately this suggestion caused widespread confusion and was opposed by Maystadt on behalf of Belgium because, so far as I could see, he did not want to make the politically unpopular revelation that the Belgian currency was weaker than the Dutch. Everyone else then became confused, at which point Maystadt adjourned the meeting to hold closed-door bilateral meetings with the finance ministers from the most significant ERM member countries.

Sadly Maystadt was not on this occasion a very effective chairman. He was somewhat distracted by some Belgian political crisis of the day involving a problem with the Belgian monarchy whose details neither I nor I suspect any Belgian can now remember. The main difficulty was that he did not want our deliberations to go on through the night as he was anxious to get back to his domestic politics.

I hung about and steadily consumed bad wine and rather good bread rolls in the long interval waiting for my colleagues to reconvene in a formal meeting. Nigel Wicks knew everyone so was able to pick up the gossip from other delegations and report back to me. We were all ringing up our Heads of Government. Mitterrand and Kohl were advising us all to reach agreement. Kohl had apparently just said *'nein, nein, nein'* to the suggestion that we might fail to agree a solution. I phoned John Major occasionally to tell him what was and was not happening. It reminded me overwhelmingly of the atmosphere on Black Wednesday the previous year, except that on this occasion there were more people present.

At about 10 p.m. Maystadt suddenly called us into full session again and announced that he had failed to broker an agreement. All obligations would therefore have to be suspended for a temporary but indefinite period. As I listened, I was convinced that this was going to be a disastrous shambles.

The chairman then asked whether anyone saw any other solution and there was a long silence. It nearly ended there. At this point I rather unexpectedly caught the chairman's eye and made a short intervention. I argued, quite briefly by my own standards, against the catastrophic consequences that this proposed suspension would have. Drawing on the British government's experience of its loss of authority after Black Wednesday, I said that suspension would be seen as a total political failure on the part of the Community. It would also be disastrous for all our ambitions for a single means of exchange and a reduction in currency turmoil within the Union and our market. I strongly argued that a further attempt should be made to settle the matter.

I think I must have spoken with quite unaccustomed eloquence which I hope did not owe too much to the bad wine. Jean-Claude Trichet was not the only person who credited me with changing the mood of the meeting entirely. My neighbour at the table whispered to me that everyone had wanted to have that discussion but had been fearful of offending Maystadt. The Danish and Portuguese now joined in passionately supporting me with vigorous nodding support from the Germans, the French and Jean-Claude Trichet. Jacques de Larosière, the quite brilliant governor of the Banque de France before Trichet succeeded him in September, made a particularly impressive and technically crucial intervention. Maystadt reluctantly agreed to go away and make one further effort and within half an hour we were back in session with an agreement that we would move from the current 3 per cent to a wider 15 per cent band with every member state still inside the system. When I phoned this triumph through to John Major he seemed slightly dismayed. It was clear he would have preferred a total collapse. I never doubted that John supported British membership of the EU but a collapse of the ERM at this point would have been a great help with his domestic political troubles.

The band-widening solution, which others had advocated earlier in the evening, was of course a ridiculous fudge and did transform the nature of the ERM. However, after the experience of Black Wednesday, I had already decided that membership of the ERM was a thoroughly pointless preparation for the creation of the single currency, and that the formation of proper rules for the management of the currency would soon overtake the supposed disciplines of that mechanism.

As a joke, the Portuguese minister had asked me as the final session ended with handshakes all round whether the UK would rejoin the ERM as we were now within the new wider 15 per cent band. I said with a smile that the time was not right, and then repeated my more usual serious line. It is a sad irony that Black Wednesday and the expulsion of Britain from the ERM might possibly have been avoided by the same technique, if only anyone had looked for a solution in the chaotic events of that day. The British government was instead consumed by a crisis from which the French government escaped unharmed less than a year later.

Most of the discussions at ECOFIN meetings were about either the technical details of creating the single currency or the day-to-day problems of the European economy, and the general direction of our reactions to those problems. There were occasional moments of light relief, though. For example, we spent some time discussing the name to be given to the new single currency and the nature of its notes and coins. These were exactly the sort of issues about which the noisier Eurosceptics in Britain were likely to get excited and I therefore joined in the debate with more force than the intrinsic importance of the subjects warranted.

I argued that the new currency should be called the florin, which was the best name I could think of that had both a general European connotation and some echoes in Britain. The florin had been the conversational name of the two-shilling coin that had circulated before we adopted today's decimal coinage in 1971 under Anthony Barber. Unfortunately I lost this argument because the Germans had jumped the gun and simply gone around saying that the new currency would be called the euro. I received some limited support from several other ministers for the florin, which I thought sounded more friendly and less artificial. However the consensus was that we had somehow slipped into an acceptance of the euro and it was not worth reopening the subject.

I did very much better on the coinage because my colleagues were sympathetic to my problems back home and quite content to let me influence the popular details of the arrangements. I argued that the coins should have national emblems on one side – a suggestion that was greeted with some incredulity, until I brought to a meeting a large collection of British pound coins which my officials had gathered. The assembled ministers studied these with interest. One objected that although it was a nice idea, there would be huge difficulty and cost in returning all the 'foreign' coins to their country of origin at the end of each working day. I explained that we had never felt the slightest need to return English, Scottish or Ulster coins or notes in that way and that they could freely circulate without disruption.

My fellow ministers were won over, but, since Britain has of course not joined the euro, no British symbol – which presumably would have been the Queen's head – has ever been used on one.

The central-bank governors insisted that the printing of banknotes was exclusively their prerogative, but designs for possible banknotes were circulated to all the ministers for their comments. The most entertaining problem was raised by our Greek colleague Yiannos Papantoniou. He argued strongly that the notes would have to be bilingual, carrying Greek as well as Latin letters. This gave rise to an agitated debate with the majority of ministers eventually insisting that Greek lettering would be baffling in Scandinavia and elsewhere. Yiannos fought hard but eventually admitted defeat. One additional reason his colleagues were so unhelpful to him, of course, was that we regarded Greek membership of the new currency zone as such a very remote possibility. I do not think that any of us imagined then that Greece would in due course join the eurozone, while the United Kingdom would become the member with the remotest prospects of membership.

Our most crucial decisions concerned eligibility for membership of the new currency zone and the rules by which the zone should be governed. This produced extremely tense and difficult debates between member states which finally reached crisis point at a European Council meeting held at Dublin Castle in September 1996, attended by Heads of Government, foreign ministers and finance ministers.

The agenda for the discussions had been set by Hans Tietmeyer, the president of the German Bundesbank. He had loyally followed the German Chancellor, Helmut Kohl, into agreeing the principle of the new currency, but he was determined to demand strict rules for its membership and its operation. That was obviously the deal that he and Kohl had made, and Kohl determinedly pressed this agenda on all present.

The key issue was the fiscal discipline to be imposed on the governments of the nation states that adopted the new currency. The Germans insisted that the Maastricht criteria should be adhered to and that penalties should be imposed on any member government which exceeded a 3 per cent budget deficit, or whose sovereign debt exceeded 60 per cent of GDP in any one year. Everyone was signed up to this in vague principle already but the French now led the way in arguing, with the support of many other member states, that more flexibility should be allowed in practice for the governments of sovereign states to make their own pragmatic judgements according to the circumstances of any given time. In other words, the French and others should be allowed to borrow more money when electoral pressures made them want to do so.

This was not really a subject upon which either Chancellor Kohl or President Chirac of France had any expertise but, provoked by their advisers, they certainly developed passionate opinions. At one point, walking through the castle, I had the privilege of being amongst a small group of ten to twenty observers watching and listening to an argument taking place between the two great men. They had no common language so they argued through interpreters but this did not diminish their heated vigour. The language was strong and the volume was high. I surveyed this public spectacle with some bemusement for several minutes before the two broke apart and stormed away, each with their respective entourage.

The deadlocked prime ministers then remitted the problem to finance ministers and central-bank governors, leading to a number of utterly unproductive discussions in a separate room in the castle. Nigel Wicks and I left a meeting at one point, no doubt to deal with some domestic query coming in from the Treasury back in London. When we returned we found that the formal meeting had been adjourned, but a smaller group was meeting in the library. Nigel and I did not realize that this meeting was of a group that had been selected by the finance ministers with some difficulty, and asked to retire to seek to bridge the differences.

When the two of us sailed into the library and sat down to join the meeting we therefore did not realize that we had invited ourselves. Fortunately I believe that we were both popular and regarded as useful so no one objected to the rather vigorous role which we both proceeded to play in the discussions, essentially on the German side.

To cut a long story short, full agreement was eventually reached between all the finance ministers which we then pressed on our Heads of Government. We agreed that the Maastricht criteria should be binding. Membership of the eurozone would only be open to those countries which complied with the criteria and had fully convergent economies that could be competitive and coexist with the major currencies in the block. Penalties were to be imposed on any government that remained in breach of the criteria for too long (a point I was personally not keen on, believing that sovereign governments would in practice never submit to them). There was also to be a 'no bailout' clause to ensure that no government would be expected to support the sovereign debt of any other member state that had got itself into trouble.

It remains my opinion that the euro would have been more successful, and the financial crisis of 2007–8 would have been less

severe, if our successors as ministers had adhered to this clear agreement, most of which was enshrined in the treaties.

It was a conference filled with tension and the only light relief
came when John Major told me he was bored and I suggested that
we slip out to my favourite pub in Dublin, Kitty O'Shea's. I urged the
prime minister to tell no one where he was going and he vowed to
me that he would not. I alerted my trustworthy driver and we shot
off for our quiet drink. Unfortunately, John had broken our pact and
– prudently – told his security detail where he was going. Within
minutes, everyone knew where we had gone and some had got there
before us. Kitty O'Shea's was, within five minutes, packed to capacity
with journalists, security men and politicians. We literally drank the
pub dry. The photo opportunity this provided meant that it was the
only moment of the entire summit to be reported in the British media.

After I left office, I watched in astonishment as Italy was admitted
to the eurozone in 2002, despite having a huge and barely sustainable
stock of sovereign debt of over 100 per cent of its GDP. When I
protested to some of my old ECOFIN friends in encounters, they
rather patronizingly told me that Italy could not be excluded on a
technicality because Rome was the birthplace of European civilization
and Italy had been one of the six founder members of the Community.

Worse still, Portugal and Greece were admitted, despite the fact
that their economies were not remotely strong enough or convergent
enough to cope with the competition they would face. Greece in
particular was admitted on the basis of totally bogus statistics which
appeared to comply with the Maastricht criteria but were obviously
not adequately challenged by any other government.

The first government to exceed the Maastricht criteria on genuine
statistics was that of Gerhard Schröder in Germany. He had an election to fight in 2002 and abandoned fiscal discipline to offer electoral
inducements and spending promises. Next came President Chirac's
French government for similar reasons. It seems that no question
was ever raised of imposing penalties on such major member states.
The other members of the eurozone followed France's and Germany's
lead with enthusiasm, entering into unsustainable levels of deficit and
sovereign debt.

The package which we had named the 'Stability and Growth Pact' in Dublin was therefore effectively dead as soon as it faced a serious challenge. I seriously doubt whether the finance ministers of my time would conceivably have gone along with such reckless policies.

When the credit crash of 2007–8 spread from New York and London to afflict members of the eurozone, banking debt was converted to sovereign debt on a grand scale as governments stepped in to prevent their countries' banking systems from failing. The 'no bailout' clause was then ignored and Germany and others began to rescue bankrupt governments in order to prevent them defaulting on their debts to German and other banks.

As I write the eurozone crisis remains unsolved and the single currency could still face yet more crises. The idea of Britain ever joining any single European currency has been killed off by years of nationalist and Eurosceptic campaigning. In the event I did not advocate joining when it was first introduced, mainly because our exchange rate was then too strong. Thereafter it became ever less attractive politically to anyone in the UK as Euroscepticism flowered, and Gordon Brown finally killed the idea of Britain joining for the foreseeable future.

I still believe Europe would have been more prosperous if our successors on ECOFIN had stuck to the rules we negotiated including the Maastricht criteria. It would have needed the leadership of Helmut Kohl, fortified by Delors, Tietmeyer, Trichet and de Larosière, to achieve it. With the exception of Angela Merkel, that quality of leadership has never re-emerged in Europe down to the present day.

20

'Un Poco Loco'
(Bud Powell, 1951)

TORY EURO WARS

The constructive debate and discussions at European Councils were extremely civilized compared with the political battle over the euro raging in London throughout John Major's period of office after 1992.

John was unable to inure himself against the personal and wounding attacks that backbenchers and newspapers hurled at him throughout this time, and the permanent warfare with his colleagues sometimes reduced him to a state of near-misery. I was unable to persuade him, as I had persuaded Gillian, to stop reading the newspapers, on the grounds that they were upsetting him too much and contained nothing he needed to know. John constantly tried to appease the right wing of our party in favour of accommodation and compromise, believing that agreement and unity could always be restored. In successive reshuffles he promoted hard-line Eurosceptics at every level including to the Cabinet. This ended the era of the 'Cabinet of chums'. Cabinet business became impossible because within half an hour of any meeting concluding, unknown Eurosceptic ministers would have briefed the press with a distorted and biased version of its deliberations, raising the temperature still further.

I was one of the ministers who rapidly decided that it was a mistake to allow any serious business affecting my department to be brought to Cabinet. I was not going to expose the details of my brief to the kind of malicious commentary that would have ensued. The then

Cabinet Secretary, my friend Robin Butler, unavailingly tried to find serious subjects for the Cabinet to discuss. He was usually charming and persuasive, but I fear that he was never able to convince me to raise any subject of any significance with a Cabinet from which all vestiges of sensible collective responsibility had vanished.

Apart from voting in divisions, I took little active part in the debates on Maastricht on the floor of the House of Commons, because other ministers handled their departmental responsibilities. The nearest we came to defeat was in July 1993, just after I had been made Chancellor, when our Eurosceptic rebels aligned themselves with Labour and proposed to vote against our opt-out from the Social Chapter. This was purely political, even cynical. Our ultra-right wing were particularly opposed to the social legislation in the Chapter, but had found an ingenious method by which they thought they could block ratification of the treaty. The result was an immediate panic and crisis of the sort that came to dog us increasingly frequently. A series of meetings between various senior ministers and whips took place against the background of advice from the chief whip, Richard Ryder, that we were likely to be defeated by twenty-five votes on the relevant vote. At first John Major and other ministers tried to devise intricate plans whereby they could simply carry on and ratify the treaty with the Social Protocol still included and then hold a vote to remove it sometime thereafter. I will not explain this further because it was plainly an elaborate nonsense based on the belief that we could somehow ride the blow and find some procedural way around it later.

From the first Michael Howard and I insisted that the government could not survive such a defeat in the House for very long and we demanded that the vote on the Social Chapter should be made a vote of confidence, putting the survival of the government at the centre of the decision.

For a couple of days, a lot of time was wasted with frequent meetings arguing about procedural and constitutional issues without getting to the point. Matters finally came to a head on Thursday 22 July after Richard Ryder came to see me at Number 11 and told me that he had done a deal with the Ulster Unionists and the Welsh Nationalists and he still thought we would lose but only by a small number, perhaps as few as three. More ridiculous meetings took place during the course of the day and things were finally resolved at a Cabinet meeting at 7 p.m. that evening. John, who had by this time come round to my way of thinking, called on me to speak first. I argued that the government could not survive for long if we did not ratify Maastricht and that we had to settle the matter now. If we left ourselves swinging in the wind over the autumn we would be ridiculed and destroyed. The whole thing had to be settled in the next few hours. A vote of confidence drafted to trigger the Act ratifying the treaty would be decisive and if carried would begin to restore the authority of Parliament and the government. I also argued that the vote must be tabled straight away and debated the next day, Friday, so that MPs would not be pressurized by the weekend's press.

Michael Howard spoke strongly in my support, as did John Gummer. Douglas Hurd had come round to my point of view and only three Eurosceptics – Peter Lilley, John Redwood and Michael Portillo – held out. The pleasant surprise was that not one of the three threatened resignation, which I had rather feared.

After the decision had been taken, I was concerned that many of my colleagues were uncertain about it. I accurately predicted that many in the press and on radio and television would doubt the government's real determination to resign if defeated. Indeed in the course of the next twenty-four hours, some joker made a very witty remark that the prime minister's car would turn around on the Mall and return if ever he set out for the Palace after a defeat. Therefore, without consulting anyone, after the vote had been announced I held a large informal press conference with many lobby correspondents in the Members' Lobby to explain then if we were defeated there would be a general election. If we won, we would ratify the treaty.

My colleagues were, as I had intended, rather bounced by public reports of my comments. All the more nervous rebels were extremely worried about the risk of forcing a general election, which would almost certainly have been lost by the government with many Conservative seats lost. The resulting pressure was sufficient to give us victory in the division lobbies, and save the treaty.

Unrelenting plotting, rumours and intrigue continued. The newspapers endlessly implied that John Major was about to jump or be pushed, which was sometimes true and sometimes the exact opposite. By the time of the 1993 party conference, the press had begun to mention me as a possible replacement for John who might be acceptable to the Eurosceptic dissidents. This seemed to me to be particularly malicious as, like Michael Heseltine, I remained the most loyal supporter of the prime minister not only out of friendship but for the practical reason that the whole government would collapse if he fell and no successor emerged. The idea that I, as a notorious Europhile even more provocative to the right-wing nationalists than John Major, could emerge as leader to reunite the party was farcical. In my party conference platform speech, which received the standing ovation I was by then always dutifully given, I deliberately put in a dramatic phrase that 'any enemy of John Major is an enemy of mine'. This dampened down the speculation about me but unfortunately did nothing to stop the plotting. Indeed, some people contrived to read a plot into even this, which demonstrates the pitch to which the hysteria had risen.

The autumn of 1994 saw another crisis. By then the main threat hanging over the prime minister and the government in Parliament was perceived to be the European Finance Bill. The 'business managers' – Tony Newton, the Leader of the House of Commons and Richard Ryder, the chief whip – had convinced John Major that the Eurosceptics were determined to repeat the exercise that they had mounted against the Maastricht Bill in November 1992, and that they were discussing tactics with the leaders of the Labour Party. The fear was that prolonged debate would dominate the House throughout the session, exposing Conservative divisions and possibly leading to defeat for the government.

I was late to see the danger myself. In the summer of 1994 I was still expressing the view that the bill, which was a Treasury matter and therefore fell to me to handle, would carry the House with little difficulty as Labour and Liberal Democrat MPs would support it in principle and only zealots would oppose it.

The bill was necessary to give effect to the deal negotiated by John Major and Norman Lamont at the Edinburgh European Summit on the future financing of the European Union through to the end of the century. Like the Maastricht Treaty before it, it had aroused little or no controversy at the time of the negotiations, and had been widely hailed as a good deal. Firm ceilings had been imposed on the Community budget and the British contribution was set to decline compared with that of other member states to a very marked degree.

The irony was that the deal was only as expensive as it was because of the need to buy Spanish and southern European support for the enlargement of the Union, of which the British were the strongest supporters. John Major and Norman Lamont had been very keen to expand the Union to include the Scandinavian countries of Norway, Sweden and Finland. They were heavily influenced in this view by Eurosceptic opinion which believed that enlargement would weaken the Union and halt the spectre of 'federalism' which they so feared. They also believed that Scandinavians and Austrians would be allied voices in the long run to restrain Community expenditure. In the short run, however, the Spanish in particular had demanded heavy compensation in the form of enormous structural funds for the supposed damage to their economy from enlargement and the completion of the single market.

By the time it came to the legislation to give effect to the deal, in the autumn, the domestic political climate had changed for the worse. I was now preparing myself for a long and difficult debate.

A little over a week before the second reading of the bill, John's 'inner Cabinet' of Douglas Hurd, Malcolm Rifkind, Michael Howard, Richard Ryder, Sarah Hogg and me met for a Sunday evening supper meeting with him at Number 10. The intention had been to discuss political strategy but the conversation immediately turned to the crisis that was building up around the European Finance Bill. John broke the news to us that he was going to make the whole bill a matter of confidence, from the first and throughout its passage. He believed that, as with the Maastricht Bill, the threat that a defeat for the bill would bring down the government and cause a general election, was the only way it would get through. I gained the impression that he had already discussed and agreed the plan with Douglas Hurd.

All of us agreed that this was bold, decisive and sensible. No one raised any doubts. It was agreed that John himself would announce it within the next day or two. Meanwhile there was no need for any meeting of the full Cabinet. We divided up amongst ourselves the task of informing other members of the Cabinet and making sure no one objected.

During the following week, the strategy showed serious signs of starting to go wrong. The Eurosceptics were understandably furious, and several backbenchers expressed their hostility to the whole idea that the government's survival should depend on the bill. More seriously, the anti-European press and media began to raise grave doubts about the constitutional wisdom and political basis of our manoeuvre. Together with more predictable left-of-centre commentators, journalists began to air the idea that the vote of confidence was all gigantic bluff. 'Only the Queen could dissolve Parliament.' 'Only the prime minister need go if the bill was defeated.' 'The Cabinet would in practice refuse to resign if the vote went the wrong way.' 'The Queen would refuse a dissolution.' 'The Conservative Party would elect a new leader who would form a new anti-European government and continue in office.' So the comments in the right-wing press and then the dangerous rumours in Parliament began to run very strongly.

Many Eurosceptics wanted to believe this. I and others, including some whips, became convinced that these ideas were rapidly gaining support to the extent that we were in serious danger of losing the bill.

I decided that I needed to reinforce the message that the second-reading debate was a matter of confidence. Feeling on the merits of the bill was now running so high amongst anti-Europeans, and the belief was so widespread that defeat would mean the end of John Major but not of the government, that defeat on a reasoned amendment to be tabled by the Opposition parties seemed to me to be probable unless something was done to steady the party before the debate.

I discussed with the prime minister the démarche I now planned. I would, quite exceptionally, give a press conference for lobby correspondents in the House ostensibly to explain the figures in full to them. I would take the opportunity to underline in the strongest terms that the survival of the government would indeed depend on our winning the votes on second reading and all important votes thereafter. I had had success with this approach a year earlier when we had faced defeat on the Social Chapter. This time John was an enthusiastic party to my plan: he was in complete agreement and urged me to carry it out. He also told me, in confidence, that he was convinced that if we were defeated on Monday, the Queen would indeed agree to dissolve Parliament and a general election would follow. Frankly, he said, he had reached the stage where he accepted that the party must either come to its senses or face the consequences.

I duly summoned a gathering in the small upstairs room in Parliament where press conferences for the lobby were held. I found the room packed with journalists. I did as I had planned, explaining the figures, and then taking an opportunity of an early question to emphasize the point that defeat on the following Monday would mean an immediate general election. Not surprisingly, many journalists did not want to believe me. Several members of the Cabinet had, I believe, let them know that the issue had never been formally discussed in Cabinet, and implied that they therefore did not feel bound by any decision that the government would resign if defeated.

In order to make my point both credible and newsworthy I therefore told the gathering exactly how the decision had been reached, and, truthfully, that all the Cabinet had been individually consulted and all had accepted the decision. The resulting reports in the newspapers fully met my expectations.

Unfortunately Robin Oakley of the BBC asked a question in which he described the 'supper club' decision as a suicide pact. This absurd phrase, which was never used or accepted by me, was also widely used in the newspapers the next morning.

The second reading was a dramatic and enjoyable late-night occasion with a high-quality and highly charged debate. I made what I believed to be the best speech I had ever made on the floor of the House, and was so confident of my subject that I extemporized a great deal, and gave way to and replied to every intervention. The bill was carried.

It had always been probable that we would withdraw the whip

from any who failed to vote for the government on a vote of confidence. The two or three that we had anticipated would not have mattered. Indeed, it would have been good for party discipline if they had had to work their way back to membership of the parliamentary party by prolonged loyal support. Eight, soon to be nine, was far too many, however, and their existence poisoned the atmosphere yet further as they organized themselves as a rebel group, achieving widespread publicity for their views and forming a focus for discontent. How quickly they could do damage was revealed in the Budget debates the following week, when they took their revenge on me and the government in the vote on the second instalment of VAT on fuel.

Although I was able to make good the damage done to the country's finances by this rebellion fairly easily, the damage done to the government was not so easily repaired. The government had looked weak, and the rebels had tasted and demonstrated the power they could wield if they acted as a group.

Michael Heseltine and I remained the Cabinet's most unswerving and stalwart supporters of both John Major and of the Maastricht Treaty. Douglas Hurd was slightly less sound on Maastricht but equally loyal to John. Unfortunately the friendship that Michael and I felt for John led us into a serious error.

By 1994 the Eurosceptics had begun to demand a referendum on our membership of the EU or at least on our membership of the single currency. Michael and I, like every politician of our generation, were fiercely opposed to this ridiculously simplistic way of trying to settle complex and hugely important subjects. In a modern, sophisticated and intricate democratic system we much preferred parliamentary government to direct democracy. Unfortunately, John convinced himself that he could settle the issue and restore order within the party by promising a referendum if Britain ever decided to join the euro.

Michael and I were implacably opposed to this in every conversation that we had with John together or separately over the course of months and years. Neither of us expected Britain to join the single currency in the near future but we did not want to put any future decision at the mercy of a plebiscite. We also did not believe that this concession would satisfy or silence the Eurosceptics.

In November 1994, Douglas Hurd, with John Major's approval, actually sent a long memorandum urging a commitment to a referendum on either the single currency or the outcome of the 1996 Intergovernmental Conference, to Michael Heseltine, Malcolm Rifkind and me. I replied with a denunciation of referenda in general and a flat disagreement that any such commitment might pacify the party. Malcolm Rifkind weighed in in support of Douglas Hurd. Michael Heseltine strongly agreed with me, adding some additional points of his own. Some colleagues leaked the idea of a referendum to the press, but this exchange mercifully killed it off and by the end of 1995 Michael and I believed that, because of our opposition, John had definitively dropped the idea.

However, early in 1996 the press began floating it again, extremely heavily. Michael and I had been lunching together from time to time in the previous months and at one of those lunches we had firmly agreed that we would stick together on European issues through thick and thin. If one of us ever felt obliged to resign, then both would.

The press speculation resulted, as usual, in a whole series of meetings between ministers which came to no conclusion. All this was against the background of heavy briefing to the by now ferociously Eurosceptic right-wing press who all demanded a referendum. Some of the newspapers made references to me as the single obstacle to the proposed move.

Eventually the then Secretary of State for Agriculture, Fisheries and Food, Douglas Hogg, almost certainly at John Major's request, raised it in Cabinet and a long discussion ensued. Michael Heseltine spoke at passionate length against the whole idea of a referendum and against the notion that a concession would ever satisfy the Eurosceptics. I spoke more briefly in his support but my anger must have been even plainer. Even our usual allies deserted us but John, realizing that this pressure had failed to move us, summed up by saying that we could not decide immediately.

I had already told John that I would resign if he committed himself to a referendum. He obviously guessed at the Cabinet meeting that I, and probably Michael, would have resigned if he had tried to bounce us into it. Others must also have picked up the mood and Michael Howard, who by now was a strong advocate of a referendum on Europe, proved that he was a good friend by coming to see me urging me not to resign if the decision went against me.

Norman Blackwell, the prime minister's special adviser, tried to act as a go-between on the issue. He had plainly been asked to search for some compromise. In conversation with him, I did accept that the sovereignty of Parliament and parliamentary democracy would be less threatened if we agreed that Parliament should first be allowed to vote on the issue and pass the necessary legislation before any referendum was held. He also made an argument that we should agree that the commitment to a referendum should be made for the next parliament only and not permanent, so that the government could keep its longer-term options open.

I might not have accepted this rather absurd compromise if I had not been heavily lobbied by all my pro-European friends in the Commons not to resign, and especially not on the issue of the referendum. Geoffrey Howe and Leon Brittan were particularly influential with me, but my great friend Jim Lester was also very eloquent on the subject, as was my then PPS, Peter Butler. It was Leon, though, who suggested a final compromise, that in return for my agreement I should get the freedom to state publicly that it remained the case that the government could foresee circumstances in which it would be in the national interest to join the currency.

These discussions formed the basis for the compromise that Michael Heseltine, John Major and I subsequently arrived at. We reached agreement on a carefully drafted and amended text in a tense meeting, which was rather like a treaty session.

I was pleased to be back on good terms with John again. Nonetheless, I made it clear to him that this was my last compromise. I would not stay in his government if the subject was reopened before the election.

John informed the Cabinet of the decision at the next meeting. He read out the statement, no one said anything in response and the policy at least was settled. The prime minister later made the statement public. However, it was a complete damp squib and did nothing at all to end the continuing conflict within the Conservative Party.

The concession was denounced by James Goldsmith's Referendum Party as inadequate and pocketed by the Eurosceptics who proceeded to argue against John in Parliament and outside it with the same fanatical fervour that they had before. Tony Blair and Gordon Brown in the meantime were utterly appalled. They had been resisting the same pressures for a referendum on the single currency from the newspapers and a few of their own backbenchers. I well remember Tony Blair's anger and disbelief when he confronted me in the corridors of the House after John's announcement. Gordon Brown, then in favour of the single currency, was equally aghast. I tried to persuade them that they need not match the promise but of course they both quite rightly felt that that was a politically impossible position to maintain.

Michael Heseltine and I had another short conversation a few days after these extraordinary events. We agreed that we had each only made a concession because separately we had become concerned about the terrible pressure on John. We each felt that he was genuinely suffering under the strain of our refusal to go along with his obsession that a referendum announcement would end all his troubles. We both merely wished that John had been right in his expectations of this useless manoeuvre.

In later years, Michael Heseltine and I always agreed that this was the biggest single mistake that either of us has ever made in our political careers. We had allowed the idea of a referendum to be given legitimacy again.

As we were settling the referendum question, Malcolm Rifkind returned to a question that had first arisen a year earlier. At that time Malcolm's predecessor, Douglas Hurd, had floated the idea, for conventional diplomatic reasons, of a White Paper setting out the government's policies and positions for the Intergovernmental Conference (IGC) on the future of the EU, due to open in 1996. The Cabinet, including the prime minister, had been opposed, on the basis that it could cause dissent within the party and Cabinet in the short term, and then tie our negotiators hand and foot at the IGC.

Now Malcolm, who was flirting with the Eurosceptics at the time, raised the issue again. A White Paper was a strong Eurosceptic demand. They wanted it to commit the government to inflexible demands and positions that would either cause the EU to become more loose and decentralized or, more likely and as they wished, cause a crisis that would isolate us and start to drive us to the edge of the Union.

Unfortunately, Malcolm had a meeting with a group of Eurosceptic backbenchers and told them that he wanted to produce a White Paper. This immediately reached the newspapers and yet another division and crisis seemed likely.

On this occasion Michael Heseltine and I allowed ourselves to be picked off separately and 'bounced' in the few hours before a Cabinet meeting. Tony Newton, the Leader of the House of Commons, was sent to see me early on a Thursday morning. In a panic he told me that the business managers were convinced that the Labour Party was about to table a Commons motion demanding the publication of a White Paper for the IGC. This would happen in the next few days and we would be defeated in the Commons vote as our Eurosceptics would all vote against us. I expressed considerable scepticism. We were establishing a pattern in which, whenever anyone wanted to persuade the prime minister to do anything really stupid, a theory would appear that the Labour Party were about to commit themselves to do it first and then join with the Eurosceptics to defeat us in the House.

However, I did not want to become impossibly churlish with my colleagues and I felt the need to behave more reasonably with the more sensible ones like Tony Newton and Malcolm Rifkind. There was also quite a good case to make that most governments would issue documents of some kind setting out their approach to the IGC, and it was difficult to make a presentable case in public against publication without alluding to the divisions within the party. I therefore allowed myself to be persuaded.

I had a quick word with Michael Heseltine outside the door of the Cabinet Room as we arrived. I discovered that he had just been 'bounced' in the same way by the party chairman Brian Mawhinney in a similar conversation. Therefore at Cabinet everyone agreed that we should have a White Paper.

In discussion, however, Michael and I made and established some useful points. The document was to set out an approach to the negotiations and to our future in the Union. It was not to be a series of inflexible demands and it should stress that it would not bind or commit our negotiators in detail. It was also to be based strictly on the agreements that had already been thrashed out within government at the interminable and numerous meetings of the large Cabinet Committee that had been discussing our position on the forthcoming IGC for a long time since Douglas Hurd's day. The drafting of the White Paper was not to reopen issues settled in that committee.

Michael Heseltine was annoyed at one point when the chief whip let out in the Cabinet discussion that he would have expected the Liberals to vote with us in any division on the need for a White Paper. I had never believed that Labour was going to commit itself to a White Paper or table a motion in any event. However, the Cabinet conclusion was quite sensible and no harm was done.

The text of the White Paper was subsequently agreed quite easily. Malcolm kept back his text as long as possible but then consulted Michael Heseltine, me and, I suspect, one or two sceptics like Howard and Portillo. The draft was quite good, in my opinion. Michael Heseltine wanted to strengthen the arguments in it about the benefits of our membership of Europe and suggested some strong amendments. I allied myself with him and we were amazingly successful. The resulting Paper had paragraphs from everyone and the tone varied from page to page but the opening pages in particular had some very rousing Heseltine pro-European messages in them. Cabinet cleared it without dissent.

Malcolm presented the White Paper publicly with a slant which enabled the Eurosceptic press to present it as a Eurosceptic triumph, but again, no harm was done. Michael Heseltine and I were more prominent than anyone in endorsing it and pointing out that we now had a clear, detailed policy which was agreed and set out our view of a 'Europe of nation states'. We tried to contrast our position with that of Labour. It was noticeable how silent most of our Cabinet colleagues were on the subject, however. In the months to come, I repeatedly referred in public to the White Paper as setting out our firm agreed policy on our future relationship with Europe. Sometimes when I did I was accused of being 'divisive' and reopening the Tory Euro-battle.

There was occasional respite from all this madness in the last few months of John Major's government. The last party conference before the election was expected to be extremely fraught and it was antici-pated that my speech would be a particular focal point of discontent because of my pro-European stance. Brian Mawhinney had warned me that I should expect booing, barracking and hostility. I was not excessively fazed by this forecast, which amazingly turned out to be entirely inaccurate. I delivered what I think was the most successful party conference speech of my career and was greeted with such prolonged cheers and ovations at the end that Gillian was reluctantly persuaded to come up onto the stage to wave to the audience and acknowledge their reception with me. John whispered to me that this had saved the general election for us. I thought that highly unlikely myself. It was the last moment of unadorned apparent success that we were to enjoy.

The political atmosphere within the Conservative Party in Parliament and in the media throughout these years could only be described as poisonous. We were doomed at the 1997 election and it was obvious from the start that Tony Blair would be swept to power with an enormous majority. The British public will not vote for a deeply divided party.

The opinion polls confirmed the view that we were heading for a landslide defeat with a majority against us of well over a hundred seats. Because of my provocative nature to Eurosceptics, I was kept out of the way on a series of nationwide tours during which I met huge numbers of candidates and members of the public. These went quite well and I would return to Central Office from time to time and report to my colleagues that I thought we were bound to be defeated but that the majority might not be as great as the polls suggested. This intelligence was not greeted terribly warmly by the

leadership of the campaign, in whom a slight sense of pseudo opti-
mism had begun to appear. The best example of this was Michael
Heseltine, who once followed me out of a meeting asking me why I
was so convinced that Labour would win an overall majority. 'Surely
you have not met anyone who had voted Conservative who will now
vote Labour?' he asked. I replied that I had met hundreds of them,
no doubt a representative sample of public opinion. 'No, no,' said
Michael, 'our focus groups show that no voters will cross from
Conservative to Labour.'

The national opinion polls did however show that we were far in
the lead on the issue of the economy. I tried to claim that a Labour
government would threaten the continuation of growth with low
inflation and rising employment, and talked of a 'black hole' in their
public spending plans. Blair and Brown skilfully avoided this challenge
by simply declaring that they would not change economic policy in
any respect. They signed up to my figures for taxation and spending
for the next three years – although I myself had intended that they
would be pragmatically revised each year in the light of economic
circumstances. I challenged them on higher rates of taxation and they
insisted they would stay unchanged. No journalist therefore believed
that the economy was an election issue and all my press conferences
descended into arguments about Europe.

John Major and Michael Heseltine were most unwisely trying to
run a 'Eurosceptic-lite' campaign to stem the flow of votes away from
us and appease the noisy rebels. Michael even produced a crude
cartoon of Tony Blair being dangled as an innocent child on the knees
of Helmut Kohl. In my opinion, this completely uncertain campaign
only exacerbated our crushing defeat at the polls. Thus was the misery
of John Major's government, which had a number of substantial
achievements to its credit, finally brought to an end.

21

'On the Road Again'
(Willie Nelson, 1980)

FOREIGN AFFAIRS

The 1990s witnessed the rapid evolution of the modern globalized economy. Nonetheless, when I first arrived at the Treasury I did not begin to realize quite how much foreign travel would be involved. European Council summits and monthly ECOFIN meetings were one part of it but British economic policymaking also involved membership of and engagement with a whole range of international organizations, chiefly the G7, the International Monetary Fund, the World Bank, and the Commonwealth Finance Ministers' Conference. I also continued my long-standing practice of making ministerial visits to key global markets, accompanied by would-be exporting and investing businessmen. I used these as opportunities to promote British exports, as well as to maintain my general understanding of foreign affairs and of the developing globalized economy with its new emerging markets. And, of course, whenever possible I tried to extend any visits by a day or two in order to fit in a little tourism or birdwatching.

Gillian would almost always enthusiastically accompany me. Throughout my ministerial career, she would spend days engaged in marvellous tourist visits whilst I was locked into my meetings. Unfortunately, whilst the grateful taxpayer paid for me to travel business class and be fresh for my meetings, we paid for Gillian's travel ourselves, and could only afford economy. We used to joke that she was 'being put in the boot', but in fact Gillian was a formidable long-distance traveller in even the most spartan conditions. She was also extremely good at being the minister's wife at the evening cocktail parties and dinners which politicians and ambassadors inflict on themselves in enormous quantities. She was very popular with my officials, and after she died in 2015, several of them wrote to me. David Smith, a British government official, recalled a vicious game of musical cushions following a dinner hosted by the chairman of a Japanese bank. The battle for the last cushion took place between Gillian and the British consul general in Osaka. Gillian won – largely thanks to the behaviour of the vice consul and ambassador, who unceremoniously obstructed their colleague and ensured that Gillian's path to victory was clear. Robin Morgan, one of the Treasury officials who accompanied us on a visit to Indonesia in 1994, remembers Gillian delicately sidestepping requests to describe her day, at a dinner with assembled dignitaries from the Indonesian government. She had been at a hospital witnessing a vasectomy operation.

Gillian was a trustee of Oxfam at that time, a position she held for twelve years in total, and on our travels she visited many of their aid projects. On our Home Office visit to Pakistan she was the only person to visit Peshawar in the rather dangerous North-West Frontier. Afterwards she recounted how delightful it was to talk face-to-face with the normally heavily veiled women who ran their children's project, who had been able to take off their veils in her company.

Our travels hugely enlarged my understanding of international politics. They also brought me into close and friendly contact with some formidable figures. Obviously I relied very much on my working relationships with the successive Treasury Secretaries of the United States. Lloyd Bentsen, a wise veteran former senator from Texas, epitomized the best of old-school politics without being in any way an expert on economic policy himself. He retired not long after I became Chancellor, and was replaced by Bob Rubin, with whom I became extremely friendly. Bob and his wife Judith turned out to be old friends of Leon and Diana Brittan, with whom they took annual holidays. Bob was a brilliant, charming, quietly spoken American with a first-class mind and excellent political judgement. I did not always agree with him, but I suspect he was invariably correct. I also got to know his assistant secretary, Larry Summers, and we developed an equally good relationship. Larry was a brilliant academic. His economic opinions were to the left of Bob's and mine but he was a very shrewd man whose advice was invaluable. He became an excellent Treasury Secretary himself in later years.

I also became close to Alan Greenspan, who was chairman of the Federal Reserve not only throughout my time but for a period of nearly twenty years. Alan was another formidable old-school politician with great economic skill and knowledge, whom the commentators usually treated with reverential awe. I came to regard him as one of the wisest men I had ever known, but we also developed an extremely good personal relationship. This was helped by our mutual love of jazz. We would often get together at the British ambassador's Residence to discuss our musical tastes and heroes, rather than make any further attempts to put the world economy to rights.

Alan had been a jazz tenor saxophonist in his youth. He gave me a colourful account of his short but quite successful music career. He recounted to me that when he left school in the 1940s he shocked his family by taking his saxophone on the road as a professional musician. He achieved modest success but the end came when he had a two-week gig somewhere in the Midwest with a rather larger group in a jazz club. The other saxophonist was Alan's old school friend Stan Getz, who later became one of the colossi of jazz history. Two weeks alongside Stan Getz made Alan realize that he had only a limited future in music. He promptly went back east and delighted his father by going to university and beginning a career on Wall Street. I suspected that Alan's account was slightly embroidered, but it was a good story over a drink, which entirely fitted the laid-back and delightful character of the man I had befriended.

Alan's reputation was damaged many years later over the financial crash of 2007–8. Some Wall Street figures who had gambled recklessly and lost tried to blame the credit boom, which they had previously enjoyed, on mistakenly loose policy by Greenspan. I regard that criticism as a facile attempt to find a scapegoat for the greed and folly of dealers in New York and London.

I also developed a good personal friendship with Manmohan Singh, then India's finance minister. He was not a professional politician but a brilliant academic and technocrat who had been educated at St John's College, Cambridge. Manmohan was serving in a Congress-led government in Delhi, headed by the shrewd if rather corrupt prime minister Narasimha Rao, but dominated behind the scenes by Sonia Gandhi, the Italian-born widow of former Indian prime minister Rajiv Gandhi. Manmohan was conspicuously honest, quietly spoken and reserved. He embarked on a spectacular and much-overdue liberalizing reform of the Indian economy which swept away a great deal of bureaucracy, reduced corruption, began to attract some inward investment and created room for entrepreneurship. He later became prime minister but his lack of political skills and the continued domination of the old Congress Party bosses limited his achievements. I saw a lot of him at the peak of his career when he was single-handedly responsible for creating the conditions for India to begin to achieve economic success in the modern world. I greatly relied upon his wisdom and good character and made sure that I usually allied myself with him in our international gatherings.

I had my first introduction to the occasional absurdities of giant summit gatherings soon after I became Chancellor, when in July 1993 foreign ministers and finance ministers were invited with their Heads of Government to a G7 summit in Tokyo. The Japanese went completely over the top in organizing this international event, at which President Clinton was the star attraction. The main motorways and urban arteries of the city were all closed to the public so that the dignitaries could travel smoothly to any meeting without being impeded by the Japanese traffic jams. Even when I was simply going out for an informal cup of coffee with a colleague I found myself in a little convoy of limousines sailing along an elevated section of motorway and gazing down on a capital city otherwise in gridlock.

After one such seamless trip I held my first bilateral meeting with the French finance minister, Edmond Alphandéry. Edmond and I would later strike up a very good relationship, but this first meeting is particularly memorable. After we emerged from our quiet chat we faced our national political correspondents and gave a press conference. Edmond, to my amazement, gave a detailed account of our discussions on matters of relevance to French domestic politics which neither of us had even mentioned during the course of our encounter. I soon discovered that this was traditional practice for ministers from all countries at such gatherings.

I also discovered that the typical course of events at the formal meetings was for us to base our discussions around a draft communiqué of conclusions. Far from being conclusions of the discussions which had actually taken place, as one might reasonably expect, this document was in fact prepared in advance by powerful advisers known as 'sherpas'. The difficulty in Tokyo in 1993 was that we had no particularly pressing subject on the international agenda at all. In order to give newsworthy substance to the communiqué, therefore, the Americans were insisting on inserting a commitment to provide huge sums of money to the Russian government to help with its economic reforms after the collapse of the command economy of the recently defunct Soviet Union. It was clear to everyone that this money was not going to contribute in any meaningful way to moving Russia from post-Communist state to functioning capitalist economy. It was in fact expensive padding for a G7 summit press release. With my fresh determination to control public spending in the United Kingdom I was very unwilling to commit a few billion to the hat that was being passed around the finance ministers. Eventually I contrived with my officials to sign up to a sum of money which had already been committed by the British government to fairly relevant programmes, so that we could conclude the meeting without either burdening ourselves with any additional public expenditure or causing a diplomatic incident.

The settings for the G7 summits were always gargantuan because we were surrounded by thousands of lobbyists and members of the world's press. The British official contingent was usually the most frugal with only one or two hundred in the whole party. Most countries brought much bigger entourages, and the Japanese in particular were accustomed to travelling with a party of up to 3,000. So many people attended the Italian summit in Naples in July 1994 that all the hotels were reserved exclusively for those attending, and all but actual residents were barred from entering large parts of the city centre. Despite these precautions we experienced a sudden power failure as every delegation installed its computers, electronic kit and so on to prepare for the great gathering.

Russia was always on the agenda. John Major and I had breakfast in Tokyo with its president since 1991, Boris Yeltsin, an occasion which was memorable mainly because Yeltsin was on the wagon – a state of affairs that did not, I think, last long. He was in fact a fairly shrewd elderly drunk who steered his country through its political problems quite well. The key Russian figure for me though was Anatoly Chubais, a long-standing Kremlin official who was by this point the Russian deputy prime minister. More importantly, he was a close political friend of Yeltsin's daughter, Tatyana, who wielded significant power during Yeltsin's later period in office. Chubais proved to be a genuine economic liberal and he was reasonably trustworthy and useful in his dealings with the G7 ministers. For a time he ran the state-owned monopoly electricity provider and later became a wealthy oligarch in his own right.

Unfortunately the Americans and their allies never devised a process for reform of the Russian economy with any real prospects of success. The Americans were obsessed with privatization and seemed to imagine that the denationalization of all the giant state enterprises would produce a healthy market economy almost as an automatic consequence. Yeltsin and his friends in the meantime were understandably determined to ensure that privatization did not result in foreigners owning all the commanding heights of the Russian economy. The introduction of private capital was therefore monopolized by Yeltsin's friends who were enabled to acquire ownership of huge enterprises at modest prices. This led to the era of 'gangster capitalism' in Russia, in which violent fights between different interests took place over the course of several years, until finally a few lucky and hugely wealthy oligarchs emerged.

I remember one visit to Moscow at this time during which I enjoyed several meals in some of the city's most splendid newly established restaurants and clubs. As an overseas minister, I was allowed to go to the special floor usually reserved for the leaders of the various economic mobs, where I observed them at close quarters as they enjoyed themselves. They would travel through the streets of Moscow to and from these desirable destinations in limousines with darkened windows, accompanied by crowds of bodyguards and aides. I suspect 1920s Chicago might have had a similar feel. I am glad to say that my officials and I never became embroiled as the Russian Federation took these first faltering steps towards capitalism.

The lasting consequences of these early post-Communist years were only too apparent in the later stuttering years of the new Russia, in which living standards steadily dropped before eventually reviving because of Russia's ownership of commodities such as gas, oil and aluminium which became the sole basis of its economy. A market economy is totally dependent on an efficient rule of law, and that has still not been established in Russia. The concepts of democracy and capitalism were each discredited by these early years of turmoil, paving the way for the emergence of Vladimir Putin and his KGB friends presiding over a more autocratic state.

The Russians were entirely consumed in both their domestic and international affairs by their desire to overcome the humiliation of the collapse of the Soviet Union and their craving to be regarded as a great power again. In response to this the G7 summits eventually became G8 summits, with Russia admitted as the eighth member. We finance ministers were not prepared to adopt this development fully, however, since Russia was our principal debtor and a difficult problem. We continued to sit as a G7 at our meetings, with Mr Chubais joining us for those sessions in which Russia was to be considered.

Tokyo was not the only G7 summit I attended that had no acutely pressing business to conclude. I remember one particularly me-andering finance ministers' meeting at a summit in Washington at which the Japanese minister suddenly intervened in the way in which elderly Japanese ministers usually did. The spontaneous discussion subsided into dismayed silence as he produced a long written text and settled down to slowly read it out for us to listen to through interpreters on our headphones, his lead official looking down over his shoulder, checking that his note was read correctly and turning each page as he reached the bottom.

I got up to stretch my legs during this performance – still listening through my headphones of course – and strolled over to the window. There I was joined by my friend Alan Greenspan. I asked Alan what he thought the whole point of this meeting was as we were all very busy people who did have serious work to do. Alan corrected me. 'The point of this meeting is that you should get to know most of these people quite well personally,' he said, looking around the room. 'It is quite possible that the moment will come when you have to deal with one or more of your peers to resolve an urgent problem. You will be able to trust some of them and discuss matters properly over the telephone because you have been forced to spend so much time with them at these gatherings.' As usual, he proved to be right.

As the global economy continued to emerge from recession and achieve some stability and growth through the mid-1990s I did discover other value to the G7. Our meetings of ministers were always attended by the head of the International Monetary Fund and by the governors of the central banks. Important discussions took place and we developed some co-operation and alignment of our policy object-ives.

The finance ministers' meetings always had a session where Michel Camdessus, the managing director of the IMF, would present his frank evaluation of economic policy and performance in each G7 country, after which discussion followed. This was effectively a process of voluntary peer review, and it was invaluable. No minister could necessarily sign up to all the conclusions of such a discussion, but I found that it was a valuable way of deepening my understanding of what was going on in our changing world.

The IMF always wanted to publish their reports on our national economies to improve the quality of international debate. I thought this was a splendid idea and, keen to improve the quality of the debate at home, I took the dramatic step, quite unilaterally, of publishing the IMF review of the British economy each year. This might have been reckless had not the background been a steady improvement in performance.

Each year, finance ministers from most nation states would also gather for the annual meetings of the IMF and the World Bank. These were huge formal affairs attended by the finance ministers of over a hundred countries surrounded by an enormous networking and fringe-meeting circus involving the leading business and financial figures of each economy. In later years when we were in opposition, I attended a meeting in Beijing in my then capacity as an adviser to Daiwa Capital Securities, a Japanese finance house. It was a fascinating, but rather pointless experience.

One of my duties when attending as a minister was to engage in a huge number of bilateral discussions, usually with people I wanted to talk to and they thus served some useful purpose. One of my strangest bilaterals took place when officials wanted me to sign an agreement that had been negotiated with the Chinese government. We were in the run-up to handing back Hong Kong to China. As the last governor of Hong Kong, Chris Patten was making desperate attempts to endow it with some democratic institutions and prospects, and at the time of this particular annual meeting had just made some move in this direction which had infuriated the government in Beijing. The minor financial agreement with which I was concerned had been elevated to the title of 'treaty'. I was meant to sign this momentous document, sitting alongside my opposite number, in a little old-fashioned diplomatic ceremony complete with a display of our national flags. The relationship between Britain and China was then so fragile that the diplomats present were not at all sure that my Chinese opposite number would attend and were full of trepidation about his likely conduct if he did, and what message any contrived conduct would imply. I dutifully attended the so-called ceremony. My Chinese colleague also duly attended, but did not address a word to me, not even hello or goodbye. We did, however, sign the documents. I left it to diplomatic experts to try to analyse the mysterious message about the next steps in Hong Kong that this bizarre episode was supposed to portend.

One of the most serious international financial problems to punctuate my period of office was the so-called 'tequila crisis' in December 1994. The Mexican economy first overheated and then crashed, threatening debt default and financial crisis for Mexico's creditors. The IMF rapidly produced an emergency $50 billion programme to bail out the Mexican government, subject to stringent economic conditions. This is the main practical value of the IMF today, and its response to this particular crisis proved to be one of its most successful rescues and turnarounds, paving the way for similar success responding to crises in the new economies of South East Asia a few years later.

It was during the tequila crisis that I really discovered how the IMF worked and what the modern role of the United Kingdom was. As the British Chancellor and as a G7 minister, representing a country that made a major contribution to IMF funds, I was indignant that neither I nor the UK Treasury seemed to be involved in the resolution of the Mexican situation for any practical purpose. The whole thing was put together and led by the United States and the IMF team.

Some of my Treasury officials seemed to share my frustration at our exclusion. I remember to my embarrassment having a conversation with the US Treasury Secretary Bob Rubin in which I rather pompously protested that he plainly had not yet understood the rules of the G7, and then tried to get involved. Bob was a considerable financial expert with a glittering career on Wall Street behind him. My recollection is that he dealt with me very politely and I trust that he was more amused than annoyed by my indignation. I blush with a little shame at the recollection. When I had acquired a bit more experience, I discovered that in the late twentieth century only the American voice and the American dollar really counted when fast-moving emergencies occurred.

The other major gatherings I attended, in a revival of a practice that had been abandoned by Nigel Lawson and Norman Lamont, were the Commonwealth finance ministers' summits. These were held annually in some exotic Commonwealth location, shortly before the IMF annual meetings. The membership of the Commonwealth was rather unbalanced, with the bulk of regular attenders being the finance ministers of small Caribbean islands. So far as I was concerned, the key players were Manmohan Singh of India and Paul Martin of Canada. Paul was an excellent reforming figure who was then rescuing his country from financial collapse and later became prime minister.

The Caribbean meetings were filled with entertaining characters and had some interesting moments but they were also a valuable way of preparing for the business of the forthcoming IMF annual meetings. I could deal in depth with major issues that concerned Manmohan, Paul and myself, in ways that sometimes produced results at the later IMF gatherings.

My fondest memory is of a Commonwealth summit in Jamaica in which I was introduced to the sinister atmosphere of then gangster-ridden Kingston, but also was able to fit in some very good bird-watching in the Blue Mountains.

The Jamaican finance minister, Dr Omar Davies, was a long-serving political boss with whom I got on pretty well. He told me of a splendid restaurant on the outskirts of Kingston where I could eat well sitting in the open air surrounded by splendid countryside. However, when I got back to the High Commissioner's Residence, where I was staying as a guest, and mentioned that I would be taking my car and officials there, it caused great consternation.

A series of diplomats proceeded to give me the most solemn warnings about the security risk of going to this restaurant, despite the fact that armed security men would accompany me there as they did everywhere else in Jamaica. I ignored their advice and relied on that of the Jamaican minister. The restaurant, whose clientele appeared to be the leading political, business and diplomatic figures in the town, did indeed prove to be the best place to eat in Kingston, and I ate there more than once. The High Commission's security advice seemed utterly baffling.

Much later, I discovered the secret to this puzzle. The story I was told was that some time in the recent past a British diplomat serving in Kingston had had a torrid affair with a female colleague also working in the High Commission. To keep his affair secret, and ensure total privacy while he was enjoying his trysts, said diplomat had taken the wise precaution of putting the highest possible security warnings against this restaurant, the lovers' favourite rendezvous.

*

This was a time when many developing countries were becoming healthier economic prospects, and it was important to make trade visits and build political contacts in them. I made numerous bilateral visits to relevant countries across the globe, but I focused particularly on Latin America where Brazil, Argentina and Chile were fast emerging as countries with which I believed we ought to engage. I also became quite involved with the economic revolution taking place in South East Asia.

My excellent permanent secretary at the Treasury, Terry Burns, became alarmed at the extent of my travels abroad with British businessmen. Despite the fact that these represented a tiny footnote in our budget as a whole, as the department's accounting officer he was concerned about the money I was spending. More significantly, I think the problem was that he was, like most leading politicians and civil servants at the time, unaccustomed to any foreign travel outside the United States and Europe. Far too many powerful figures in the 1990s seemed to believe that the world could be fully understood through visits to Washington and Brussels alone. He therefore insisted on accompanying me on one of my visits to South East Asia.

I am glad to say that Sir Terry was eventually satisfactorily impressed by my efforts to open up financial markets in China and Malaysia, and to address the consequences of change in Hong Kong with the party of leading bankers and financial advisers that I took with me from the UK. However, our travels were a huge cultural shock to Terry, who had never been to Asia before. He had taken with him an early example of a laptop so that he could keep in almost hourly contact with the activities of the office back home and with what he considered to be the real civilized world, but right at the beginning of our trip he dropped this exciting new bit of kit and broke it. This, I think, led to the almost permanent sense of discomfiture that was quite apparent thereafter. Terry was perpetually nervous about the relaxed way in which I and my other officials and diplomats approached matters and did not participate in any more such trips, confining himself to crossing the Atlantic to Washington through the rest of our time together.

It was on this visit that I met the near-autocratic prime minister of Malaysia, Mahathir Mohamad. I already knew his finance minister, Anwar Ibrahim, who was a delightful man and a leading figure in debate at the G7 and the IMF as he tried to introduce economic reform in his country. I spent some very enjoyable days with Anwar in Kuala Lumpur, and then visiting his home state. Unfortunately, shortly after our visit, Anwar quarrelled with his prime minister, who ruthlessly deposed him as his heir apparent, subjected him to cruel false allegations and then contrived his imprisonment. This absurd behaviour robbed Malaysia of a very fine potential leader.

My contact with Mahathir on this visit produced one startling revelation. At the time Rupert Murdoch, whose presence in the British media I was beginning to resent, was trying to gain entry to the television market in Asia and was therefore looking for the support of the leaders of Asian nations. Mahathir had been accused of corruption in a small article in the *Sunday Times*, and I still do not know whether this was in any way accurate or not. He went out of his way to boast to me as a visiting British politician that he had personally demanded and obtained from Rupert Murdoch the dismissal of Andrew Neil, the editor of the *Sunday Times*, in reprisal for the publication of this irksome story. I had first met Andrew when he had been a Young Conservative activist in the early 1970s, and he had since then had a career as one of the most spectacularly successful journalists of his generation, having taken the *Sunday Times* to new heights as an influential political and reporting newspaper, with a huge circulation. Andrew had indeed been dismissed by Murdoch for reasons unknown to me and, so far as I was aware, unknown to Andrew. I have no idea whether Mahathir's boast to me was really true. However even the fact of him claiming this was an insight into the ways of a man who for too long dominated the politics not only of Malaysia but of the region.

On one ministerial visit to Zimbabwe, I was probably the last British minister to have a long informal one-to-one discussion with President Mugabe. He struck me as a very intelligent and articulate man. He was in effusive mood and told me how much he would welcome more British and other foreign investment into his country. I took this with a pinch of salt as he had just emerged victorious from an election campaign which he had conducted on overtly racialist lines, attacking foreign investors. Nevertheless we discussed the question of land reform and he pressed me for British financial help for this, arguing, as he always had, that on independence the British government had in principle promised this. I knew that our Foreign Office denied this but I actually was prepared to discuss the prospect of some financial aid for this purpose if it would ease political tensions. However, the talks reached no conclusion because we flatly disagreed about the use of the funds. I offered help so long as farmers selling land were willing sellers and received market value as compensation. President Mugabe was not prepared to contemplate either of these conditions and so our talk ended. Mugabe thereafter embarked on his appalling policy of misappropriation and seizure of white land. Mary Soames, Churchill's youngest daughter and the wife of Christopher Soames, the last governor of Southern Rhodesia, always told me that she had been friendly with Mugabe and was amazed that he had turned out as he did. I suspect I was one of the last people to meet him before he deteriorated into the ageing and declining dictator he has since become, which at least gave me a little insight into the qualities that he must once have had.

The closest relationship that I developed through my bilateral visits was in Mexico, which I had first visited as education minister, and where I became a personal friend of the president, Ernesto Zedillo. I think our friendship was cemented on the occasion when Ernesto and his wife dined at Number 11 with me and Angela Knight, my excellent economic secretary who had kindly agreed to partner me in Gillian's absence, one bitterly cold winter's night. Ernesto and his wife arrived in warm and extremely expensive-looking coats but on removing his, Ernesto realized he had left his suit jacket in his car. He was very embarrassed so I took my jacket off as well and the two of us sat at dinner shivering in our shirts.

Zedillo's path to the presidency had been remarkable. An economist by training, he then served briefly as education minister in the Institutional Revolutionary Party (PRI) – our terms in education overlapped by a few months – before resigning in 1993 to help run Luis Colosio's campaign for the presidency. Colosio was dramatically assassinated while campaigning in the immediate run-up to the election, forcing the PRI to find a new candidate. However, an obscure Mexican election law decreed that no one who had held public office in the last six months could be elected president. This ruled out almost the entire PRI Cabinet, except the slightly marginal figure of Zedillo. He first became the PRI's presidential candidate, and then in December 1994 president, with 50 per cent of the vote – in the time-honoured tradition of the PRI which had been in power continuously in Mexico for seventy years.

I watched Zedillo embark on a very impressive process of political and economic reform. In doing so he confounded all the expectations that he would prove a technocratic flunky for the rather menacing figure of his immediate predecessor Carlos Salinas. Zedillo's efforts eventually bore fruit in making Mexico's the most successful economy in Latin America, paving the way for its admission to the North American Free Trade Agreement. Zedillo also paved the way for genuine democracy in his country, although that had the unfortunate effect of making his successor as the candidate of the Institutional Revolutionary Party the first PRI candidate to lose an election. Sadly, all Latin American progress tends to be punctuated by disappointment and setbacks.

I had many opportunities to further my birdwatching on my foreign visits but these could be complicated by the insistence of my hosts that I be accompanied by security and other watchers. I had particular difficulties in Japan, where birdwatching is an almost unknown Western interest, regarded as deeply eccentric. On one trip Gillian and I were driven by our government escort an enormous distance through very attractive-looking birdwatching territory to a large natural-history museum. We were there shown in to a collection of stuffed birds in cases. I tried to explain that my interest was in searching for birds with binoculars in the wild. The Japanese were totally nonplussed. They explained that there were many more birds in the museum than could be found in the open air and they would be much easier to study at close quarters.

On another occasion in Japan we were taken to a splendid nature reserve but only allowed to birdwatch in considerable comfort. I recall with pleasure sitting in the middle of a forest in freezing temperatures in a hide overlooking a stream. The hide was glass-fronted with central heating, keeping us extremely warm. Two Japanese women in traditional costume served us with tea and light refreshments as we sat at the front of the hide gazing at the rich variety of species in the bushes by the stream.

On yet another attempt at Japanese birdwatching, I was driven with a large escort of armed guards in separate vehicles to a wonderful reserve where a huge flock of cranes was gathering in a migratory movement. This was one of the finest birdwatching venues in the world, and I looked forward to parking, getting out of the vehicle, and observing the birds with the telescopes at the visitor centre. Unfortunately my security escort swept our whole convoy past the visitor centre and directly over the ground towards the flock of cranes, who not surprisingly rose into the air very noisily and scattered to the far distance. Japanese policemen then jumped from the other vehicles and ran about waving their arms in the air trying to instruct the birds to return to be inspected by their honoured guest.

Fortunately in most countries, thanks to the persistence of the embassy staff, it did usually prove possible to explain to our hosts that I really was making a private and informal trip to observe wildlife in its natural habitat.

I was also often lucky enough to be able to visit jazz clubs when staying in cities in Europe, America or even behind the Iron Curtain. The most memorable of these came on one occasion when I was visiting Chicago. I was the guest of the British consul and his wife in their comfortable Residence. I must confess that I found them very rigid in their behaviour and somewhat stuffy. I was therefore pleasantly surprised when they suggested that we spend an evening at a jazz club. We sailed in the diplomatic car into the South Side of Chicago which is a very colourful part of the city not usually visited by foreign tourists at night without exceptional care. We pulled up outside an old crumbling brownstone and went through its doors into an atmosphere which reeked of cannabis smoke, and through which we were able to make out a large packed crowd seated around a neglected-looking dance hall. We stood out somewhat, as we were the only white people in the building and certainly the only people wearing suits. The band was an eccentric but famous ensemble led by a man who called himself Sun Ra, performing very original modern jazz music with considerable elan to an enthusiastic crowd. We took our seats at a small table which appeared to have been held for us, and listened for a time without arousing too much curiosity from the other members of the audience. To my amazement, during one number, the consul suddenly took his wife by the arm and they moved onto a small dusty patch of dance floor where they began to perform a very high-quality quickstep. We emerged from the gathering as a sensational success.

With hindsight, I am amazed that I was able to combine all this fascinating worldwide political travel with the domestic pressures of macroeconomic policymaking for an economy in recent recession and the parliamentary duties of a Chancellor of the Exchequer. I suppose that I was already an experienced minister, at what proved to be the peak of my career. I like to persuade myself that I was able to broaden my knowledge and understanding of global politics in the process, but only others can judge whether this had any worthwhile effect on my political contribution. I was delighted to be able to participate so fully in foreign affairs during this key period for the emergence of the modern globalized economy and was only sorry that I was too pro-European for even John Major to be prepared to enrage the Conservative Party by appointing me Foreign Secretary. That is a job I would love to have done.

22

'Time Out'
(Dave Brubeck, 1959)

OUT OF OFFICE

On the night of the 1997 general election I was in Nottingham for the overnight count. While the slow process continued, I listened to the predictable results across the country as we were completely massacred. The highlight in the news was Michael Portillo's defeat. My percentage majority at the last election had been identical to Michael's and a similar swing would have defeated me too. However, the East Midlands was rather different from North London and I was returned with a reduced but quite comfortable majority. I remained fairly unruffled by this as I had believed throughout the campaign that heavy defeat was quite inevitable after the ridiculous warfare within the government over the previous years. The British electorate does not vote for divided parties.

Gillian and I had always made sure that we did not become so accustomed to Number 11 Downing Street, or Dorneywood, the Georgian mansion that is traditionally the Chancellor of the Exchequer's country home, that we came to regard them as our own permanent homes.

It was so strange living in these places that there was, however, little chance of this. My two children, who were then young adults, greatly enjoyed using Number 11 as a home from time to time but there were considerable downsides. One night Kenneth was woken to find himself in the middle of a fully armed security rehearsal for dealing with a terrorist attack. On another occasion, Ken's ancient Eastern European-built Skoda broke down on Downing Street. Ken phoned the AA and explained that his name was Ken Clarke, his car was a Skoda, and it had broken down on Downing Street, whereupon the telephone operator, thinking that this was a childish hoax, hung up. It was with considerable difficulty that Ken was able to persuade any mechanic of the reality and location of his plight.

Every two or three weeks we would try to spend a family weekend at Dorneywood and we often invited friends. There we became passionate players of croquet, which is a splendidly competitive sport. The best players we ever invited were John Gummer and Martin Suthers, who demonstrated that 'sons of the manse' are always the best players of this ferocious game. Years later, John Prescott acquired a taste for the croquet lawn there, but he had to stop playing after some embarrassing publicity over his recreation. I was never therefore able to take up his invitation to come over sometime and play him at 'that game of yours', which promised to be an extremely competitive match as he believed he had achieved some prowess.

We always referred to Number 11 as the 'tied cottage' and I insisted that the only certainty for the future was that sooner or later I would become an ex-Chancellor. Electoral defeat hardly came as a surprise in May 1997, so we were prepared in every way to move back to our own homes in Nottingham and London. I had even arranged for a removal firm to come and collect our possessions when the defeat was announced.

However, the morning after our defeat, the strange conventions of a British election made the Downing Street staff, who were usually courtesy itself, behave very badly. I was detained in Nottingham and Gillian had to travel to London to supervise our move. The staff insisted to Gillian that she and all of our possessions should be out of the building by noon. Apparently Tony and Cherie Blair had arranged to visit to inspect the accommodation before deciding whether to live in the usual prime minister's flat behind Number 10, or at Number 11. The staff chivvied and pestered Gillian rather mercilessly to hurry up and get out before the Blairs arrived.

Had I been there to help her, I would have dismissed these demands in a firm and peremptory fashion. I knew Tony and Cherie perfectly well and I was quite certain that they would not be remotely worried to find Gillian or me there when they made their tour of inspection. Indeed, they would undoubtedly have been friendly and helpful. Gillian was more conformist and, with the help of my PA Debbie, desperately attempted to move out, but failed. They were whisked out of the back door as the Blairs arrived.

The Number 11 accommodation, as used by Chancellors hitherto, was actually far superior and more comfortable than the accommodation in Number 10. The Blairs therefore made the sensible decision to move into what had been our home.

Gillian, with her enthusiasm and talent for cooking, had particularly enjoyed the huge if rather plain kitchen at Number 11 which gave a full and clear view down the length of Downing Street from its extensive windows. Her only indignation with the Blairs came when she discovered that Cherie had insisted on having the kitchen rebuilt and redecorated. Gillian rather sniffily thought that she had destroyed a perfectly good kitchen, which was ideal for a serious cook.

Ironically, given that I hadn't been there at all that day, a new myth sprang up around me, based on newspaper reports that I had personally moved our furniture out of Number 11 in a hired van. These stories were accompanied by a photograph of me putting a piece of furniture into a van. The picture clearly showed hedgerows and trees which anyone who cared to could have established were not native to Downing Street. They were actually taken when I moved a piece of my mother-in-law's furniture from Sidcup into our home in Nottingham. However, so far as the popular press was concerned, this quite harmless myth persisted ever after.

John Major resigned from the leadership immediately after the result was announced. I was not surprised and indeed felt almost relieved on his account. He had been tortured by the constant abuse and pressure to which he had been subjected throughout his premiership and I believed, correctly as it turned out, that he would return to his normal and happier self once he was released from the chains of office.

The Conservative Party was therefore plunged into a leadership election which, as for every leadership election since Ted Heath's time, was to be decided by a transferable vote system in a series of ballots of its MPs. Six candidates put themselves forward: William Hague, John Redwood, Peter Lilley, Michael Howard, Stephen Dorrell, and me. Michael Heseltine held back for reasons then unknown to me. Michael Portillo and Malcolm Rifkind, who had previously been named as possible candidates, had lost their seats and so could not stand. Chris Patten's term as governor of Hong Kong had not yet ended so he too was ruled out. As the Chancellor of the Exchequer I was the obvious choice and, at the outset, the pundits' odds-on favourite. I thought I would probably win.

I persuaded Michael Jack, David Curry and Ian Taylor to lead my parliamentary campaign and found that I had an army of enthusiastic young campaigners eagerly supporting me from the headquarters we established in the Methodist Hall opposite Westminster Abbey. I am afraid my style of campaigning was a disappointment to them. I was exhausted after my nation-touring efforts in the general election campaign – politics is nothing if not a test of stamina – and partly for this reason I was not terribly receptive to their attempts to involve me in a national media campaign. In fact, I was rather churlish about it. I saw no point in appealing to journalists and the general public when our electorate consisted solely of MPs, most of whom knew quite enough about me already. With hindsight, I was probably wrong and they were probably right because a good campaign might have influenced some of the new MPs. In a portent of every one of the three leadership elections I ran in, my keenest supporters also wanted me to modify my strongly pro-European opinions or to obscure my sympathy for the principle of the single currency. With my usual opinionated stubbornness I disappointed them again and refused to do this. I could see no point at all in aspiring to be prime minister on a platform of political opinions that were not mine.

Although a nationwide opinion poll of party members put me miles ahead of the field and it seemed that I was also the bookmakers' clear favourite, this had little or no effect in Parliament, where the decision was for MPs alone to make. For that reason I became steadily less confident of success.

The problem was that the party in defeat was even more consumed with European passions than it had been in government, and the Eurosceptics were convinced that now was the time to seize control. They had good reason: the membership of the parliamentary party had undergone a dramatic transformation on 1 May 1997. Many senior pro-European MPs had resigned and many had been defeated. In conversation in the House of Commons we sounded like survivors coming back from the Western Front as we regretted that so-and-so had just failed to make it and lamented the loss of this friend or that. The 1997 intake of new MPs, who became known as 'Thatcher's Children', was a fairly talented bunch, but much more Eurosceptic than previous cohorts, altering the balance of the party considerably.

I led the field in first preferences in every ballot except the third and final vote, but as the campaign wore on, I soon reached the view that this was an elimination contest to see which Eurosceptic was eventually going to defeat me. Stephen Dorrell dropped out in my favour before the first ballot but even his few supporters did not all transfer to me. When Michael Howard and Peter Lilley dropped out after the first ballot, they urged their supporters to vote for William Hague. As successive candidates were eliminated the field crept steadily closer onto my heels.

The nearest I came to the possibility of success was early on, before the first ballot, when it was announced that, because he was so young and inexperienced, William Hague was going to renounce his candidacy and back Michael Howard. Michael had become one of the most unpopular members of the last government because he had put over his iron-fisted law and order policies in a rather unattractive way. He had also squabbled very publicly with his Minister of State, the excellent and liberal Ann Widdecombe, who did him enormous damage by letting slip her opinion that he had 'something of the night about him'.

Unfortunately William Hague's friends rallied when they heard the rumour and overnight succeeded in persuading him to draw back from his commitment to Michael and maintain his candidacy. Michael promptly became the first of us to be eliminated, in the first ballot. William's change of heart ended what was probably my best ever chance of becoming leader of the party.

John Redwood was eliminated in the second ballot, leaving William and me to contest a third and final round.

It was at that point, facing William Hague in the last vote, that I and my team began to see the writing on the wall. Our first thought was for me to approach Michael Heseltine and offer to stand down in his favour if he would enter the contest. I believed that he was less unpopular than me with the right wing of the party and had a better chance. He was very tempted, and we agreed that this would happen and nearly put it into effect for twenty-four hours. He asked for time to consider and I later discovered he had gone away to take advice from his doctor. After a full medical check, he was advised that his health was not up to the workload of being Leader of the Opposition. He therefore reluctantly backed out of the contest and I carried on. Twenty years later, Michael remains remarkably healthy. It was probably the best chance that he had ever had of achieving his ultimate ambition, missed because of this discouraging – and inaccurate – advice.

Matters European then became particularly relevant. It was obvious that if John Redwood's supporters transferred to William at this stage, William would overtake me and win. I cannot now remember who came up with our last desperate idea of the Clarke–Redwood pact into which we entered to try to prevent this, but someone discovered that John objected to William's candidature for reasons to which I was never party. A plot was therefore devised for John and me to enter into an alliance and ask his supporters to vote for me in the final round.

Half a dozen of us gathered in Tim Sainsbury's house just around the corner from the House of Commons. Assisted by Tim, not only a colleague but an ally, we drew up and agreed a document setting out the terms for this novel alliance. It was not in fact as ridiculously fanciful as it seemed to the outside world. John and I usually agreed on domestic matters and we had similar views on economic policy in particular. The key to our pact was that we solemnly agreed that Europe was to be an open issue with no binding party policy. The two of us, and other MPs, would stick to our respective opinions and attempt to reduce Europe's profile in the party's campaigning.

Although John and I believed that this might work, we were

singularly unsuccessful in persuading others. There was trouble with his supporters almost straight away. His campaign manager throughout had been Iain Duncan Smith, who had been conspicuous by his unexpected absence from the meeting at Tim Sainsbury's house. It soon became obvious that Iain's reservations were shared by most other Redwood supporters. Even worse, one or two MPs who had previously voted for me defected to William in disgust at this Nazi–Soviet agreement.

Most significantly Margaret Thatcher was induced by her close entourage of Eurosceptic aides to join vigorously in William Hague's campaign. Redwood's supporters were summoned one by one to meet her and were lectured sternly on the wickedness of voting for a dreadful pro-European like me. The only difficulty, apparently, was that Margaret scarcely knew William and only really remembered him as a schoolboy who had spoken from the floor at the 1977 party conference. At one point Margaret stormed out of the St Stephen's entrance to the Commons and was confronted by a group of children in front of a television camera. She seized the moment to impress upon these children, and through them the nation, the importance of backing William. Someone had just explained to her the way in which he actually spelt his name. She used this new-found knowledge to impress upon the children, 'Remember the name William Hague – H-A-G-U-E.'

The final result, after some brief moments of hope, matched my expectations. I was disappointed, of course, but by this time not all that surprised. William won comfortably and embarked on a period of opposition to the Blair government at the height of its popularity. In some ways this was as big a blow to William's career as it was to my own. If I had defeated William in the 1997 leadership election I would have led the party through five stormy and divided Europe-obsessed years and lost to Tony Blair in 2001. William would have sailed into the leadership in the wake of that defeat and, providing he had opposed the invasion of Iraq, he would probably have defeated a very vulnerable Blair in 2005.

After his victory, William immediately and generously asked me if I would serve on his front bench. This seemed entirely genuine, rather than a nod to convention, although I do not recall whether he mentioned a particular role. I told him, however, that I had no intention of going back onto the Opposition front bench. I remembered from the 1970s how truly frustrating a role it was, and had no need of more frontbench experience. I further explained that I did not expect that I would ever be a minister again and that I planned to continue as a backbench MP and find something else to do.

My move to the back benches produced some odd consequences. At the autumn party conference in Blackpool that year, John Gummer persuaded Gillian and me to stay with him at a low-cost, basic, very clean Blackpool boarding-house almost opposite the back door into the Winter Gardens Conference Centre. It was convenient and away from the constant political scrum at the five-star hotel where the Shadow Cabinet and leading lights were staying. When journalists discovered where we were they decided that we had fallen on hard times and were living rough. The place was besieged night and day by journalists and photographers who tried to talk their way in for a photograph of our room. The welcoming Blackpool landlady (a Mrs Caplady, I think) was overwhelmed and distressed by the experience and slightly turned to whisky to soothe her nerves.

Gillian and I had not fallen on hard times at all. In May 1997 I had immediately been invited by my old chambers in Birmingham and London to resume my place. I politely declined these kind offers. I had been a minister for almost twenty years and had no trace of a practice to resume. Whilst I probably would have been able to make a living from instructions from solicitors keen to present their clients with a celebrity counsel, I would have needed an extremely good junior to back up my advocacy as a silk, not least to explain to me the many changes in procedure and the law since I had last practised almost two decades earlier. Although it could have been a good source of income I had no expectation of being able to put together a sufficiently serious practice.

Instead I was toying with a move into the world of business. Indeed, I soon received some very good offers to join large and reputable companies as a non-executive director.

The first was Unichem, a successful pharmaceutical wholesale company whose chief executive, Jeff Harris, approached me and offered me the chairmanship on a generous salary. He and I both thought that my experience as Health Secretary would give me familiarity with the business, and he had ambitions to take the company into the European market: like me he naively assumed that the EU would soon move to a single market for pharmaceuticals.

Unichem was a successful and specialized business based on warehousing in completely hygienic conditions and immediate delivery of any medicine to any pharmacist at any time. Its little vans were a frequent sight across the country as they made their twice-daily deliveries of medicinal drugs to retail pharmacies. My old friend Geoffrey Rippon had greatly enjoyed being chairman of Unichem, and thinking I would too, I accepted the offer. It was rather startling to begin my non-executive career as chairman of the board and I had to conceal my L-plates carefully for the first few months.

I stayed with Unichem for ten years, and did indeed hugely enjoy and benefit from the experience. Our attempts to move into Europe were frustrated in Portugal and Italy particularly by their restrictive protectionism, but we eventually entered the European scene through a merger with the Franco-Italian company Alliance Santé which was owned by Stefano Pessina, an Italian entrepreneur who lived in Monaco. Stefano became a good friend and he and his partner Ornella Barra, who was also a director of the company, knew everything that there was to be known about the specialized world of pharmaceutical wholesaling. With their help we traded as Alliance Unichem and steadily strengthened our position across the Continent. I left as Alliance Unichem merged with Boots, the Nottingham-based nationwide pharmaceutical retailer. We had grown so quickly and Boots had so stagnated that the companies merged on an almost fifty-fifty basis of valuation as Alliance Boots. When my colleagues and I had approached the Boots board a few years earlier and suggested a merger on a thirty-seventy basis in their favour, they had treated us with rather patronizing disdain.

I was also invited to become deputy chairman of British American Tobacco (BAT). Pat Sheehy, my old acquaintance from Home Office days when he had helped me on police pay, was now the chairman of BAT, a conglomerate combining a tobacco business with a range of other operations including a big insurance arm. Pat, who autocratically ran the company as both chairman and chief executive, had decided to split the tobacco business from the rest to see if they would do better as two separate specialist companies. He kindly offered me a choice between the tobacco company and the insurance business, rather assuming that with my background as Chancellor I would opt for the insurance. As a lifelong smoker, I thought the idea of a global tobacco business sounded much more fun than the world of Zurich insurance and was delighted to become deputy chairman of the new BAT. The new chairman and chief executive was the excellent Martin Broughton, who became a friend as well as a comfortable business partner.

This was another hugely enjoyable experience despite the fact that I found myself on the receiving end of steady political sniping as the health hazards of tobacco were becoming clearer and the tobacco industry was being demonized throughout the Western world. I entirely accepted that tobacco was indeed the principal cause of lung cancer and a serious contributor to other cancers and heart disease. However, as someone who had smoked since the sixth form at school and who now greatly enjoyed cigars, I took the libertarian view that it was the duty of companies and governments to ensure that everyone was clearly warned of the medical risks of smoking, but that fully informed adults should then be perfectly free to choose their own lifestyle. I maintained this position firmly against our increasingly aggressive critics, and I still do.

In the well over a hundred different countries in which it operated, BAT was managed by a splendid array of pleasant and enterprising people. The company attracted extrovert, gregarious and resilient individuals who were able to withstand the constant criticism associated with its product. The company also maintained the highest ethical standards of almost any organization that I had ever been connected with. Amongst other things, I became the chairman of our Corporate Responsibility Committee. I took the view that our product was so controversial that we had to be purer than pure in every other aspect of our business activities. We strove to be a model employer and to uphold impeccable business standards in everything we did.

This involved resisting some strong pressures. Trading in some of the corrupt markets that we entered involved competing against international companies who were following very dubious standards. BAT resisted these pressures completely. An intended investment in Vietnam, in the course of which I travelled to Hanoi and Saigon, or Ho Chi Minh City, was abandoned when it became obvious that the Communist rulers of that country expected large bribes in exchange for permission to invest. A few years later they appeared to accept that we would not pay, and a successful investment was eventually made. We had a similar experience in Russia where we ran an extremely successful cigarette manufacturing and distribution business without political protectors or recipients of favours. Most extraordinarily, we even managed to open a factory manufacturing tobacco in Nigeria without, as far as I was aware, compromising our standards in any way.

Tobacco's critics followed much lower ethical standards in their campaigning than the company did in conducting its business. The campaigners were so convinced of the merits of their cause and so zealous in their determination to vilify and destroy our product that they believed the end justified the means, making wild allegations without any factual basis at all. We were accused of using child labour on our tobacco plantations. We did not own any plantations and we actively tried to stop child labour on the farms from which we purchased. We were accused of deliberately marketing our products to children when we were in fact actively campaigning to tighten laws against sales to children. Despite our pressure, governments, including our own, declined to enforce the criminal law against people selling cigarettes to children, or to raise the age at which sales were legal, because of their fear of upsetting the retailers and newsagents.

Whichever country I went to I learnt to expect that the staff would be international, as was the main board based in London, so that you could never anticipate the nationality of the leading figures in any subsidiary in any territory. The multinational and multicultural experience of working with such keen and energetic people was extremely worthwhile.

I followed my previous practice of taking Gillian with me on most of my business trips and, as I had as a minister, I worked while she enjoyed some fabulous tourism and visits to Oxfam projects. When time allowed we continued to indulge our respective passions for birdwatching and flower photography, becoming worldwide travellers on a scale far broader than we had ever expected. The happy result is that I have been lucky enough to have seen well over 3,000 species of bird in my lifetime.

One of the most exciting moments of my new career as a 'tobacco baron' was the discovery that BAT had just bought a Formula One racing team. As I've already mentioned, I had been a keen supporter of Formula One motor racing since my son Ken had asked to go to a motor race when he was a small boy and I had taken him to a Grand Prix at Silverstone. He and I had both since become petrol-heads, with regular visits to Silverstone and Brands Hatch and sometimes to Barcelona. Gillian had accompanied us for the first two years when Ken was still in short trousers. We had however dropped her from attendance after she fell peacefully and calmly asleep in the middle of the immense din and excitement of one of the races at Silverstone to which we had taken her. Now I found that my new company was about to engage directly in this global competition.

In my opinion, it had been a foolish decision to buy a racing team when we could perfectly well have simply sponsored one. Formula One racing is phenomenally expensive and it is extremely difficult to find anyone capable of keeping the costs at a sane level. Before I joined the board, Martin Broughton and my colleagues had been persuaded to acquire a team from a man called Ken Tyrrell who gratefully escaped with a few million pounds as his price. Our new acquisition provided us with a factory, a huge team of technicians, a championship driver, Jacques Villeneuve, and a manager, Craig Pollock, who was a personal friend of Jacques Villeneuve and a former ski instructor, but who had little or no experience of running anything. Having persuaded the BAT board that it would achieve instant success with Villeneuve, they were about to sail into their first race confident that they would finish first and go on to win many championships.

I of course was delighted to attend the races and I was also the person least surprised by the total uselessness of our team in its early stages. As I was the only genuine petrolhead on the BAT board, I soon became chairman of the board of our subsidiary, British American Racing, which was the name of our team. I maintained this role for many years and derived great pleasure from it, however frustrating it could be. It took a long time to remove Craig Pollock. When we eventually did, he was replaced with Dave Richards who, though scarcely capable of spelling the word budget, did understand motor racing. He introduced some common sense and drive into our team, which gradually improved. Villeneuve doggedly stuck with us for many years without noticeable success and in 2003 we acquired the young Jenson Button as one of our drivers after his short and unsuccessful spells with Benetton and Renault. Eventually in 2004 and 2005 we succeeded in persuading our engine-making partners Honda to take the team off our hands and relieve us of the financial drain. Thereafter the team, with whom I continued to keep in touch, went on to have great success, briefly owned by a leading designer, and then by Mercedes.

Ken and I had several happy seasons of globetrotting to circuits the length and breadth of the world. Motor-racing people are a friendly and cheerful lot and for the most part very congenial, and I got to know many of them. I remained a good friend of the diminutive Bernie Ecclestone who was the autocratic mastermind who first invented and then ruled over the whole Formula One circus. Bernie had fought his way to the top having left school at sixteen, and as a result he was treated rather scornfully by the old establishment of motor racing. I rather sympathized with his aggressive resentment of the grandees at Silverstone who should certainly have treated him with more respect. I admired Bernie as a brilliant entrepreneur with an amazing pocket-dynamo personality, and did not begrudge his huge personal fortune because he was the only person who had realized that this strange activity involving straw bales at the corners and men dressed in duffel coats could be turned into a global, glitzy, mass-marketed, profitable business. He was the best second-hand-car dealer that Bexleyheath had ever produced, with the most amazing business acumen, and I always thought that he was probably a bit opportunistic rather than dishonest.

Away from the excitements of the motor-racing circuit I also joined the board of the Foreign and Colonial Investment Trust which was the biggest investment trust in the United Kingdom and which exposed me to the world of investment and the City. At one point Alliance Unichem, BAT and F&C were all FTSE 100 companies, with BAT the fourth-best performing FTSE 100 company over the decade that I was there.

I also became a non-executive director on the board of the *Independent* newspaper, owned by the magnificent Tony O'Reilly. The *Independent*, which was left of centre and sometimes idiosyncratic, had introduced new standards of genuine independence into British newspapers. Unfortunately it always lost money, but with the acquisition of the then hugely profitable *Belfast Telegraph* in 2001, we were able to cancel out its losses.

Tony O'Reilly had begun his career as a notable rugby player and was now one of the leading public figures and businessmen in the Irish Republic. He was a lively, warm and outgoing man and I got on extremely well with him and his wife Chryss. I used to joke that I was the token Tory on the board but I actually enjoyed good friendships with my colleagues, including the formidable left-wing female combination of Helena Kennedy and Margaret Jay.

At first I was only on the board of the British subsidiary but subsequently I went onto the board of the main company which involved travelling to meetings in Dublin and further afield as the company owned important and successful newspapers in South Africa, Australia and New Zealand, and a stake in a large-circulation newspaper in India. On one memorable occasion Tony insisted that we needed to have a board meeting in New Zealand which turned out, by 'lucky chance', to coincide with the All Blacks–England rugby match. We all obtained tickets to watch England being given a good thrashing.

I added to my portfolio a role with an asset-management company run by my old stockbroker friend Christopher Saunders, another with a hedge fund run by a dynamic Frenchman, and a brief year advising the Japanese finance house Daiwa until it pulled out most of its London assets to cover losses in Japan. Apart from the income, which was on a scale that no politician could ever earn when in government, I acquired a much wider experience of the financial and business world than I had ever conceived of. I was constantly obliged to reflect that it was unfortunate that I only acquired this valuable experience after I had been Chancellor of the Exchequer and not before.

These were of course the years when, despite the public assertions of my successor as Chancellor, Gordon Brown, the British economy was going through an artificial boom before its eventual bust. Happily, though, the companies I worked for all did well and were not affected by this febrile atmosphere. The one thing that did disconcert me was the spiralling executive remuneration levels and the increasing income gap between those at the top of British companies and those at the bottom. As chairman of one or two remuneration committees I tried to exercise a certain hairshirt restraint but it proved almost impossible. The bigger companies had adopted a clever new fashion of appointing consultants to advise on executive pay levels each year. The consultants would always advise that their client company's executive pay was in the middle or towards the bottom of the range. The other non-executives on the remuneration committee would always believe, correctly in our cases, that the executives were excellent and that they should be moved into the 'top quartile' of the league table. Most other companies would do similarly, so that the next year the consultants would report that we were once more in the middle or towards the bottom. This process produced the most startling increases in the level of executive pay. I expected uproar at our annual meeting when we first awarded a chief executive a £1 million salary, but nothing happened and the process continued. In my opinion it needs to stop. Those people like myself who believe in free-market economics should be just as concerned as socialists to ensure the fairness of the system, and we ought to be particularly keen to make sure that no indefensible gap arises between the very well paid and the ordinarily paid. But I was only able to exercise a tiny modicum of restraint on the boards on which I served – other non-executives tended to regard my caution as eccentric and I could not get the remuneration committees to support me. This problem has not been corrected to this day. The only contribution from the government at the time was Peter Mandelson's declaration that he was 'intensely relaxed about people getting filthy rich as long as they pay their taxes'.

Over the years, it has increasingly become the fashion for MPs to be full-time politicians, and MPs are sometimes criticized for having outside interests, jobs or sources of income. I was never much troubled by this and was not attacked particularly personally apart from by tobacco lobbyists, but I genuinely disagree with this view. I continue to believe that there are far too few MPs in Parliament with outside interests. This both narrows the experience of our political leaders and reduces their independence from their parties and the whips.

Despite my business ventures, I remained actively engaged in Parliament and politics in Westminster and in Nottinghamshire. The result was that during my decade in opposition I was every bit as workaholic as I had always been during my two decades in government. I did, though, have much more liberty in my politics. I could follow the subjects that most interested me and I was also able to be more detached from the sclerotic infighting to which the Conservative Party was still subjecting itself and which gave William Hague a quite dreadful experience as leader. Euroscepticism was in the ascendancy, added to which there was a new division between Hagueites and Portillistas – Michael Portillo had lost his seat in 1997 but re-entered Parliament in 1999 and became Shadow Chancellor – involving rather vague arguments about the socially reforming direction in which the party might now travel.

This was all a great shame as William was in fact an extremely able and forceful performer. He regularly defeated Tony Blair in the weekly exhibitionist debating contest that was Prime Minister's Questions where he displayed a splendid wit and penetrating oratory and constantly made Blair uncomfortable. Unfortunately, PMQs has less impact on public opinion than it is credited with and Blair remained a tremendously popular and charismatic figure in the world outside Westminster. The Major government had become so unpopular and discredited by the time it had collapsed that Tony had been gifted a lengthy honeymoon period during which the public believed he could do no wrong and were quite determined not to go back to Conservative government.

Sadly, though, Tony Blair and New Labour had little idea of what they intended to do with the colossal political power that they had won. They had scant policy of any significance on the public services such as education or health, and had pledged to continue the same economic policy that I had pursued as Chancellor. They were more obsessed with constant campaigning than we had been, and introduced spin doctors such as Alastair Campbell, politically appointed press officers, message discipline and a short-termist sloganizing style based on an obsession with the daily media agenda. This change in the political culture has persisted and has contributed greatly to the increasingly shallow and short-term nature of political debate and the indifference and hostility of much of the general public to politicians and the political establishment.

One thing that Tony did seem clear on, however, was that he wanted to prepare for Britain to join the single European currency, which was due to be launched on 1 January 1999. He therefore started to have fascinating and very private meetings with me and Paddy Ashdown, then the leader of the Liberal Democrat Party, in order to plan how to win over British public opinion to support this.

Paddy and I were both insistent that we could only visit Tony in total secrecy. We would both have been undermined if any of his entourage had leaked our visits to the press. As a result we would enter the complex of buildings by the Cabinet Office entrance on Whitehall and make our way through the labyrinthine corridors to some small room in or around Number 10. I was assured that only one member of Tony's staff knew that he was holding these meetings and that he had not even told Alastair Campbell about them.

Our discussions were all about how to campaign on the subject of the single currency to persuade the public of its merit in the face of a bitterly hostile press. We only occasionally touched on technical and policy issues. Unfortunately, Tony was convinced that all the campaigning should be done by Paddy, Michael Heseltine (who was not party to these discussions) and me with the support of the Confederation of British Industry and the rest of the business community. We were particularly keen that as prime minister he should take the lead. Otherwise I in particular was only going to make news as a participant in purely internal Conservative wars. Our discussions were generally very friendly and extremely interesting but never really reached any positive conclusion. Over time, I became aware that Tony's difficulties stemmed from his already deteriorating relationship with Gordon Brown, who had finally been persuaded by his close aide Ed Balls to oppose the single European currency.

When we did finally begin to outline all-party projects in which Tony vaguely undertook to take a part, it all came to nothing. In 1999 Michael Heseltine and I appeared on a much-publicized public platform with Tony and Gordon at the IMAX cinema in Waterloo to proclaim our support for a common means of exchange in our new single market. Gordon spent the event pretending, by means of rigid body language and a shorter speech than everyone else's, that he wasn't there, and afterwards ostentatiously detached himself from any related activity. Tony never followed up on it in any practical or visible way.

It soon became quite exasperating that whilst he kept pressing Paddy and me to take a higher profile, he himself would do nothing.

Tony always showed obvious and sincere enthusiasm in our private discussions and said that Britain coming to terms with the European Union and joining the single currency was one of the great aims of his premiership. After one meeting, walking back through the corridors with Paddy, I complained about the situation. Paddy replied, very shrewdly I now think, that 'The trouble with Tony is that he always believes what he is saying when he is saying it.' I was often reminded of that phrase years later in debates on the invasion of Iraq, when Tony continued to express the most sincere belief in the existence of weapons of mass destruction in Iraq, while everybody else had long ago ceased to believe in what was obviously a delusion.

However, I now rather began to lose interest in the prospect of Britain joining the single currency at its birth as I was convinced that we could not join at sterling's then inflated exchange rate. Tony was meanwhile stymied by his Chancellor, who instructed his press officer Charlie Whelan to brief the press that he and Tony had agreed that they would not join the single currency until the Treasury had studied the project. A long and academic study was then carried out by officials, some of whom I still knew. I once asked one of them what conclusions they were reaching and he explained to me that they were waiting to be told by their Chancellor what conclusions he wanted them to reach.

At one point, Peter Mandelson came dashing into my room in the House of Commons, to tell me that the exercise had finally been concluded, and that Gordon was about to announce that the UK did not pass any of the 'five tests' that he had thought up in a taxi and announced at the start of the process. Peter asked me for ideas on how to stop this but I was unable to offer any suggestion to thwart Gordon's cunning plan, which had obviously succeeded. The prospect of joining the single currency vanished – perhaps fortunately, since the eurozone was getting into problems, because it was ignoring all the sensible rules that had been laid down for it. Incidentally, so far as I am aware it is completely incorrect to assert, as Eurosceptics have continued to do, that anyone had ever declared or intended to declare that some cataclysmic disaster would hit the British economy if we failed to join the euro.

Tony is a highly intelligent man and he did eventually start to produce a clear agenda of enterprising reform. In particular he adopted the policies of the third-term Thatcher government on education and health. Andrew Adonis vigorously implemented the Baker education reforms, first as an aide to Tony Blair in Downing Street, and then as a minister, with changes of nomenclature from 'grant-maintained schools' and 'city technology colleges' to 'academies'. Alan Milburn, as Secretary of State for Health, pursued my reforms of the NHS with skill and courage, and modified and improved the internal market, decentralization of control and the emphasis on outcomes and patient interests in the light of experience.

Unfortunately by the time he had worked out his agenda, the bizarre personal warfare between Tony and Gordon Brown had intensified to such an extent that he no longer had the political power he had

had at the outset to fully implement it. I still adhere to the perhaps old-fashioned view that it is wise to work out why you want to be prime minister and what you propose to do before you campaign to gain the office.

While he battled with his Chancellor, Blair was at least little troubled by the Conservative Party, which continued to indulge its taste for the civil warfare it had so enjoyed in the years running up to our 1997 election defeat. In 2001 our election campaign, like that of 1997, was fought against the background of infighting and division. Disastrously, William in desperation took up the old Eurosceptic clichés as the principal subject of the campaign, including a zealous focus on a countdown of the number of days left to 'save the pound'. The arguments about the single currency roused frenzied opinions from ultra-Europhobes in the press and in Parliament that were of little interest to most ordinary human beings. Blair had already committed himself to a referendum if his government ever did apply to join the single currency, so any sensible elector could see that the general election was not the decision point on that question anyway.

I so disdained the 'save the pound' policy that I fought the 2001 election on an independent policy platform in Rushcliffe. I deliberately kept well away from the national campaign, instead focusing on door-to-door campaigning in my own constituency as I thought personal contact was the only worthwhile way of trying to influence votes. In order to avoid publicity about causing party splits I also shunned all national journalists except Don Macintyre of the *Independent*. Don accompanied me on my door-to-door campaigning one day, hovering behind me as I stood on the doorsteps of East Leake. He was eager to hear my constituents' views on the single currency. I told him I did not think anyone would mention it: the tiny number of people with any interest in it already knew my views. In fact no one mentioned the pound or the euro all morning. The only hot topic for debate was aircraft noise from East Midlands airport.

So determined was I not to get involved in the national debate that when the BBC's Michael Crick descended on me one Saturday morning when I was doing a walkabout in the shopping centre of West Bridgford, I wouldn't talk to him. I continued to shake hands and chat with constituents but refused to end my silence about the national campaign. Michael was as determined as I was and so we provided *Newsnight* with some entertaining footage of him chasing me with a microphone round and round a bus shelter while bemused locals looked on.

The Blair government had had an enjoyable first term of office which now concluded with a second electoral triumph for them. The Conservative Party in its turn suffered its inevitable second election massacre. With a sigh of relief William Hague promptly resigned the party leadership; he later told me that he would never again in any circumstances lead a political party.

The real achievement of the first Blair government of 1997–2001 was to cement the Thatcher revolution permanently into place. Any other Labour leader would have wasted a lot of time trying to reverse our supply-side and trade union reforms which had created a more successful modern economy and society, but Tony was a great admirer of both Margaret Thatcher and her government. After a short interval under Gordon Brown, which I describe in the next chapter, Blair was succeeded by David Cameron, an even greater admirer. The result was a welcome continuity in British politics which had in its previous phase been marred by alternating periods in office for ideologically opposed parties.

Would Margaret have approved of the work of her disciples, Tony and David? Surely not. Margaret had stronger and clearer ideas, a greater interest in public policy, and a bigger sense of the national interest than either of them. And Blair introduced, and Cameron enthusiastically adopted, the mass-media campaigning tactics that she had always despised.

23

'Plucked Again'
(Duke Ellington, 1950)

OPPOSITION AGAIN

Following William Hague's resignation as leader after the 2001 general election, the Conservative Party went on to the pleasure of yet another leadership election, in which we could argue about Europe and other matters dear to the hearts of our MPs and activists all over again.

I decided to have another go. The other obvious contender was the then right-wing hard-line Eurosceptic Michael Portillo and I could see no other credible candidate who could argue for liberal centre-right internationalist government. I thought the 'save the pound' general election campaign had been a pathetic disaster and that I had a reasonable chance of persuading the party to return to mainstream politics. Gillian took it for granted that I would run, as did all my friends.

My campaign team was largely the same loyal group of supporters as I had had in 1997, but other things had changed considerably. Technology had moved on, so although I have still never operated a computer myself, this time I was persuaded to have a website, and a so-called rebuttal unit. I never did discover what we put on the website. The voting system had changed too. MPs were to vote in a series of ballots to reduce the field to two candidates, who would then subject themselves to a vote of the voluntary membership. This was all part of the reforms that party chief executive Archie Norman had carried out on William Hague's behalf. The idea had been to democratize the party and to attract new members by giving the voluntary membership a key decision-making role. This was well intentioned but unfortunately did not work. The reforms didn't attract new members and the party henceforth proceeded on the basis that it was to be governed by an elderly voluntary membership which provided an ever-diminishing and less representative reflection of the Conservative vote in the country, let alone the public in general.

The full field comprised Michael Ancram, David Davis, Iain Duncan Smith, Michael Portillo and me. Impartial pundits accepted that the obvious leading candidates were Michael Portillo and me: no one else standing had good public exposure or similar levels of ministerial experience. I certainly felt that Michael was a formidable opponent.

He was, though, unfortunately dogged by absurd and malicious media rumours about his private life. This gossip dominated the reporting of his campaign at the expense of any of his other views or qualities, and it plainly hurt him. I was infuriated by this nonsense which I was sure was untrue and in any case irrelevant and felt very sorry for him. All the candidates participated in a TV debate, in which I observed Michael going completely into his shell and failing to engage in any of the political arguments. I think it was his experience during this campaign that eventually persuaded him to give up his political career altogether.

I was of course dogged by the usual and perfectly mainstream controversy about my pro-European views and throughout the campaign I continued to exasperate my friends and supporters by adamantly refusing their requests that I should modify them. I have always maintained that if Portillo and I had got through to the final stage, the Conservative Party would have been required to choose between two of its more unpalatable prejudices. The outcome would have been determined by whether the party was more Europhobic than homophobic or vice versa. Faced with the choice at that time, they would almost certainly have plumped for me.

This was not, however, to be. Michael Ancram and David Davis having fallen out of the race after the first and second ballots, I came first in the third MPs' vote by a small margin, but Iain Duncan Smith reaped the benefit of Michael's distractions and beat him into third place by one vote. The final contest for the voluntary members' vote between Iain and me then took place over a period of three months with a series of debates across the country in which I took part with vigour. Most members of the general public and the majority of voluntary members of the Conservative Party had never heard of Iain Duncan Smith and knew nothing about him. He won the contest by a large majority. I am quite convinced that this was because our members were delighted to be able to avoid making a choice about Europe or anything else by voting for someone who was neither Kenneth Clarke nor Michael Portillo. My considered reaction to the defeat, after my initial disappointment, was that the Conservative Party had gone mad and that I would be a happier man enjoying my new business career.

Unfortunately the choice of Iain Duncan Smith, or IDS as he became known, proved to be an extremely poor one. The unknown man did not develop the skills of a national political leader quickly enough, and after two disastrous years the parliamentary party voted him out in order to avoid the ignominy of coming third in the next general election.

I firmly believe that if Archie Norman's system had been in place in 1997 I would have won the leadership then. I had a higher public profile than the other candidates and the voluntary party faithful would have voted for me as the heir apparent. But my parliamentary colleagues wouldn't have me and chose the unfortunate William Hague instead.

In 2001 I obtained more MPs' votes than any other candidate and would certainly have won a run-off amongst MPs against Iain Duncan Smith. If – and it is admittedly a big if – I had then succeeded in persuading the party to oppose the invasion of Iraq we might have beaten a fading Tony Blair in 2005. But this time our increasingly Eurosceptic voluntary membership wouldn't have me and instead chose Iain Duncan Smith.

It remains my view that the leadership of major political parties should be decided by a secret ballot of that party's MPs. The parliamentarians know the candidates and their views best and by working alongside them have been able to appraise their potential. As I write, the Labour Party is experiencing the fallout of allowing members of the public to pay a small sum of money to the party in order to cast a vote in its leadership election. The result was the election of Jeremy Corbyn, with views opposed by almost all of the MPs that he is expected to lead.

The closing date for the ballots for the leadership election had been 11 September 2001 – the day of world-changing tragedy when fanatic Islamists blew up the World Trade Center in New York. I supported the subsequent wave of feeling for our Atlantic alliance and the invasion of Afghanistan.

Two years later, I was not surprised by President George W. Bush's decision to invade Iraq in 2003 in order to overthrow the regime of Saddam Hussein. I had long been debating these matters in private meetings with powerful Americans – right-wing Republicans particularly – at the annual Bilderberg conference, which I had been attending since I was first invited in 1993. The conferences, taking their name from the hotel in Holland where the first meeting took place, were the principal activity of an institution that had sprung up in the 1950s with the aim of helping Western Europe and North America to understand each other better and to work together on geopolitical matters of critical importance. They attracted the highest quality of genuinely leading political and business figures from the United States and Europe. Bilderberg was the outstanding political gathering of the several conferences of this kind that I attended.

I had been attending international forums such as the Institute of Political Affairs since the 1970s, but in the early 1990s I began to be invited to other great international gatherings such as the annual – and very important – World Economic Forum conferences at Davos and the aforementioned (and rather more secretive) Bilderberg meetings. Officialdom had panicked when my Private Office revealed that I would be travelling to these affairs alone, and the Cabinet Secretariat had strongly urged that I must attend accompanied by a private secretary or not at all. It was ruled quite impossible that I might talk to important people on great issues of politics without any official briefing to guide me or a Civil Service secretary to take careful notes.

I am afraid I treated this advice with cavalier disdain and was probably responsible for the growing practice of ever more ministers attending the Davos political circus.

After my visit in 1993, when Tony Blair had also been invited for the first time, I became a regular attendee at the Bilderberg conference. I eventually took over from the former Foreign Secretary Peter Carrington as the British representative on its steering committee, arranging invitations for other leading British figures.

Rather strangely, Bilderberg acquired a most sinister reputation amongst left-wing conspiracy theorists. The names of those who attended and the subjects we discussed were no secret. We did however keep the proceedings fairly secret, and we certainly ensured that there were no leaks of any kind as to what had actually been said by any of the leading public figures who attended. This insistence on being able to talk frankly and informally in total confidence led to the notion that Bilderberg was some kind of secret plot to rule the world. I would have been delighted to be party to such a plot so long as it was well intentioned and in accordance with my own views. Sadly, Bilderberg was merely a political conference attended by people with widely differing political views and we never attempted to reach any policy conclusions or unanimous opinions of any kind.

The dominant personality at Bilderberg was Henry Kissinger, and several other veteran luminaries always attended alongside each year's newcomers. In the early years of the new century many of the leading neocons of the American Republican Party, newly in power in Washington, took part. People like Paul Wolfowitz and Richard Perle were regular attendees, as were others who were very close to the centre of foreign affairs policymaking in the US. I soon became aware, certainly from 2001 onwards, that the Bush administration, inspired by Vice President Dick Cheney and Defence Secretary Donald Rumsfeld, were planning to install a new government in Iraq.

The neocon arguments were reasonably worthy and almost idealistic in their own terms. They believed that when the Cold War had ended the United States had become the world's only military superpower. They felt that Bill Clinton had been negligent in failing to use that unstoppable military might to do good and to spread democratic liberal values. They now wanted to put this right, and chose Saddam Hussein in Iraq as their first target. They would invade, defeat the Iraqi army with ease and then sweep on to Baghdad where cheering crowds of Iraqis would welcome them as a liberating army. The subsequent election would produce a pro-American and pro-Israeli government led by Ahmed Chalabi.

The wider repercussions – claimed the neocons – would then produce further desirable change. President Assad in Syria would respond to the 'shock and awe' campaign by deciding to become the liberal reforming pro-Western leader that some Western politicians, including Peter Mandelson, had first hoped that he would be. 'The brave students of Tehran' would be inspired to rise and overthrow the ayatollahs and restore democracy to Iran. The whole of the Middle East would be transformed and Israel's future security safeguarded.

In one detailed conversation I had with one of the leading neocons, he went even further. The next phase would be to produce democratic change in the Gulf States, and in particular in Saudi Arabia. I do not think that he or the others contemplated military attack but rather believed that political pressure and intervention should be used to get rid of a medieval feudal dictatorship and replace it with a more secure modern democracy.

One of us was clearly living on a different planet. I had to accept the plan's curious idealism but I was left completely incredulous at its simplicity. Although I am not an expert on the Middle East, I feared that it did not remotely contemplate the political, tribal and cultural complexities of the region and its population. Unfortunately I was hearing all of this from the very men who were determining the Bush administration's foreign policy.

The plan's frightening naivety was further revealed in discussions with the neocons about the future government of Iraq. A military commander would be installed at first to oversee the transition to democracy whilst Mr Chalabi fought his election campaign, and then would remain in place, protecting Chalabi and ruling through him, for some years after that. There were constant references to General MacArthur in post-war Japan. I regret to say that I found that analogy, which plainly gave confidence to those working on the forthcoming military attack, quite ridiculous. I had met Chalabi, who had been living in exile in the US for some years, at a Bilderberg conference. I thought he was a rogue and a crook (he was a dodgy Iraqi businessman with a conviction in Jordan *in absentia* for bank fraud) and I failed to see why anyone thought he would win votes and public support in Iraq.

As a result of my experiences at Bilderberg I was used to arguing these issues long before it became clear that Tony Blair wanted the United Kingdom to take part in this invasion shoulder to shoulder with the Americans. He was a most unlikely ally of the ultra-right-wing President George W. Bush. I once challenged him about the president's obvious stupidity, and his complete domination by Cheney, Rumsfeld and their acolytes. Tony was amused but the most robust defence of Bush's intelligence that our normally persuasive prime minister could muster was, 'He is not as stupid as you think.'

Blair's difficulty in pursuing his dear wish of standing alongside President Bush was that the British Foreign Office put particular importance on the legality of the use of military force in international law. Military commanders were just as anxious to be reassured that their behaviour was lawful. Since regime change is not a legitimate basis for warfare in international law, Blair required an alternative, legal pretext. This resulted in the claim that Saddam Hussein possessed so-called weapons of mass destruction which he could use against the West. I never discovered any diplomat or intelligence agent who believed this claim, or that it was likely to come true in the near future. Eventually Saddam was forced to accept UN weapons inspectors, but the US and UK then managed to secure the passage of UN Resolution 1441 condemning him for not co-operating with the inspectors.

It was against this background that I began to engage in the debate in Britain about our participation in the proposed invasion. Several inquiries have now been carried out into the events that led up to it. However, my own impression was that Blair had decided at a very early stage that he would take a leading part in this military adventure. No doubt he accepted the Cheney case. I also think that he was perhaps attracted by the idea of participating in such a huge event on the international stage, seeing himself as the articulate advocate who would be able to influence US policy and mobilize international opinion behind an inarticulate American president.

The debate in Britain and in the House of Commons became increasingly alarming. Iain Duncan Smith led the Conservative Party into fervent support without much consultation with colleagues in the Shadow Cabinet or the party. The American neocons had always been the only people to have taken a serious interest in him on his visits to the United States and he was a natural convert to their cause.

I was opposed from the first. However, Tony Blair successfully avoided serious discussion on the floor of the House of Commons throughout most of the run-up to the war. Eventually, in late February 2003 when preparations were far advanced, he persuaded the House to vote for a motion in bland terms which was assumed to be based on the need for a further resolution at the United Nations before any attack could be authorized. I made it clear in my speech that I regarded the case for any military action as unproven, and the consequences as deeply concerning: 'Any war will be won easily . . . However, we should consider alternatives because of the consequences of war. How many terrorists will we recruit in the greater, long-standing battle against international terrorism? . . . What sort of leadership will replace that which might be deposed? . . . The next time a large bomb explodes in a Western city, or an Arab or Muslim regime topples and is replaced by extremists, the government must consider the extent to which the policy contributed to it. That is why Hon. Members should pause and why, unless evidence is produced for a breach and a material threat, my judgement today is that we should not go to war.' I abstained on the vote.

Blair had indeed persuaded a reluctant Bush to give him support in the hopeless quest to get a second resolution passed by the UN but he continued to make preparations for invasion after the predictable failure of his efforts.

The final debate on 18 March was a dramatic occasion in which I voted against the war. The final debate which gave Blair a parliamentary vote to authorize the war was only held at the last possible moment when everyone participating knew that British forces were assembled in the Middle East and that an invasion was going to take place in the next couple of days. About thirty-five Conservative MPs rebelled against the leadership and joined Labour voters in an outnumbered opposition lobby.

I continued to speak against the invasion after it had happened. The most prominent opponent of the invasion was the Labour Party's Foreign Secretary, Robin Cook, who resigned from his post to lead the opposition cause. I had always had great difficulty with Robin in the past. In the 1980s, when he had shadowed me at Health, he had always seemed to extend his political affinity to every contact between us, even behind the scenes, which prevented us from ever getting on friendly terms. I now warmed to him and, as I was the most prominent Conservative opponent of the war, we established a good personal relationship, which continued until his untimely death in August 2005.

The Conservative rebels on 18 March included my old friend John Gummer, who a few years later would hold a reunion dinner at his house in London for those of us who had opposed the party line. That evening brought home to me the astonishing variety of Conservative opinion that we represented: we extended from the far right to the far left of the broad Conservative coalition. Such a collection of people would never have agreed on any other major issue but we were all united in our opposition to the war in Iraq.

I regard the decision to invade Iraq as the most catastrophic foreign-policy decision taken by a British government in my lifetime, putting the Suez debacle completely into the shade as a minor error by comparison. Tony Blair, however, had totally convinced himself of the truth and worthiness of his cause and he spoke with eloquent and passionate sincerity throughout. The most striking exchange that I had with Blair was when I intervened in the middle of a brilliant speech that he was making in the House. He had been blazing with passion before giving way to hear me ask him whether he had considered the consequences of the appalling instability which the invasion would probably cause across the whole Middle East. He replied with vehemence and obvious incredulity. He laughed at my suggestion and derided the idea that the tyranny of Saddam Hussein was providing stability of any kind. I fear that the extent of the political collapse and anarchy in the years since then shows that I myself had under-estimated the risks.

I think that more Conservative MPs would have voted against the authorization of the war in the key vote if it had not been for the obvious imminence of actual engagement and the spirit of patriotism flowing through the country. Several friends, including Sir George Young, told me the day before the debate that they felt bound to follow the convention that Conservatives never voted against the British Army when it was engaged in operations in the field. Despite their serious reluctance, they therefore voted with Blair. He certainly won the argument in the country – at first, at least – and I recall an opinion poll showing that 70 per cent of the public supported the invasion when it went ahead. I occasionally recalled this in later years when it became the norm to form policy on a range of subjects in response to opinion polls.

Iain Duncan Smith's demise as leader came later in 2003, by which point his performance had become so catastrophic generally that a sufficient number of backbench MPs used the party's constitution to demand a vote on the leadership. I had absolutely nothing to do with the organization of the campaign against him, but I did vote against him in the ballot. Sadly his defeat was inevitable. Public support for Blair as prime minister was fading but the Conservative Party was in no condition to defeat him.

On the day that IDS was defeated, I was immediately approached by Michael Howard who asked me over the telephone whether I was going to stand in the forthcoming leadership election. I told him 'no' quite firmly. The party had become far too right wing and was utterly obsessed with Europe: as a pro-European enthusiast I would have been defeated if I had stood yet again. In any event, I also believed that the party's move to the right meant that we had no hope whatever of winning the next general election. Michael Howard would at least provide us with capable and professional leadership and produce a respectable defeat, rather than a catastrophic one. When I next got home Gillian was extremely annoyed with me when I recounted my conversation with Michael. She had been watching him on television saying firmly and apparently sincerely that he had not yet given any thought to whether he would be a candidate. In the event Michael was the only candidate who stood and was elected unopposed by the parliamentary party on 6 November 2003.

Michael conducted himself very competently inside and outside the House of Commons in the eighteen months that remained in the run-up to the 2005 general election. However, we would have done much better in 2005 if we had conducted the right campaign. Blair's standing was badly damaged, mainly due to the Iraq War, but unfortunately we could not take advantage of this. The leadership of the party had been firm supporters of the invasion and Michael Howard was one of the last remaining neocons prepared to give it his strong and continuing backing.

Michael also adopted the new fashionable campaigning tactics that Blair had introduced into British politics. He hired Lynton Crosby, an Australian 'guru' who was believed to be an expert in the best American methods of election campaigning. Together they fought a terrible campaign based almost entirely on resistance to immigration. This was probably an accident. Michael raised the subject early in the campaign in a bid to assuage anti-foreign prejudice against immigrants but, as was entirely predictable, this was taken up and enlarged by the popular media so that immigration ran rampant throughout the campaign. The party leadership was seemingly unable to redirect the debate and I encountered constituents who were steadily becoming more hostile to what they presumed was the prejudiced position that the party was adopting. My own campaigning did not touch upon the issue at all and I was comfortably re-elected to a Parliament in which Conservatives remained in a clear minority.

Throughout the campaign, Michael Howard's right-hand man in Parliament was David Cameron, who after a short stint as Michael's special adviser in 1993–4 had left to work at Carlton TV and then won a parliamentary seat in 2001. I admired David's ability but associated him with the conduct of the campaign. However, a chance remark he made to me in the corridor after leaving a One Nation group dinner gave me cause to reflect upon his personal position. This group of fairly moderate Conservative MPs had been giving

David a hard time about the tenor of the party's Opposition campaigning and David now asked me not to assume that he agreed with everything that was being said by his boss. I was reassured that, although he had been loyal to his leader in the discussions that evening, some of his own opinions continued to be as liberal as I suspected.

After our 2005 general election defeat Michael announced that he would stand down and I put myself forward as a candidate for the third and last time. I had the same band of enthusiastic supporters as ever. Once more I argued that the party had become too right wing and that we needed to appeal to the centre ground again if we ever wished to return to power. Once more, I refused in any way to tone down or to modify my views on the desirability of Britain remaining in the European Union. I hoped that the experience of losing the general election so heavily might cause the party to think about returning to its more centre-right mainstream tradition. As my campaign literature put it, 'If you are sometimes fed up and angry with our plight – as I am – you have a choice. You can give up, bail out, and call it a day. Or you can get stuck in, decide to fight, and give it your all. That is what I intend to do.'

The Conservative Party conference in early October was timed to be a key event between our general election defeat in May and the leadership contest, which formally started the day after the conference, on 7 October, but which had informally been going on throughout the summer.

In the long months between May and October, a wide range of potential candidates had made announcements about their intentions to stand, or not to stand, or to support one candidate or another. By the eve of the conference, five candidates appeared to be in the running: David Davis, David Cameron, Liam Fox, Malcolm Rifkind, and me.

David Cameron's candidature had been surprising because he was widely regarded as being far too young and inexperienced – although he was ably supported by George Osborne and other younger Members. Over the summer, my supporters and David Cameron's had tried to arrange a pact between us so that we did not divide our moderate vote. However, at a meeting arranged by Stephen Dorrell between David and me and groups of our respective parliamentary supporters, it became clear that while each of us was quite happy to combine with the other, we also each expected to be the number one candidate with the other as his deputy. David was as stubborn as I was and no agreement was reached. In any case, by 6 October, David Davis had established an enormous lead in all the polling of membership and it seemed certain he would be elected.

The conference changed all that. All five of us made platform speeches and four of us did extremely well. I made a very successful speech myself and secured a good standing ovation. David Cameron, Liam Fox and Malcolm Rifkind received equal ovations, with Malcolm making the best speech in my opinion. Unfortunately for Malcolm, his public standing had considerably diminished during his absence for two whole parliaments between 1997 and 2005 and his candidature was largely disregarded. David Davis, on the other hand, made the worst speech of his life. His biggest weakness had always been his public speaking and on this crucial occasion he made a dull and rambling speech which was poorly received.

David Cameron, however, made a quite brilliant platform speech in which he spoke fluently and convincingly and without notes. His standing ovation was no more enthusiastic than Malcolm's, Liam's or mine. However, he made an enormous impact because he was so surprisingly powerful and effective and he immediately began to be taken much more seriously. The 2005 conference was as decisive for Cameron as the 1963 conference had been for Alec Douglas-Home more than forty years earlier.

My candidature quickly began to fade, and by the time we returned to Parliament a couple of days later I found several of my friends were transferring their support to David. I realized that this was a sensible position for any Conservative MP in the large One Nation wing of the party. David's platform was almost identical to mine but he had none of the controversial political baggage that I had collected and he was far more likely to be able to give the party a fresh start.

The result was that I slipped to fourth place in the first ballot and David Cameron and David Davis went into the run-off. David

Cameron comfortably won amongst the membership at large because of his brilliant conference speech and the impact it had had on the broader electorate. Indeed, I voted for him myself.

Standing for the leadership of the Conservative Party is the only one of my many bad habits that I have ever given up. After David's election I decided I would contest no more, and looked forward to being a more satisfied Opposition MP with a dynamic party leader who could both rebuild the party and was undoubtedly a credible prime minister-in-waiting.

David had made only one mistake in the course of his leadership campaign. His team obviously could not bring themselves to believe that he was on his way to victory without the hard-line Eurosceptics and he was persuaded to reach out to them. He won their support by pledging to take the party out of the centre-right European People's Party (EPP) group in the European Parliament. This was totally unnecessary in terms of winning votes but David had to make good on the pledge immediately he took over as leader. It took him a long time to restore good relations with Europe's most important leader, the centre-right German Chancellor Angela Merkel, and her Christian Democratic Union party. In the meantime David slowly cobbled together a curious alternative group made up of all sorts of stray right-wingers including a mysterious Latvian nationalist, Roberts Zile, a maverick independent Swede and an ultra-right-wing Polish nationalist party, Law and Justice, run by a pair of very un-orthodox twins. The only respectable allies that he was able to find were in the fairly sensible Civic Democratic Party in the Czech Republic. This bedevilled David's relationship with Europe when he took power as prime minister in 2010, and resulted in him being unnecessarily blindsided at various points in important negotiations. It also drew him back into flirting with the Eurosceptic faction inside the parliamentary party, an approach which had comprehensively failed John Major.

Europe was at the forefront of the work I did during the 2005–10 parliament. I took an active part in protracted debates about a proposal to reform the treaties of the European Union – the Treaty of Rome and the Maastricht Treaty – and create a new European constitution. The reforms themselves, extending qualified voting to every significant subject and thereby making the Union much more effective, were highly desirable. However, the constitution came to disaster as various member countries held referenda and rejected it. In particular the French public gave it a resounding '*non*'. The idea of a constitution was abandoned and the key reforms re-emerged in 2007 in a new Treaty of Lisbon which member states were invited to ratify.

I took an even more active role in the 2008 parliamentary debates on the ratification of this new Treaty of Lisbon. The British party leaders – Gordon Brown, who had finally and disastrously succeeded in taking over the premiership from Tony Blair, David Cameron and Nick Clegg – were in a state of confusion because all three of them had foolishly promised that they would hold a referendum before ratifying the constitution, and by implication the successor treaty.

I, on the other hand, had never acknowledged the need for a referendum at all. I spoke in favour of the treaty and voted with the Labour government in every vote for which I was present, while the Conservative front bench adopted a series of quite absurd hard-line points of opposition.

In the course of all this, I established a very good relationship with Jim Murphy who was then Minister of State for Europe and leading on the legislation needed to ratify the treaty. In conversation, he expressed his amazement to me that most Conservatives could adopt such extreme and eccentric positions on practically every aspect of the debate. As just one example, in a debate on energy policy, which was not really varied in any way by the treaty, our frontbench spokesman had implied that the whole thing was a conspiracy to ensure that our energy supplies could be diverted from Birmingham to Berlin if ever the desire to do so arose. I welcomed Jim to an understanding of the bizarre nature of Conservative Euroscepticism.

For the purposes of the debate, I had a copy of the only authoritative consolidated version of the treaties, which put the Lisbon amendments into their full context. When I had tried to obtain a copy of this document from the Vote Office of the House of Commons,

I discovered that they did not possess one and no other MP had requested one. I had to go to the offices of the European Commission in London, which were ironically in the former HQ of the Conservative Party at 32 Smith Square, in order to track it down. In the course of the debates I realized that I was one of a tiny minority of the MPs debating the treaty in an agitated fashion who even possessed a copy of its commitments.

All three leaders found reasons to break their referendum promises and Parliament eventually ratified the Lisbon Treaty in July 2008. However, the rather unfortunate consequence of my dogged support of the government on Lisbon was that I was the most rebellious Conservative MP in the House of Commons for that session of Parliament.

As well as being active on the subject of Europe, I also took a very close interest in macroeconomic policy throughout my thirteen years in opposition to the Blair and Brown governments. My participation in debates and frequent criticism of Gordon Brown's Chancellorship rapidly led to a deterioration in my personal relationship with him. This was a shame, as we had actually been on very good terms when he had shadowed me as Chancellor: it has always been my belief that there is no reason to let political differences prevent friendly relations. I am afraid that Gordon's temperament did not permit him to be quite so relaxed about criticism and challenge when our roles were reversed. Even his best friend would not deny that Gordon was prone to extreme sensitivity which on occasions verged into paranoia. He seemed genuinely hurt whenever I did not agree with him and our friendly chats in the corridors of the Commons came to a fairly swift end. He instead took to doing a passable imitation of Edward Heath during the 'great sulk', and for many years grunts and nods were the best response that I could get from him. In exactly the same way as Heath had, after he fell from office Gordon immediately resumed friendly terms and on the rare occasions when he came to Parliament and we bumped into each other we would make a point of having long and interesting conversations.

The subject matter of our disagreements was certainly fascinating. For the first three years of his Chancellorship, between 1997 and

2000, Gordon stuck rigidly to the figures for taxation and public spending that I had published before the election. This was in line with the election commitments he and Blair had made. Frightened of risking the Labour Party's reputation for economic responsibility, Gordon fought, for public purposes at least, to adhere absolutely to my figures with no flexibility at all. I on the other hand had always proceeded on the basis that I would have an annual spending round involving debates with my Cabinet colleagues in which I would be able to switch some spending from one department to another in line with unexpected events, without threatening the overall figures. Brown's approach, which he described as 'prudence' at every opportunity with depressing and almost comic regularity, left him completely unable to switch spending between departments for three years, and therefore unable to correct the inevitable pressures that sprang up, principally in the NHS.

In reality Gordon tried to get around the difficulty he had created for himself by resorting to ingenious methods of accounting, favouring policies that involved expenditure that was off balance sheet and so not part of the published figures.

Gordon did of course inherit years of steady growth from me as well as sensible tax-and-spend figures. This delivered the budget surplus needed to reduce the level of public debt at the top of the economic cycle.

The comfortable situation I had handed over also coincided with, and was complicated by, a crazy financial bubble which produced a huge upswing in the markets based on the naive enthusiasm of the robotic lemmings who dealt in securities. These overpaid and suggestible individuals became obsessed with the IT revolution and poured money into ridiculously speculative ventures if they seemed to have a 'dot com' angle. The dot com bubble, the first of two periods of South Sea Island financial madness during the New Labour government, extended to every aspect of investment, with dot com innovations producing automatic and false increases in company valuations, and all sensible valuation or risk assessment abandoned. I saw the mania first-hand at BAT and Alliance Unichem, where the boards came under constant pressure from our major investors to embark on gimmicky dot com policies to give a boost to our share price.

The market soared, and Brown's tax revenues soared with it. While the bubble lasted the Treasury received a huge boost to its tax revenues, mainly as a result of enormous surges in credit and in City of London incomes. The New Labour government, sticking rigidly to its 'prudent' plans, was unable to use these windfall gains in any way other than to pay down the national debt. At one point both the Americans and the UK seemed well on course to pay off their entire respective stocks of debt, and pension-fund managers and others began to express alarm at the potential effects on their investment policies of neither government needing to issue bonds of any kind. Inevitably, though, the bubble burst and the crash came. Fortunately it did not have serious immediate consequences, but it did cause a collapse in the Treasury's tax revenues and brought an end to the era of 'prudence'.

After their promised three years of prudence, Blair and Brown rushed into an amazing boost in the level of public spending, and even allowed much of it to appear on balance sheet in the public accounts. Indeed they almost raced each other to make public spending announcements, with Tony Blair rushing to a television station to announce that the government would raise NHS spending to the European average of percentage of GDP, to the considerable annoyance of Gordon Brown, who had been preparing to take personal credit for a slightly differently formulated pledge to pour money into the NHS himself. There followed many years of increases in expenditure in most areas of government. This certainly produced a good climate of opinion for the government as a high proportion of the money went into huge increases in the number of public-sector jobs, and public-sector pay and pensions in particular were raised to new heroic levels. Inevitably, there were also some improvements in the levels of service to the public.

Even now, a great deal of expenditure was kept off balance sheet by ingenious accounting devices. Unfortunate Treasury officials were quite unable to stop the Chancellor from allowing public bodies to use the private finance initiative (PFI) to fund big capital projects. I had spent a great deal of time developing this policy but I had accepted advice about the strict discipline that would be needed, so that private finance was only so described if it involved a genuine and full transfer of risk to the private investor who was intending to design, build or manage a particular project. We had had great difficulty persuading banks of the need for this. Financiers hoped that the government would give them a guaranteed return on any contract that they financed, in line with the usual extravagance of public-sector commercial dealings. I resisted, which is why our government never succeeded in placing any significant number of PFI contracts.

That we failed to place any significant contracts whilst we were in government was also partly because Labour had attacked the wicked capitalist idea of private financing of public projects, and so financiers were justifiably worried that they might be cancelled. In practice, the Labour government embraced PFI with naive enthusiasm and placed enormous numbers of contracts for new hospitals and colleges and public projects with a total indifference to the costs or risks involved and using inexperienced civil servants to negotiate terms.

Gordon Brown also carried out an amazing expansion of the welfare state by expanding a benefit known as tax credits. This was a system whereby government topped up the incomes of employees on low pay, introduced at a modest level in time for the 2001 election. In order to keep the expenditure off balance sheet Gordon gave the new benefit its bizarre title and insisted that it should be paid out by the Inland Revenue, rather than by the Department of Work and Pensions. When I challenged him in the House of Commons he denied that it was public expenditure and said that, based on its home in the Revenue, it was a tax measure and was actually 'negative expenditure'. Gordon was eventually persuaded to give up his accounting device and after a few years it was deemed to be public expenditure.

The Inland Revenue had in my time been an excellent department for collecting sums of money from unwilling taxpayers. It was, however, quite unsuited to paying out weekly benefits to wage earners on restricted family budgets. It made a huge number of errors in calculating the tax credit due, because the payments were based on estimates of family incomes, estimates that regularly turned out to be wrong. The hard-pressed recipient was then expected to be able to repay any overpayments.

Gordon continued to increase benefits in all kinds of general and particular ways, so that in the end a huge proportion of the working population received a government wage or salary on top of their employer's pay. The government really began to subsidize the depressed wage levels paid by weaker or less scrupulous employers, resulting in the UK developing a low-pay, low-productivity economy in more difficult economic years.

Examples of unjustified or unwise expenditure abounded and I began to intervene with speeches in Budgets and economic debates urging the case for fiscal discipline. During the times of economic and financial boom this was not a widespread or popular position. I did though often find myself near to agreement with my old Cambridge contemporary Vince Cable, who had entered Parliament as a Jenkinsite Liberal Democrat in 1997, and who like me spoke on behalf of his party urging fiscal restraint.

In the last years of the Blair government this all took a further alarming turn. The Western world entered into another, even bigger financial bubble with an explosion of uncontrolled credit in Wall Street and the City. The credit boom of 2006 led to the most extraordinarily reckless lending to householders and to businesses at very low rates of interest. Banks in the United States and Britain made use of misleading devices to remove debt from their balance sheets. The sensible system – if done on a modest scale – of securitization of debt was turned into a monstrous arrangement to disguise risk from published accounts. Inevitably the credit boom led to a credit crash with banks throughout North America and Europe facing insolvency from which they had to be rescued by their governments. A huge crisis of sovereign debt, household debt and collapsed financial systems swept from its starting point in America and Britain through the developed world.

The credit boom had of course produced another immense surge in tax revenues for the Treasury. Gordon had not only spent this bonanza but had also continued to run a deficit on top of the bloated revenues to finance yet more electorally popular projects and policies.

When the boom inevitably turned to bust, and the collapse came, Britain was left with the worst fiscal deficit of any government in the G20 as a percentage of our GDP. Many people suffered as we experienced the longest and deepest economic recession since the war, from which it took many years to begin to make a recovery.

I cannot claim that I had seen all this coming. Although I was involved with one or two asset-management companies and hedge funds I did not have huge experience or expertise in this area.

I had, though, been alerted to the dangers of crazy credit creation at a meeting of various European political and economic policy-making figures at a conference arranged by my old friend the former French finance minister Edmond Alphandéry. There, the former World Bank chief executive Jacques de Larosière interrogated the various overexcited financiers and politicians present with considerable skill. He played the innocent and asked how risk was being managed in one or two of the ingenious accounting practices that he described. He was, of course, confronted by people who patiently and wearily explained to him that he was out of date, and did not understand the new paradigms. I took little part in this discussion but it slowly dawned upon me that Jacques was the great voice of common sense in the whole debate. When the overpaid young started telling us veterans that 'this time it is different', I began to worry.

I had also certainly commented on the complete uselessness of those who were supposed to regulate risks in this field. Gordon Brown's great new creation of the Financial Services Authority did not seem to understand that it had any macroeconomic regulatory role at all and, so far as I am aware, never queried the absence of any sensible risk management from almost all our great financial institutions. But I had not fully appreciated the greed and incompetence of the great bankers of the English-speaking world.

The next Conservative Chancellor, George Osborne, had to tackle the task of returning the British economy to economic sanity and health. He inherited a position so far removed from the one I had handed over to Gordon Brown that his problems made my own, back in the 1990s, seem like a walk in the park.

24

'Straight Life'
(Art Pepper, 1979)

MINISTRY OF JUSTICE

I am quite sure that it was George Osborne who in 2009 persuaded David Cameron to ask me to join the front bench again. George had had almost no knowledge of or background in macroeconomic policy when he became Shadow Chancellor in 2005, but he was making a good fist of handling his portfolio. He was a quick learner and he swiftly began to establish some authority. However, he and David understandably felt under pressure because they were widely regarded as novices, their inexperience contrasting sharply with the undoubted economic knowledge and presence of former Chancellor and prime minister Gordon Brown.

George also got himself into trouble when he quarrelled with Peter Mandelson, over conversations on board a luxury yacht belonging to the Russian oligarch Oleg Deripaska. This was made public in an absurd flurry of media-promoted political gossip, shaking George's standing, and it was against this backdrop that George and David approached me, presumably in a bid to restore some appearance of experience to the Tory front bench.

I was enjoying my business career and was not in any way expecting ever to resume a ministerial role. I obviously would have to give up my various non-executive directorships, which I was enjoying very much, and I was also dubious about whether I could fit into the new Blairite style of politics which the Conservative Party had now adopted. However, David pressed me in a friendly and persuasive way and eventually succeeded. We agreed that I should shadow Peter Mandelson at the Department of Business and that I would serve in Cabinet for about two years if we won the election: I was not going to endure the tiresome business of being a Shadow minister unless I could have a last taste of substance.

Peter Mandelson was a man with whom I had always got on extremely well and whose abilities as a political strategist and policymaker I greatly admired. In fact I liked him much better than any member of the Labour Party did, apart from Tony Blair himself. Tony had once told me that his two goals as prime minister had been to get the British public to love Europe and the Labour Party to love Peter Mandelson. He also admitted that he had failed in both aims. Peter had been doing an excellent job in the European Commission as the trade commissioner and had only allowed Gordon Brown to persuade him to return to British public life in order to play his part in saving from disaster the New Labour 'project' to which he had devoted his life. Peter was an impressive Secretary of State for Business but his return to government was always going to be difficult because Gordon had blamed Peter for the original 'Granita pact' – the deal done over dinner in 1994 at which Gordon had been persuaded to step aside to allow Tony Blair to become leader of the Labour Party. Ever since then they had detested each other with a deep and bitter loathing.

I shadowed Peter in a responsible way, preparing myself to be Secretary of State for Business and a supportive ally of George Osborne if we managed to regain power. I accommodated Peter's general enthusiasm for plotting and conspiracy by having meetings with him in his room in the House of Lords on an almost weekly basis, at which we would discuss the important issues he was considering and try to reach agreement. I would then support him in every decision that was genuinely in the national interest – rather than pointlessly, or for party political reasons, opposing decisions that would be of value to the economy when we took power – and vigorously oppose him where we disagreed. I found myself in opposition mode far more frequently in the last few months as Peter became more desperate, and began to spend money like a Bourbon monarch.

The steady collapse of Gordon Brown's government made Peter's attempt to save New Labour a thoroughly hopeless task. As I observed Gordon get into ever more trouble in the House of Commons it was plain to me that he was cracking up under the strain. Gordon had always been a workaholic, keeping bizarre working hours and trusting no one. Under pressure, he was also inclined to a degree of paranoia and suspicion. Watching him in the Commons in the summer before the eventual 2010 election I thought on occasions that he was so pale-faced and tense that he was almost dysfunctional, and I really did fear for his well-being. He managed to recover and fight a respectable general election campaign in 2010, but his government was in ruins and he was quite unable to win an overall majority.

David Cameron and George Osborne fought a reasonably good and responsible campaign. I thought at the outset that we were going to win, because the Labour government was being held accountable for Britain's collapse into the worst financial crisis of my lifetime and into the deepest and longest recession since the Second World War. This was justified: the financiers had been reckless and greedy, but the government, and the regulators, had been useless. I did, however, think that George was a little politically reckless in modestly trailing a desire for cuts in public spending, a point on which I thought we should obfuscate. He was right and responsible and I was wrong. George's approach gave his policies a democratic legitimacy which they would otherwise have lacked.

Unfortunately, the British public could not quite forget the absurd excesses committed by the Conservative Party in its previous Eurosceptic and right-wing frenzies, and it became clear that many electors were hesitant about putting Tories back into power. My old friend Nick Clegg took advantage of this, helped significantly by the innovation of the televised leaders' debates, which he deftly used to portray the main political parties as 'the old politics' at a time of intense disillusionment with politics and politicians. The only time I was given a central role in a press conference at party HQ, I therefore took the opportunity to make some outspoken remarks about the dangers of coalition government. I firmly believed that the tribalism of British political parties would make a successful Continental-style coalition impossible.

My warnings though went unheeded by the public, and on the morning of 7 May 2010 we found ourselves the biggest single party in a hung Parliament. I was certain – despite my misgivings about coalitions – that a minority government would not be able to achieve anything at all useful in the British parliamentary system. At hurried small gatherings of Shadow Cabinet members I therefore urged strongly upon David Cameron that it was his duty to try to form an effective coalition with the Liberal Democrats. After the skilled, friendly and rapid negotiation of a coalition agreement, in which I played no part, we found ourselves returning to office with David Cameron as prime minister. For the first time in my life I was now a member of a coalition government.

The business portfolio had to be given to my old friend Vince Cable, who was the best expert on economic policy in the Liberal Democrat Party, although he was also the most left-wing social democrat in the new Cabinet. I had no idea what was going to happen to me when I was summoned to meet David Cameron in Number 10, and I am not sure that David did either. David very generously was obviously prepared to honour his promise to give me two years in government. He was also plainly concerned about what on earth he might be able to do with me. His first approaches to me were rather nervous but he brightened up enormously when he threw out the suggestion that I might become Lord Chancellor and Secretary of State for Justice and saw that I was quite delighted with this idea. I explained that it would give me an opportunity to return to the enthusiasms of my youth, and I would also welcome the chance to reacquaint myself with the law and the legal profession, within which I had quite a lot of friends. And so, to my great surprise, I found myself holding a new office with responsibilities in areas which interested me but which I had never remotely expected to hold.

Having received the glad tidings from Downing Street that I was to become Justice Secretary, I discovered that no Number 10 official knew where the headquarters of the department was. I returned to my office in Parliament for some lunch, and to try to find out.

Eventually my old friend and driver ever since my days as a junior transport minister, Roy Gibbons, was despatched to come and take me over to Petty France.

I was astonished to discover that the Ministry of Justice occupied the bleak and ugly concrete fortress that Sir Basil Spence had provided for the Home Office. However, a vast refurbishment had been carried out by the Labour government. No expense had been spared in the cause of providing modern brighter offices and rooms and converting the building's former car park into a vast and magnificent glass-covered atrium. It had become traditional for officials to turn out en masse to welcome their new ministers and a huge crowd of officials were waiting for me in the glorious new atrium. To my embarrass-ment, I realized that I had been expected for some time: this was the third or fourth time they had all turned out. Nevertheless, I was ushered in smoothly by my new permanent secretary, Suma Chakrabarti, and shown my new and rather smart office, accompan-ied by my wide-eyed Opposition aides who would now become my special advisers. David Hass had joined me from George Osborne's office when I had rejoined the front bench. He was a former BBC man and became my media adviser with a particular interest in prisons policy. He was a good friend and trusted working companion. Kathryn Laing, whom I had recruited from a field of applicants, was very young and highly intelligent and acted as my close adviser and confidante on policy and political matters. The two of them were not only a good influence on me, but were also more than capable of protecting me against the demands that soon began to come from Downing Street to make me more compliant with the bizarre modern practices of twenty-first-century control-freak government and political campaigning.

First things first. Before I was able to get down to the real business of running the Justice Ministry, I was despatched to Ede & Ravenscroft on Chancery Lane ('We supply ceremonial robes for all occasions') to be fitted out in the eccentric costume required by all Lord Chancellors. Part of the role was to make public appearances about five times a year wearing a most marvellous outfit. The robe was at least as mag-nificent as that of the Chancellor of the Exchequer and with the full-blown accessories of wig and silver-buckled shoes provided quite a spectacle. It was similar to the garb I had worn a few times as a QC in the 1980s, so I was relieved to discover that modern technology had come to my aid in the business of actually putting on these extremely complicated items of clothing. Velcro enabled knee breeches and other key elements to be fastened without fiddling with endless buckles and belts, which were still present but were now mainly ornamental. And I discovered to my great relief that the final innovation was a smart set of full black tights which gave the required smooth effect without the need for wearing ladies' suspenders. In my opinion, I could still show a shapely calf when wearing tights with my knee breeches. I also still remembered how to put on a full-bottomed wig without it sitting up awkwardly and making me look like a basset hound.

The splendour of my passage on ceremonial occasions was enhanced greatly by the young officials in my excellent Private Office who would also don eighteenth-century costumes and turn themselves into my purse- and mace-bearers, and a court attendant who was my Tipstaff. They would precede me as I processed to private and public occasions of which the most solemn was the State Opening of Parliament.

My role in this ceremony was to present the Queen's Speech to Her Majesty who would be seated in her robes on the throne in the House of Lords. I resolved to do this without stumbling or falling by following the practice which Her Majesty had ordered Lord Hailsham to follow twenty-five years earlier. This was to turn around and walk sensibly down the steps of the throne and back to my place rather than complying with the ancient duty of stepping backwards to avoid turning my back on my monarch.

I am actually a great supporter of British traditional ceremonial, though I prefer it when other people dress up and provide the entertainment. But I am a notoriously bad and sloppy dresser and found it slightly ironic to be playing the role of the splendid Lord Chancellor myself. I have also always been particularly amazed that the British engage in these things at closed private gatherings as much as public ones: my annual ritual encounter with the lord mayor and the aldermen, all of us in our magnificence, sipping on the 'Loving Cup' and nibbling at the 'Loving Shortbread' on silver platters, took place with very few witnesses in the ceremonial rooms of the House of Lords.

My daughter Susan brought my six-year-old granddaughter Sophie to witness one of these mayoral ceremonies. They were almost the only people sitting in the huge and magnificent Royal Gallery when a mace-bearer threw open the end doors and shouted 'Make way for the Lord High Chancellor.' Little Sophie loudly and clearly shouted, 'I think we should stand up now,' and solemnly watched my procession go by, my two dutiful relatives standing to attention. She also enjoyed the shortbread.

Once all the excitement of my arrival in the department had died down, we all settled around the boardroom table, and I was introduced to the key members of my new team. Darren Tierney, a cheerful Irishman and a great pleasure to work with, was my new private secretary. He had assembled a keen team of extremely young officials to help him, and was eventually succeeded by the equally capable Mark Sweeney. After some opening remarks, Suma handed over to Darren to discuss 'diary matters'. Darren asked me about the rhythm to my week and when I sought clarification said, 'Well, things like, when do you usually travel to Nottingham, do you want time set aside for lunches with journalists,' and then – perhaps casting around for a third idea – 'or, do you need time carved out for the gym?' Suma shot Darren a withering look as I leant back in my chair and told my new private secretary, 'I don't think that will be necessary.'

The next question was about what I wanted to do in the new department, which was responsible for the entire civil and criminal justice system, including criminal justice policy, the courts, and the prisons.

I had not the first idea of what the Conservative Party had been doing in terms of justice policy in opposition but someone handed me a printout of the key section of the Conservative Party website, of which I had never previously been aware. It seemed to include a lot of expensive commitments to build more prisons and extend sentences, particularly for knife crime. My instant reaction was that this was merely an extension of the reactionary and counterproductive policies which every Home Secretary after me, from Michael Howard onwards, had pursued. While crime levels had been falling in every Western country over the last two decades, regardless of sentencing policy, incarceration levels in England and Wales had risen steadily, roughly doubling from about 45,000 to 80,000 since I had been Home Secretary. This had been based entirely on Michael Howard, David Blunkett and the rest trying to respond to the various campaigns in the tabloid press, in particular the *Sun*. Thereafter I did not consult my party's election website again.

It was clear to me that the continuing financial crisis meant that the Ministry of Justice budget would have to be cut dramatically. This would require us to stabilize the prison population, or preferably reduce it, to close some of the more unacceptable prisons we had, and to significantly reduce the legal-aid budget. These policies were not just forced on me by fiscal reality: happily, they were what I believed in. I quickly resolved that they would form the basis of my programme.

The first months of the government were entirely consumed by the Treasury's need to deliver a sharp reduction in public-expenditure plans and tackle the debt crisis. I had no negotiations of any kind with George Osborne but I was determined to make the biggest contribution that I could. I therefore settled down with my new permanent secretary Suma Chakrabarti to draw up our proposals. I was happy to discover that Suma was a dominant force in the department and was personally as keen as I was to reduce the level of public expenditure in the wider public interest. He readily produced a number of radical proposals to which I made additions, and we thrashed out for ourselves the figure we believed we could deliver. This was quite an achievement: in my entire experience of being in government, I had never encountered an attempt to reduce spending on anything to do with law and order.

To be fair, equally remarkable reductions were put forward by Theresa May as Home Secretary, from a department that was accustomed to recruiting more and more police officers each year. It was unfortunate to say the least, however, that once we began to run into serious press troubles with our efforts to reduce the prison population and achieve the agreed spending reductions, the prime minister's entourage suddenly become rather less zealous than they had been in pursuit of a headline figure.

The immediate impact of these reductions was made very noticeable to me in my everyday work. A proportion of the savings inevitably had to come from reducing the excessive number of officials employed by the department and I had the slightly sad experience of walking through a large open-plan area full of empty desks every time I came into the office.

The really significant savings, though, were to come from prison and legal-aid reform.

I believed now no less than I had as Home Secretary that prison was the proper penalty for serious, persistent and committed criminals. Equally, I continued to regard it as a wholly unsuitable place to detain unpleasant waifs and strays whose problems were mainly caused by personal inadequacy, drug addiction or mental-health issues. I found that the prisons were now full of such people, often deprived of proper attention for their drug or alcohol problems, or for their inability to obtain work because of their lack of basic numeracy, literacy and other skills. Incarcerating such individuals alongside hardened criminals merely served to toughen them up and to introduce them to serious villains with whom they could associate upon release. This no doubt explained why almost 50 per cent of offenders were returned to jail within twelve months of leaving. The impression that I had formed from my experience of the criminal classes as a barrister was that the best chance of a young inexperienced offender turning himself into an honest man was if he could acquire upon release a girlfriend, a flat and a job. (The problems for women offenders, of whom there were very few, were quite different and very difficult. I worked hard at continuing my predecessor's policy of reducing their number by finding other ways of tackling the distressing personal problems they almost all had.)

I worked to improve health facilities in prison hospitals and to ensure that mentally ill prisoners should, if possible, be admitted by the NHS into suitable institutional care. I also did my best to encourage prisoner education because of the astonishing proportion of inmates who were functionally illiterate and innumerate and had never had a job. Most importantly I strove to expand private-sector training opportunities for prisoners, to prepare them for future employment. The pioneers in this last policy were the remarkable retailers, Timpson, who specialized in shoe repairs, key cutting and engraving. The major obstacle to faster expansion of this programme came, as ever, from the sheer lack of space in the prison estate which had been caused by the bloating of the prison population.

Realizing that my liberal and reforming instincts were not shared by several of my Cabinet colleagues, I used the crisis of public spending and government debt to my advantage. I argued with shocked colleagues that we could not afford to carry on with the former policies and often used the anecdotal claim that it was more expensive to keep a man in prison than it was to send him to Eton, which seemed an appropriate comparison. I was also greatly assisted by the fact that we were in coalition with the Liberal Democrats. I was already on very good terms with all my Liberal colleagues, particularly Nick Clegg, Vince Cable and Chief Secretary to the Treasury Danny Alexander. In my suddenly converted opinion, we were much more successful throughout our five-year term in coalition than a single-party Conservative government could have been.

I was also able to sell to my colleagues as a cost-saving measure the introduction of more privately owned and managed prisons. This policy, which I had introduced as Home Secretary in the early 1990s, had been allowed to lapse in recent years. Although it certainly could yield savings, the main attraction for me was that it introduced a widening range of providers who would introduce new methods and new ideas for the incarceration and the training of offenders. I did not and do not believe that public-sector management is necessarily inferior or superior to private-sector management: indeed, some of the contracts that we put out to tender were awarded to the Prison Service. I do, however, believe that an element of competition and even choice for the Secretary of State is a valuable incentive to improve outputs and performance. There were some very good private-sector prisons and there were also some very bad ones, but the overall management ethos of these institutions was stimulated by bringing in new approaches. I have no idea why my eventual successor Chris Grayling promptly cancelled this policy upon taking office. My more 'right-wing' colleagues were often wetter than me on free-market matters.

Another major reform I implemented was to the bloated legal-aid system. The availability of legal aid across the whole range of litigation had increased enormously since my time in practice. There were also now at least ten times as many lawyers, the amount of litigation had exploded, and the length of any single piece of litigation – civil or criminal – was at least twice what it had been in my day. Britain now had by far the most expensive state legal service in the world.

Some lawyers have argued that we should have a National Legal Service to match the National Health Service but we had never been able to afford that. Legal aid was provided to those deemed unable to afford any legal advice of their own, and people had to have very little income indeed to qualify. As a result the British civil legal system has never been open equally to all citizens. Only the very rich and the very poor have ever been able to cheerily contemplate going to the courts to resolve disputes.

The department had been trying to sell savings in the cost of criminal legal aid to my predecessor, Jack Straw. They had devised a curious proposal to put out legal-aid criminal work to competitive block tendering which was also to be accompanied by a substantial reduction in the fees paid to lawyers for individual cases. I flatly rejected this and left criminal legal aid undisturbed.

I took a different view on the amazingly wide availability of legal aid for civil litigation. Family law especially had exploded and I had a particular concern about the vast amount of contentious litigation that now surrounded the break-up of many marriages. Courtroom battles are the worst possible way of reaching a civilized resolution between former spouses who have come to hate one another. Frequently one spouse, usually the wife, would be devoid of assets and income and therefore able to obtain legal aid in order to mount numerous claims against a former husband who would be obliged to pay for any resistance. I therefore cut back severely on legal aid for these cases and promoted mediation as a more civilized, sensible and cost-effective way to resolve such claims.

I was also particularly cheese-paring on human rights including immigration cases. No one prizes more than me the virtues of justice being done in every case of this kind. Unfortunately, this had been turned by some specialist practices into something of a racket, in which fanciful claims and repetitive appeals were brought. I therefore reduced the scope for legal aid for repeated appeals in these cases.

Inevitably, this proved to be a highly contentious issue for some sections of the legal profession and I was reminded that lawyers were amongst the most powerful and well-represented pressure groups within both Houses of Parliament.

When Chris Grayling took over from me as Justice Secretary, he was not at all interested in reforming the prison system in a liberal direction, nor in reducing the prison population. Inevitably therefore he had to return to seek more savings from the legal-aid system. He revived the disastrous proposals for criminal legal aid, which dragged him into prolonged and unsuccessful controversy during much of his term of office.

Reading the copious briefing required to get me up to speed on my portfolio, I also quickly decided that one no-brainer cost-saving reform was the closure of a large number of courts which were extremely underused. I decided to get on with this as quickly as possible. I therefore announced in the summer of 2010 the intended closure of over a hundred underused and redundant court buildings across the country, after a short period of local consultation in each area. The furore this rather mild spending decision caused amongst the Downing Street entourage underlined their extreme naivety about what was to come. The prime minister's most eccentric but usually creative adviser, Steve Hilton, was furious at what he regarded for some reason as an attack on his localism agenda. David Cameron's mother, who unbeknown to me was herself a magistrate, became a figure of major concern. My planned written statement was pored over in Number 10 and attempts made to delay it. Eventually I got fed up with this, published the statement and handed the whole policy area over to my highly able junior minister, Jonathan Djanogly. He handled the whole thing beautifully, with barely a murmur of dissent. We saved the prime minister's mother's courthouse, in the light of the response to the public consultation. In fact, all the most vigorous opponents of the policy seemed to come from within Number 10.

Part of my problem in persuading colleagues to adopt a more sensible criminal justice policy was that some of them had a mordant fear of the right-wing press, and in particular of the *Sun*. Rupert Murdoch's representative on earth as far as I could work out was Rebekah Brooks, a former editor of the *Sun* who would later become notorious, but at this point was merely famous and powerful. As far as I am aware the only encounter I ever had with Rebekah took place at the 2010 Conservative Party conference, shortly after we had returned to office. I had been induced to abandon the enterprising bed-and-breakfast independence of my Opposition years, and was holed up at enormous expense along with the rest of the Conservative members of the Cabinet in the Radisson Edwardian in Birmingham.

The prime minister sent word to me that he thought I should meet with Rebekah Brooks, who was by now a key executive in the Murdoch empire, and evidently a figure of great influence with my young friends who were running the government. She was obviously accustomed to meeting with Home Secretaries and Justice Secretaries and having her advice taken seriously.

During her time at the *Sun* Rebekah had perfected the 'celebrity victim' style of campaigning. This comprised front-page stories based on cases in which a reasonably attractive, usually female victim had experienced an unpleasant crime. The presumption of innocence until proven guilty was discarded, to be substituted by prurient and hysterical reporting. This would increase after sentencing, when the judge would be subjected to extreme abuse because of his supposed leniency. Each campaign would require the introduction of a new law imposing longer minimum sentences for the offence in question.

Tony Blair's Home Secretaries and Justice Secretaries had responded with unbelievable deference, producing a collection of ever more prescriptive sentencing laws, usually named after the unfortunate victim. This had contributed to a complete mess – for example, it seemed completely bizarre that the minimum sentence for murder with a knife was significantly higher than that for an equally vicious murder with a poker.

So, it was with great interest that I accepted my summons and duly turned up on the top floor of the Radisson, to be ushered into an extravagant part of the hotel near the prime minister's suite and with floor-to-ceiling windows looking across the skyline of Birmingham. On the table in front of me was an array of rather delicate Marie Antoinette-style cakes of various pastel shades, and behind them the figure of Rebekah Brooks who appeared to be dressed as if for riding, in long shiny boots with trousers tucked into them, and her trademark cascade of red hair.

We engaged in friendly conversation for some time, during which she gave me her views about the governance of the realm, until eventually she got to the point of this particular audience, which was her conviction that what would sort out the overcrowding problems of the criminal justice system was some prison ships. Failing that, she would be interested in the introduction of military-style boot camps. It now became clear why my political advisers David and Kathryn had been fending off remarkably similar suggestions from Downing Street over the last few weeks. I shared with Rebekah my view that prison ships would not only be rather expensive, they would also be a totally unproductive, inhumane and useless addition to a penal system. With no space for worthwhile activities of any sort, their only purpose would be to warehouse offenders in utter boredom, until they were thrust back out into their communities, no better and probably worse than when they had arrived. We reached no great conclusions and I took no action on Rebekah's suggestions. Indeed, I never met her again.

Court closures and prison ships were only the beginning of my difficulties with Number 10. Sadly, David Cameron had become fully converted to Tony Blair's general style of government, which involved bringing in a large number of political advisers, effectively to create a full-blown department in Number 10. Previous prime ministers had managed with a small Civil Service Private Office, a handful of high-powered political advisers, and of course access to the great mass of officialdom that inhabited the Cabinet Office. The huge entourage that now gathered around David largely comprised young people from think tanks, or from the PR industry or journalism, some of whom were rather out of their depth. Most of them regarded their sole mission as to second-guess and direct the work of Cabinet ministers.

I simply refused to be part of this system and acted as a Cabinet minister in the way to which I was accustomed. I gave media interviews and made public statements without bothering to seek permission for a slot in the 'grid' (the managed media timetable planned by Number 10). I did not use slogans or take guidance on the 'line to take'. After some time I discovered that my special advisers were constantly fending off Downing Street aides, urging them to get me under control. I told Kathryn that she should simply say that she could do nothing to stop me and suggest to them that they take their complaints up directly with me. No one from the prime minister downwards ever so much as mentioned my disregard of 'message discipline' to me. I assume my veteran status gave me special dispensation.

I also discovered within my first few weeks that policy aides from Number 10 were in the habit of visiting my department and holding meetings with my civil servants at which policy proposals would be developed and prepared. I put an immediate stop to this and instructed the permanent secretary that these people were no longer to be admitted, and that departmental civil servants were not to hold meetings with them without my consent. I said that if anyone wanted to come over from Number 10 to discuss policy, I would happily chair a meeting myself. They never came again so far as I was aware, and there was no take-up of my offer. I did receive occasional complaints, indirectly, and was told that these meetings were essential because the prime minister was anxious to make a speech on criminal justice as soon as possible. I declared myself perfectly willing to meet with the prime minister myself if he wished to discuss policy or the possible contents of a speech. That ended all further talk of the direct supervision of my department, and the prime minister's speech was placed firmly in the long grass.

There were particular advisers in Number 10 who were a constant source of difficulty because they flatly disagreed with my approach. Andy Coulson, formerly editor of the *News of the World*, was the prime minister's director of communications and played a leading part in his relations with the media and the wider public. He had obviously been appointed as Rupert Murdoch's representative in Number 10 and sought to exert great influence. I constantly strived to develop a reasonable personal relationship with him and our occasional lunches together at least allowed us to avoid excessive strain. My other chief opponent was Patrick Rock whom I had last known, and never previously quarrelled with, as special adviser to Michael Howard at the Home Office. He had now become David Cameron's deputy director of policy, with particular responsibility for criminal justice. Throughout all my contact with these two individuals it was quite obvious that there was no political meeting of minds between us.

All three of my principal challengers on the subject of 'law and order' were eventually arrested and committed for criminal trial themselves. At the time of writing, Rebekah Brooks has been acquitted of the charges against her, Andy Coulson has served a prison sentence, and Patrick Rock has been convicted on child pornography charges.

Serious reform, and progress on our spending settlement, both turned on a draft Criminal Justice Bill containing a whole raft of proposals on legal aid, sentencing and offender management. I had of course followed the rules of collective clearance and presented my proposals for the bill to a proper meeting of the Home Affairs Cabinet Committee, where I had persuaded some difficult colleagues to clear it. I was no doubt helped by the fact that the Home Affairs Committee chairman was Nick Clegg, and its deputy chairman was me.

My proposals had involved abolishing several mandatory sentences – i.e. offences for which judges were required to impose a particular minimum sentence. The circumstances and severity of different cases involving the same legal offence could vary hugely, as could the circumstances of the offender. I was strongly of the view that these aggravating and mitigating factors should dictate the sentence, and that judges therefore needed a wide degree of discretion to impose the sentence that the public interest demanded. Standardization and conformity with basic norms would continue to be ensured by the work of the Sentencing Council, presided over by a senior judge, which laid down guidelines and advice to ensure consistency from court to court.

The prime minister was shocked when he found out about these measures – and about some of the other measures that the Home Affairs Committee had cleared for my bill. He insisted that I came to see him. At one point in our first one-to-one meeting on the topic he explained that I was planning to repeal 'Ben's Law'. This was a reference to legislation Jack Straw had introduced in 2009, which had increased the minimum sentence for murder with a knife from fifteen years to twenty-five. David was appalled that I was contemplating reversing this, and even more shocked that I had never heard of 'Ben's Law'.

Newspapers then started a campaign against another one of my proposals, which someone had leaked, to offer a discount of up to a third in an offender's sentence if they entered a guilty plea before their trial had started. The principle of a discount for an early plea was a long-established part of the criminal justice system, and this proposal to increase and regularize it was wholly justifiable. Early pleas save witnesses and victims the trauma of being forced to testify, and save the taxpayer the expense of a trial. The proposal would help to deliver the financial savings to which we were committed, and, just as importantly, was key to the liberal, reforming penal policy and reduction in the prison population which were my overriding object-ives. As I went out to argue my case, I was reminded that my reforming policies had sparked lively controversies in every department in which I had ever served.

This all turned into a tricky face-to-face negotiation with the prime minister, with David insisting that I should drop both my abolition of mandatory minimum sentences and my proposals on early guilty pleas. Although I did not threaten directly to resign he must have guessed that I saw little point in carrying on as Justice Secretary if I was expected simply to follow the childlike precepts of some of my predecessors.

Fortunately, as so often happened in moments of apparent political crisis, a solution emerged from one of my aides, working frantically away on my behalf back in the office. On this occasion the splendid idea came from the brilliant Kathryn Laing. It centred around another controversial sentence, the Imprisonment for Public Protection (IPP). The IPP, introduced in 2003 by the then Home Secretary David Blunkett, was a complete injustice of a sentence and was causing huge logistical problems for prisons. The idea was that an offender would be given a minimum sentence, after which they would be eligible for release, but only if they satisfied a Parole Board hearing that they were no longer a danger to the public. Since they could not be released if they couldn't pass this test, it was a completely open-ended, or indeterminate, sentence.

The difficulty was that it is almost impossible for anyone, however professionally experienced, to predict with confidence the future behaviour of any prisoner upon release from jail. The retired judges who comprised most of the Parole Board had also become terrified of media denunciation if ever anyone they had released went on to commit a serious offence. We were therefore faced with rising numbers of offenders – in the thousands – languishing behind bars for many years after the end of the sentence handed down to them. In my view this was a complete travesty and counter to all the assumptions of fairness on which the British justice system was based.

I had not up until this point been brave enough to advocate the total abolition of IPPs, thinking it a bridge too far for Downing Street, and instead had just sought to cut the scope for awarding these sentences. The settlement that I was now persuaded to propose to the prime minister was that I would give up on some of my ideas on mandatory sentencing and early guilty pleas if, and only if, he would agree to the total abolition of IPPs. We had several slightly fractious meetings to discuss this, over the course of several months.

David was just as stubborn in a political argument as Margaret Thatcher had always been, as was I. However, he was always friendly and jovial and never offensive, as she had sometimes been. At one meeting in his House of Commons office he explained that he was quite prepared to have a liberal-minded Justice Secretary, but he did not want that to be apparent to the public. What he wanted was what he described as a 'retributional shield' of tough-sounding initiatives, behind which liberal, reforming moves could be hidden. I was never entirely sure that this sort of thing would work, but we did arrive at a happy compromise, based around the abolition of IPPs, which enabled me to continue for another slightly quieter year at the Ministry of Justice.

The last hurdle was a bizarre final request from David that I find some new mandatory minimum sentences to introduce. With the greatest reluctance, I went away to consider this last demand and eventually came up with two proposals. These combined severity of offence and previous convictions in such a way that no one would ever qualify for them who was not already doomed to be sentenced by any sensible judge to at least the mandatory term that was proposed.

I was still very reluctant though, and I tried them out on my old friend from the Midlands Circuit, Igor Judge, by now the Lord Chief Justice, at one of my regular meetings with him at the Royal Courts of Justice. To my surprise Igor was unperturbed. He asked whether the two new proposals would include what he called 'the usual get-out clause'. This was a provision that had been slipped by the parliamentary draftsman into every previous mandatory sentence, that the term should be imposed unless it would be 'unjust to do so in all the circumstances'. Igor thought the prize of abolishing indeterminate sentences was as important as I did and he persuaded me to settle for this less than satisfactory deal.

The bill eventually appeared as the Legal Aid, Sentencing and Punishment of Offenders Bill. Number 10 insisted at the last minute on including the word 'punishment' in the title to make it sound sufficiently tough.

When I finally presented the LASPO Bill to the House of Commons I described indeterminate sentences as an unmitigated disaster and a disgrace. I was pleased and surprised when David Blunkett, who had introduced them in the first place, said that they had never worked as he had expected and dampened down all opposition to their repeal.

I took the final precaution of making public my total opposition to the principle of mandatory sentencing in a statement which was picked up by some of the newspapers about twenty-four hours before the bill's report stage. Rather surprisingly there was little serious comment about the total contrast between my statement of principle and my bill's utterly pointless new mandatory sentencing provisions. I at least satisfied my conscience somewhat by my public declaration and the bill duly rolled forward with various other worthy reforms in it of interest only to lawyers and campaigners.

An odd footnote was a minor dispute I had with Boris Johnson, who was at the time the London mayor, and seeking a second term of office. When my bill was finally passing through Parliament, he wound up a number of Conservative backbench peers to support an amendment to create what he described as a sobriety scheme. The idea was that anyone arrested for being drunk could be sidetracked out of the courts and into a different sort of sentence which required regular checks to prove that you had become and remained sober. The problem was that Boris had absolutely no idea how this scheme would work in practice, and met my efforts to put to him even the most elementary questions, such as how much it might cost, with totally bizarre responses. The first time that we met and Boris found himself unable to answer a straightforward question he clowned about, ringing the Met commissioner on his mobile and asking him to convince me. The commissioner professed to be keen on the scheme, but I was not sure he had done much thinking about it either. The second time we had arranged a telephone call, and I was rather surprised that when faced with a similar fairly high level of questioning, Boris put his phone on speaker and asked someone from the office to come and answer questions on his behalf. This was rather irritating because I was facing the real possibility of defeat in the House of Lords on this relatively minor and almost entirely unthought-through amendment. Boris has many fine qualities, but attention to detail is not one of them.

It would be difficult to find two more contrasting styles than that of Theresa May, then Home Secretary, and myself. Apart from the media obsession with our shoes, our personal way of doing business could not be more different, she rather formal, organized and precise, me rather more noisy and relaxed. We in fact agreed far more than the parody of our relationship, and our respective brands of Conservatism, suggested. She was not the author of 'the nasty party' speech for nothing.

However, on human rights law we really did not see eye to eye. This was brought home in spectacular fashion when we got into a bit of a 'cat flap' over an argument she put into her party conference speech that the courts had found in favour of someone's appeal against deportation because they had a right to a family life, which had been proved, based on the fact that they owned a cat. I was immediately asked whether I agreed with her description of the case, and as I did not believe that any judge had ever made a finding based on cat ownership, I said so. This was manna from heaven for the bored journalists hanging around the conference centre. They turned the whole episode into a huge media scrum, the main lasting result of which was some rather fine cartoons of my Hush Puppies and Theresa's kitten heels attacking each other. The Royal Courts of Justice quickly confirmed publicly that there was no such case.

In contrast, Theresa and I agreed far more than was ever publicly understood on the subject of the Justice and Home Affairs opt-out. This was an EU concession that Tony Blair had negotiated whereby the UK could decide, if it wanted, to opt out of EU measures on justice and policing matters. For very practical reasons, both Theresa and I thought that opting out would sometimes be disastrous: crime does not respect borders, and international co-operation is a crucial important tool in fighting it. International crime is usually much better organized than international criminal justice. We therefore carefully agreed between ourselves that we would use the opt-out to get ourselves out of some of the less useful EU justice measures, but that we would stay in more than thirty valuable ones. In this instance, it was Nick Clegg and David Cameron who held the whole thing up, so that it was not until nearly a year after our agreement that our general approach was published. Finally, Nick and Theresa succeeded in bullying their Cabinet colleagues into agreeing our approach.

On questions of political strategy in particular Theresa and I usually agreed quite quickly. I used to joke with her on these occasions that

I was not as left wing as I was believed to be, and she was not as right wing as she pretended to be. Her own joke, when asked how she got on with me, was to say 'I lock them up, and he lets them out.'

There were countless other issues that I had to deal with as Lord Chancellor and Justice Secretary involving legal issues both at home and abroad, but these are only of interest to a specialist reader. The other great political controversy that I was engaged in concerned the role of the European Convention on Human Rights and the Court of Human Rights at Strasbourg. Right-wing members of my party often believe that these are creations of the European Union and are fiercely opposed to the court's jurisdiction over the United Kingdom. I am a committed defender of the Convention which was actually drafted by British lawyers after the Second World War to put in place overarching standards for the political and legal systems of post-war Europe. It comes under the aegis of the long-standing institution the Council of Europe, its remit extends to such countries as Russia, Azerbaijan, Ukraine and Georgia, and it is one of the main levers that exists to maintain some liberal and democratic standards and protect the citizens of those countries who do submit to its judgements. The United Kingdom only loses about 2 per cent of the small number of cases that go there and they are usually trivial ones about such matters as whether an air hostess can wear a crucifix when wearing her uniform on duty.

The growing band of right-wing Eurosceptics in the Conservative Party and the tabloid press maintain a constant barrage of campaigning against this wicked European institution, which they believe protects foreign criminals and terrorists against our laws. I have always fiercely resisted these arguments, which are in my opinion utterly unfounded, but there are problems with the court because of the length of time that it takes to resolve cases when, for example, some suspected terrorists are trying to resist extradition. The United Kingdom did not lose any such case in my time but some achieved a great deal of publicity.

While I was at the Justice Department, the British government held the presidency of the Council of Europe for six months. As a consequence of this, I presided over a meeting of justice ministers during our presidency, held in Brighton. There I was greatly assisted by my good friend Dominic Grieve, the Attorney General, who shared my views on the Convention and the rule of law. We actually achieved complete unanimity from every government on a statement that we called the Brighton Declaration, which sought to begin to address the delays in hearing cases and to allow the Strasbourg court to have more regard to national legal systems. We regarded this as a triumph. Needless to say the right-wing press and the hard-line Eurosceptics took no notice whatsoever of this important step.

I greatly enjoyed my time as Lord Chancellor and Justice Secretary and I was delighted to be able to contribute to restoring the country's finances, and to start to implement some of the liberal penal-reform policies I had first thought about as Home Secretary twenty years earlier. I regretted, though, that I was never able to implement the more radical reforms on my agenda because of the nervousness of David Cameron and Downing Street over any appearance of liberal change. It was a pleasure and surprise to me a few years later when, after a period of traditional law-and-order fervour from my successor Chris Grayling, David appointed his old friend Michael Gove, who revived and expanded my liberal agenda with commendable enthusiasm.

25

'My Favourite Things'
(John Coltrane, 1961)

CABINET OFFICE

I had agreed with David that I would only serve for two years as a member of his government, and as that term came to its end I expected to return to the back benches. I warned my two special advisers, and advised them to seek the next job in their own careers. David Hass, who had enthusiastically thrown himself into training for prisoners, took my advice and returned to the world of public relations. Kathryn Laing – who had immersed herself in the policy issues at the Ministry of Justice, working closely with its civil servants, and who was one of the most intelligent people that I have ever worked with – decided to take a chance and stayed with me.

It was actually two and a half years before David conducted his first major reshuffle. I was the first minister to be summoned, which strengthened my assumption that he was going to ask me to retire – something I was perfectly prepared to do without any fuss at all. To my surprise, and I suspect to the surprise of most of his entourage at Number 10, he asked me to stay on at Cabinet level as Minister without Portfolio in the Cabinet Office. Surprised and grateful, I accepted this. I was very much the veteran. My old friends Sir George Young – who had become chief whip on Andrew Mitchell's resignation following his unfortunate encounter with the Police Federation at the Downing Street gates – and Vince Cable were the only other members of the government who were remotely near to my own advanced age. Now that I no longer had a department or public service to lead, I regarded myself as mainly there to give the benefit of my 'wit and wisdom' to Cabinet proceedings. David acted up to this role, by keeping me in my position in the middle of the giant oval Cabinet table, almost opposite him and alongside Nick Clegg. I regularly took part in discussions, although I tried to curb my natural garrulous habits, which I was only too aware were getting worse as I got older.

David had started his term of office by declaring that he wished to revive a proper tradition of collective policymaking in Cabinet. Unfortunately, he never succeeded in delivering this, and the level of collective discussion declined throughout the parliament. David and George Osborne were huge admirers of Tony Blair's style of government and often referred to him as 'The Master'. They wholeheartedly shared his inclination for personal decision-making by the prime minister and his close advisers across the whole range of policy. David also, as Tony had, believed in constant political campaigning as the daily style of politics and in exerting control-freak discipline over his colleagues, with steady injunctions about the use of set policy lines and slogans on all public occasions, of the kind which has given a certain 'talking clock' style to many twenty-first-century politicians.

The Cabinet met for just ninety minutes, on one morning each week. This was an almost comically inadequate time within which to discuss any important subject. Various junior ministers were invited to attend Cabinet, although most of them were not expected to say anything as, elbows pressed into each other, they tried to fit around the table. David also followed the Blairite practice of lining the walls with Number 10 press and political advisers. The room was always extremely crowded.

I had always regarded it as part of my role in David's government to insist on raising difficult current issues which rarely made it onto the Cabinet agenda of their own accord. Vince Cable, the most left-wing member of the Cabinet, was also inclined to raise tricky or troublesome matters. My more cautious and ambitious junior colleagues felt less able to do this, but I know they were generally grateful for my attempts to raise topics which they would otherwise have been debarred from debating.

The opportunities for this unfortunately became ever more squeezed by the introduction of agenda items which were mainly designed to inform the Cabinet of what was happening in a particular department, rather than to invite discussion on any particular issue. David always explained this to me as a consequence of being in a coalition government where frank and open discussion was more difficult because it was taking place between political rivals. Although the divisions between the two coalition parties were often smaller than the divisions within them, there was some justice in this. Inevitably, as the parliament progressed there were many issues which the coalition partners came to from different starting points, and increasingly all the big decisions were finalized by private meetings of a gang of four known as the 'Quad' comprising Cameron, Osborne, Nick Clegg and Danny Alexander, with the Cabinet Office ministers Oliver Letwin and David Laws as their political sherpas.

I was also newly a member of what seemed like dozens of Cabinet Committees, many of which stemmed from Oliver Letwin's enthusiasm for drawing up spreadsheets against which departments could be held to account for delivery of the policies they had been inveigled to introduce by Downing Street and the Treasury. As a result, with the exception of the Home Affairs Committee, where I remained deputy to Nick Clegg as chairman, most did not actually discuss policy. Instead they were used to haul junior ministers over the coals in respect of the minutiae of delivery. I had experienced this from the other side of the table while at the Ministry of Justice, where I had insisted on meetings with me personally, and no more than once a quarter. As we put our colleagues through their paces in Cabinet Committees, or listened passively to colleagues' progress reports in Cabinet, I yearned fondly for the days of the Thatcher and Major governments when Cabinet would take up three hours over a whole morning each week, at least, and we held lively and effective collective discussions.

Apart from William Hague, who had been in John Major's Cabinet for the last couple of years, I was the only minister who had served in any previous Cabinet. For my other colleagues, presidential government with short and cursory collective meetings was normality. Since it had been in place since Tony Blair had first arrived in 1997, far too many senior civil servants also believed that this was the normal process. My old friend Robin Butler had been Cabinet Secretary when Blair took office and had once described Blair's first Cabinet meeting to me. It had had no agenda except a briefing from Alastair Campbell on the 'line to take' for events the following week. Robin said he had tried to change this and, when he had heard that Gordon Brown was about to make the Bank of England independent of government, had suggested that it should first be discussed in Cabinet. Tony's response had apparently been, 'What has it got to do with them?'

All my allies from the Blair government in opposing the Iraq War had complained to me that that decision had never been adequately discussed in Cabinet. Nor did David Cameron ever discuss his startling and catastrophic decision to call a referendum on Britain's membership of the EU in Cabinet.

In my opinion, this is a disastrous way to run the government of a complex modern nation state. It is a reaction to the hysterical constant 24/7 chatter that now dominates political debate. Media handling and public relations are now regarded as the key elements of governing, and a small army of advisers who are supposed to be PR experts but who are of frankly variable quality have far too big a role in policy-making. Next week's headlines are given more priority than serious policy development and the long-term consequences for the nation.

In previous governments the best test of my policy proposals had been the reactions and challenges from my Cabinet colleagues in collective discussion, which had often modified and improved my plans. The Thatcher government would never have pursued our political agenda if she or anyone else had paid too much notice to newspapers or opinion polls. In the short term, British public opinion is always opposed to radical change of any kind. (The 2016 referendum result, which seems to refute this, was an angry protest vote rather than a vote *for* anything.) Ultimately, voters judge governments by the effects of their policies and the general competence of the team.

On moving from the Ministry of Justice I retained responsibility for an intriguing piece of legislation which, in the end, aimed to regularize the accountability of the intelligence services.

Its beginnings, however, had been rather less straightforward, originating in the disastrous fallout from Tony Blair's and George W. Bush's 'War on Terror' and the associated disgraceful internment of suspects in the Guantánamo Bay detention centre without charge or trial. Some of those detained, and subsequently released, were British citizens, who quickly began to bring compensation claims alleging British involvement in their mistreatment. By the time the coalition government took office in 2010 this had become a real problem. We faced a series of sensational claims about the British intelligence service's alleged involvement in outrageous practices of abduction, ill treatment and torture of terrorist suspects in Iraq, Afghanistan and elsewhere, which needed to be resolved in such a way that the extremely important work of the intelligence services was not compromised.

The new coalition government came up with a three-part plan fairly quickly. We would settle the civil claims from the Guantánamo Bay detainees, for a considerable sum of money. We would have an independent inquiry, led by a former judge, which would seek to investigate what had gone on during the period of alleged abductions and internments, and draw some conclusions. And we would introduce legislation to – somehow – enable the government to defend itself by putting some of its evidence before a judge in closed court in future cases.

The first step, before the legislation, was to deal with the outstanding cases from the Guantánamo Bay inmates. These were nearing the stage of open court and we had decided that we would not seek to get emergency legislation onto the statute book in time to affect their hearings. We therefore had to settle these claims and pay compensation, since the government could not effectively defend itself in open court without compromising national security.

The former detainees insisted that a minister had to be personally involved in the settling of their claims. I therefore found myself presiding at a meeting with all the detainees who had brought a claim, and was involved in negotiating the final details of the settlement. The settlement was covered by a confidentiality undertaking. Unfortunately I made an error a few weeks later when answering a

Parliamentary Question when I blurted out the total figure of compensation that we had paid.

The planned independent inquiry was duly set up under a retired Appeal Court judge, Sir Peter Gibson. The inquiry made steady progress, but the whole thing became complicated the following year when fresh allegations emerged of British intelligence involvement in cases of alleged illegal rendition of Colonel Gaddafi's enemies and their families. In two separate incidents, individuals had allegedly been kidnapped with British involvement and returned to Libya where they had predictably been subjected to torture by Gaddafi's agents. These cases were reinforced when Gaddafi fell in October 2011 and Libya collapsed. Journalists searched the abandoned office of one of his leading thugs and discovered correspondence allegedly from the British intelligence service claiming credit for the delivery of the regime's enemies.

These were new revelations to the British public and to the government.

I was faced with strong arguments that the judicial inquiry should be ended or suspended whilst the police investigated the Libyan cases. I have deeply regretted ever since that I agreed with this and in January 2012 asked Sir Peter Gibson to produce an interim report and then end his work. I was unsure about the need to suspend the inquiry pending police investigations but I was influenced by a slight concern about Sir Peter's health. I thought that it might help if he was allowed to produce his interim report and then after a reasonable interval another judge could take over.

Unfortunately, the police investigations appeared for some reason to go on for years. One civil case was settled in 2012 and the Crown Prosecution Service finally decided not to bring charges in the criminal investigation in 2016. The promises I gave to the House of Commons, with the agreement of the prime minister, that a fresh inquiry would eventually resume, were later modified to say we would decide whether a further inquiry was needed once the police had finished their investigations and Parliament's Intelligence and Security Committee had finished its own report on the issues. It remains to be seen whether anything further is done.

As Lord Chancellor I had many inconclusive discussions about the third part of our plan with David Cameron and the Home Secretary Theresa May. The central question was how a judge could be permitted to hear evidence from the intelligence service when it sought to defend itself against claims from people who alleged that the British government had been involved in their torture or mistreatment. I was often at odds with Theresa in particular on the subject. We were all agreed that our spies could not possibly give evidence about their secret work in open court. Intelligence services necessarily require the highest possible standards of secrecy and whilst the identity of individual officers could no doubt have been protected, the information that would have to have been given by witnesses being questioned in open court would have been of enormous value to many enemies of the United Kingdom, who would have been delighted to receive a detailed account of the methods and practices of the British intelligence agencies (MI6, MI5 and GCHQ). However, Theresa wanted the Home Secretary to be able to decide that a court should hear the claims in closed secret sessions, with her certifying that this was required in the interests of national security. I was more sensitive to the needs of open justice and the rule of law in the liberal society we were meant to be defending. I believed that any decision to hold a closed hearing should always ultimately be the decision of a judge not the government.

In the meantime, the Home Office, Foreign Office and the intelligence services argued that we were being exposed to extortion and blackmail because they were obliged to pay out compensation claims rather than submit the evidence to refute the claims.

I was still involved in this deadlocked debate when I became Minister without Portfolio at the Cabinet Office because David then made me a member of the National Security Council which he had set up when he first took office. The NSC was a very worthwhile innovation. Its discussions were high quality and sensible, and it genuinely brought the key decision-makers – political, military and intelligence – around one table to discuss the many difficult problems that we were facing in regard to national security and foreign affairs.

However, our inconclusive ministerial meetings and the arguments about this continued. Theresa May and I were not able to reach an agreement because MI5 were particularly exercised by the proposals and inspired the Home Secretary to take a very strong line. This was not, in fact, an example of the public perception that Theresa and I represented right-wing versus left-wing Conservatism. Rather, while I have no doubt that both our positions were based on our sincere appraisal of the public interest, I took a more legalistic view and she took a more authoritarian one.

What had particularly provoked the intelligence agencies into this illiberal attitude towards closed hearings was that our close allies the Americans had now begun to worry about the litigation risk, and were threatening to downgrade the intelligence-sharing relationship. I will be sparing with legalistic detail of this horrendously complex debate: suffice to say that both the Americans and the agencies had really got themselves into a lather on this subject, and for a time it was difficult to have a reasoned discussion.

The agencies were very keen on legislation to protect themselves against allegations of all kinds. My motivation, rather, was my conviction that a much greater degree of accountability should be introduced into the political control of the intelligence agencies. I still remembered Roy Jenkins' advice when I became Home Secretary and found myself responsible for MI5: 'You will never know what those people are up to,' had been wise words, well justified by my experience in that role.

I was and am in no doubt that the United Kingdom needs to have powerful, effective and efficient secret and intelligence agencies which can provide us with information that is absolutely vital to the defence of the country and the safety of its citizens. The challenge is always to ensure that a proper balance is achieved with the need to remember that we are defending a democratic liberal society which respects the rule of law.

Dominic Grieve, the sometimes marginalized Attorney General, and I had practically identical views on all this. Gradually, we managed to successfully argue our case, on the grounds not only that putting any branch of government above the law was entirely counter to all

British traditions of fairness and justice, but also, that we were prepared to entertain the thought that some of these claims could be well founded. The danger, if the government insisted on secret proceedings, would be the temptation to use that secrecy to hide occasional incidents of incompetence and malpractice from the public gaze.

I had argued strongly all the way along that I wanted to be the minister responsible for the passage of the legislation, with joint responsibility alongside Theresa May for the actual policy content. Somewhat to my surprise, David suddenly agreed to this and then supported me in the main areas of friction that presented themselves. I remain convinced that this was a sensible decision. Through almost the entire passage of the bill arguments continued between those like me who saw this as a chance to increase the accountability of even the most secret parts of the state, and others who thought it an opportunity to remove the ability of the courts to look at those secrets at all. The Home Office version of the bill would not have achieved a parliamentary majority.

Taking this highly controversial, very sensitive and very difficult legislation through Parliament was fascinating. The bill included a significant increase in the power and independence of the parliamentary committee responsible for reviewing the intelligence and security agencies, which I hoped would in future play a much bigger role in investigating and forming a view on the individual actions and legality of what the intelligence services were doing in the name of the government. Nonetheless, much of liberal opinion was opposed in principle to the idea of closed court hearings and a great deal of hard discussion and careful drafting was needed to get sensible people onside in sufficient numbers to give a majority. The House of Lords was particularly difficult, with a large number of legal peers, some of whom were quite unrealistic about the need to protect the country from genuine terrorist threat. Fortunately, I was able to win the support of some of the people I regarded as key, such as my old friend James Mackay who had been the inscrutable Lord Chancellor under both Thatcher and Major, Eliza Manningham-Buller who had been head of MI5, and Harry Woolf, the former Lord Chief Justice. With their help I was able to get a sensible version of the bill onto the statute book.

Despite the fact that it had been extremely uphill work, MI6 responded to the passage of the bill by giving a drinks party for me and my team on the MI6 headquarters terrace on the south bank of the Thames. As I surveyed the magnificent view in the company of the 'Chief', it occurred to me that the agencies seemed perfectly satisfied with the new abilities to defend themselves in court, which they now had.

I also involved myself in a whole variety of policies which I largely selected on the basis of my personal interests and hobbies.

David Cameron had invited me to take on a trade representative role but I had declined, mainly because I wanted to remain in touch with and be able to influence domestic events, rather than globetrotting on a semi-permanent basis. I did, however, feel strongly that the government needed to drastically improve its support for British exporters. Our export performance was unenviable, particularly in the newly emerging markets of the world where we had been left far behind by the Americans, the Germans, the Japanese and others. The country had been running a dreadful balance of payments and current-account deficit for some years.

I insisted that I would only become involved in selected sectors of the economy in certain important markets. Given my experience at the Department of Health and at Alliance Unichem I offered to take the ministerial lead in promoting health-care exports to Brazil, China and India, where I believed that the potential market was enormous, and the strength of the British offer very good. I was also persuaded to add the energy sector to my activities in Brazil. Brazil was intending to exploit vast reserves of oil at considerable depth under the sea off its coast, and there were many specialist companies in the UK particularly in Aberdeen with world-leading niche expertise in oil exploration and extraction from the seabed.

The government's export and inward investment support organization, UK Trade and Investment, was slowly becoming much more effective under the coalition, which was giving it a higher priority and appointing executives with private-sector backgrounds. Health care was a particular speciality and I helped to develop a small sub-agency called Healthcare UK, which, under the able leadership of Howard Lyons, concentrated on the promotion of British companies with the expertise required to design, build and manage health-care facilities and deliver primary care health systems. We made good progress on health in China and good progress in Brazil on oil and gas. Unfortunately Brazilian development was ultimately completely halted because of allegations that the state oil institution Petrobras was involved in corruption and misbehaviour on a grand scale.

My efforts in Brazil also came complete with several healthy doses of farce, not least when Air France lost all my luggage due to a light dusting of snow in Paris where we changed planes. The result of this was that I spent the majority of that particular trip travelling round a rather sultry Rio in my aged tweed jacket and corduroy trousers. I am proud to say that the only new item of clothing I purchased was a pair of trainers in which to go birdwatching, my usual brown shoes not really being suitable for the Brazilian jungle.

Happily, my luggage had caught up with me in time for me to act as David Cameron's representative in Santiago at a meeting between EU Heads of Government and the Heads of Government of the South American and Caribbean countries. Our ambassador explained on my arrival that the British Embassy had had some difficulty persuading the Chilean organizers of this great summit that I should be accorded the seniority which our diplomats felt was warranted. This was largely due to my wholly untranslatable title of 'Minister without Portfolio'. One enterprising young diplomat then had the bright idea of throwing in the fact that I was a Queen's Counsel. The news that I was a legal adviser to the Queen had an immediate impact, and I immediately soared up the diplomatic rankings. There was one rather perturbing effect, however, which was that I was allocated a fleet of Chilean bodyguards who lined up outside my car when I arrived at the conference and then marched along either side of me as we processed to the venue – my anxious aides stumbling over them to try to brief me on some vital new matter. By far the greatest downside was that these bodyguards insisted on accompanying me on my half-day's birdwatching. It took some hard negotiating to get them to drop the fleet of siren-wailing cars which they had wanted to travel in. Instead they piled into a minibus with me, and I took them off to admire the condors floating on the currents of air high above the mountains overlooking Santiago.

Apart from my involvement in British exports, I was keen to see financial crime and fraud properly investigated and prosecuted. I shared the general dismay of the population at the outrageous conduct of various institutions and individuals that had led to the credit crunch and credit crash, and at the failure to hold any of those responsible to account. I remembered my days in the Home Office when I had first discovered how these complex cases were largely beyond the capacity of the criminal justice system. And from my days at the Treasury, I was also accustomed to the ferocious lobbying of the banking and financial services industry against any suggestion of personal responsibility for ill-gotten gains acquired by sharp practice.

I therefore contrived to get myself involved in the reconstruction and revival of the Serious Fraud Office. Over the past decade the SFO had declined to a dreadful extent. When I enquired about its failure to prosecute anyone for notorious frauds in the LIBOR and foreign-exchange markets, I was told that the SFO had regarded this as a purely regulatory matter not suitable for criminal sanctions. As the people involved had taken part in hugely profitable theft of other people's money by rigging markets, and as – in some cases – they had openly boasted about this in emails, I found this impossible to accept. The SFO had just acquired a new chief executive, David Green, and I encouraged him to begin the process (which should have begun long, long before) of prosecuting individuals for serious criminal activity in the financial markets.

My other major activity, at David Cameron's invitation, was as the lead for the government on the proposed EU–US Free Trade Agreement (also known as the Transatlantic Trade and Investment Partnership). The Doha Round, a proposed World Trade Organization agreement intended to lower trade barriers, had collapsed in 2008 after years of negotiation, with potentially disastrous consequences for global trade. Ever since, attention had switched to bilateral deals between those governments that supported the removal of trade barriers. David was every bit as enthusiastic about this as I was. The growth of trade following the removal of barriers had been a major stimulus to economic growth and advance in recent decades. If no worldwide agreement was possible, then leading powers needed to take the initiative in producing deals wherever they could. Nothing was more important than the proposed deal between the two biggest economic blocs in the world, the United States and the European Union, and negotiations were beginning to get under way.

They were being carried out by the European Commission on behalf of the EU as a whole. However, Britain was the leading European member in support of liberal economic and trade policies and we should and could have exercised considerable influence in promoting progress on the deal on both sides of the Atlantic.

I therefore made visits to both Brussels and Washington to try to get up to speed with the negotiations and encourage all our political and diplomatic contacts to be supportive of a deal if it could eventually be delivered. A trade agreement between the United States and the European Union would cover almost half of the world's GDP. Not only would it promote growth, investment and jobs on both sides of the Atlantic, it would also lay down a basic framework for future deals between the EU and other countries, particularly China, which Cameron and I were both very keen to pursue in due course.

Negotiations had also started with Japan in response to the openness of the government of Prime Minister Abe, and on one of my visits to Brazil I got various Brazilian ministers to agree that they would like to discuss an EU–Brazil trade deal in due course if their Mercosur South American trading bloc could not be induced to begin negotiations.

I also found myself fulfilling some ornamental purposes. While I was at the Cabinet Office, Sayeeda Warsi and I represented the government at the inauguration of the new Pope, Francis, in March 2013. As someone who had a distinguished CV but was no longer burdened by the heavy duties of a departmental minister I was clearly the ideal candidate. The two of us, one a Muslim and the other an agnostic at best, sat in St Peter's Square with front row seats at the extraordinary ritual ceremony complete with wafting incense and vast numbers of bobbing scarlet-robed cardinals.

After I had left the government, the Chinese suddenly decided to celebrate the seventieth anniversary of their VJ-Day. It was intended to be something of an anti-Japanese political orgy. If we had sent nobody it would have offended the Chinese. If we sent too senior a person it would offend the Japanese, which presented the Foreign Office with a dilemma. An ex-minister with a distinguished CV again proved ideal. Other Commonwealth countries did the same thing. The upshot was that I found myself on the podium in Tiananmen Square a few seats away from President Xi and President Putin, amongst others, watching a fantastic military rally with goose-stepping troops, aircraft flying overhead, and rockets and missiles passing by us on trucks. The resemblance to the kind of thing that fascist regimes staged in Europe in the 1930s was uncanny, although of course the president was keen to stress that the rally was entirely anti-fascist.

These were both somewhat surreal occasions and very enjoyable for a veteran politician at the end of his career. I was pinching myself throughout.

Altogether, I had a sufficient volume of work to enable me to continue to enjoy my full-time political activities as much as I ever had. But two particular incidents marred my very contented enjoyment of my role.

The first came in January 2013 when I was shocked to read in the newspapers that David Cameron had, without warning so far as I as a member of the Cabinet was concerned, announced that he intended to hold a referendum by 2017 at the latest on Britain's continued membership of the European Union. I later discovered that other members of the Cabinet had been similarly surprised by this news, which they too learnt from their morning newspapers.

I thought this was reckless and irresponsible. I had always been totally opposed to the idea that a referendum is a useful way of taking decisions on hugely complex political and diplomatic issues in a sophisticated nation state in today's world. A quick campaign and a vote on a broad-brush simple question which obscures a myriad of sub-issues within it about the role of Britain in the world and the best base for our future economy has always seemed to me to be reckless beyond belief.

I therefore quickly found myself in a small room with David Cameron and Ed Llewellyn, his chief of staff and right-hand man, arguing about the merits of this decision. It was obvious that David had taken it mainly for reasons of party management, because he had had to contend for years with the constant backdrop of right-wing nationalist Conservative backbenchers agitating on Eurosceptic causes. He also saw it as a way of reducing votes for the right-wing populist Nigel Farage and his UK Independence Party at the next general election, due in 2015. He explained that he was convinced that the announcement of a referendum would calm the whole issue and bring the constant bickering to an end – at least for the time being – so that we could concentrate solely on the serious business of government in the run-up to the next election. Apart from my views about the irresponsibility of this gamble, I certainly doubted whether offering Eurosceptics the prospect of a referendum was going to calm anything down.

David further explained that he intended to delay the vote whilst he embarked on a process of reform of our relationship with the EU. He was clear that he intended to advocate remaining in the Union, but he thought that the majority would be increased in the referendum if he could illustrate that he had achieved important improvements in our relationship with Europe. He was remarkably vague about the reforms that he particularly wanted to achieve.

I have no doubt that David was concerned about my fury at finding myself part of a government that had taken this foolish and extremely risky decision. However, I had no intention of resigning. I saw no point in making my fundamental issue of principle the issue of the referendum itself, on which David had now burnt his boats anyway by making it such public knowledge. Instead I firmly intended to concentrate on trying to get the right result from any referendum, now that we apparently were likely to have one.

In order to calm me down, David offered to let me see a draft of the speech that he was going to make to formally announce his decision. He assured me that no one else outside his office was being allowed to see this draft, let alone comment. I strongly suspect that he gave that assurance to several other people who were given a chance of making a contribution. I did look at and work on the speech, and I was to an extent reassured and pleasantly surprised by its very pro-European arguments. I hope that I made some modest contribution to making it even more pro-European in tone, with an emphasis on the benefits that Britain derived from membership of the EU. I also tried to strengthen the commitment to economic reforms which I and most pro-Europeans had always favoured. The speech emphasized the need for the extension of the European single market to services and other areas, and the need for deregulation or better regulation in Europe. It also advocated the delivery of international trade agreements by the EU, including the EU–US trade agreement upon which our government was so keen. Thereafter I leapt upon those reforms as desirable things to pursue because I knew that, not only did I agree with them, but we had many allies in other governments across Europe who would support us in seeking such reforms.

These economic reforms also proved to be the policy of the incoming new European Commission. They had actually been the policy of President José Manuel Barroso and his Commission but he had received precious little support in any detailed particular or in practice from any member-state government, including the British, in trying to deliver them. The British negotiations might, I hoped, give added impetus and some practical effect to these policies under a new presidency.

David then made a dreadful error by making a thoroughly bad first impression with the new president of the Commission, my old friend Jean-Claude Juncker. Juncker had been the favoured candidate of the centre-right grouping in the European Parliament, known as the EPP. It was this group from which David Cameron had unnecessarily and damagingly withdrawn the Conservative Party, in order to appeal to the Eurosceptic wing of the party during the leadership election in 2005. David had asked me what I thought of Jean-Claude's candidacy, to which I had replied that I thought he would be perfectly fine, although I conceded that there were conceivably stronger candidates. By this time, I had known Jean-Claude for over twenty years and we had attended Council meetings together, first as employment ministers and then as finance ministers. I still dropped in to see him occasionally on my visits to Brussels and Luxembourg, and probably knew him better than any other British politician did. I greatly admired his skills as a wheeler-dealer and negotiator of sensible compromise on key policy issues. The fact that he chain-smoked and ignored the law against smoking indoors also meant that he always conducted political discussions in the smoke-filled atmosphere which I have always believed leads to better political decisions.

Unfortunately, David had asked the same question of another old friend of mine, Angela Merkel, whom I had first met at meetings of her Christian Democratic Union party and Conservative MPs under the auspices of the Konrad Adenauer Institute. He had somehow erroneously got the impression that she would prefer someone else. He had also always overrated Chancellor Merkel's ability to ensure the agreement of the governments of twenty-six other member states, let alone the European Parliament. In order to demonstrate his new tough and assertive nationalist line towards Europe, David now chose to launch a scandalous attack on Jean-Claude for his alleged excessive drinking and other defects. Jean-Claude was particularly hurt by false suggestions that his father had been a Nazi collaborator during the Second World War, which left wounds within the son which never subsequently healed.

The virulence of the British opposition and the bid for influence by the European Parliament combined to make Juncker's election inevitable. Almost immediately after his assumption of office, I was asked to ring him up and congratulate him and seek to establish a foundation for a sensible professional relationship with the British government thereafter.

I have also had contact with Jean-Claude subsequently. Fortunately David Cameron put in a lot of work to establish a proper relationship. Jean-Claude will never forgive him for the attacks. However, he is an even firmer believer in the European project than I am and he was quite easily persuaded that his Mr Fixit skills and his diplomatic and leadership powers should properly be employed in trying to enable the British to win their referendum. Unfortunately, like everybody else, he was unsuccessful.

As public debate on our membership of the EU went on, David continued to follow his established practice of giving a strong Eurosceptic tone to his every public utterance on the subject. In fact, since Margaret Thatcher, the only serving prime minister ever to have made pro-European speeches or remarks had been Tony Blair. David resolutely stressed the failings and problems of the EU in all his remarks, which naturally fed the anti-European current in public discussions and media reporting. In particular David began to feed the arguments that Nigel Farage was making about the immigration problems which he claimed were being caused by our membership of the EU. Farage always realized that xenophobic and dog-whistle racist arguments would win him more votes than any arguments about the workings of the Union. This dynamic was at its worst when the delay on free entry for Bulgarians and Romanians that had been imposed on them from the date of their admission to the EU came to an end. David simply endorsed the fears being raised in the right-wing tabloids about the huge numbers of Bulgarians and Romanians, including gypsies, who were supposedly now about to enter the UK. Worse, he joined in the attacks on the Blair government's previous decision to admit Poles and Czechs straight away when their countries had joined the EU in 2004. David denounced the decision to allow in Poles in particular as a dreadful mistake. The Bulgarian scare stories slightly fizzled out on 1 January 2014 when free movement for Bulgaria began. Two MPs made a much-publicized visit to the first plane that landed in the UK after the embargo was lifted. The vision of Bulgarian hordes fell rather flat when only one Bulgarian intending to look for work in the UK emerged from amongst the passengers. When migrant pressures built up in later years, towards the date of the referendum, the previous complete failure of the government to explain the benefits that migrants were bringing to the economy and the contribution that they were making to rising prosperity helped to feed the idea that excess numbers of foreigners and the loss of control of our borders was somehow a key problem.

My sense of political ease within the Cameron government never fully survived the lurch into a referendum. But there were other problems, too, including the declining level of collective responsibility within the government. Little serious discussion was now taking place at the short Cabinet meetings, which were sometimes taken up with ministers making presentations on routine aspects of their departmental policy. Actual decisions were being taken by the gang of four led by David Cameron and Nick Clegg. The so-called 'political Cabinet meetings' which I had helped to persuade David to hold for the Conservative Cabinet ministers became ever less important. Invariably they now started with long presentations by political aides such as Lynton Crosby on the state of public opinion, the latest opinion polls and the line to take in any public exchanges. Efforts to raise questions or opinions about substantive matters were not encouraged.

I still participated widely in the debate in the national media, which I have always considered one of the privileges enjoyed by those lucky enough to achieve political office. However, it became increasingly obvious that Downing Street objected to my media appearances and performances because I never bothered to get approval before I made them, and I never deployed the corny slogans and narrow lines to take that other more junior ministers were induced to follow. This came to quite a head when the Downing Street advisers made more determined efforts than usual to stop me appearing on the BBC's political flagship programmes *Question Time* and *Any Questions*.

I had been a regular performer on these two programmes for decades, and in fact had been one of the first ministers ever to appear on *Question Time*, back in the early 1980s. Until that point, it had been decreed that ministers should not appear on these programmes in case they were asked questions outside their own departmental responsibility. The result was that, in the first difficult years of the Thatcher government, the Conservative case would be argued by eager but not always adequate backbenchers against the leading spokesman of the Labour Opposition. This tradition came to an end when Michael Heseltine appeared on *Question Time*. However by the time I first appeared in 1982 officialdom had not yet adjusted. I was therefore presented with a briefing for my appearance which gave me some extraordinary advice. Arguments about the independent nuclear deterrent were high-profile political controversy at the time. When, out of mild interest, I turned to the page on the nuclear deterrent I found that I was advised to say to my nationwide audience only that 'This is a matter for my Right Honourable friend the Secretary of State for Defence.' I took a very Heseltine view of this kind of briefing and thereafter engaged in regular television and radio controversy on the major political subjects. The Dimbleby brothers who have chaired the two programmes for many years – and Robin Day before them – seemed, together with their teams, quite happy to have me appear two or three times each year from then on.

However, thirty years on from my first appearance, I knew that Downing Street was becoming less than happy with my regular appearances. In the spring of 2014, I had arranged with the producer of *Question Time* to appear on an edition of the programme to be broadcast from Welbeck College in Nottinghamshire which was convenient for my own home. At the last minute I was told by Downing Street that this had been cancelled because the programme had accidentally booked two Conservative ministers. Downing Street assured me that the producers had promised to try to book me on another occasion.

I was rather startled by this as it been arranged for several months in advance, so I rang up the producer to find out what had gone wrong. She was amazed at my query. She had been told by the Downing Street press office that I was ill and unable to attend. The press officers had kindly offered to help the programme by finding somebody else to take my place.

This was a silly and childish incident and I was reinstated on the programme and took part in the normal way. I was, however, particularly annoyed by being plotted against and deceived in this way, and my personal attachment to continued office in the government was undoubtedly diminished.

I had no reason to expect that I was going to continue for much longer in any event, because my advancing age made it increasingly evident that I ought not to continue. Eventually another reshuffle took place and I was indeed invited to stand down. I readily agreed, as it was obviously a sensible decision from the point of view of both the government and myself. I parted from David on extremely good terms and my letter of resignation expressed the genuine pleasure I had derived from my unexpected bonus four years of office.

My first intention was to retire to the back benches for the last year of the parliament and then retire from Parliament altogether. The Boundary Commission had proposed drastic national changes which involved splitting my constituency into four pieces, each in a different parliamentary seat. It would have been senseless for me to start to fight a new constituency at my time of life. When a coalition squabble with the Liberal Democrats forced the boundary changes to be put off I was genuinely in two minds about what to do. I consulted my executive officers in Rushcliffe, who were all good personal friends, and asked them for their frank advice. If they had been remotely hesitant, I would have retired immediately. But instead they enthusiastically urged me to do one more full parliament. They wanted to wait to select my successor when the new boundaries were finally settled. I now resolved to become a cavalier and maverick backbench MP for my final parliament.

Things were seriously complicated by a sudden deterioration in Gillian's health in the months leading up to the election. Gillian had been struggling with cancer for ten years. However, she had been successfully treated for her first problems and had continued to live a fairly normal life because her lymphoma was in remission and not causing her too many difficulties. We enjoyed the Christmas of 2014 with our family but in the New Year her lymphoma suddenly flared up again. From there on Gillian became increasingly ill, and I began to have serious concerns for her and had to devote much more time to being with her. I hesitated about continuing with my parliamentary candidature but she said that it was entirely a matter for me and I allowed things to drift on.

I fought the general election in a fairly low-key way as I was beginning to become lame with an arthritic ankle and I was also spending a lot of time at home with Gillian. I did little campaigning in my own constituency, where things appeared calm and I appeared to be popular. I did, though, spend many days in the marginal constituencies surrounding mine. These key seats in the Midlands in the end proved decisive in an election in which the Labour Party was wiped out in Scotland by the Scottish National Party and the Conservative Party won back many seats from the Liberal Democrats in the South of England. Because they had supported a Conservative-led coalition for five years, the Liberal Democrats were punished by those voters who had previously supported them, believing that a Liberal candidate had a better chance of beating the Tory than Labour. As a result, they were almost completely destroyed.

I visited six constituencies that were very close Labour–Conservative battles. Labour expected to win most of them and we expected to lose them. I conducted very interesting shopping-centre walkabouts and other public campaigns which gave me an insight into what was happening.

The nationwide campaigns of the two main parties were both appalling and there was strong public hostility to all politicians. David Cameron and the Conservatives were unpopular but, amongst the wavering working-class voters who might have voted Labour, there was distinct opposition to the idea that Ed Miliband and Ed Balls could be trusted with the economy, and grudging acknowledgement that George Osborne had done a competent job in pulling us back from the disaster that the last Labour government had left behind.

I also encountered a surprising surge of feeling in places like Derby, Ilkeston and Broxtowe that a Labour government would be dominated by and dependent on the Scottish National MPs who were obviously about to be elected. Nicola Sturgeon was one of the most liked and successful TV campaigners in Nottinghamshire and Derbyshire but the voters of the Midlands did not want her to control their government.

I was comfortably re-elected in my own constituency. To general amazement, the Conservatives won all the marginals across the Midlands and in parts of the North-West, and even won in Derby North where I had campaigned for our candidate but had never remotely expected her to win. I reflected that the mood of the floating voters of the

North Midlands was something along the lines of 'I suppose we will have to have the bastards back again as they are the only competent people available.'

Gillian's health continued to decline during the campaign and she was becoming inactive and confined to home. By an enormous irony, the last thing that we did together was to travel to our polling booth in my constituency to cast our votes. This really was the exemplar of a life in which Gillian had willingly made huge sacrifices to support me in my political career.

When I returned home from my count in the small hours of the morning, I found that Gillian's health had deteriorated further. A few hours later I got her into my car and rushed her to hospital. She was very quickly admitted to intensive care. She managed to recover sufficiently to go onto a general ward but was never able to return home. I started to make preparations for her to be cared for at home before realizing that this was not going to happen.

After a bedside gathering of my children, my granddaughter and me around her bedside, we received the message a few hours later that she had died peacefully on the afternoon of 8 July 2015. We were devastated by the loss but I think that I was made closer to my children and grandchild by our bereavement.

Gillian's funeral was held in West Bridgford in my constituency and a huge number of people came. Our old friends from Cambridge and elsewhere travelled from all over the country. The people there from the Nottingham area included all the people she knew from her activities in Oxfam, people from the local branch of the Parkinson's Society which she had helped to establish and of which she had been the president, and all her friends from her other activities. My old friend Martin Suthers, who had known us both at Cambridge and been our birdwatching companion on holidays and regular companion at our home, gave a very eloquent and moving speech. Jill Tanner, as far as I know a completely non-political woman who I suspect never voted Conservative, which was of no concern to Gillian and me in our friendship with her, was equally remarkably eloquent in paying tribute to Gillian's contribution to quilting and other activities.

Parliament had only reassembled a few weeks earlier. It was

therapeutically very valuable to me to keep busy, which I was able to do in my determination to be a reasonably independent backbencher for my last few years. My political activities in future would be conducted in a more solitary way, however, as I had lost my lifelong companion and beloved wife who had been so important to me in her more active days.

26

'Sack o' Woe'

(Cannonball Adderley, 1960)

REFERENDUM

Ministers were just as astounded as MPs to discover that the Conservative Party had won an overall majority in the 2015 general election. Our victory was a by-product of the collapse of the Liberal Democrat Party and the English reaction to the rise of the Scottish National Party. The government was fairly unpopular but it was able to form a new single-party administration.

In a conversation with George Osborne in the first few weeks I do, however, remember agreeing with him that our slim working majority of twelve seats would not prove to be enough to deliver all the difficult decisions that a responsible government would have to try to push through.

The new government made some patchy progress in various areas, and the economy continued to grow fairly sporadically. George continued to have considerable difficulty in making enough headway with eradicating the unsustainable deficit and moving towards one day reducing the stock of sovereign debt to a more sustainable level. He produced popular Budgets which were a triumph on the day and were acclaimed by the newspapers as demonstrating his obvious position as the next prime minister. Parliamentary proceedings would then turn to some tough measures designed to reduce excessive levels of welfare spending, which would immediately be denounced by lobbyists and interest groups and defeated. George's political reputation would then plunge and he would be derided for his lack of political wisdom in producing the measures that had been tucked away in his Budget, celebrated with such praise only a few months before.

I tried to help a little by speaking up inside and outside the House in favour of cutting back the extraordinary levels of government subsidy for people in not particularly low-paid jobs, or to defend the downwards correction of errors in distributing disability benefits, which had been unintentionally increased for most recipients. It was to no avail. Recovery was fitful and based on a rising level of consumer debt. The performance of our economy internationally was feeble. We steadily acquired the biggest current-account deficit in our history which would have created a sensation thirty years before when it was described as the balance of payments and hounded Harold Wilson.

All these economic difficulties, and the ongoing battles over reforms in the health-care and education systems, were however dwarfed by the looming problem of David's casual and short-termist promise made in January 2013 to hold a referendum on British membership of the European Union. Unfortunately now he found himself prime minister again he would have to follow through on his pledge.

Although the commitment was for a vote by the end of 2017, David decided to go as quickly as possible and increased the pace of his negotiations for EU 'reform' in order to get the vote over in 2016. He assumed that thereafter he would be able to concentrate on the rather more worthwhile overall objectives that he had set himself for his political legacy, of improving social mobility and meritocratic opportunity in modern Britain. Unfortunately, when he had blithely announced his intention to call a referendum three years earlier, David had failed to predict what the political landscape would look like by the time of the vote.

A mood of angry protest was sweeping through every Western democracy, which is why in the 2015 general election the SNP had swept Labour out of Scotland and the UK Independence Party had come third in terms of vote share with 12.6 per cent, albeit fortunately winning only one seat thanks to our first-past-the-post electoral system. (Under a proportional system UKIP would have taken more than eighty seats.) The political class was unpopular, the establishment despised, and a large group of people were dissatisfied with their stagnant living conditions and their children's poor expectations. This was all compounded by a wave of migration in the summer of 2015. It is strange that no one had predicted that huge numbers of people would flee warfare, anarchy and violence in several countries in the Middle East and North Africa, and pay smugglers to transport them across seas and through borders in search of a better life in northern Europe, particularly in Germany, Sweden and the UK.

The public reacted to tragic scenes of desperate people drowning in the ocean or trudging along distant roads or living in squalid camps with a mixture of compassion and fear. There was a widespread feeling that it was the duty of prosperous countries to give refuge to those fleeing warfare in particular. Nonetheless a large section of the population did not wish to give them refuge in this country and were anxious at the sight of the numbers of people living in wretched camps in Calais or fighting to get onto lorries through the Channel Tunnel, striving to reach England.

David had never really had a clear idea of what he wanted to get out of his EU reform negotiations: they had mainly been a tactical device to kill the time and explain the delay between calling the referendum in 2013 and holding it years later. I had initially urged him, with some success, to use the negotiations to press for sensible reforms like extending the single market, signing trade deals with the Americans, and deregulation. However, David now – extremely unwisely, in my view – added immigration to the list of subjects that he was trying to negotiate with the EU. In public debate British ministers echoed the hostility of sections of the public to waves of immigration and supported Nigel Farage's slogans by claiming that they wished to regain control of our borders. No serious effort was made to explain that Brussels was not responsible in any way for decisions about whether Afghans, Syrians and so on could live in the United Kingdom. No minister developed the argument that EU nationals such as German academics, Italian construction workers and Romanian nurses were not a threat to the British economy but were in fact working in the country and contributing to our recovery and the delivery of public services. In the public debate, ministers

echoed Eurosceptics in challenging the whole principle of free movement of labour as part of the single market – a principle which the
same ministers had previously advocated and attempted to extend.

At one point, early in 2016, I made a visit to Brussels myself to
have a meeting with several people including Jean-Claude Juncker
and Ivan Rogers, the excellent British diplomat tasked with trying to
achieve a reasonable deal. I also met one or two key people in the
Commission and the European Parliament. The European politicians
I talked to all knew that I was a sound pro-European and I believe
that the ones who knew me well trusted me. I tried to impress upon
them that, in my opinion, there was a serious risk that the British
might vote to leave the Union and it would be extremely dangerous
to leave David Cameron empty-handed with nothing to say on the
various issues that he had chosen to raise. Most of these issues were
either trivial or symbolic but it was vital that he should be enabled
to return home and claim success. I do not know whether I was
instrumental in ensuring that something was produced or not. I
certainly found a worrying mood amongst some of the European
negotiators who were taking it for granted that Britain would vote to
remain in the Union because it was so obviously in the country's
economic self-interest.

Eventually, David was able to negotiate a peculiar alteration to
in-work benefits for EU nationals in the United Kingdom so that a
four-year delay would apply before workers from the Continent could
qualify for these payments in the UK. It was not clear that this would
reduce the number wishing to work in Britain, and nor was it
explained that EU citizens would as a result be working alongside
British colleagues who were receiving higher incomes for doing the
identical job. It did, however, give David Cameron something to say
on the subject of immigration.

I think that David Cameron and George Osborne had vaguely
believed that the whole process could be turned into something of a
personal triumph, based on their demonstration of the British government's negotiating skills in producing a package of improvements. In
the event the so-called reforms were a damp squib in the public

debate back in the UK, and they fairly quickly ceased to feature at all in the referendum campaign.

The day after he had announced his reform package to the nation on 19 February, David finally set the referendum date for 23 June 2016. The whole subsequent months-long campaign period was unsatisfactory from the start and it became clear that David's decision to hold a referendum had indeed been an irresponsible gamble.

The overriding problem was that for more than a decade the right-wing tabloid press, supported by vehement Eurosceptic political debate, had created an atmosphere of sustained hostility to the European Union. Even Tony Blair had only tried to counter this with occasional pro-European speeches, and usually only when he was overseas. Leading Conservative figures had constantly adopted a tactic of faintly echoing every prevailing criticism of the EU and David Cameron had particularly taken this tone when reporting on his progress or lack of it in his 'reform' negotiations.

I had been involved in 2015 in various discussions over the formation of an all-party pro-European campaign group. My principal collaborator had been Peter Mandelson. He and I were desperately anxious to oversee the emergence of a powerful pro-European voice to make the positive case for Europe in the campaigning, and various efforts were made by a committee, mainly using money supplied by Lord Sainsbury, to try to put such an organization in place.

Partly because I thought that younger political figures should be involved, but mainly because of Gillian's terminal illness, I had withdrawn from this role and handed my position over to my old friend Damian Green who, because he had quarrelled with David Cameron and had been surprisingly returned to the back benches, was available. A reasonably respectable all-party campaign eventually emerged with the strange title of 'Stronger In'. However, in the event, both party leaderships declined to get involved in cross-party campaigning and David Cameron, George Osborne and Downing Street ousted the all-party campaign from prominence in the later stages of the debate.

In these last few months, the atmosphere of the national campaign became thoroughly poisonous. The mass media turned the entire process into a struggle between personalities, and particularly between Cameron and Osborne on one side and Boris Johnson and Michael Gove on the other. This Tory war erupted because of a last-minute decision by the colourful Boris Johnson to join the Leave camp. Almost immediately he became its de facto leader so far as the media were concerned.

I had known Boris for years and like most other politicians I was amazed by his last-minute decision to take that side in the campaign. I knew four other MPs who had each personally been told by Boris that he was going to support the Remain campaign. I also thought that I knew him well enough to know that, although Eurosceptic in many of his views, he did not believe that it was in Britain's interest to leave the Union and the single market. I could only conclude that he had made his decision based on a simple calculation of the best tactics to achieve his overriding ambition to succeed David Cameron as prime minister. He had correctly worked out that the majority of the ageing activists who remained amongst the dwindling number of Conservative Party members would favour leaving, and he therefore believed that a vigorous show would win him their support in the next Conservative leadership election. I do not think that it crossed his mind that the Leave campaign might actually win. Presumably he expected that once Remain had won, he would be given a leading post in David Cameron's government from which he would be well placed to succeed David when he eventually retired.

The public debate therefore hinged heavily on personalities in the last month or two, with Boris providing hugely enjoyable photo opportunities for the newspapers on a daily basis without producing very many concrete arguments in his utterances. I soon began to dub the whole three-ring circus the 'Boris and Dave Show'.

The arguments and the exchanges accompanying this show at the national level rapidly became unpleasant and extremely simplistic if not untruthful. The issues that dominated public debate were economic arguments raised by the Remain camp and anti-immigrant arguments raised by Leave. I shared the expectation of the Remain leaders that the outburst of economic warnings from every respectable international and national body pointing out that Britain would make itself poorer by leaving the biggest single market in the world would persuade the sensible centre ground of public opinion. Unfortunately the IMF, the OECD, the G20 finance ministers, the British Treasury, the Bank of England and the prime ministers and presidents of all Britain's allies in the world were quickly dismissed when their warnings were publicized. Their reasoning was rather erudite and perhaps a little obscure, but their arguments were disregarded and they were instead attacked for being foreigners. All reasoning from the vast majority of economists at home and abroad was eventually sweepingly rubbished by Michael Gove with the absurd phrase that 'we have had enough of experts' and by the assertions of all Leave campaigners that economists often got things wrong. Broadcasters retained 'balance' in their reporting by matching all the statements of prestigious organizations and individuals with the eccentric opinions of the one or two economists who could be found to contradict them.

Unfortunately George Osborne and Downing Street responded by producing extraordinarily simplistic presentations of the economic case. I'm sure that they were guided by their so-called expert campaigners who told them that people found broad economic assertions by great institutions too distant from their own lives. People therefore needed to be given specific and straightforward explanations of the impact on their own lives and pockets. The result was a series of claims that the average household would lose £4,300 each year and similar fancies which were easily derided. The ultimate blow was when George decided to produce a draft emergency Budget, raising income tax and cutting spending on the NHS and other public services, which he said he would be bound to deliver in the event of a Leave result. This was dismissed with enraged mockery and did enormous damage to George Osborne's political reputation because of its obvious absurdity.

Meanwhile Nigel Farage and the right-wing press continued to repeat ad nauseam their claims that we had lost control of our borders and were facing a potential flood of immigrants. One or two large-circulation tabloid newspapers produced an anti-foreigner or anti-immigrant story every day of the campaign. Ludicrous claims were made particularly about the risk of crime and terrorism if we did not restore a 'fortress Britain' quality to our territorial borders. A key moment came when prominent Conservative Leave campaigners realized that this was the only subject likely to win them significant numbers of votes. People like Boris Johnson and Michael Gove in effect gave respectability to the political arguments of Nigel Farage who was no longer a particularly popular or attractive advocate of these views to the British public. Once Boris and Michael began to promulgate the absurd nonsense that millions of Turks might eventually pour into the UK, the level of concern about immigration was raised to new heights.

I do not believe that the British public were swept along by dog-whistle racism and xenophobia into personal dislike of immigrants. The United Kingdom, in my opinion, has the most tolerant society and the highest quality of community and race relations of any country in Europe. There was of course a small minority of people who had voted for the extreme racist right in the past but they were not the great bulk of the people tempted by Leave. The Leave campaigning did however convince very many voters that the sheer number of people arriving in the United Kingdom was causing intolerable pressure on our public services. There was a simplistic appeal in the argument that our problems with schools, hospitals, welfare and so on could most quickly be solved by merely turning more foreigners away. Ironically, this argument was often most effective in parts of the country that had absolutely minimal immigration.

I campaigned myself at many meetings and gatherings across the country and I did quite a bit of broadcasting. I accepted requests from the Conservative In campaign and from Stronger In to speak to public meetings whenever they asked me. I continued to stress the greater political influence that Europe gave us in the world and the increased prosperity that membership of the biggest single market in the globalized economy gave us. I was a very minor figure in the national campaign, however. As a veteran politician, I understood this; the leading figures of the day quite properly led the debate. Michael Heseltine was more annoyed than I was by the fact that Downing Street in particular made little or no use of us. We were thought to be too pro-European and provocative to the Eurosceptics who they fondly imagined were going to be reconciled to the government and the party when the results eventually came in.

None of my serious arguments received media publicity of any kind and I was not alone in this experience. Only personal insults of opponents or simplistic slogans about economic disaster or waves of migrants had any news value. I tried to avoid all these things and only twice was reported nationally. Once, in response to a question about whether David Cameron would resign if he lost the referendum, I replied that he 'wouldn't last thirty seconds' after a Leave victory. Once, when pressed about Boris Johnson, I made a silly joke that Boris was just 'a nicer version of Donald Trump'. Donald Trump was then emerging as the Republican contender for the US presidency surging on a wave of angry protest voting very similar to that of the Leave campaign.

My judgement in the last few days of the campaign was that the public were now angry and confused and that the result was therefore completely unpredictable. In the early days everyone I met had agreed, regardless of their instincts on membership, that they felt uninformed on this huge question and they wanted to know more about the subject. Once it became clear that the national campaign was not going to add any accurate information to any citizen's understanding, the anger and sense of protest became worse. The behaviour of most of the leading politicians during the campaign fed the underlying current of hostility and contempt for the London-based political class that had been a growing problem in the past few years.

In the event, the older voters and particularly the blue-collar working-class voters of the North and the Midlands joined with the 'small "c" conservative' older people in the shires to give the Leave campaign a narrow but clear majority. London and Scotland proved to be the only strong bases for the Remain vote. I cast my own postal vote in Lambeth which had the highest Remain majority in the whole United Kingdom. My constituency of Rushcliffe was a lonely island in the East Midlands with my constituents voting 58 per cent Remain and 42 per cent Leave. Shocked politicians from both sides reacted with bewilderment and amazement to this astonishing result.

David Cameron did indeed resign about four hours after the result of the referendum became clear, which was the only honourable thing for him to do. Like a gambler on a lucky streak, he had stayed at the table for one too many hands and lost it all. He would have suffered an absurd loss of authority if he had tried to continue as the prime minister of a government enacting policies against which he had been vigorously campaigning for the previous four months. The whole circus therefore moved on to a leadership battle inside the Conservative Party. The Labour Party, which had been largely irrelevant in the national debate on the referendum, added to the entertainment with a mass revolt against Jeremy Corbyn, who had provided rather tepid leadership for the pro-European efforts of his party. The public was subjected to yet more diverting arguments about personalities, raising to a new height of frenzy the mad and wild atmosphere that had been seizing the whole political life of the country since the last weeks leading up to the referendum.

Theresa May's contribution to the campaign, like my own, had been almost non-existent so far as the public were concerned. The Home Secretary had actually made a substantial speech at one point supporting the argument for Remain. It was not reported, except for a chance phrase in it about the possibility of Britain leaving the European Convention on Human Rights which was quoted by right-wing newspapers because it made her sound like a Eurosceptic. I knew that this was not her view and I obtained a full copy of the speech to see exactly what she had said. The ECHR was of course nothing to do with Britain's membership of the European Union and came from the Council of Europe, a quite separate organization dating back to post-war Britain.

After reading it closely, I could see that Theresa had made a long and very good speech in favour of Britain's membership of the Union. It was the best and most authoritative speech that I had read about the security case for our membership because she had expert knowledge and had been a defender of the arrangements that we had established in the European Union for fighting cross-border crime and gathering intelligence on international terrorism. It also went on to make an excellent case for the economic benefits of remaining in the EU. The result was that, like every other serious pro-European campaigner, she had found that no media platform of any kind had taken the slightest notice of her views. However, the impression that she had been a lukewarm pro-European proved of enormous benefit to her in the subsequent leadership election.

As a Conservative MP, I had a vote in the first stages of this leadership election but I took no active part. I watched with amazement as the Notting Hill set who had been at the heart of the Cameron government politically slaughtered each other in childish imitation of all the nastier aspects of political life. Once Boris Johnson and Michael Gove lay dead on the stage, Theresa May emerged as the only conceivable candidate of prime-ministerial quality amongst those left standing.

I did accidentally provide a moment of great public entertainment during the slightly delirious days of the leadership campaign. I did several interviews one morning from studios near Westminster trying to be statesmanlike on the issues facing my party and the qualities of the different contenders. These created no stir at all. After one interview on Sky television, however, I stayed in the studio to chat with my old friend Malcolm Rifkind who had appeared with me. Two veterans like ourselves should have been alert to the danger that cameras and microphones might still be switched on or might be activated once the journalists saw us talking privately. The result was an extremely funny video clip in which I made very disparaging comments about most of the leading contenders but actually gave a great boost, I was later assured by all her thrilled and amused campaigners, to Theresa May. I chatted away to Malcolm, saying she was a 'bloody difficult woman' then immediately going on to add 'but you and I worked for Margaret Thatcher'. I did also then say that she was a good thing and that I always got on with her. I made it clear that I was going to vote for her after I had cast a vote in the first round to encourage a young contender called Stephen Crabb who was bound to be eliminated. My rather trenchantly expressed views on the ridiculousness of the idea of Boris Johnson being prime minister, on the extremely stupid things being said by another contender Andrea Leadsom, and on the treachery and wild views on foreign affairs of Michael Gove, cannot have been a great help to their campaigns.

When Sky television released this candid chat a few hours later, I returned to the House of Commons to be greeted by MP after MP laughing as they approached me and saying how much they had enjoyed the whole performance. Three-quarters of the Conservatives who came up to congratulate me also politely said that they had agreed with every word that I had said. My son, who is an IT expert, rang me up in amusement to say that it was the first time that he had ever known his low-tech father to go viral on YouTube and the social media. Theresa, at a hustings for Conservative MPs which I did not attend the following day, made a skilful and positive use of my description of her as a 'bloody difficult woman' in one of her answers.

A few days later, on 13 July 2016, Theresa May emerged as a new prime minister of a totally reconstructed government. At least this ended the period of two or three weeks during which we had had no government capable of doing anything. We still, though, had no policy to deal with the biggest political and economic revolution that the country had faced for forty years, and no functioning Opposition. Like other MPs I embark on the period of four years that this parliament has to run in the hope that Theresa will prove to be a commanding and effective prime minister who manages successfully to overcome the amazing combination of difficulties that the UK faces in its foreign policy, security and economic well-being. This will require her to manage a fractious party in an overexcited and difficult mood, and a divided and anxious country.

I have been repeatedly asked whether I could remember any madder period of political life in the United Kingdom during my career. I have pondered this and have done my best to think back to the miners' strikes of the early 1980s, Black Wednesday in 1992, the Maastricht debates in 1992 and 1993 and so on, but the answer is obviously 'no'. It is my opinion that democracy is not functioning satisfactorily in any Western country on either side of the Atlantic. Modern mass media, and constant superficial PR-dominated political campaigning, have produced an angry backlash from the public in almost every democratic country in the West. Populists with extreme political stances and simple solutions to every complex problem have emerged to threaten the old party system of the traditional governing class. In 2016, Britain was hit by the consequences of this in a quite startling and unexpected overturning of just about every political belief and principle of the preceding decades. David's chancer-like gamble, taken for tactical internal party-management reasons, turned out to be the worst political mistake made by any British prime minister in my lifetime.

EPILOGUE

My political career has coincided almost exactly with the beginning and the end of Britain's membership of the European Union. Fifty years ago, when I became a very active Conservative student, I campaigned in support of Harold Macmillan's application for the United Kingdom to join the then European Community. In my last parliament I find myself taking part in the discussions about how Britain will leave. It is far from being the only issue to which I have devoted myself, but it has been one of the key political principles upon which I have founded my career. I still firmly believe that Britain should be involved in the development of the Union, but – alas – it seems that this is not to be.

I can, however, take pleasure in the fact that I have been lucky enough to enjoy the sensational period of success in the life of the United Kingdom that our membership of the EU has helped to deliver. The country has indeed modernized itself. This was my obsession when I first became politically active – I saw Britain sunk in stagnation and disillusion in the post-war world, unable to comprehend how we would cope in the changed global circumstances and unable to match the rising economic success of our neighbours. I have been in politics during the period in which the country has recovered its self-confidence and become a competitive modern economic power, and in which the quality of life of every section of our population has been improved. Today's multinational and multicultural society is altogether a stronger and more attractive culture than the one we had fifty years ago. British governments have played a crucial role in many parts of the world defending our interests and helping to promote our values. The younger generation in Britain enjoys an altogether more expanded horizon in which opportunities are available to most people to achieve things which their parents and grandparents would never have imagined.

I remain an optimist and I am not now plunged into gloom expecting all this to be reversed. Although I am politically depressed and angry about the course of events of the last year or two of my career, I remain determined to try to make a contribution, however small, to our efforts to minimize the damage and to restore our destiny in the light of this unprecedented circumstance. In the short term I fear that the country is probably going to go into recession. The prospect of Brexit has been a shock to the global economic system as well, so there are obvious dangers that other countries will also fall into difficulties. There is a real threat that this will feed the rise of populist extremism and the retreat into isolationism and nationalism which is one of the besetting problems of contemporary Western democracies. The European nations still all have to decide how to establish a safe and secure and reasonably amicable settlement with Putin's Russia. We face threats of anarchy and political collapse on Europe's doorstep in the Middle East and Africa. Fanatic religious terrorism is going to hit the streets of all Western cities for some years to come. There is hardly a lack of any agenda for a politician today and it is hardly surprising that, as a political addict, I remain gripped and fascinated by the problems as they emerge.

Brexit will probably dominate whatever years I have still to be involved. As I write this, we have a new government led by Theresa May. No politician or pundit has any idea what Britain's exit is going to mean. In any practical area the decisions will have to be made and new legal arrangements negotiated. I await a huge raft of decisions, legislation and consequences in the fields of economic policy, trade, defence, intelligence, security, criminal justice, environment, fisheries, agriculture, transport, energy. The future political status of such disparate places as Ireland and Gibraltar and Scotland is all to be decided.

Perhaps more than any other career, political life always gives an individual the possibility of being engaged on subjects of the most huge and profound importance for every citizen, and of being involved in and influencing the great historical events of their time. Every politician aspires to make a difference on these subjects and to these events, to whatever trivial extent. I will continue to try to make a difference if the possibility continues to present itself, just as I have in the past.

If I have achieved any success in politics, it is almost entirely due to the most extraordinary luck that I have had compared with practically every other career politician of my generation. My luck did not take me to be prime minister of my country. It certainly, however, gave me a fulfilling and fascinating public life which I was equally lucky to be able to combine with a private life of great satisfaction and security with my supporting family and my loving wife.

Appendix

My Brexit Speech, 31 January 2017

Since this book was completed in July 2016 and first published in October of the same year, the debate about Brexit has – inevitably – continued. It is now clear that Britain's withdrawal from the European Union will dominate not only the next two years, but possibly the next ten – or even longer. As my speech in the Chamber on 31 January 2017 demonstrates, I am still passionately committed to the European project, and was the only Conservative MP to vote against the government in their bid to trigger Article 50. That process has now begun and we await the outcome. All that is certain is that the negotiations will be extremely complex. Political careers are a rollercoaster and mine has been no exception and, though there are many who disagree with me, it was cheering to have a week in which I seemed to have rather a lot of fans. It's obvious to me that some of the sixteen million remain voters were boosted by the fact that somebody was still on their side, refusing to see why on earth they should be abandoned. I still believe that the sixteen million were right. And my reasons for this cannot be better expressed than in the speech I gave, so it is reproduced here for anyone who wishes to revisit it in full.

*

Mr Kenneth Clarke (Rushcliffe) (Con) Speech at Second Reading of the European Union (Notification of Withdrawal) Bill (Day 1) Tuesday 31st January 2017

Mr Speaker, you will not be surprised to hear that it is my intention to vote against the Second Reading of this bill, if a vote is called, and to support the reasoned amendment, which I think will be moved very shortly by the Scottish Nationalists.

Because of the rather measured position that the hon. and learned Member for Holborn and St Pancras (Keir Starmer) had to present on behalf of the official Labour Party, it falls to me to be the first Member of this House to set out the case for why I believe – I hope that I will not be the last such speaker – that it is in the national interest for the United Kingdom to be a member of the European Union, why I believe that we have benefited from that position for the past forty-five years and, most importantly, why I believe that future generations will benefit if we succeed in remaining a member of the European Union. It is a case that hardly received any national publicity during the extraordinary referendum campaign, but it goes to the heart of the historic decision that the House is being asked to make now.

It so happens that my political career entirely coincides with British involvement with the European Union. I started over fifty years ago, supporting Harold Macmillan's application to join. I helped to get the majority cross-party vote for the European Communities Act 1972, before we joined in 1973, and it looks like my last Parliament is going to be the Parliament in which we leave, but I do not look back with any regret. We made very wise decisions. I believe that membership of the European Union was the way in which we got out of the appalling state we were in when we discovered, after Suez, that we had no role in the world that we were clear about once we had lost our empire, and that our economy was becoming a laughing stock because we were falling behind the countries on the Continent that had been devastated in the war but appeared to have a better way of proceeding than we did.

I believe that our membership of the European Union restored to us our national self-confidence and gave us a political role in the world, as a leading member of the Union, which made us more valuable to our allies such as the United States, and made our rivals, such as the Russians, take us more seriously because of our leadership role in the European Union. It helped to reinforce our own values as well. Our economy benefited enormously and continued to benefit even more, as the market developed, from our close and successful involvement in developing trading relationships with the inhabitants of the Continent.

The Conservative governments in which I served made very positive contributions to the development of the European Union. There were two areas in which we were the leading contender and made a big difference. The first was when the Thatcher government led the way in the creation of the single market. The customs union – the so-called common market – had served its purpose, but regulatory barriers matter more than tariffs in the modern world. But for the Thatcher government, the others would not have been induced to remove those barriers, and I think that the British benefited more from the single market than any other member state. It has contributed to our comparative economic success today.

We were always the leading government after the fall of the Soviet Union in the process of enlargement to eastern Europe, taking in the former Soviet states. That was an extremely important political contribution. After the surprising collapse of the Soviet Union, eastern and central Europe could have collapsed into its traditional anarchy, nationalist rivalry and military regimes that preceded the Second World War. We pressed the urgency of bringing in these new independent nations, giving them the goal of the European Union, which meant liberal democracy, free market trade and so forth. We made Europe a much more stable place.

That has been our role in the European Union, and I believe that it is a very bad move, particularly for our children and grandchildren, that we are all sitting here now saying that we are embarking on a new unknown future. I shall touch on that in a moment, because I think the position is simply baffling to every friend of the British and of the United Kingdom throughout the world. That is why I shall vote against the bill.

Let me deal with the arguments that I should not vote in that way, that I am being undemocratic, that I am quite wrong, and that, as an elected Member of Parliament, I am under a duty to vote contrary to the views I have just given. I am told that this is because we held a referendum. First, I am in the happy situation that my opposition to referendums as an instrument of government is quite well known and has been frequently repeated throughout my political career. I have made no commitment to accept a referendum, and particularly this referendum, when such an enormous question, with hundreds of complex issues wrapped up within it, was to be decided by a simple yes/no answer on one day. That was particularly unsuitable for a plebiscite of that kind, and that point was reinforced by the nature of the debate.

Constitutionally, when the government tried to stop the House from having a vote, they did not go to the Supreme Court arguing that a referendum bound the House and that that was why we should not have a vote. The referendum had always been described as advisory in everything that the government put out. There is no constitutional standing for referendums in this country. No sensible country has referendums – the United States and Germany do not have them in their political systems. The government went to the Supreme Court arguing for the archaic constitutional principle of the royal prerogative—that the executive somehow had absolute power when it came to dealing with treaties. Not surprisingly, they lost.

What about the position of Members of Parliament? There is no doubt that by an adequate but narrow majority, leave won the referendum campaign. I will not comment on the nature of the campaign. Those arguments that got publicity in the national media on both sides were, on the whole, fairly pathetic. I have agreed in conversation with my right hon. Friend the Secretary of State for Exiting the European Union that he and I can both tell ourselves that neither of us used the dafter arguments that were put forward by the people we were allied with. It was not a very serious debate on the subject. I do not recall the view that £350 million a week would be available for the health service coming from the Brexit Secretary, and I did not say that we are going to have a Budget to put up income tax and all that kind of thing. It was all quite pathetic.

Let me provide an analogy – a loose one but, I think, not totally loose – explaining the position of Members of Parliament after this referendum. I have fought Lord knows how many elections over the past fifty years, and I have always advocated voting Conservative. The

British public, in their wisdom, have occasionally failed to take my advice and have by a majority voted Labour. I have thus found myself here facing a Labour government, but I do not recall an occasion when I was told that it was my democratic duty to support Labour policies and the Labour government on the other side of the House. That proposition, if put to the hon. Member for Bolsover (Mr Skinner) in opposition or myself, would have been treated with ridicule and scorn. Apparently, I am now being told that despite voting as I did in the referendum, I am somehow an enemy of the people for ignoring my instructions and for sticking to the opinions that I expressed rather strongly, at least in my meetings, when I urged people to vote the other way.

I have no intention of changing my opinion on the ground. Indeed, I am personally convinced that the hard-core Eurosceptics in my party, with whom I have enjoyed debating this issue for decades, would not have felt bound in the slightest by the outcome of the referendum to abandon their arguments – [Interruption.] I do not say that as criticism; I am actually on good terms with the hard-line Eurosceptics because I respect their sincerity and the passionate nature of their beliefs. If I ever live to see my hon. Friend the Member for Stone (Sir William Cash) turn up here and vote in favour of Britain remaining in the European Union, I will retract what I say, but hot tongs would not make him vote for membership of the EU.

I must move on, but I am told that I should vote for my party as we are on a three-line whip. I am a Conservative; I have been a decently loyal Conservative over the years. The last time I kicked over the traces was on the Lisbon Treaty, when for some peculiar reason my party got itself on the wrong side of the argument, but we will pass over that. I would point out to those who say that I am somehow being disloyal to my party by not voting in favour of this bill that I am merely propounding the official policy of the Conservative Party for fifty years until 23 June 2016. I admire my colleagues who can suddenly become enthusiastic Brexiteers, having seen a light on the road to Damascus on the day that the vote was cast, but I am afraid that that light has been denied me.

I feel the spirit of my former colleague, Enoch Powell – I rather respected him, aside from one or two of his extreme views – who was probably the best speaker for the Eurosceptic cause I ever heard in this House of Commons. If he were here, he would probably find it amazing that his party had become Eurosceptic and rather mildly anti-immigrant, in a very strange way, in 2016. Well, I am afraid that, on that issue, I have not followed it, and I do not intend to do so.

There are very serious issues that were not addressed in the referendum: the single market and the customs union. They must be properly debated. It is absurd to say that every elector knew the difference between the customs union and the single market, and that they took a careful and studied view of the basis for our future trading relations with Europe.

The fact is that I admire the prime minister and her colleagues for their constant propounding of the principles of free trade. My party has not changed on that. We are believers in free trade and see it as a win–win situation. We were the leading advocate of liberal economic policies among the European powers for many years, so we are free traders. It seems to me unarguable that if we put between us and the biggest free market in the world new tariffs, new regulatory barriers, new customs procedures, certificates of origin and so on, we are bound to be weakening the economic position from what it would otherwise have been, other things being equal, in future. That is why it is important that this issue is addressed in particular.

I am told that that view is pessimistic, and that we are combining withdrawal from the single market and the customs union with a great new globalized future that offers tremendous opportunities for us. Apparently, when we follow the rabbit down the hole, we will emerge in a wonderland where, suddenly, countries throughout the world are queuing up to give us trading advantages and access to their markets that we were never able to achieve as part of the European Union. Nice men like President Trump and President Erdogan are impatient to abandon their normal protectionism and give us access. Let me not be too cynical; I hope that that is right. I do want the best outcome for the United Kingdom from this process. No doubt somewhere a hatter is holding a tea party with a dormouse in the teapot.

We need success in these trade negotiations to recoup at least some of the losses that we will incur as a result of leaving the single market. If all is lost on the main principle, that is the big principle that the House must get control of and address seriously, in proper debates and votes, from now on.

I hope that I have adequately explained that my views on this issue have not been shaken very much over the decades – they have actually strengthened somewhat. Most Members, I trust, are familiar with Burke's address to the electors of Bristol. I have always firmly believed that every MP should vote on an issue of this importance according to their view of the best national interest. I never quote Burke, but I shall paraphrase him. He said to his constituents, 'If I no longer give you the benefit of my judgement and simply follow your orders, I am not serving you; I am betraying you.' I personally shall be voting with my conscience content, and when we see what unfolds hereafter as we leave the European Union, I hope that the consciences of other Members of Parliament will remain equally content.

INDEX

PICTURE ACKNOWLEDGEMENTS

All photographs are from the author's collection, with
the exception of the following:

Page 7 top right © *Liverpool Daily Post*
Page 7 bottom © Keystone/Getty Images
Page 8 top © PA/PA Archive/Press Association Images
Page 8 bottom © Phil O'Brien/EMPICS Sport
Page 9 bottom left © Popperfoto/Getty Images
Page 11 top © Michael Stephens/PA Archive/Press
    Association Images
Page 11 middle © Neil Munns/PA Archive/Press
    Association Images
Page 12 top © Peter Macdiarmid/Getty Images
Page 12 bottom © Jeff Overs/BBC News & Current
    Affairs via Getty Images
Page 14 top left © David Jones/PA Archive/Press
    Association Images
Page 14 top right © Mike Egerton/EMPICS Sport
Page 15 top left © Andrew Winning/PA Archive/Press
    Association Images
Page 16 top © Dan Kitwood/Getty Images
Page 16 bottom © John Stillwell/PA Archive/Press
    Association Images

extracts reading groups
competitions books new
discounts extracts
competitions events extracts discounts
books
new events
events books
new extracts
new reading groups
interviews reading groups
events extracts extracts books
discounts events
new books events
events
discounts extracts discounts
reading groups
www.panmacmillan.com
extracts events reading groups
competitions books extracts new
books